BLACK
EDWARDIANS

BLACK EDWARDIANS

Black People in Britain
1901–1914

JEFFREY GREEN

FRANK CASS
LONDON • PORTLAND, OR.

First Published in 1998 in Great Britain by
FRANK CASS PUBLISHERS
Newbury House, 900 Eastern Avenue
London, IG2 7HH

and in the United States of America by
FRANK CASS PUBLISHERS
c/o ISBS, 5804 N.E. Hassalo Street
Portland, Oregon, 97213-3644

Website http://www.frankcass.com

British Library Cataloguing in Publication Data

Green, Jeffrey
Black Edwardians : Black people in Britain, 1901–1914
1. Blacks – Great Britain – History – 20th century   2. Blacks
– Great Britain – Social conditions   3. Great Britain –
History – Edward VII, 1901–1910
I. Title
305.8'96'041'09041

ISBN 0–7146–4871–X (cloth)
ISBN 0–7146–4426–9 (paper)

Library of Congress Cataloging-in-Publication Data

Green, Jeffrey, 1944–
Black Edwardians : Black people in Britain, 1901–1914 / Jeffrey
Green.
p.   cm.
Includes bibliographical references and index.
ISBN 0–7146–4871–X (cloth). – ISBN 0–7146–4426–9 (pbk.)
1. Blacks – Great Britain – History – 20th century.   2. Great
Britain – History – Edward VII, 1901–1910.   3. Great Britain – History –
George V, 1910–1936.   I. Title.
DA125.A1G69   1998
941'.00496–dc21   98–16242
                                                CIP

Typeset by Footnote Graphics, Warminster, Wilts
Printed in Great Britain by
Bookcraft (Bath) Ltd, Midsomer Norton, Somerset

For Susan, Sue and George

Contents

List of illustrations

Acknowledgements

EVIDENCE of the Black presence in the British Isles is spread widely. Much has been retrieved through the families and friends of the people detailed in these pages, who agreed to be interviewed, answered letters, and loaned documents and photographs. My understanding owes a great deal to Frank and Evelyn Alcindor, Amy Barbour-James, Leslie Brown, Olive Campbell, Percy Chen, Joe Deniz, Geoffrey Dove, Marjorie Evans, Ronald Green, Don Johnson, Margaret Othick, Richard Savage and Leslie Thompson.

I am indebted to the following individuals who provided clues and evidence, and shared information: Tony Barker and Stephen Bourne for information on entertainers; Peter Calvert for his contacts with Yorkshire veterans who spoke about the pygmies; Marva Carter who took me to the Herndon Home in Atlanta; E. B. Davies of Walthamstow School who led me to two veterans in 1983; Ian Duffield for copies of the correspondence of John Archer; Christopher Fyfe for his knowledge of Sierra Leone and his discovery of the tombstone of Dr D. P. H. Taylor in Banjul; James Gibbs for details of African students at Queens College, Taunton; my ex-wife Maureen for finding postcards; Robert A. Hill for informing me of Thomas Johnson's 1908 autobiography; Christopher Jackson of the Children's Society, London; David Killingray for information on Amgoza Lobagola, Klikko and Bandele Omoniyi; Hazel King and Ivor Wynne Jones for details of the African Institute, Colwyn Bay; Bernth Lindfors for copies and gifts of showbusiness ephemera, and for telling me that Ira Aldridge papers were in Evanston, Illinois; Rainer Lotz for information on entertainers who travelled around Europe, notably James and George Bohee, Belle Davis, Louis Douglas and Will Garland; Josephine Love whose hospitality enabled me to use the Azalia Hackley Collection in Detroit, and for her explanation of the vibrant community life in Atlanta in the 1900s; Doris McGinty for searching street directories of Washington DC; Barbara Ponton for details on Thomas Johnson; Paul Reed for information on Black men in the British army in 1914; Howard Rye for sharing the results of his searches in street directories, birth and marriage registers, and other details of entertainers; Donald Simpson for leading me to Amy Barbour-James and guidance at the library of the Royal Commonwealth Society; and Brian Willan, authority on South Africa, who provided evidence located in Nigeria that convinced me that Dr J. J. Brown needed a full investigation.

Archivists and local studies librarians searched and permitted me to search in street directories, scrap books, electoral registers, burial registers, catalogues and local newspapers. Cemetery records led me to the family of Dr Alcindor. Wanderings in graveyards supplied the fresh air that is the only disadvantage when working in those wonderful institutions, the newspaper library of the British Library, the London Library, Rhodes House (Oxford), and the Public Record Office.

I am grateful for the staff of the Schomburg branch of the New York Public Library, the public libraries of Boston, Dallas, and Detroit, the Moorland-Spingarn Research Center and the library of Howard University, and Northwestern University for assistance during my time in the United States.

My thanks to Paul McGilchrist for inviting me to visit the Royal College of Music archives with him, in search of Coleridge-Taylor; to Bill Tonkin of the Exhibition Study Group for a free run of his postcard collection; David Clifford for sharing his enthusiasm for the music of Coleridge-Taylor; and to Christopher Fyfe for reading the draft manuscript and for his excellent recommendations.

Introduction

IT has long been presumed that the Black people who could be found in Britain in the first decades of the twentieth century were students destined to return home when qualified, or sailors who had found temporary homes in cities close to the sea and ships. Others were a handful of doctors and semi-permanent students, entertainers usually from the United States, and visiting delegations seeking greater understanding. A few; people of no consequence except when colonial agitators or unemployment stirred discontent. Which was all very comforting to the masters.

Reality was quite different. A veritable gazetteer of place names of the British Isles had a Black presence in Edwardian times. Wrexham, Colwyn Bay and Swansea in Wales; the cathedral city of Lincoln, the island of Jersey and the south coast resort town of Bournemouth are some of the places where Black people have now been traced. York, Leeds, Harrogate, Bradford, Beverley, Hull and Scarborough in Yorkshire had Black residents or visitors, as did the outer areas of London including Acton, Edgware, Leytonstone and Croydon. Rural areas with a Black presence included Hampshire, Wiltshire, Cornwall, the Lake District, St Albans and Sussex towns such as Rye, Brighton and Crawley. Dublin, Belfast, Newry, Cork, Ennis and Fermoy in Ireland; towns such as Dundee, Manchester, Aberdeen, Grimsby, West Hartlepool and Wigan had Black residents.

Edwardian Britain's widespread population of African birth or descent was resident at the centre of the world's largest empire, participating in the affairs of the leading industrial nation. Some knew no other land and others were self-motivated migrants. There were ambitious professionals, youths anxious for an education, parents concerned about the future, adults seeking tranquility and workers seeking more money, as well as the descendants of earlier generations. All of this was a surprise to me as I followed up clues in papers I first handled in Charleston, South Carolina, in 1979.

It was jazz historian John Chilton who first alerted me to the London years of Edmund Jenkins, a South Carolina-born musician who had studied in Atlanta before moving to England in 1914. Like many instrumentalists of the 1920s jazz era he had been trained at the orphanage in Charleston founded by his Baptist minister father.[1] Edmund Jenkins progressed to study at London's Royal Academy of Music from 1914 to 1921, where he won prizes, medals and scholar-ships.[2] Tracking his friends revealed a middle-class Black community in Britain reaching back into the late Victorian years. I spoke to the children of people born in Victorian times: 1867, 1873 and the 1880s (and even 1856).[3] This was my grandparents' generation.

I rediscovered something that my grandmother had made clear to me when, around 1962, I was studying history at school. She had been adult when King Edward had reigned; I was reading about the 1910s campaign for women's votes. She told me that she had worked, as a servant, for a Votes For Women suffragette (Martha Louisa Vass always called them suffragists) whose protests included chaining herself to railings in London. Grandma Vass remarked that she worked every day, late into the night when there were dinner parties, and had just one Sunday afternoon off every second week. Women's rights based on women's wrongs had no place in my textbooks.

Her neighbour told me, when I asked him what he had done on a Saturday night when he had been my age, that he had put on his best boots and walked to Mayfair to see 'what the toffs were doing'. This was another working class to that in my school books. When I stumbled over the Black presence in Edwardian Britain I was thus slightly prepared to face facts not found in history books.

What delayed a proper investigation was a deep-seated belief, one that was and is widespread in Britain, that people of African birth or descent were 'from' somewhere else and thus could only be in Britain on a temporary basis. Such sojourners had no place in the history of Britain, it seemed. This was innocently encouraged by studies of the Black people who had led their peoples to independence, for the triumphs of the early leaders of Kenya, Tanzania, Nigeria, Ghana, Trinidad, Guyana and Jamaica had followed years abroad, often in Britain.[4] They were known through their writings and biographies, whereas little was known of humbler individuals.

The interconnections of Black leaders in Britain, France and the United States, detailed in Imanuel Geiss's *The Pan-African Movement* of 1974[5] and Ayo Langley's *Pan-Africanism and Nationalism in West Africa* of 1973[6] showed that Black people had long made links outside Africa and the Caribbean – the colonial lands where the Black majority had no votes, few rights, no control and little influence.

But mundane matters such as finding accommodation, paying the rent and earning a living had not been addressed – let alone what it must have been like to experience a sense of isolation as a person of colour in a White society. And were there other aspects to the Black experience of Britain? Surely there were Black people whose lives, like my grandmother's, received little public attention. Grandma Vass knew next to nothing about Africa, as I discovered in 1968 when I told her my employers were sending me to Uganda. When I lived in Kampala it was something of a surprise for me to be accused of exploiting Africa and Africans through imperialism. My response, that Britain's tropical empire had been of no benefit to my grandparents and their children, and that my presence in Uganda six years after independence was due to an official work permit, did not really resolve the matter.

I spent months travelling around the United States, an ambition created by my interest in jazz and the Black culture which had nurtured it. On returning to London in 1971 I started to read histories of Whites in Africa and biographies of the Victorian traveller-explorers who had done so much to stimulate British involvement in tropical Africa. I was attempting to discover why the British had ruled Uganda, and other African lands, with such apparent ease. Meanwhile the men and women who had worked with me in Kampala were being murdered, robbed, forced into exile: for Idi Amin had seized power and had instituted a tyranny that surely surpassed the British empire. Had this resulted from British imperialism?

After all, British imperialism in Uganda began officially in 1894 – within a lifetime of 1971. It was possible that children who, in the 1880s, had witnessed Stanley emerge from the rainforests of the Congo to reach Lake Albert, could have celebrated Uganda's independence. I read a biography of Harry Johnston, linguist, artist, writer and early governor of Uganda. In 1982 I met an elderly man, sunning himself on a bench in the Sussex churchyard where Johnston had been buried in 1927. I asked him where the grave was, and that led to conversation. He had known Johnston – Sir Harry Hamilton Johnston, knighted by Queen Victoria, whose land laws had affected my work in Kampala. 'That little bugger', he said – suddenly I was back in Grandma Vass's home and hearing another version of history.

I became less surprised by aspects of history I had not anticipated. In seeking information on Edmund Jenkins, who lived in London and Paris from 1914 until his death in 1926, I had assumed that veterans would easily recall an American of pure African descent whose accent must have been similar to the then US president Jimmy Carter. I discovered that some who had sound memories had forgotten Jenkins was black. This was true of other Black people in the memory of Whites – strikingly when a 1930s group photograph had the sole Black male arrowed to guide me. It was not an African descent that veterans recalled. I tried to assess if this ethnic invisibility resulted from wishful thinking, and concluded that generally race had not been among the main reasons for the person to be recalled. Indeed, I started to believe that Black people had been part of the British landscape.

One way of checking was to ask veterans; nearly every person I have met in Britain, when asked, recalled Black people before the 1940s. Marjorie Evans recalled west Africans in traditional cloth in Edwardian Croydon; Leslie Brown told me about his doctor father who lived in London from 1905, and of S. S. A. Cambridge and his three daughters in the 1910s. Pop Chandler remembered West Indian soldiers near Bethune in France in the winter of 1917, and my father told me that he had seen members of Louis Armstrong's orchestra in south London around 1934. A veteran in Epsom recalled Dr Harold Moody and Dr Gunn Munro before 1936, and another in Cheshire volunteered that a West Indian doctor named Donaldson had practised in Manchester in the 1930s. Councillor Edward Nelson was remembered in Cheshire. The sporting fraternity recalled boxer Len Johnson, born in Manchester in 1902. I ceased noting those who had thrilled to the singing of Paul Robeson in the 1930s, and those who had met the racing tipster Prince Monolulu. I understood why the children's street game of 'Touch a Nigger for Luck'[7] had survived generation after generation. There had been a widespread and continuous Black presence in Britain for years.

There was no major research into this Black presence in Britain's history until Kenneth Little's *Negroes in Britain*, published in 1948.[8] Little had studied the 'coloured community in the dockland of Cardiff' which he numbered at some seven thousand. Suggesting that 'Negro people had become established in small numbers during the '90s' he then detailed events in Cardiff after the 1914–18 war. The second part of his book was an overview of the Black presence in Britain from the sixteenth century. Recent books have also avoided the Edwardian period, which was a period of change.

By the 1910s both Germany and the United States had overtaken Britain's economy, and had a substantial lead in modern industries, notably electrical engineering, chemicals and vehicles. But Britain's financial investments around the world, in shipping, railways, banking, insurance, and trade remained colossal. One quarter of the globe's population dwelled in lands that were part of the British Empire. Those lands and investments made Britain the envy of the world and the Edwardians were rightly proud of that status.

Pride in the empire did not mean knowledge of it and its peoples, for widespread ignorance was exhibited in the newspapers of the 1900s and 1910s. This helped my research, as I followed a path that would worry some historians. I looked at the yellowing pages of old newspapers, usually weeklies published in some town in a district where I had not located a Black presence through other sources. More times than not I found a report on the activities of a Black person.

Even when focusing on one aspect of Black activity in Britain I sped read other pages and found additional aspects of Black history. One example was the American song-and-dance show *In Dahomey*, a London theatrical success of 1903. The *Westminster Gazette*'s 'A Colour Line in London? Publicans and "Nigger" Customers' of September 1903 revealed anti-Black actions in central London; the *Daily News* noted 'The Coloured Man's Complaint'. I then looked in the London *Weekly Dispatch* and found 'Black Man's Rights. Racial Question In the West End. Complaint Against a Publican'. My *In Dahomey* research was published in a New York music journal.[9] I met Paul B. Rich and mentioned this colour-bar incident, and he recommended I approached Sheila Patterson, who edited *New Community* for the Commission for Racial Equality in London. My research paper was accepted and duly published.[10]

It was the first of several articles that dealt with Black people active outside the field of music. The acceptance of these articles and the encouragement of professional historians confirmed that what I was uncovering was both of value and often quite unknown.

I also spent time reading memoirs, biographies and letters of people, centred on the 1900s and 1910s, but soon without such a time restraint. I noted that Black people were mentioned from time to time. Sometimes they were not mentioned but appeared anyway, as with the photograph of 'Nursemaid at the seaside, c. 1896' in Frank Dawes's *Not in Front of the Servants: Domestic service in England 1850-1939* (1975).

A biography of Charles Darwin revealed that the future author of *Origin of Species* had studied taxidermy, in 1820s Edinburgh, with a 'blackamoor' named John Edmonstone from British Guiana.[11] Ruth McClure's *Coram's Children: The London Foundling Hospital in the Eighteenth Century* (1981) noted that this charity had taken in 'a mulatto child and also the child of Black Peggy, a Negro girl'. In the mid-nineteenth century the Russian writer Alexander Herzen took refuge in London where he met and employed 'a Negro, a lad of seventeen'.[12] Among the ninety-four who sailed from England with Captain James Cook in the *Endeavour* in 1768, a round-the-world voyage that brought knowledge of Australia and New Zealand to the British, were botanist Joseph Banks and his four servants – two were Black: Thomas Richmond and George Dorlton.[13]

The Diary of a Prison Governor: James William Newham, 1825-1890 seemed unpromising but the entry for 18 June 1887 recorded the death in Canterbury prison of Arthur Roberts 'a negro prisoner' who had almost completed a fifteen month sentence for uttering conterfeit coins.[14] A history of Llandudno, the Welsh seaside resort, noted that around 1900 the town's 'first coloured immigrant came as a storeman at the turn of the century. He was Joe Taylor who married and settled down after arriving in the area with a travelling fair.'[15]

The memoirs of poet Osbert Sitwell noted a 'negro, locally known as "Snowball", who limped with a pitiful exoticism through the winter streets, trying to sell flowers' in Scarborough at the turn of the century and that his elder brother had a rug, 'unusual in design and bold in colour, he had commissioned at the age of seven from an old negro whom he found in the workhouse at Scarborough'.[16]

Seventeenth century English music provided 'The Fair Lover and His Black Mistress' in which Nigrocella, from the West Indies, is serenaded 'Were I as black as Leda's hair, You should not thus endure'. Composer John Blow had been the organist at Westminster Abbey.[17]

Newspapers revealed details that I could follow up elsewhere, although their references to Black people were often because of crimes or alleged crimes. Newspaper reports were generally patronising, often offensive, but they provided valuable clues.

Basic education had been introduced across England in the 1870s and most Edwardians were literate. All manner of publications were aimed at the masses. Metropolitan scandal sheets such as the *Illustrated Police News* carried reports of serious accidents, crimes and allegations of crimes, adding a literal touch of colour if the incident involved a Black person. An October 1907 report noted:

> Attacked by a lion. An exciting scene occurred at a circus at Newport on Thursday night. A negro lion-tamer was leaving a cage in which he had been putting a lion through some tricks when the animal sprang at him and caught him by the arm. He released himself, but not before his arm had been badly mauled.[18]

Other publications, such as *The Sphere* and *Tatler*, sought a different audience. A mid-1905 edition of the former, which had four pages devoted to King Edward's grand-nephew's marriage (he was the Crown Prince of Germany) and three to the Spanish king's visits to France and Britain, included a splendid photograph of 'An African Diplomatist Presented to the King', showing 'The Hon. J. J. Thomas, who was presented at the recent levee held by his Majesty, is a member of the Sierra Leone House of Assembly'.[19]

The provincial press noted incidents involving Blacks that had taken place outside the circulation area of the newspaper. Thus in 1905 a north Yorkshire newspaper reported on an incident in Lincolnshire, fifty miles away. 'Three persons stabbed by a Negro at Grimsby' was the headline. The short report named him as William Savoury.[20] When an African American was awarded a scholarship to Oxford it was mentioned in London's sports press.[21] A breach of promise court case in Scotland was reported in distant Yorkshire.[22]

Evidence of the Black presence was scattered. It was easy to see why much of it had been missed.

Much of the writing that passes as the history of Black people is on the themes of slavery, exploitation of Africa and of Africans, plantation society, anti-slavery protest and anti-colonial protest. Their focus is largely on the lives of Black people but not on Black people in Britain. However, even the apparently clear cut exploitation of Blacks by Whites has not been free of myths. Nowadays no informed person would state, as history professor Sir Reginald Coupland did in 1933, that 'all slaves in England . . . were recognized as free men' from 1772, for Black people remained subject to their slave status in Britain into the late 1820s.[23] This myth of a liberal and free Britain survived into very recent times.

Other myths have had a long life and still affect perceptions of people in history. The myth of Britain's all-powerful global empire has not entirely disappeared. New legends are being formed, new history is being developed. For the majority of people in late twentieth-century Britain the Black presence is very recent, stemming from the migrations that began in 1948 as Little's book was published.

A study of early twentieth-century Britain's Black residents and visitors, many of whom were alive in 1948, suggests that the migrations following the 1939–45 war might have followed a pattern. But people from the tropical empire who, over the centuries, had moved to the British Isles did not fit into any historical niche once coercion, notably in the centuries of slavery, had ended. Failing to find evidence of a later Black presence in Britain has warped history.

The result has been a simplified version of Black British history; those Blacks who lived in Britain before the 1830s were victims of an imperial and slaving society. Those who influenced the move towards African and Caribbean independence were freedom fighters.

The nature of empire was hardly questioned. How could there have been sufficient force to intimidate the millions all the time? How did so few rule so many? The image of a White world dominating Blacks received a blow when I was informed by Amy Barbour-James, born of pure-African descent in London in 1906, that her Guyana-born father had been an officer in the Gold Coast [Ghana] post office. A study of colonial records, both printed and in the Colonial Office files at the Public Record Office in Kew, revealed that he had been one of dozens of Black West Indians working in the African empire. Had they all made a home in England, like John Barbour-James? How was it that he and the other Black colonial officials had been overlooked? Like the memoirs and the newspapers, the evidence was to hand.

The *Gold Coast Report for 1904* noted that the police had 'four West Indian superintendents' and the annual *Blue Book* named them as T. S. Coppins, A. W. Downer, W. H. Simmons and C. T. Webb. The earliest appointment, that of Thomas Coppins, dated from 1898. Five years later the report stated that 'a proportion of the sanitary inspectors will, in the first instance, be drawn from the West Indies'. The *Gold Coast Civil Service List, 1909* noted West Indian teachers and sub-officers of police 'seconded from the West Indies'. Yet the 'European population' of the Gold Coast was only 1,715 in 1909.[24] This did not seem the all-powerful empire of legend. Was the empire sustained by myths? It must have been; and those myths still have influence.

Because the empire was such a dominating force, there was no prohibition against Black visitors and settlers in Britain. If visible minorities in Britain experienced substantial elements of racism and culture-conflict, what stopped that information reaching back to the tropics? If the King Edward's imperial domains were underfunded, his subjects milched and their economies warped in the interests of Britons, what had financed the travellers and settlers?

How could a Black minority earn a living if the majority of Britons despised them? How had it been possible for Amy Barbour-James to lead a life that was in no large way different to that of Whites? Indeed, did the majority despise the Black people who lived among them? Perhaps no Whites in Britain worried about Blacks? Was it better to be Black and in Britain than to live in the tropical empire? Such questions were raised as I discovered more about the men, women and children of African birth or descent who had found a home in Britain in the first fifteen years of the twentieth century.

Black people were active in many ways and in many places, in early twentieth-century Britain, overcoming encounters with racism, bigotry, ignorance and bias at all levels. Even the small adults from the Congo rain forest, who appeared in a demeaning display in theatres and halls all over Britain for more than two years, triumphed as people despite the odds.[25]

My contacts with the children, neighbours and friends of Black Edwardians involved reaching back into the nineteenth century. This was not a just a search in archives, old newspapers and memoirs, but an often spirited contact with witnesses. One example was when I investigated the Congo pygmies. I was introduced to two ladies in their nineties who remembered the Africans living in their Yorkshire village in 1905–7. Edwardian history, as my grandmother had made clear, was not that long ago.

East Grinstead
November 1996 – June 1997

NOTES

1. J. Chilton, *A Jazz Nursery: The Story of the Jenkins' Orphanage Bands* (London: Bloomsbury Bookshop, 1980).
2. J. Green, *Edmund Thornton Jenkins: The Life and Times of an American Black Composer 1894-1926* (Westport CT: Greenwood Press, 1982).
3. The mother of Marjorie Evans (half-sister of Anglo-African composer Samuel Coleridge-Taylor) had been born in Dover in 1856. Her Black son was born in London in 1875. She died in 1953 and my informant, Miss Evans, was expecting to celebrate a life of one hundred years in November 1996, as this was written.
4. Kenya's Jomo Kenyatta had studied in the 1930s London and worked in Sussex; Julius Nyerere had studied in Edinburgh before leading Tanganyika at independence; Nigeria's Nnamdi Azikwe studied and taught in the USA in the 1920s; Ghana's Kwame Nkrumah also studied in America; Trinidad's Eric Williams studied at Oxford and taught in the USA; Jamaica's Norman Manley studied at Oxford.
5. I. Geiss, *The Pan-African Movement* (London: Methuen, 1974).
6. J. Langley, *Pan-Africanism and Nationalism in West Africa 1900–1945: A Study in Ideology and Social Classes* (Oxford: Clarendon Press, 1973).
7. The first child to touch a Black person walking along the street was deemed to have acquired good luck for the remainder of the day. One version necessitated spitting on the pavement first, and was explained to me in 1981 by a Paddington veteran recalling the 1910s, who was full of respect for the local 'Black doctor', John Alcindor, who had died in 1924.
8. K. Little, *Negroes in Britain: A Study of Racial Relations in English Society* (London: Kegan Paul, 1948).
9. J. Green, 'In Dahomey in London in 1903', *Black Perspective in Music* (New York), 11, 1 (Spring 1983), pp. 22–40.
10. J. Green, 'The Coloured Man's Complaint', *New Community* (London), 11, 1/2 (Autumn 1983), pp. 175–8.
11. A. Desmond and J. Moore, *Darwin* (London: Michael Joseph, 1991), pp. 28, 91.
12. A. Herzen, *My Past and Thoughts* quoted by E. Newby (ed.), *A Book of Travellers Tales* (London: Picador Books, 1986), pp. 229–30.
13. P. O'Brien, *Joseph Banks: A Life* (London, 1987; repr. Collins Harvill, 1994), p. 68.
14. P. Coltman (ed.), *The Diary of a Prison Governor* (Kent County Council, 1984), p. 37.
15. I. Jones, *Llandudno: Queen of the Welsh Resorts* (Cardiff: John Jones, 1971), pp. 53–4.
16. O. Sitwell, *Left Hand Right Hand!* (London: Macmillan; Reprint Society, 1946), p. 87; O. Sitwell *The Scarlet Tree* (London: Macmillan; Reprint Society, 1951), p. 287.
17. Harmonia Mundi recording HMO 215. My thanks to Stewart Pearson.
18. *Illustrated Police News* (London), 26 October 1907, p. 2.
19. *The Sphere* (London), 10 June 1905, p. 236.
20. *Scarborough Evening News*, 7 August 1905, p. 3.
21. *The Sporting Times* (London), 23 March 1907, p. 2; J. Green, 'A Black Edwardian Rhodes Scholar', *Oxford* (Oxford), 40, 2 (December 1988), pp. 71–6.
22. *Beverley Guardian*, 14 October 1905, 'Edinburgh lady and a Negro Doctor'; see index: Dr Nurse.
23. F. Shyllon, *Black Slaves in Britain* (London: Institute of Race Relations, 1974).
24. *Gold Coast Report for 1909*, pp. 30–31 notes mining companies employed 585, merchants numbered 574, officials were 438 and that missions numbered 118. These reports and lists were consulted at the library of the Royal Commonwealth Society, then in London.
25. J. Green, 'Edwardian Britain's Forest Pygmies', *History Today* (London), 45, 8 (August 1995), pp. 33–9.

— 1 —

Imperial exhibits

THERE was uncertainty. Did the nineteenth century end on 31 December 1899, or one year later? That it was the end of an era was clear when Queen Victoria died on 22 January 1901, for she had ruled Britain since 1837. Her son and heir was to be crowned Edward the Seventh, monarch of the world's leading nation state which claimed imperial rights over one quarter of the inhabitants of the globe.

His coronation was to be a splendid affair, a ceremony that might outclass the old queen's jubilee of 1897. Kings, rajahs, presidents, chiefs, emperors and prime ministers were summoned to witness the coronation. Indian troops were brought to Southampton to wait their moment when they would join in the parade before hundreds of thousands of spectators. Medals, ribbons, spurs, helmets, shined brass and mirror-like boots: a splendid display of power. From the corners of the earth, from Africa, from Europe, from Asia, from America, came the curious, the rulers and the ruled.

The American socialist and novelist Jack London witnessed the coronation parade of 9 August 1902. He had been in London for some weeks, observing the poor in the East End. He wrote in *The People of the Abyss* that he would have enjoyed Edward's coronation had he arrived from America and stayed in a luxury hotel until the pageant. The socialist waited with countless others behind the soldiers who lined the route. He wrote that he was thinking that five hundred peers owned one-fifth of England and, with their colleagues and servants, spent nearly one-third of the country's wealth.

The king returned to his palace. The generals who had ridden in the parade had fought famous battles in India, Africa and China. Behind them came soldiers from Canada and Australia, from New Zealand and Bermuda, from Fiji, Borneo, Sierra Leone, Nigeria, Cyprus, Jamaica, Malta, Hong Kong, St Lucia, South Africa and India – warriors and lackeys, conquered peoples and proud settlers. The parade was almost over and the crowds were drifting away when Chinese and Africans marched along. They were cheered; and then the rain fell.

It was splendid, but merely decorative. Behind the pomp were

several myths and illusions. The very symbol of the British nation and
its empire was half-German; and his queen was Danish. The generals,
splendid on their horses, had taken years to defeat a few thousand
White farmers. Indeed, in one week in 1899 the apparently mighty
British had nearly been swept out of southern Africa. The cavalry,
which prided itself of being elitist and was officered by aristocrats, had
played no major part in that war and was never needed in battle again.

The five hundred land-owning aristocratic families who had upset
Jack London were of lessening importance. Britain now had more
people living in towns and cities than in the countryside, and much of
its wealth was created by manufacturing industries and commerce.
Edward's kingdom depended on coal; coal mining and distribution
employed one male worker in ten. The nation's cotton mills depended
on foreign cotton, largely American; its woollen mills relied on wool
from the antipodes. These raw materials were transported in British-
built ships, fuelled by Welsh coal, financed by British banks and
insured in London.

The mass of Britons were literate, for compulsory education had
been introduced in the 1870s. Conditions in towns were improving,
with safe, uninterrupted water supplies to be found in nearly every
town by the late 1890s.[1] There was a growth in legislation aimed at
assisting the weakest members of society, leading to school meals
(1906) and school medical inspections (1907).[2] Inexpensive urban
transport systems enabled numbers of workers to move some distance
from their employment, and a growing network of theatres provided
entertainment for the multitudes. Gas and electricity were replacing
oil lamps; horses were being replaced by petrol engines; the nation's
railway network was almost complete; contacts were made through
swift communications – letter, telegram and the telephone. Newspapers reported news from near and far, enabling the stick-at-homes
to learn of events in distant lands including, of course, those in
Britain's empire.

A child attending a British school in the 1900s could learn of the
empire from Lionel Lyde's *A Geography of the British Empire*.[3] Many
did, for it was published in 1900 and had reached its eleventh edition
by 1915. Professor Lyde's introduction proclaimed that the empire
covered about one-fifth of the land of the globe and that Britain's
merchant navy was equal to all the other countries in the world put
together. Of Barbados Lyde wrote 'even negroes are obliged to work –
on the plantations or in catching and salting flying-fish'.[4] He made
no mention of slavery. The size of Britain's tropical African empire
was 'not known with any approach to accuracy' whilst 'the oldest
possessions, Gambia and Sierra Leone, are also the least valuable'.[5]

Lyde detailed southern Africa with its new (founded 1885) city of

Johannesburg on the gold fields, and the lands to the north, then called Rhodesia after Cecil Rhodes who had financed the settlement of Europeans there in the 1890s. That invasion had led to war. The professor noted that 'the Matabili were savage warriors' and the 'Mashonas are peaceful to cowardice'. The stone ruins of Zimbabwe, here called 'Zimbabye', were said to be 'probably of Persian origin'.[6]

Turning to tropical Africa the professor wrote that the Gold Coast had given a name to the English guinea coin but now exported gold dust, palm oil and rubber, ignoring the cocoa that was to make this Britain's richest tropical colony by the 1920s. East Africa was described on one page. Zanzibar's long involvement in the East African slave trade was mentioned, probably because the British had helped end it, whereas they had been major exploiters in the western African slave trade for three centuries.

There were other potent influences on the British view of Africa and Africans. Missionary tales were published in adult and youth editions. They and stories of British explorers in Africa were awarded as prizes in schools and dispersed at meetings.[7]

One of the most enduring images of Blacks had been created by the 1850s novel *Uncle Tom's Cabin*. Descended from that anti-slavery book were numerous stage acts, songs and dramas. Following emancipation in the United States there were Cabin acts involving genuine Black people, although many Whites in burnt cork make-up continued to present libellous images of Blacks on the stage.[8] Cabin shows, lively musical entertainments set in a bogus American South during planta-tion slavery times, were a standard part of Britain's entertainments. Blacked-up performers (Nigger Minstrels) in song-and-dance shows, often using *Uncle Tom's Cabin* themes, presented Blacks as foolish dandies, happy to sing and play the banjo. Hundreds earned a living in minstrel shows for decades.[9]

The minstrel acts included people of African descent. Other enter-tainments also presented genuine Black men, women and children to the British. Residents of any town that had a theatre would have had almost regular opportunities to see Black entertainers, and smaller towns had halls where touring groups and individuals earned a living. Spectacular public entertainments which ran for months brought both images and real people before the ticket-purchasing multitudes. These imperial exhibitions were in part a display of power. As with the coronation in 1902, groups of 'natives' were seen by crowds of Britons in the centuries-old tradition of parading captives from foreign lands as evidence of military success. In Edwardian Britain displays of Black people also supported the widespread belief that White people in general, and Britons in particular, were superior. Blacks, and Whites, in show business lived in the public eye, and their doings were thought to be of interest. Reports in the press reveal aspects of the lives of imperial exhibits and display contemporary opinions.

The exotic African was to be seen in the lively show *Savage South Africa* in London in 1899.[10] One of the performers in this enactment of the recent warfare between Rhodes's settlers and the Ndebele was Peter Lobengula. The show closed in 1900. Lobengula remained in Britain, touring to Manchester with his English fiancée Kitty Jewell. Reports that the pair were to marry led to newspaper comments 'Black scandal' and 'Black peril'; their divorce led to further comments, which reveal the prejudice of the British.

The Times of 28 January 1902 reported on the court hearing of the application for a dissolution of the marriage of Peter Lo-Ben and Florence Kate Lo-Ben formerly Jewell. He was accused of cruelty and adultery with a Maud Wilson. Described as the son of the late king of Matabeleland, he 'had been extremely cruel to the petitioner and at one time had bitten her finger, and another time had tried to stab her with an assegai'. The president of the court remarked 'Well, what did she expect. He was but a savage'. Lobengula was also said to have lived off her earnings as a prostitute.

The African married an Irish woman, settled in Salford near Manchester, worked as a coal miner and raised a family. He died of phthisis (a tuberculosis encouraged by coal dust) on 24 November 1913, shortly after obtaining the right to vote, for his country of origin was now a domain of the British empire. The local press was interested in the prince who had become a coal miner and that his claim for civil rights had involved the government minister for colonial affairs. 'Several coloured gentlemen' attended his funeral at Agecroft cemetery. By 1920 his widow and four children were buried there. Another son, who died in 1977, expressed no public interest in his father's royal status.

Another African who was an imperial exhibit was the man known as Frantz, or Klikko the Wild Dancing Bushman. On display in London in 1912, and again from October 1913 after a spell in France, the exploitation of the South African so upset a stagehand at the Palace theatre in Maidstone that he alerted the Aborigines' Protection Society.[11] The performer was traced to Gravesend and then to Cambridge. The act ended with the African being gagged and carried off the stage, jerking convulsively and foaming at the mouth. A novel public performance to many, but an outrage to the stagehand and to the liberal protection society, it was so disquieting to the Variety Artistes' Federation that it blacklisted the act, which remained within the law. The African and his manager appeared in East Ham (London) and in the summer of 1914 at Dublin's world's fair. His photograph was published as a postcard.[12] He was still working, in Margate, in 1915.

Such 'savage' Blacks were not the only manner in which Edwardian Britons saw citizens of the empire. Much larger audiences saw some forty Jamaicans in London in the summer of 1905. The band of the West India Regiment played at the Crystal Palace exhibition centre for several weeks, to a possible audience of 966,325, the total of paying visitors to the exhibition.[13]

The year before 2,417,928 entry tickets had been sold for the City of Bradford Exhibition, where 'the most interesting black race in the world' was displayed. Men, women and children from Somalia lived in the grounds of the exhibition for the summer months, carrying out, in public, a range of activities that were pictured on at least nine postcards sold at the show. The 'native doctor' Chakim, his wife and six children are posed in one picture. Thirteen women and children appear on another; eleven adults are on a third card. Five are a 'native family'; fourteen children are posed at school. 'Washing day' has no adult males. One of these cards, mailed in Keighley on 17 October 1904, has the comment 'these people are what we saw at the exhibition last week but I do not care for them'.

These people were, in fact, seasoned entertainers, employed by the Continental Syndicate. A fire at the showground on 30 August damaged some of their accommodation, and the reports in the *Bradford Daily Telegraph* reveal something of the truth behind the image. Sultan Ali's apartments, a store room, and two apartments occupied 'by a couple of warriors and their families' were damaged by the fire. Personal belongings in the store room were valued at nearly three hundred pounds (the price of a modest house). The goods, which included items purchased in France, had been insured.

The exhibition closed at the end of October 1904. The *Bradford Daily Telegraph* duly reported on 'the tribe's departure', noting that half of the men wore 'English suits'. 'The manner in which they have "picked up" English . . . was astonishing.' Sultan Ali was quoted as stating that normally they traded sheep, and added that 'after their experience in Bradford they will not take kindly to the occupation. It is on the cards that the "village" will be a feature of the Liege Exhibition next year.' The reporter also noted that they had remained staunchly Muslim during their months in Yorkshire.

This was not their only strength. The paper had a headline 'Somalis Besiege the Town Hall', for a difference of opinion over gratuities had led many of the Africans to seek redress at the city's town hall. Because of this demonstration the group were late for their train. The two carriages reserved for the Somalis and their belongings had to be uncoupled, and added to the next train to Hull. There was no disgrace over the demonstration, for the lord mayor and other august personages were at the station to bid them farewell. The 'Somali Village' had

Somali War Dance,
Coronation Exhibition, London, 1911

1. Somalis on show in London, 1911

acted out a simple life in Africa but the Africans had taken advantage of their time in France and in England, and had not abandoned their faith or their sense of justice. It seems likely that those who went on to appear in Belgium had been in Britain, and probable that some at Bradford had toured abroad before.

In 1910 at least twenty-eight Somalis were in a village presentation at the Maritime Gardens in Portobello, Edinburgh. Postcards include one of four musicians. The following year saw Somalis at the Coronation Exhibition in London, when a postcard of seven men in an alleged war dance was sold.

The most famous of these African groups were the Senegalese, who certainly numbered over one hundred when they had their 'village' in London in the summer of 1908. Opening in May 1908, the Franco-British exhibition was in purpose-built grounds at the White City in west London. The *Evening News* commented that 'large eyes roll at you from ebony faces' and that 'the coloured lady who composes a meal of rice and scraps of meat serves it without cutlery. The black fingers of the family are thrust into the pot.' The leading African was Mamadou Seek and the priest was Assame Parge.[14]

The propriety of such living exhibitions was raised in *The Times*, which concluded that the 130 Senegalese, who had already been in France, were experienced; and that the government of France needed no gratuitous advice on how to run their empire.

There were photographic postcards, of course. The village itself, a blacksmith at his forge and two dozen Africans posed as 'the Senegalese at home' are some that have survived. The group that sailed from Liverpool for Africa in November included, according to the passenger list, fifty-eight adults, twenty-six aged between one and twelve, and two babies. The family names Sow and Benga were quite common.

Three African men, possibly from Durban in South Africa, were also photographed at the Franco-British Exhibition. They pulled rickshaws. There were other Blacks at the showgrounds, some visiting, for these exhibitions were immensely popular, being instructive and amusing. Other African elements could be found in the Gambian and Nigerian sections, the latter displaying Benin bronzes, tropical products and minerals. The Olympic Games of 1908 were held at the exhibition, but they lacked the media attention and mass audiences of more recent times.

When presenting African villages the promoters did not tell the public that the living exhibits were seasoned travellers and semi-professionals. The image was the reality. In the summer of 1908, fifty miles south of London, something of the reality became exposed. Struggling with spelling and lettering at his lodgings at 18, Kensington

2. Senegalese village at the Franco–British exhibition, 1908

3. South Africans at the 1908 exhibition

4. Ethnic villages included children

Gardens, Brighton, Brausfoot Maroosa wrote to the Colonial Office, London, on 7 August. 'I was brought over here from Sierra Leone' he wrote, adding

> I like to go home again. Sir would you kindly help me to back again. We are here for two weeks. We have tried all best and I find we cant do any good here so we like to go home if we have the chance.

The Colonial Office asked the local police to check the story, and to find out how many Africans claimed to be natives of Sierra Leone –

5. Women featured in the Dahomey Warrior troupes

and thus qualified for official assistance. Were they destitute, they asked. The Africans were bogus, for their act, as Maroosa had written, was 'the Dahomey Warriors'. The people of Dahomey, far from Sierra Leone, had fought French imperialists and acquired a reputation for courage; which gave them a commercial value as imperial exhibits in Britain. Maroosa and his colleagues from Sierra Leone were assisted back to Africa after the Freetown legislative council voted, on 9 September, to repatriate the out-of-work warriors.[15]

Dahomey Warriors, surely from that French colony one thousand miles east of Freetown, travelled all over Edwardian Britain. They appeared in grand exhibitions and in public halls in towns and cities. There were warriors in Scarborough in early August 1905, for example.[16] Postcards are far from rare: a woman with two children; 'Princess Gumma'; 'Princess Fassie (of the Dahomey Warriors)'; and a

Dahomey Village, Imperial International Exhibition, 1909, White City, London

6. The Dahomey village at London's White City, 1909

group of nearly forty on a card that states their manager was Angazza Bogolo. Three adults appeared on the card mailed in Durham's Bishopmiddleham in August 1905 with the note 'Saw these people on Saturday – they look interesting dont they.'[17] There was a Dahomey Village, duly pictured on a postcard, at the Imperial International Exhibition in London in 1909.

Africans were presented as conquered peoples and, paradoxically, as warriors and soldiers. The London weekly the *African World* advised its readers on 2 May 1908 that King Edward would be reviewing the Royal Naval and Military Tournament at Olympia, west London, due to open on 21 May. One hundred 'native soldiers of the West African Regiment' from Sierra Leone would participate in that show. They were to present Africa: warriors, medicine men, a devil dance and how soldiering was conducted in Africa's tropical forests. They had all volunteered to make the journey, and were to be accommodated at Olympia.

Two weeks later the *African World* published a photograph of the soldiers marching, in bare feet, in London. The *Daily News* also reported that the African soldiers had arrived and that 'in the Strand the traffic was held up while the dusky warriors passed'. The band numbered two dozen. A lieutenant and a sergeant were White. 'During the whole time they are in London they will not be allowed out of Olympia except in the charge of a European' seems to have been stated to assure imperialists that Londoners would not lead them astray. Or was it to assure Londoners that they were safe from inquisitive natives? They did leave the exhibition grounds, on 1 June, when they were inspected by the king at Buckingham Palace.[18]

Yet another group from Sierra Leone was appearing at a London exhibition in 1908. Eight Mandingo children worked at the Toy City and Fun Fair at Earls Court. Both the *Daily Mirror* and the *African World* mentioned what must have been a publicity stunt in December 1908. Wearing grass skirts and blankets, they visited parliament where they were welcomed by members including John Burns, who was greeted by Chief Ti-To. Ti-To knew that Burns, destined to be the first working man to be a member of a British government, had tried his fortune in west Africa where he had saved his father's life. The African thanked the socialist. The newspapers also reported that the group was reluctant to travel on the underground railway back to the exhibition.

NOTES

1. F. Smith, *The People's Health 1830–1910* (New York: Holmes & Meier Publishers, 1979), p. 228.
2. A. Davin, *Growing Up Poor: Home, School and Street in London 1870–1914* (London: Rivers Oram, 1996), p. 209.
3. L. Lyde, *A Geography of the British Empire* (London: Black, 1915).
4. Ibid p. 40.
5. Ibid p. 42.
6. Ibid p. 64.
7. H. Stanley, *How I Found Livingstone* (London: Sampson Low, 1890), a 'prize for general attention and industry' awarded in Buckingham in 1890 [author's collection]; *The Story of the Life of Mackay of Uganda, Pioneer Missionary, by his Sister* (London: Hodder & Stoughton, 1898), a prize for 'good answering in scripture' awarded in Carrickfergus in 1898 was the seventh edition 'completing 26th thousand' [author's collection]; E. Hume, *David Livingstone: The Man, the Missionary, and the Explorer* (London: Sunday School Union, nd; 3rd edition) was awarded by a Clapham (London) Presbyterian Sunday School [author's collection]; W. Livingstone's *Mary Slessor of Calabar, Pioneer Missionary* (London: Hodder & Stoughton, 1917) was a remarkable albeit later book, the author's 'Xmas 1917' edition being the eighth of that year. It was republished over forty times and had a children's edition. It was also possible to read novels set in Africa by one-time travellers, such as V. Cameron, *In Savage Africa* (London: Nelson, 1903).
8. R. Toll, *Blacking Up: The Minstrel Show in Nineteenth-Century America* (New York: Oxford, 1974).
9. H. Reynolds, *Minstrel Memories: The Story of Burnt Cork Minstrelsy in Great Britain from 1836 to 1927* (London: Alston Rivers, 1927).
10. B. Shephard, 'A Royal Gentleman of Colour', *History Today* (London) April 1984, pp. 36–41.
11. N. Parsons, 'Frantz or Klikko, the Wild Dancing Bushman', unpublished paper presented in February 1989 at the University of London. My thanks to David Killingray for supplying a copy.
12. My thanks to Bill Tonkin of the Exhibition Study Group.
13. *Daily Gleaner* (Kingston, Jamaica), 3 October 1905.
14. *African World* (London), 23 May 1908, p. 117.
15. Christopher Fyfe kindly advised their fate.
16. *Scarborough Post*, 5 August 1905 noted the group at the Arcadia had been augmented for the public holiday weekend.
17. Jeffrey Green collection.
18. *African World* (London), 2 May 1908, pp. 615, 617; ibid 16 May 1908, p. 75; ibid 6 June 1908, p. 193.

— 2 —

Imperial visitors

THE Colonial Office in London was responsible for the administration of many of the peoples of the British Empire, especially the lands of the Africans and their descendants in the Caribbean. There was little parliamentary support for empire building despite the efforts of Joseph Chamberlain, the secretary of state for the colonies. The Colonial Office was cheese-paring, budgeting expenditure cautiously. The underdeveloped colonies had little or no surplus income to invest, so many if not most of the modernising or Westernising activities resulted from actions by other people.

Britons interested in imperial development included traders and merchants, missionary groups, individuals who believed that the future of Britain required its surplus population to be settled overseas, and a sprinkling of dreamers, reformers and idealists. They invited Black people to visit Britain, arranged tours and meetings, showed them industrial and social activities, and thus enlarged their understanding of the British and Britons' awareness of the people of the tropical empire. There were invitations from the Colonial Office, too. Those who accepted these invitations often came as representatives of their people, not as supplicants. It is clear that these imperial visitors saw more than their supposed masters had intended.

One example of a visitor who was far from content to keep to the role expected by his hosts was Lewanika, ruler of the Lozi of western Zambia (then known as the Barotse of north west Rhodesia). His people's lives were centred on the Zambezi river, fortunately some distance from the settlers who had accepted the invitation from Cecil Rhodes to make a new life in Rhodesia in the 1890s. Lewanika established direct links with the Colonial Office (and thus parliament at Westminster) through a treaty. He also avoided armed conflict with the White invaders, and did not abandon traditional religious values despite efforts by missionary Francois Coillard. Coillard believed that the conversion of Lewanika would encourage many of the Lozi to take up Christianity, and so the pressure on the Black monarch was considerable.

Lewanika was a leader of his people, not a stooge of Rhodes and his

minions. He was sagacious, anxious to care for his people. To the
White settlers of Rhodesia he was merely another African chief, of
course.[1]

Something of Lewanika's personality is seen in the memoirs of Colin
Harding, who escorted the African leader and his party to England in
the summer of the coronation year. Harding, who had been associated
with Rhodes and had fought in the 1890s wars in Rhodesia, was an
administrator in Barotseland from 1899. On holiday in England with
his 'Cape boy' John Norton,[2] he was sent to Cape Town where he met
Lewanika, his ngambella (prime minister) and others of the group
he and Norton were to accompany to London as witnesses at the
coronation. Welcomed at Southampton by Lord Kintore and a
representative of the Colonial Office with a message from the British
king, the group went to Sherborne in Dorset and then to the small
Somerset town of Marston Magna where flags were flying and church
bells were ringing to greet the Africans.[3]

Edward's coronation had to be postponed as he needed an
operation for appendicitis; his African guests fretted. Harding took
them to nearby Yeovil in early June 1902. The *Western Advertiser*
reported that Lewanika had tea with the mayor, magistrates and
members of the corporation. The mayor 'presented the dusky
potentate with a beautifully-bound copy of a book containing the
photos of all the Lord Mayors and Mayors of England and Wales'. He
was also given a box of gloves.

On 18 June the *Advertiser* reported that the 'dusky monarch of
Barotseland' had visited the Royal Counties Show at Reading, where
he had been greeted at the railway station by the mayor. The African
was admired – 'a most intelligent face, and his physique is very fine
indeed'. The 'native members of his suite were rather picturesquely
attired in a kind of semi-military uniform'. Lewanika was cheered by
the crowd at the showgrounds.

On 9 July the weekly humorous magazine *Punch*[4] published a poem
about Lewanika, which began 'A Christian I gladly would be. But I've
twelve little reasons against', namely his wives. The polygamous
monarch duly met Edward the Seventh. Was the African being
humoured in order to avoid further costly warfare in Rhodesia?
Lewanika was far from naive: even the comments of Harding reveal
that he had strong motives. But Harding made no mention on a visit he
made with the Africans to Goudhurst in Kent, an omission that
exposes the partial nature of autobiography.

Lewanika had two sons at Bethany House School in Goudhurst.
They had been there since mid-1901.[5] Their father's visit, with
Mokamba the ngambella, Sekota (a servant) and an interpreter on
8 July 1902 is recorded in a photograph and on a memorial stone.

MR. A. E. TALBOT. NGAMBELLA. PR. IMASIKU. SEKOTA INTERPRETER. PR. LUBASI.
MR S. KENDON.   COLONEL HARDING. KING LEWANIKA.   REV A. G. MANN.

King Lewanika's visit to Bethany House School, Goudhurst, July 8, 1902.

7. Lewanika of the Barotse, with his prime minister and interpreter, visit his sons
Imasiku and Lubasi at their school in Goudhurst, Kent, July 1902 (Skene Catling)

A local newspaper reported that the small town's streets were decorated in honour of the imperial visitors and that the headmaster had said that Imasiku and Lubasi were popular at the school, where they studied the same subjects as the others except Latin, and had quickly mastered English. Bethany House's archives show that the pair attended the school into 1904 and that Lubasi was in contact with it in 1909.[6] Imasiku headed the Lozi of Barotseland from 1945, after the death of his father's successor.[7]

Harding, who was to train the Barotseland police, wrote of 'the childlike simplicity of the Barotse nature'.[8] He also mentioned the 'young and noisy crowd [which] had gathered round the entrance of our Wilton Crescent [London] abode', that King Edward's son (the future George the Fifth) had also met the African leader, and that the party had been guests of Colonial Secretary Chamberlain at the naval review at Spithead. There were meetings with the newspaper magnate Alfred Harmsworth, and with 'most of the distinguished guests who had gathered in London for the Coronation'.[9]

'Hardly a day passed without Lewanika or his Prime Minister making some reference to the contemplated discussion' with Chamberlain over the status of the Lozi now that their lands had become part of Northern Rhodesia, which was administered by Rhodes's British South Africa Company, in association with the Colonial Office.[10] Despite Chamberlain's assurance that a proposed hut tax would not be implemented without Lewanika's consent, when the group returned to Africa they found that it was being arranged. By Lewanika's death in 1916 'most of his power had been shorn... Lewanika retained few or no administrative rights over his people or the most fertile and valuable portion of the Barotse Kingdom', Harding wrote.[11]

A letter written by B. P. Kuaate, Lewanika's secretary on the British visit, has survived. Dated 20 August 1902, written in good English in a clear hand, it was headed 90 Sloane Street, which was an expensive neighbourhood in central London. It asked a doctor for receipts for over thirty pounds.[12] It seems that the Lozi were using Harding; who thought his Black companions depended on him.[13]

Sekota or Sikota Kwandu, who had visited Goudhurst, was interviewed half a century later. His comments on the coronation of 1902 appeared in the *Northern Rhodesian Journal* of 1953,[14] the year that Edward's son's grand-daughter was crowned Elizabeth the Second. Kwandu named his fellow steward as Amba, and the two interpreters as Khoatle and Iwakutili. He recalled the weeks waiting for Edward to recover from surgery, during which time the Lozi visited Sheffield where they toured a foundry and met the mayor; and visited Manchester, again meeting civic leaders, touring a cotton mill and a fish plant (apparently dealing with eels). They went to Scotland where they received Edward's command that Lewanika 'ought to be welcomed as a member of the Royal Family'; and visited both Glasgow and Edinburgh. They were back in London two days before the coronation, which Lewanika witnessed inside Westminster Abbey. Kwandu waited outside where the proceedings were explained to him 'by one of the Princes from Ireland'. Two days later the African leader had a coronation medal pinned on his chest by the British king-emperor.

The French protestant missionary Francois Coillard had asked Lewanika if he was at all embarrassed at the prospect of meeting Edward the Seventh, to be told 'Oh no, when we kings get together we always find plenty to talk about.'[15] On their return Mokamba said 'The great ones honoured us; the [Christian] believers showed us affection; but the people of the world despised us because our skins were black.'[16]

One example of the latter aspect of the experience of Black Edwardians can be seen in *Punch* on 13 August 1902. 'The merry little shoe-black who greeted one of our Dusky Visitors with the question "Shine your face, Sir?" expects to be out of the hospital in a fortnight.'

The crowds outside Lewanika's lodgings exhibited curiosity over the imperial visitors. This can be seen in other Black Edwardians' experiences of Britain in 1902. Ham Mukasa and Apolo Kagwa were guests for the coronation, too. Mukasa's account was published, in English, in 1904. *Uganda's Katikiro in England, being the Official Account of his Visit to the Coronation of His Majesty King Edward VII* was translated and edited by Ernest Millar, the official interpreter and a Church Missionary Society missionary in Uganda. Like Harding, Millar owed a great deal to Africa and Africans.

His missionary society employers had been active in Uganda since the mid-1870s. They had come into conflict with local beliefs, pagan and Muslim, as well as Catholic missionaries who were seen as an advance guard for French imperialism. Civil warfare, in which Mukasa and Kagwa were successful leaders, and the threat of French empire-builders led to Uganda becoming a protectorate of Britain in 1894. The British ignored the wishes of the Baganda's traditional decision makers, and nominated the infant Daudi Chwa to be the future kabaka or king. That region of Uganda was then ruled through three regents, the most influential being Apolo Kagwa, the katikiro or prime minister. Kagwa and his secretary Ham Mukasa were to observe the natives of England and Scotland in the summer of 1902.

The two Ugandan visitors were sophisticated and made a physical impression, for Kagwa was over 6 foot three inches tall and Mukasa had a weak leg and so wore a surgical boot. They were not hicks from an Africa of European legend, but proud Africans whose historians

8. Ham Mukasa (left) and Apolo Kagwa from Uganda travelled widely in
Britain in the summer of 1902 (Royal Commonwealth Society)

traced the Baganda's descent through more than thirty kabakas and
five centuries. Their ways had deeply impressed European travellers
from the first such visitor in the 1860s.[17] Both men spoke English
and Kagwa's son Sepirinya Kadumukasa was being educated in
Cambridgeshire.[18]

After attending a service at St Paul's Cathedral on 15 June, the two

Africans walked to Lambeth Palace. They were followed through the streets. 'I saw a great many little English boys following me to see what a black man was like.'[19] He wanted to talk with them but Millar said he should not. The eighty street urchins were not the right people; after all, the trio was on its way to meet members of the Church Lads' Brigade at a palace. On another Sunday in London they emerged from church to find 'a great number of persons both small and great, who were not accustomed to black people' had come to stare at them.[20]

Mukasa was impressed by the masses of people in London ('like locusts in numbers'). On 27 June 1902, when he joined the crowds visiting soldiers from Asia and Africa ('Soudanese, Swahilis, Baganda, Kavirondo people, Abyssinians, Masai . . . to the number of four hundred') at their temporary barracks at north London's Alexandra Palace, he observed 'if one were to fall down he would be trodden to death'.[21]

This was a justified fear, for the previous Saturday had seen one hundred thousand spectators looking at these uniformed men, who included 150 members of the West African Frontier Force, Caribbeans and a 'full-blooded negro rifleman from Central Africa'.[22]

When Mukasa and Kagwa attended a gathering at the Bishop of London's home in Fulham, 'we two and an Indian were the only black people there'.[23] They were taken to a play at Drury Lane and a variety show at the Hippodrome, and visited a hospital in Balham where they inspected an X-ray machine and observed that industrial and street accidents were hidden costs of life as lived in an urban industrial society. Mukasa visited an orphanage, and commented that England's violent past was displayed in the military equipment, prison cells, execution axe and traitors' graves at the Tower of London.[24]

They visited explorer-author Henry Stanley at his home, where they observed bananas (a fruit yet to be imported in quantities sufficient to reach the masses) and that women left the room after dinner. They met Uganda's ex-governor, Harry Johnston, and admired his Swahili. They went to the headquarters of the Church Missionary Society and its president, member of parliament Sir John Kennaway, and 'saw the room in which Namukade and Kataluba (the envoys sent over by [kabaka] Mutesa in 1878) had lived, and also the man who had looked after them'.[25] They were photographed at Westminster by Sir Benjamin Stone, MP.[26]

As the weeks ticked past while the king-emperor regained his strength, the two Ugandans, like Lewanika's group, were taken round Britain. Southampton at the end of June, then Birmingham where they visited a plating works with ten thousand workers and the BSA bicycle and rifle factory with a larger workforce. Mukasa observed that it had produced five thousand rifles weekly during the recent war in South Africa.[27] They moved on to Britain's premier port, Liverpool, where they were taken over the *Oceanic* which had three hundred crew. On 5 July they were welcomed at the town hall by the mayor, and were escorted round the council chamber and the courts. They observed cattle boats from Ireland. Then they went to Cambridge which had 'great colleges where sons of the rich are taught'.[28]

Moving south they visited future missionary nuns and priests at St Joseph's College, Mill Hill, on the edge of London. They spoke to six Franciscan sisters at St Mary's Abbey, about to depart for Uganda, who heard Kagwa state that he hoped they would teach women and children, and nurse the sick. The male students at Mill Hill were welcomed as future teachers of English: Kagwa used Luganda in his speech.[29] Bishop Henry Hanlon, who had lived in Uganda in the 1890s, translated. Kagwa was capable of making his speech in English. Did the bishop note that these Catholic missionaries were wanted as teachers, not as religious zealots? The Ugandans moved to Hampstead where they stayed with Millar's brother, before leaving for Carlisle on 10 July.

They had their photographs taken at Carlisle's agricultural show; then went on to Glasgow where they were greeted by the lord provost and taken round the city's prison, university and hospital before joining the provost for dinner. They attended a Sunday service at the city's cathedral and on Monday 14 July they went down a coal mine. They also visited an iron foundry and a furnace, and met five magistrates with whom they discussed how to punish drunkards. Mukasa observed that workers at a sugar factory near Greenock 'had faces like black men, because the charcoal made them very black'.[30] Kagwa made a speech at the town hall and visited a shipyard.

On 16 July they were in Edinburgh, meeting civic dignitaries and seeing the impressive Forth bridge. Southwards to Newcastle 'where they make cannon'; visiting an armaments factory employing twelve thousand, Mukasa noted machinery which did 'all kinds of work just like men'. They toured a ship with guns that 'would carry fifteen miles'. Kagwa fired a practice round, as did one of the daughters of their host, William Cruddas. They had welcomed their stay at his home and that they were not made 'to sleep in a strangers' house, which they call in English a "hotel"'. The next day they visited a pottery where 'they make plates of earthenware for the rich'.[31]

They moved far south to Hertfordshire where Kagwa and Mukasa were guests of prime minister Lord Salisbury at Hatfield House. There were 'a great many kinds of people, Chinese, Indians, Moors, South Africans, and a king who was black like we are'. This was Lewanika, who 'was not a Christian, and did as he liked'. The three thousand English people there drank tea 'as they stood up, as is their custom'.[32] Salisbury's son, Lord Cranborne, escorted Kagwa round the premises.

Back in central London the Ugandans met with members of the Anti-Slavery Society at the Westminster Palace Hotel on 6 August, a matter ignored in Mukasa's book, possibly because domestic slavery still continued in Uganda. This meeting was detailed in the society's quarterly journal.[33] On 7 August they went to Windsor to greet the soon-to-be-crowned Edward. There they met Ras Makonnen, the leader of the delegation from Ethiopia. Makonnen's cousin was the Emperor Menelik who ruled from 1889 to 1912. Makonnen presented Edward with a zebra.[34]

Mukasa noted that Makonnen 'had with him about ten companions'.[35] Probably because of Millar's editing, as with that earlier meeting with rival Catholic missionaries, we know little of this connection, and can only guess that the two Ugandans met William Henry Ellis, for we do know that Ellis met Makonnen in London.[36] Ellis, an American of African descent born in Texas in 1864, was no stranger to Europe. He was the first Black broker on Wall Street. He was invited by Makonnen to visit Ethiopia following their meeting in London, and he duly went there in October 1903.[37]

Ethiopia was not a British colony. Indeed, following the massive defeat of Italian invaders in 1896, it continued its independence. The Cameroons had been a German colony since the 1880s, although Baptist Missionary Society workers from the 1850s and traders, who used the West African steamship service which turned round at the fine harbour of Dualla, had given the coastal region strong English connections. There were two Cameroon Africans in Britain in 1902. Reported as King Manga Bell and Rudolph Bell, they were escorted round Manchester by the representative of a trading firm who took them to the town hall where the mayor greeted them. The editor of the monthly *African Times* of October 1902 questioned their alleged royal status.

Status was crucial. Three worthies from Sierra Leone, who could not wait for Edward to recover, returned to Africa before the coronation. But in Plymouth, as the *African Times* reported on 8 September 1902, Bai Farima, Pamayanha and secretary Prince Fioma had benefited from the latter's rank as a leading Freemason in Freetown. This masonic connection enabled them to mix as equals with others of that order in Plymouth.

The Colonial Office files reveal that Bai Farima, the chief of Kwaia, had gathered two hundred pounds from his people and had requested an invitation to Edward's coronation. The application from the governor of Sierra Leone bears the comment that there was no objection 'if we can find a presentable bear-leader to take him about'.[38] Dr Hood, who had been district commissioner at Kwaia, had agreed to be in charge of Farima and his colleague. Fioma was already living in England. Three tickets for the ceremony in the abbey was 'rather a large order' but seats were available for the procession and the naval review.

Hood took the visitors to his home in Ashbourne, where they were joined by Farima who came from the nearest city, Derby. He was described as a cousin of the sub-chief Pamayanha. It was not all sweetness and light for these imperial visitors. Farima complained, on his return to Africa, that Hood shouted at him and had struck him. Hood denied striking the chief, and explained that he had 'had a very unpleasant time with the Chiefs who do not seem to appreciate what has been done on their behalf'. Their real grievance was that the money they had received from their people had been taken from them, and used to pay various expenses. The officials decided that this was wrong, and that nothing should be deducted for the visits to the Hippodrome, Madame Tussauds and other entertainments, only those sums spent by the visitors on themselves.

The mass of Britons who saw the imperial visitors seem to have left no comment, so we can only guess at what went through the minds of the thousands of factory workers, mill hands, miners, street urchins, churchgoers, travellers on the railways, businessmen, officials in town halls and courts, hospital personnel, aristocrats, parliamentarians, clerks and the Church Lads' Brigade boys.

The visitors saw poor and malnourished people, grimy workers, hotel maids and porters, prisoners, orphans and what remained firmly in the memories of those first days in Britain: White men sweeping the streets.[39] Mukasa noted at the Westminster Palace Hotel:

> The work of the servants is this: the men do the cooking, the women make the beds and bring the early tea, and water for washing the face, and clean the boots, and they turn on the bath-water – but we would not let them do this, but did it for ourselves; they also wash the clothes, and lit the fires for us when it was cold.[40]

The contrast between the reality of life in Britain and the images created in the empire was substantial. Class was a crucial element in Edwardian society, with royal Blacks obtaining similar widespread respect as other monarchs.

There were Blacks who had been knighted by Queen Victoria, notably Sir Edward Jordan, a Jamaican who was mayor of Kingston in 1859, and Canadian governor Sir James Douglas, who had been born in British Guiana.[41] The first African knight was Samuel Lewis, who was as much at home in Britain as Sierra Leone, where he had been born in 1843.[42]

Lewis had studied in Sheffield and London, qualified in law, and was a major figure in legal matters in British West Africa, which led to him representing African cases in British courts. Knighted in 1896, he was mayor of Freetown, a mason, and a Sunday School teacher. His business interests extended from Africa to Britain. Sir Samuel's son Samuel was educated at Canterbury College in the 1890s and then qualified as a lawyer.

Terminally ill with cancer, Sir Samuel and his wife Edith sailed to England with an introduction to the leading medical authority Sir Patrick Manson from the colonial governor. He underwent surgery but died on 9 July 1903 near Harley Street. He was buried in Acton cemetery where his widow's poem 'Memories are treasures none can steal, Death leaves a gap no one can fill' remains clearly inscribed on his memorial: which makes no mention that he was an African.

Another West African with high-ranking contacts in Britain was the alake of Abeokuta. With three companions the alake reached Plymouth on 22 May 1904, where they were met by Southern Nigeria's governor William MacGregor. The Africans took the train to London where they stayed at the Westminster Palace Hotel. Yet again there were crowds who gathered outside the hotel to have a glimpse of the imperial visitors.

This was noted by the *Anglo-African Argus*, a short-lived London weekly that may have been edited by an African. It certainly paid a great deal of attention to the Nigerian ruler and his colleagues. On 4 June 1904 the *Argus* reported that the Nigerians had visited the zoo and two variety theatres, and had met King Edward on 30 May. They went to the military tournament on 1 June, visited the business district or City of London, and attended the Royal Counties Agricultural Show at Guildford in Surrey where the alake 'made a local firm happy' with his order for six ploughs. They left London for Liverpool, where they met John Holt, a veteran of trading with western Africa.

The Africans stayed at Liverpool's Adelphi, visited the recently-founded School of Tropical Medicine, and later met its founder Alfred Jones whose commercial interests in the tropics included the Bank of British West Africa (founded 1899), the Elder Dempster shipping company which carried most of Britain's freight and passenger traffic with west Africa, and substantial investments in the now developing marketing of Jamaican bananas in Britain.[43] The alake went to Oldham, where he toured an iron works and a cotton mill. On 13 June the mayor of Liverpool welcomed the African leader to the Royal Exchange where he was 'heartedly cheered on making his appearance in the visitors' gallery'. The four wore traditional dress, which led to criticism.

They met up with groups with interests in Africa, including the Church Missionary Society in London, and the Royal Society for the Prevention of Cruelty to Animals, which elected the alake a vice president. From London they travelled via Norwich to Aberdeen, where, the *Anglo-African Argus* reported, they were welcomed 'by large crowds of people'. They spent two days in that Scottish city, where university students attacked their carriage and dislodged the alake's headwear. This was not reported in the *Argus* but Dr T. E. S. Scholes, a Jamaican-born author resident in London (to whom we shall return) was to comment 'Imagine such an indignity to have been offered to a prince of European blood. . . . But these young gentlemen are the future moulders of British opinion.'[44] The *Lagos Standard* saw this as racist. The students were fined for their insulting conduct.[45]

Reaching Edinburgh there was a more positive contact with students, for, as the *Argus* reported, 'a number of African students resident in the Scottish capital were among those who welcomed him'. One was Ayodeji Oyejola, who graduated in medicine in 1906 and returned to Nigeria where he worked in a hospital that was built for him by the alake.[46]

The activities of Gbadebo, the alake, were mentioned in many British newspapers for it was the custom in Edwardian times to list the daily routines of British and visiting royalty. The *Bradford Daily Telegraph*, for example, reported on 7 July 1904 that

> The chieftain has been much gratified by the gift of a Bible from the King. This is to replace one which was presented to the Alake's father by Queen Victoria, and which was accidentally burned.

The Nigerian visitors left Britain on 9 July.

The following year another Nigerian visitor, described by the Colonial Office as 'a well known member of the native community of Lagos', wrote a ten page typewritten letter to the Colonial Office. Dated 10 October, it was from 114 Rodenhurst Road in Clapham Park, south London. C. J. A. Sapara Williams made several suggestions for improvements in the colony. He suggested that a college to train teachers should be established in Lagos, and that governors of the colony should exercise continuity of policy.[47] Williams, whose arrival on a ship reaching Liverpool had been noted in the *African World* of 16 September, was one of several Black visitors who attempted to change imperial policy by making contact directly with the Colonial Office when in Britain. He made contacts with resident Blacks, as will be shown.

It was not easy to campaign for reforms, for those with a good education who lived and worked in the tropical colonies had few employment prospects as teachers, doctors or lawyers outside the colonial service itself. The colonial public works departments used expatriate engineers and the medical services favoured White doctors.

Private practice depended on the patients paying fees, and those who could afford such treatment were Whites who preferred their own colour or Blacks like Sir Samuel Lewis who could afford to travel to Britain for treatment.

Teachers had employment in mission schools and a handful of government schools. In the Caribbean wealthy people sent their children to elitist schools where the teachers were often White, or sent them to boarding schools in England. Ambitious Africans such as Lewis, Kagwa and Lewanika had children at school in Britain, so there were few financial certainties for Black-led private schools in Africa. Who would employ an independently-minded Black teacher? Few White children were resident in the tropical colonies. Government employment could be risked by actions deemed offensive to the colonial authorities.

Employment in the colonial civil service involved lengthy leaves, for the system assumed that senior staff would be expatriate Britons who required 'home leave' for health and family reasons. As Blacks obtained higher positions, despite a long history of Black West Indians in posts in Victorian west Africa, now their status changed.[48] By 1909 African and Asian doctors in British West Africa were paid at a rate lower than Whites. No matter what qualifications or length of experience, inexperienced White doctors were automatically superior to coloured medical men.[49]

In the British West Indies there had been Black doctors in both private and government service for decades. Some, as we will see, worked in Africa. The tropical empire had no medical schools, so doctors and professional nurses had to train in the British Isles or elsewhere in the empire (usually Canada, notably in Montreal and Halifax). United States qualifications were not valid within Britain and the empire: a further disadvantage for Blacks there was that their studies had to be at Blacks-only colleges in an overtly racist society. There were West Indian doctors in America – and in Africa, the British Isles and the Caribbean.

Long leaves enabled doctors in the Colonial Service to depart for Britain, where they could renew contacts made during their student years and catch up with professional developments. They could also submit to further examinations, as can be seen with Frederick Telemachus Wills of British Guiana. He had qualified as a doctor at Edinburgh in 1895, and became an MD there in 1911, the year he published a research paper on bacilli.[50]

Another such imperial visitor was Dr Joseph Skeele Myers Nurse. He made a fool of himself in Scotland, but that did not justify the contempt seen in newspaper reports. Like the rowdies of Aberdeen with the alake, the incident would have been reported completely differently had all the people been White.

Nurse was of Basseterre in St Kitts, and educated in Scotland where he had qualified as a doctor. He had married a Miss Wilson in 1891, when he also knew Bella Mackintosh. His wife died, the doctor left Scotland in 1896, and wrote from the Caribbean to Miss Mackintosh. In May 1900 he was again in Scotland, apparently promising to marry her in 1902. He wrote from the West Indies, returned to Britain, and in February 1901 married a Miss Dickens. In October 1905 Miss Mackintosh's claim for breach of promise was heard before the Court of Sessions in Edinburgh.

The doctor was represented by a lawyer in his absence, who told the court that he had merely lodged with the lady, paying for his accommodation and making no promise to marry her. It was suggested that there was something unlikely in the idea of a Scottish woman marrying a Black man, for it was said that Dr Nurse 'is a negro with thick lips, the woolly hair and the general appearance of the negro'. Nurse's lawyer asked Miss Mackintosh 'He is just a "nigger"?'. The jilted Scot was awarded five hundred pounds, a substantial sum for 1905 but less than her claim.[51]

The Jamaican *Daily Gleaner* noted the matter on 1 November and Dr Scholes noted it as he prepared the second volume of his *Glimpses of the Ages*.[52]

Not all Black medical men visiting Britain had such publicity. Indeed, a Jamaican doctor who rose to become principal medical officer for Southern Nigeria by May 1906 is only known to have been of African descent because he was described as 'rather dark' in the memoirs of Nobel Prize-winner Ronald Ross.[53] Ross had been aided in his investigations linking mosquitoes and malaria by Dr William Henry Williams Strachan. The two doctors met on the boat taking Ross to Sierra Leone at the end of the 1890s. Strachan had qualified at Guy's in London in 1882, returning to Jamaica before transferring to Nigeria. Dr Strachan was listed on the *Burutu* which reached Liverpool on 25 March 1905.[54] He retired to Jamaica in 1911,[55] the year after his twenty-three page *A Guide to the Preservation of Health in West Africa* was published in London. Constable also published his *Lessons in Elementary Tropical Hygiene* in 1913. He died in Brockley, south east London, in 1921.[56]

What Dr Strachan did in Britain in 1905 and why he was in London when he died are unresolved. The traditional leaders treated as royalty were in the public eye, and thus can be traced. Those who upset or were accused of upsetting local susceptibilities, like Dr Nurse, can be traced. How many imperial visitors were like Dr Strachan: not reported other than on a ship's passenger list?

Scheduled steamship services that linked west Africa and the northern Caribbean to Britain owed a great deal to Alfred Jones whose ships carried freight and passengers from Panama and Jamaica, and from the Cameroons to Gambia, to Liverpool. Such journeys took weeks, and imperial visitors had to have funds for the fare and time. Lewanika had taken months to get to England from the upper reaches of the Zambezi via Cape Town. Lacking Colonial Office subsidies or local imperial government support, any independent travellers from southern Africa had to overcome substantial costs in time and money to reach the centre of the empire. Nevertheless a group of Sotho men were in England at the beginning of 1907, attempting to express their views to the decision-makers.

Three representatives of the Sotho, with two servants and interpreter Joseph Gumede, formed the delegation which intended to restore recent rights to their people. Many of the Sotho had been dispossessed by the Boer republic of Orange River in 1892, with land rights only in the Basutoland Protectorate as defined by the British in 1884.[57] The Afrikaner republic was finally conquered by the British in the 1899–1902 war, and the region was absorbed into the British Empire, ruled from London. The delegation hoped that the British would permit the Sotho to have rights over its traditional lands.

In 1904 their king, Lerethodi, who earlier had been assisted by an American of African descent named Conrad Ridehout,[58] was visited by a Trinidad-born barrister named Henry Sylvester Williams. Of African descent, educated in Canada and London, where he lived with his English wife and their three children,[59] Williams was described as 'a well-known barrister' in the London weekly *South Africa* on 12 January 1907 when it detailed the Sotho delegation's arrival in Britain. Also linked to these imperial visitors were Dr Evans Darby and others of the League of Universal Brotherhood (Williams was a committee member).[60]

Williams had done a great deal to publicise the Sotho visitors, with reports circulated by Reuters news agency. *John Bull Overseas* of 15 February noted 'The Basuto chiefs now in London seem, however, to have a strong case'.[61] The Port of Spain (Trinidad) *Mirror*, copying London's *Daily News*, reported that Gumede had said

> We are now British subjects, and the question is, shall we remain in a state of servitude, as we were under the Boers, or claim our ordinary rights as British subjects? We have done all we could in South Africa, and this is our last hope. We will not be discouraged until we see the King.[62]

The visitors went to the Colonial Office on 18 January 1907.

The civil servants and ministers had to adjust to such delegations: Lesisa, Moloi and Lequila appear to have been aware through Williams that towards the end of the previous year a similar delegation had visited the Colonial Office. Led by an Indian barrister and representing Asian settlers in the Transvaal, the other defeated Afrikaner republic, its protests centred on the Transvaal's law that prohibited Asians from owning land. The law was vetoed by Colonial Secretary Lord Elgin.[63]

The Africans, their London friend Williams, one or two liberal members of parliament and members of the League of Universal Brotherhood met Elgin in January, who heard Williams speak for over an hour.[64] The Colonial Office contacted the High Commissioner in South Africa (Lord Selborne) and the matter was referred to the local South African legislature: which was elected by Whites only, and had already proposed that Sotho people anxious to farm should work for wages for Whites and cultivate smallholdings for themselves.[65]

The imperial visitors had waited and, when Lord Elgin's reply was received, they announced it at a meeting of the League on 27 March. Also present was Keir Hardie, the first socialist member of parliament: known through Williams who was a member of the Fabian Society. Both had been involved a year earlier with a Gold Coast delegation.[66] The group is also known to have attended a meeting at the Arundel Square, London, church of League member Revd Charles Garnett. Williams and Gumede also attended the official opening of parliament by Edward and his queen.[67]

The Sotho returned to a now largely self-governing South Africa where voters were male and almost totally of European birth or descent. Their racial attitudes led to the reintroduction of land laws that prohibited non-White ownership.[68] Williams, as we will see, was elected to a London council later that year, but then returned to Trinidad where he died in 1911. The Indian barrister moved to India where he led the nationalist movement and became one of the twentieth century's international achievers – Mahatma Gandhi.

Other South African delegations made visits to the centre of the empire: in 1906 and, a Sotho one again, in 1909. Six Sotho posed with Lord Mottistone at Westminster on 25 February 1909.[69] They requested that Basutoland was not to be included in the Union of South Africa.

The South Africa Act was approved by parliament, with some of the lands of the Sotho and the Swazi, and the semi-desert lands of Bechuanaland, remaining colonial protectorates. It took generations before Blacks in South Africa obtained voting rights.

African delegations came from other regions of the continent. One which made contact with lawyer Williams was that headed by the Barbados-born president of Liberia, Arthur Barclay, in August 1907. The Liberians – USA-born Thomas McCants Stewart and Frederick Johnson accompanied the president – were staying at a hotel in Northumberland Avenue in central London, where they met with Williams.[70] McCants Stewart was a lawyer too, very much involved with disputes with both France and Britain over the Black-led republic's boundaries.[71]

President Barclay, the head of this African republic recognised by Britain and France in the late 1840s, visited the Foreign Office, the Colonial Office and Buckingham Palace.[72] One result of this group of Black visitors was that Williams went to Liberia in 1908. Another was that the republic obtained a loan, secured against duties charged by the Liberian customs, through a commercial operation headed by Sir Harry Johnston, the retired governor of Uganda.[73] Johnston devotes a few pages of his 1923 autobiography to this matter,[74] although his two volume *Liberia* had been published in 1906.[75] In 1971 the historian Charles Wilson described the loan as the 'grand old sport of nigger-cheating'.[76]

The other independent Black African state was Ethiopia, then called Abyssinia. A group of Ethiopian visitors were in London in August 1908. Included in that group was Lij Yasu, reported as 'Lig Eyasson' in the *African World* of 1 August 1908. Grandson of Emperor Menelik, nominated heir to the ancient Christian kingdom in 1909, he ruled Ethiopia from 1910 to 1916.

The sight of well-dressed, top-hatted, coach-riding Black dignitaries en route to Windsor, Buckingham Palace or the empire's administrators in Whitehall was far from unusual in the 1900s. The Ethiopians who attended the coronation, in June 1911, of Edward's son and heir George the Fifth, were recalled in 1948:

> The arrival of the Abyssinian envoys lit with an African splendour even this darkness. Their lion-skins and cloaks of gilded feathers impressed me more than anything I saw that morning. And it was almost the first time that, thus watching its living representatives drive by and dismount, I realised the continued existence of Ethiopia into the modern world.[77]

Other Britons would have become wiser through seeing imperial visitors.

There were more royal Africans in Britain in 1913. Ham Mukasa returned, with Musaloslala, Simewo, Belazio and Daudi Chwa, the future kabaka of Uganda. The young prince was on his way to Britain 'for educational purposes', the *African World* advised its readers on 10 May 1913. On 7 June it published his photograph and said that the delegation was staying at the Westminster Palace Hotel. Attending the future kabaka was tutor J. C. R. Sturrock.

The African Society planned a formal dinner on 20 June; Sir Harry Johnston gave a formal interview to the *Pall Mall Gazette*; the Africans visited parliament on 12 June and the law courts on 18 June. With

9. Daudi Chwa toured Britain in 1913 with his tutor. On his return to Uganda he became kabaka or king

Sturrock they visited St Joseph's at Mill Hill on 20 June and met Bishop Hanlon.[78]

The African Society dinner two days later was presided over by Charles Lucas, assistant under secretary at the Colonial Office. Also present was the anti-slavery activist and Church Missionary Society treasurer Thomas F. V. Buxton. This London gathering mixed the major elements in Edwardian imperialism: parliamentarians, liberals, special interest groups, colonial administrators – and imperial visitors.

The Africans had an audience with the king-emperor at Buckingham Palace. The *Daily Graphic* reported 'the visitor and the chiefs wore picturesque native dress. The King shook hands with the young monarch and his tutor.'

The five Ugandans visited Cambridge and Leicester before reaching Manchester at the end of July 1913. Manchester was the British centre of the cotton industry and the British Cotton Growers Association had its offices at 15 Cross Street. The association reported to the Colonial Office, whose files reveal that the visitors had been escorted round the spinning mills of Sir E. Armitage and Sons, lunched with the mayor at the town hall and visited both the Royal Exchange and the city's docks (linked to the oceans by ship canal to Liverpool). The association hosted a formal dinner at the Midland Hotel.

On 30 July, with the ever-present Sturrock, they toured Schwabe and Co's calico printing works and then visited Platt Bros. 'The prosperity of Uganda means also the prosperity of Lancashire' announced the *African World* on 2 August. Commercial cotton growing was new in Uganda, owing a great deal to Buxton's Church Missionary Society and the imperial investment in the East African railway from the Indian Ocean to the eastern shores of Lake Victoria. The CMS had arranged for supplies of seeds, with Luganda instructions. In 1905 just fifty-four bales had been exported; the anticipated crop for 1913 was 40,000 bales, valued at half a million pounds.[79] The cotton mills of Lancashire were no longer dependent on cotton grown in lands outside British control, which is why the imperial visitors were so welcome in Manchester in the summer of 1913.

The Africans had been in Scotland, including a weekend in Fort Augustus, before reaching Manchester.[80] They moved on to Ireland. From the Grand Hotel in Belfast Sturrock recommended that Lewis Harcourt, the Colonial Secretary, should send birthday greetings to Daudi Chwa. The telegram reached him on time, in Dublin, on 8 August. Within one year the touring youth would be installed as kabaka.

Sturrock suggested, in October 1913, that the Whites who travelled with the Ugandans to Africa should be persons totally committed to their safety, and requested that the Foreign Office arranged that their luggage would not be searched by the customs authorities of the countries they had to pass through to reach Naples for their ship to Mombasa. The group's tour had cost the Colonial Office just over eighty-five pounds. Sturrock refunded the balance of the advance.[81] The visit seems to have been instructive and inexpensive, and imperialists must have been content. The opinions of the visitors, and the thoughts of the mill hands and other ordinary men and women they observed in Scotland, England and Ireland, are unknown.

A few months earlier the Colonial Office had been troubled by a less august group of Africans in Britain. Four Nigerians visited Britain in late May and early June 1913, and were reported as being impressed by the 'wonderful assortment of articles' in Gamages department store in London.[82] These visitors from Calabar were not merely shopping, but were 'on a mission of protest to the Colonial Office' over 'ancient rights of the natives'. They had royal status – Prince Bassey Duke Ephraim was the successor to the last king of Calabar, and his companions were Prince James Eyo Ita, Chief Inko Goodhead and Chief Richard Koto.[83]

Unable to comprehend that Africans were more aware of Britain and British ways than Britons were of Africa, even the *African World* reported 'they were clad in European dress, and talked English with ease and fluency'. Ephraim had been educated in Britain for six years, departing in 1892.[84] They had links with Buxton and the Anti-Slavery Society – but so did many civil rights groups in the empire. They used them to be critical of Nigeria's governor, and their opinions were being heard in polite society, in offices and drawing rooms of Edwardian decision makers and among people of influence including the liberal *Daily News*.

Nigeria's governor was Frederick Lugard, whose machinations were known to the pro-imperial *African World*. On 7 June this weekly reported a 'fog' and 'conflicting statements' from Lugard and the four visitors. It also criticised Lugard for failing to make public his proposed land reforms which had so upset the four from Calabar.

The fault was in the imperial system, with parliament and the Colonial Office. As Lewanika had discovered, the men in charge in the empire acted independently, protected by their employers if their colony was quiet and cost little. Lugard ran the massive colony of Nigeria without much reference to the Colonial Office. As a soldier in Uganda and western Africa he had become famous, and he now had a reputation as a brilliant administrator. The myths of empire were so easy to construct that generations of Britons and Africans were tricked into believing in Lugard. He fooled the Colonial Office, who gave him a unique contract as governor of Nigeria, Britain's largest colony. He was allowed to spend much of each year in Britain, not in Africa.[85]

This contract enabled him to be in Britain, to counter the charges made by Ephraim and others. Lugard's wife, Flora Shaw, had admired the imperial ambitions of Rhodes and had written on Africa for *The Times*. She had also written the standard reference entry on Nigeria in the *Encyclopaedia Britannica* of 1911, which praised Lugard's achievements.[86] The Lugards constructed their image in Britain whilst, back in Africa, weeks away by ship, administrators waited for the governor's decisions.

The bullying and expansionist regime of Joseph Chamberlain had a worthy successor in Lugard, but there were some who saw through the myths. S. H. Jeyes, in his 1903 study *Mr Chamberlain*, commented that Chamberlain 'has had to suppress turbulence and savagery' in West Africa, adding 'where Mr Chamberlain's hand has not been forced by native truculence, he has been led into conflict by the ardour of his subordinates'.[87] 'Lugard failed to take the Colonial Office sufficiently into his confidence .... [and] left the Government to learn from the newspapers' over the attack on Kano in 1903.[88]

One example of Lugard's self-promotion took place in 1913 when he claimed to have found the ideal place for the terminus of the new railway in eastern Nigeria. He proposed naming it after the Colonial Secretary, which is how Port Harcourt was named. The man who had surveyed the area was Lieutenant R. H. W. Hughes, who would destroy his career if he challenged the governor.[89] The four Africans were not so restricted.

Lugard's land reforms paid no attention to traditions which had been part of local practices for centuries. They also ignored treaties between governments of Britain and African communities. The four visitors from Calabar were not the only Nigerians to travel to London to protest. Led by Abegboyega Edun, a larger group from Abeokuta sought justice and understanding in London in June 1913. Abeokuta was a semi-independent state, guaranteed by a treaty signed in 1893.[90] The *African World* again commented that the leader was sophisticated and that he had 'a range of English, and an enunciation possessed by not too many Londoners'.[91]

Edun, a Methodist of the third generation, obtained support from the Free Church Council whose secretary, the Revd Frederick Meyer, distributed tickets for a London reception in honour of the Nigerians on 13 June 1913. Meyer had been closely connected to the Pleasant Sunday Afternoon association and was a leader in the Brotherhood Movement,[92] a Christian group that was sympathetic to Black endeavours.[93]

Most of the protestors were farmers, with one Lagos merchant named S. H. Pearse. Thirteen of this 'remarkable fine set of men' as the *Liverpool Echo* observed, left Liverpool on the *Dakar* on 2 July, wearing African style clothes. Ten of them, photographed at Harrods in London, were shown on page 500 of the *African World*. They were Abebiji Risawe, Chief Shobgun, Edun, Sanusi Ekerin, Oduntan Labinjah, Ezekial Adebiyi, and chiefs Demisokun, Dada, Ombukjo and Ajero. Much of the rest of that page detailed their comments on Britain. They had been appalled by London's traffic. During a visit to Sheffield 'a large crowd gave them a cordial welcome'.

Edun returned to London and spoke to members of the Brotherhood Movement in Tooting. He and his companions had other contacts with

Britain's middle classes but Lugard was the victor: the colonial territories of Northern Nigeria and Southern Nigeria were amalgamated into one massive colony, under governor Lugard.[94]

These visiting protestors had seen various aspects of Britain's industries as well as meeting Harcourt and Lugard, and visiting the Bible Society. They went to Reading and toured the biscuit factory of Huntley and Palmer, and Sutton's seed warehouse. They went to Crosse and Blackwell's tinned groceries factory, expressing great interest in tinned fish which were exported to Nigeria. They also visited a brass foundry, went to Sheffield, and to Liverpool where they witnessed Nigerian palm oil being processed into soap at Lever Brothers.[95]

Ten months later another group of imperial visitors arrived from Uganda. On 4 May 1914 they were presented to King George at Buckingham Palace by Bishop Henry Hanlon, who shared their faith. One month before the Bishop had informed the Colonial Office that the four visitors were to be in Britain for two and a half months, and asked for £250 to defray expenses.[96]

When the British imposed their rule on Uganda in the 1890s after civil disruption on religious lines, they selected Daudi Chwa, the infant son of Kabaka Mwanga, as the future kabaka and arranged a regency of three leading personalities. Mwanga was exiled to the Seychelles where he died in 1910.[97] The leading regent was Apolo Kagwa, a Protestant, who had witnessed Edward's coronation in 1902. The Catholic regent was Stanislas Mugwanya, who came to England with his son Benedict, accompanying Prince Joseph or Yusufu, Daudi Chwa's cousin.[98] The fourth visitor was Alexis the Pokina of Buddu.

On 27 May they visited Mill Hill, meeting future missionary priests. In central London the Colonial Office took little notice of the group, who were ciphers now that Daudi Chwa had reached maturity and thus seemed to have ensured Protestant rule. Hanlon's request was rejected for the visit was not official and lacked the governor's recommendation. Indeed governor Frederick Jackson was on holiday in Sussex and made no attempt to meet the four.

Hanlon's request was reasonable, for Catholic missions were teaching over 13,000 children[99] in Uganda without any government funding. Uganda had been brought into the empire twenty years before through conflict between France and Britain over the headwaters of the Nile and pressure from Christian missions. It was no longer important. Indeed, when Germany and Britain went to war in August 1914 governor Jackson contacted the Colonial Office to see if he should return to his colony immediately – he must have been crestfallen when he received instructions to continue his holiday into October.[100]

While the four Catholic Ugandans were in London, five South

Africans were making the long voyage from Cape Town.[101] Internal self-government of the four colonies as the Union of South Africa had been approved by Britain despite the visits of the Sotho in 1906 and another group in 1909. Elected by male Whites with some exceptions, the South African government had passed the Natives' Land Act in 1913. This reserved almost ninety per cent of the land for Whites. In denying pastoral and agricultural peoples access to land it was hoped to press Africans to labour in the gold and diamond mines that were the basis for South Africa's expanding economy.

The Natives' Land Act was the cornerstone of the apartheid decades. Testimonies and evidence of evictions resulting from that act had been collected by Solomon Plaatje, who was one of the five imperial visitors. With him in England were John Dube, a churchman from Natal who had been to the USA; Thomas Mapikela from Bloemfontein who had been in a delegation to Britain in 1909; Walter Rubusana, recently the sole Black in South Africa's parliament; and Saul Msane, newspaper editor and brilliant chess player, who won many games on the ship as well as the sweepstake, on his way to England.[102]

Like the four Ugandans they lacked official status. They were members of what would soon be the African National Congress, which had gathered money for their protest. In late June 1914 they finally met Lewis Harcourt, the colonial secretary, who took no notes and recommended that they speak to premier Louis Botha in Pretoria.[103]

The delegation had considerable journalistic experience and so turned to London's press, finding sympathy at the liberal *Daily News* and the *Westminster Gazette*. The nonconformist church and the Brotherhood Movement were very supportive, but the Aborigines' Protection Society was not at all concerned despite a long history of outspoken criticism on such matters (as we have seen with Klikko the Dancing Bushman). The South Africans addressed meetings, fed information to members of parliament who used it to embarrass the government, and talked with all manner of Britons across England.

Dube left first, and in August 1914 he cabled for the others to return. Their fares were to be paid by John Harris, secretary of the Aborigines' Protection Society. His terms were rejected by Plaatje,[104] who remained in England into 1916 when his *Native Life in South Africa* was published. During those years Plaatje met with other Black people in Britain, as will be disclosed.

He and the other imperial visitors had made the same basic error. They had believed that the British cared about their empire and its peoples. They knew little about it, cared less, had no plans for its equitable development, and regarded Black people as inferiors.

NOTES

1. G. Caplan, *The Elites of Barotseland* (London: Hurst, 1970); G. Clay, *Your Friend, Lewanika* (London: Chatto, 1968); C. Mackintosh, *Coillard of the Zambesi* (London: Fisher Unwin, 1907).
2. C. Harding, *Far Bugles* (privately published; 2nd ed., 1933), pp. 105, 114.
3. Ibid p. 119.
4. *Punch* (London), 9 July 1902, p. 17; see also *Punch* 30 July 1902, p. 63 and 3 September 1902, p. 153; Harding, *Far Bugles*, p 124.
5. My thanks to Skene Catling and Bethany House School.
6. My thanks to Skene Catling.
7. Caplan, *Elites*.
8. Harding, *Far Bugles* p. 119.
9. Ibid pp. 121–2.
10. Ibid p. 123.
11. Ibid p. 136.
12. Jeffrey Green collection.
13. See T. Ranger, 'The Invention of Tradition in Colonial Africa' in E. Hobsbawm and T. Ranger (eds), *The Invention of Tradition* (Cambridge University Press, 1983; repr. 1989), pp. 239–43 on Lewanika's successor's determination to attend the coronation of Edward's grandson, George the Sixth, in 1937.
14. Donald Simpson, librarian of the Royal Commonwealth Society, produced these sources. I remain very grateful for his support and assistance which encouraged me in these researches, which, as I used his library, often had him greet me by quoting a comment once made to archaeologist Mortimer Wheeler, 'still digging?'.
15. Mackintosh, *Coillard*, pp. 430–1.
16. Ibid.
17. A. Maitland, *Speke* (London: Constable, 1971), pp. 152–8.
18. H. Mukasa, *Uganda's Katikiro* (London: Hutchinson, 1904; repr Freeport NY: Books for Libraries, 1971), p. xix; N. Motani, *On His Majesty's Service in Uganda: The Origins of Uganda's African Civil Service 1912–1940* (Syracuse NY: Syracuse University Press, 1977), pp. 7–8.
19. Mukasa, *Uganda's Katikiro*, p. 12.
20. Ibid p. 59.
21. Ibid p. 103.
22. *African Times* (London) 7 August 1902, p. 121.
23. Mukasa, *Uganda's Katikiro*, p. 81; see also p. 178.
24. Ibid pp. 90–99.
25. Ibid p. 80.
26. B. Stone, *Sir Benjamin Stone's Pictures: Parliamentary Scenes and Portraits* (London: Cassell, 1906). My thanks to Mike Wells.
27. Mukasa, *Uganda's Katikiro*, p. 96.
28. Ibid p. 119.
29. H. Gale, *Uganda and the Mill Hill Fathers* (London: Macmillan, 1959), p. 231 using *St Joseph's Advocate* (Autumn 1902), p. 174.
30. Mukasa, *Uganda's Katikiro*, pp. 129–40.
31. Ibid pp. 145–8.
32. Ibid p. 151.
33. *Anti-Slavery Reporter and Aborigines' Friend* (London) August-October 1902 p. 129.
34. A. Mockler, *Haile Selassie's War* (Oxford University Press, 1984; repr. London: Grafton Books, 1987), pp. xxiv, 385.
35. Mukasa, *Uganda's Katikiro* p. 190.

36. S. Jacobs, *The African Nexus: Black American Perspectives on the European Partitioning of Africa, 1880–1920* (Westport CT: Greenwood Press, 1981), p. 199; G. Shepperson, 'Notes on Negro American Influences on the Emergence of African Nationalism', *Journal of African History* 1, 2 (1960), pp. 299–312 repr. Okon Edet Uya (ed.), *Black Brotherhood: Afro-Americans and Africa* (Lexington MA: Heath, 1971).

37. L. Harlan and R. Smock (eds), *The Booker T. Washington Papers, Vol 6, 1901–1902* (Urbana IL: University of Illinois Press, 1977), courtesy the London Library.

38. Public Record Office [PRO] CO 267/463, courtesy Christopher Fyfe.

39. I am indebted to Leslie Thompson, who recalled the shock he had arriving from Jamaica in 1919 when seeing this; see also William Hoffman, *With Stanley in Africa* (London: Cassell, 1938), p. 274.

40. Mukasa, *Uganda's Katikiro*, p. 54.

41. D. Lorimer, *Colour, Class and the Victorians: English Attitudes to the Negro in the mid-nineteenth century* (Leicester University Press, 1978), p. 217; P. Newman, *Caesars of the Wilderness* (London: Viking-Penguin, 1987), chapter 12 details the Guiana-born Scotland-educated Sir James Douglas who governed Canada's western province of British Columbia from 1858 to 1864. His 1863 knighthood came two years after Jordan's.

42. J. Hargreaves, *A Life of Sir Samuel Lewis* (Oxford University Press, 1958).

43. P. Davies, *The Trade Makers: Elder Dempster in West Africa 1852–1972* (London: George Allen & Unwin, 1973), pp. 73–128.

44. T. Scholes, *Glimpses of the Ages, or the "Superior" and "Inferior" Races, so-called, Discussed in the Light of Science and History, Vol 2* (London: John Long, 1908), p. 177.

45. H. King, 'Mojola Agbebi' in Rainer Lotz and Ian Pegg (eds), *Under the Imperial Carpet: Essays in Black History 1780–1950* (Crawley: Rabbit Press, 1986), p. 100.

46. *West African Mail* (Liverpool) 29 April 1904 p. 101 has his photograph; King 'Agbebi', pp. 99–100.

47. PRO CO 147/178/36210; *African World* (London) 16 September 1905, p. 248.

48. Secretary of State, *Circular to the West African Governors* 3 April 1903, responded to the acting governor of Sierra Leone's request of 25 September 1902 for a general ruling about leave entitlements for West Indian negroes in the colonial service. It was decided that any system that had to decide 'whether a particular individual was white or coloured would obviously be inconvenient in practice' and it was thought best to include the specific leave details in the employment contracts for posts that would be 'filled by coloured men'. These would 'apply principally to engine-drivers, schoolmasters, policemen, overseers and other officials of similar class who are engaged in the West Indies'. The classification was thus on class lines.

49. C. Fyfe, *A History of Sierra Leone* (Oxford University Press, 1962), pp. 614–15; Public Record Office CO 879/99/918, dated 2 December 1908, notes 'A further petition from native medical students at Edinburgh has now been received, asking for reconsideration of the decision which prevents them entering the West African Medical Staff'.

50. C. Delph and V. Roth, *Who Is Who in British Guiana 1938–1940*, 2nd ed. (Georgetown: Daily Chronicle, 1940), p. 423.

51. *Beverley Guardian*, 14 October 1905, p. 2.

52. Scholes, *Glimpses of the Ages*, vol. 2, p. 181.

53. R. Ross, *Memoirs* (London: John Murray, 1923), p. 378.

54. *African World*, 1 April 1905.

55. *Colonial Office List, 1921*, p. 761.

56. *West Kent Argus*, 14 June 1921.

57. J. Marlowe, *Milner: Apostle of Empire* (London: Hamish Hamilton, 1976), pp. 29, 50–51.

58. C. Page, 'Conrad A. Ridehout, Afro-American Advisor to the Chiefs of Lesotho and

Pondoland, 1899–1903' in R. Hill (ed.), *Pan-African Biography* (Los Angeles: Crossroad Press, 1987), pp. 1–10.

59. J. Hooker, *Henry Sylvester Williams: Imperial Pan-Africanist* (London: Rex Collings, 1975); O. Mathurin, *Henry Sylvester Williams and the Origins of the Pan-African Movement 1869–1911* (Westport CT: Greenwood Press, 1976).

60. Mathurin, *Williams*, pp. 132, 134–5.

61. Hooker, *Williams*, p. 94.

62. Hooker, *Williams*, p. 94, quoting *South Africa* (London) of January 1907.

63. Mathurin, *Williams*, p. 134.

64. Ibid.

65. Ibid pp. 133–5.

66. Ibid pp. 132, 135.

67. Hooker, *Williams*, p. 96.

68. Mathurin, *Williams*, p. 134.

69. Stone, *Pictures*.

70. Hooker, *Williams*, p. 97.

71. Mathurin, *Williams*, p. 141.

72. Ibid.

73. Ibid p. 143.

74. H. Johnston, *The Story of My Life* (Garden City NY: Garden City Publishing, 1923), pp. 373–8.

75. H. Johnston, *Liberia* (London: Hutchinson, 1906). R. Oliver, *Sir Harry Johnston and the Scramble for Africa* (London: Chatto, 1957), pp. 341–3 notes Johnston's commercial interests in Liberia and his visits there 1904–6.

76. C. Wilson, *Liberia: Black Africa in Microcosm* (New York: Harper & Row, 1971), p. 108. L. Harlan, *Booker T. Washington: The Wizard of Tuskegee, 1901–1915* (New York: Oxford University Press, 1983), pp. 284–9 shows US Black views on Johnston.

77. O. Sitwell, *Great Morning* (London: Macmillan, 1948; repr. London: Reprint Society, 1949), p. 109.

78. Gale, *Uganda and the Mill Hill Fathers*, pp. 299–300; photo opposite p. 297.

79. *African World* 2 August 1913, p. 711.

80. Ibid 26 July 1913, p. 659.

81. CO 536/66.

82. *African World* 31 May 1913, p. 216.

83. Ibid p. 232.

84. Ibid 7 June 1913, p. 285.

85. I. Nicolson, *The Administration of Nigeria, 1900–1960: Men, Methods, and Myths* (Oxford University Press, 1969: repr. Oxford: Clarendon Press, 1977), chapter seven.

86. Ibid p. 171.

87. S. Jeyes, *Mr Chamberlain: His Life and Public Career* (London: Sands, 1903), p. 592. My thanks to Charles Kay.

88. Ibid pp. 601–2.

89. Nicolson, *Nigeria*, pp. 186–90.

90. M. Crowder, *The Story of Nigeria* (London: Faber, 1962), p. 220.

91. *African World* 7 June 1913, p. 285.

92. W. Fullerton, *F. B. Meyer: A Biography* (London: Marshall, Morgan & Scott, 1933), pp. 97, 112.

93. South African protestor Sol Plaatje (q.v.) found help and audiences among the Brotherhood Movement, and the 1930s coach trips for Black children from London to Epsom were funded by the Brotherhood Movement in Epsom.

94. Crowder, *Nigeria*, pp. 220–21.

95. *Anti-Slavery Reporter* October 1913, pp. 99–102.

96. CO 536/74.
97. H. Ingrams, *Uganda: A Crisis of Nationhood* (London: HMSO, 1960), pp. 49–52.
98. Gale, *Uganda and the Mill Hill Fathers*, pp. 194–6, 306. 'Daudi Chwa was virtually nominated by the [British] Administration and not elected by the Chiefs'.
99. Ibid p. 306.
100. CO 536/74.
101. B. Willan, *Sol Plaatje: South African Nationalist, 1876–1932* (London: Heinemann, 1984), p. 173.
102. Ibid pp. 174–6.
103. Ibid pp. 177–8.
104. B. Willan, 'The Anti-Slavery Society and Aborigines' Protection Society and the South African Natives' Land Act of 1913', *Journal of African History*, 20, 1 (1979), pp. 83–102.

— 3 —

The working class

THE death of Six-Fingered Jack, aged 79, in the workhouse in
Malmesbury, Wiltshire, was reported in mid-1902.[1] The destitute
Black man had been a navvy, working with pick and shovel to build
dams, railways, canals, docks and tunnels. Workhouses were prison-
like, administered by boards of guardians drawn from the tax-paying
classes, who kept expenditure to a minimum to deter the poor.
Members of the working classes, down on their luck or no longer fit
enough to sell their labour, found accommodation in the workhouse
when all else had failed.[2] Blacks have been traced in Edwardian
workhouses.

Black women have been traced working as servants in Edwardian
homes, in a sisterhood that employed around one million females in
the 1900s.[3] One in every four women had paid work in the 1900s, with
forty per cent of female workers in England and Wales in 1901 being
domestic servants.[4] No longer a major part of the agricultural workforce, Edwardian working class women also laboured in the
manufacture of clothing and in the production of textiles. These three
sectors employed over seventy-two per cent of the female workers of
England and Wales. Domestic service was an employment that
provided security and 'to some extent, a life in service was sheltered
from the cruel world outside.... Few other members of the English
working class in Victorian and Edwardian times could boast of such
security.'[5]

Servants would sometimes accompany their employers abroad, and
it was far from uncommon for African- and Caribbean-born servants
to travel to Britain, as we have noticed with Lewanika and the Sotho.
African-American servants attended their masters and mistresses too.
Evidence of their presence comes largely from reports of failings or
allegations of crimes in contemporary newspapers, as well as the
passenger lists of ships arriving at and departing from British ports.
Other sources include biographies, memoirs, photograph albums and
applications to the Colonial Office from stranded colonials lodged in
workhouses or seeking charity.

The experiences of Black servants in Edwardian Britain were varied.

John Norton, Colonel Harding's 'Cape boy servant' who was with his master in Sherborne, Dorset before the pair went to Cape Town to chaperone Lewanika to Edward's coronation, was well liked by the grooms at the hotel and got drunk with them. Harding thrashed him; and wrote 'I never informed Johnny that if he had been so disposed he could have sustained an action against me for assault.'[6]

In May 1905 a 'supposed slave' named Jack Simla was resident in the workhouse at Saunderton, between High Wycombe and Thame in Buckinghamshire, two hours walk from Naphill where he had been working. The West African 'little negro boy' had been in Britain for eighteen months, employed by a White who 'had brought him back with him from South Africa'. Neighbours had encouraged Simla to run away, the *Penny Illustrated Paper* also reported. This was 'a result of a misunderstanding. The little fellow has returned to his friend and mentor.' The pair posed in a photograph published on 20 May 1905.

Thirty miles from Naphill, at Bricket Wood in Hertfordshire, the treatment of four African servants led to a court case in September 1908. Details were published in the local and national press. The accused was the wife of a highly-educated man, hence the *Liverpool Courier*'s 'Black Maid's Allegation: Lady Convicted of Cruelty' and the *St Albans Post*'s 'Chief Justice's Wife Convicted for Beating a Black Servant'.[7] It was revealed that the Africans, unlike Jack Simla, had not been paid.

As with the Naphill servant, neighbours had befriended the Africans. Cow keeper Alfred Stevens and his wife had made friends with two of the Black girls who had moved into the Bungalow, Bricket Wood, with Mary and Algernon Willoughby Osborne around Christmas 1907. Mary Osborne had written to Stevens after he had expressed his belief that the girls were not getting enough to eat. His letter had asked 'would you find English girls to endure what they do?', according to *The Times* of 12 September.

Walking past the Bungalow Stevens had seen Mary Osborne beating thirteen-year-old Gambia with a stick. He told her to stop or he would inform the police. The following day police constable King and an inspector from the National Society for the Prevention of Cruelty to Children (NSPCC) called. They were told by Gambia (who was from that country) that she had been sat on and beaten by Mary, a fellow servant, and then by her mistress, on the steps and inside the house. On 26 September Dr T. P. G. Wells examined her, and noted 'severe' force had been used. The NSPCC represented the child and brought charges against Mary Osborne. The case, which lasted four days, was heard at nearby St Albans.

The four African servants had been in England before. They had been rescued from slavery and placed in a convent institution in West

Africa, where Willoughby Osborne had undertaken to look after them until they were twenty-one. Gambia had been with them for five years, but had never been to school in Britain. A governess had been employed to educate the other three, who were older. Their mistress admitted that this arrangement combined philanthropy and 'certainly a convenience', but disputed that there were any savings as fares to and from Africa were costly. The court was informed that African servants were usually male, and that the Osbornes had two other children in their charge, in Africa: one was Mary's baby.

'Gambia herself, in good English, detailed the assaults committed upon her. In cross-examination, she admitted she had made a statement to Mary reflecting on Mrs Osborne's moral character', which the *Liverpool Courier* noted was about her chastity. The longer report in the *St Albans Post* stated this remark was to the coachman.

The Black teenage servant seemed to be a gossip and a petty thief, but her mistress was no angel. Mrs Osborne admitted that she had torn up Gambia's bible, which she had purchased with house-keeping money (she already owned four bibles). The NSPCC inspector had questioned Mrs Osborne about the walking stick; she had retorted that she would 'flog them every minute, every hour, every day with it if they don't obey'. She denied making that remark, but the police constable testified that he had heard her.

Dr Wells testified that Gambia's body had marks that 'suggested severe blows having been administered'. He admitted that he had not examined a Black person before, and added that the skin of Black people was tougher than that of Europeans. A Dr Lightfoot from Watford told the court that he had examined the girl four hours after Dr Wells, and could find nothing to indicate a flogging. 'He had had considerable experience among black people.'

Algernon Willoughby Osborne stated that had he known that the servant girl had made a remark about his wife's chastity he would have given her a worse flogging. His wife, probably sensing that the humanitarian and Christian ethics of cow keeper Stevens were not unique in Hertfordshire in the early autumn of 1908, said she was sorry she had used a stick. After thirty-five minutes the verdict came: guilty of cruelty. As she had been provoked the costs of the case were to be paid by her victim (and thus by the NSPCC).

Osborne was the British official responsible for the administration of law in Southern Nigeria. This colonial chief justice had been called to the Bar in 1904 after an education at Winchester (motto: Manners Makyth Man) and Oxford. He was paid £1,800 a year according to the *Colonial Office List*. He went on to work in the Gold Coast, and continued in the colonial service into 1913 at least. The *African World*'s report of this trial had his remark 'the only way to correct black people was to flog them'. It ignored the evidence that the four were unpaid, having swopped slavery in Africa for a similar status in Hertfordshire.

Questions were asked in parliament: reported in *The Times* of 23 October as 'Nigerian Girls in England'. The House was informed:

> The Secretary of State is also taking steps to secure that these girls shall be sent back to the colony and that their resettlement there shall be arranged under the supervision of the Governor or some other suitable authority. (Cheers).

On 16 October that year an African servant named John Prince, employed by a Dr Bayfield now in London after a spell in West Africa, tried to cash a telegraphed money order at a post office in New Oxford Street, London. Asked about his identity, the twenty-one-year-old African dashed out and threw the telegram away. Arrested, he was put on trial at the Old Bailey. His lawyer told the court that Prince had Bayfield's authority to cash the payment. The doctor denied that, and the 'very good' servant was found guilty of theft. Sentencing was postponed as there had to be an investigation to ascertain if he could be sent 'to his own country'.[8]

The relationships between master and servant could be strong, almost inter-dependent. This is seen in the 'Death of a British Slave' report in the *Anti-Slavery Reporter* of mid-1903 by Charles Allen, retired secretary of the Anti-Slavery Society. Ann E. Styles had died 'a few months ago' aged eighty, in Hampstead, north London. Freed from slavery in Jamaica in 1834, she had left the Caribbean with her White mistress around 1840. She had worked for that woman, and then her son and her daughter. 'Remarkable for her devotion and heroic strength of character' Ann Styles had found a home in England for over sixty years.

We know more about Aumore Ashaker, whose behaviour led him to prison. The monthly *African Times* had recorded on 6 December 1899 that he was 'an unworthy native' who had appeared before magistrates at Bedford, accused of stealing a bicycle. On 7 February 1902 the *Daily News* of London reported that he had appeared at Clerkenwell sessions the day before, facing a charge of threatening to kill a London hotel keeper. 'It was stated in the land of his nativity prisoner had been selected as a promising preacher. In this country, however, he had been living by fraud.'

The Times had his name as Ashaku, that he came from New Calabar (eastern Nigeria) and his family from Sierra Leone, and that he had attended a school in north Wales 'and had for the last year or two been living by fraud'. The *Argosy* in Georgetown, British Guiana, reported on 15 March 1902 that when arrested Ashaker possessed gilt-edged visiting cards proclaiming him to be the Revd Claude Bevington Wilson of Balliol College, Oxford.

The African had been living with a woman from Yorkshire in Claremont Street, near King's Cross, London, at the beginning of the coronation year. Earlier he had lodged in Chiswell Street with William Child, who 'had at times helped him with money and in other ways'. The woman's brother came to London and went to Chiswell Street where he contacted Child who accompanied him to Claremont Street. He persuaded his sister to return to Yorkshire.

When the African got home he was understandably upset, and wrote a note to Child stating that he had a revolver, bullets and apparently the intention to use them. Child took the unsigned note to the police, who arrested Ashaker as his handwriting matched that on the note. He was found guilty and sent to prison for a year. He was described as 'living in London by fraud and by blackmailing white women'.

One month later the *Finsbury Weekly News and Chronicle* of London reported that a 'coloured man' had been 'putting himself about as Sergeant Gordon', pretending to be a military hero. The genuine Sergeant William James Gordon was a Jamaican who, serving in the West India Regiment in West Africa, had been awarded the Victoria Cross for extreme bravery in 1892.[9] His impersonator was Isaac Brown, who was sentenced to twelve months with hard labour for this deceit. The police had found 'a khaki tunic on which were the ribbons of the Victoria Cross, the Gold Coast, and South Africa' at Brown's lodgings.

It is not known if the women who worked as Abomah 'the African giantess' were African, although they were of African descent. Postcards state that she was seven feet four inches tall. Posed next to a much shorter adult White male, these postcards have been located mailed in October 1903 and as late as 1915. Nothing has been traced on where Abomah worked.[10]

An equally sparse amount of information has been uncovered on the 'Englishman who is a Darkie', reported in the London *Weekly Despatch* of 27 December 1903. During the trial of a piano maker named Bonner, accused of theft, a witness was 'a man of colour' who informed the court that he had been born on the *Great Eastern* thirty-five years before, had been christened in Cape Town, and had worked as a miner, a cook and a blacksmith.

There were Blacks in Britain's working class who were temporary residents in Britain. The lack of schools and underdevelopment of the tropical colonies led to Black railway workers serving apprenticeships in British workshops and yards. The *Anglo-African Argus* of 26 November 1904 noted that railway engineers, boilermakers and

10. Entertainers included Abomah the African Giantess

blacksmiths had been sent to England where 'climatic conditions are against them'. Alfred Jones, the bustling entrepreneur, had proposed establishing a school for African railwaymen in Lagos. A careful study of photographs of Edwardian Swindon, Grantham, York, Crewe, Peterborough and Ashford should reveal Black railwaymen in the 1900s.

One way to solve British West Africa's lack of skilled workers was to import them, and, to overcome the image of those lands being the 'white man's grave', the Colonial Office recruited from the British West Indies. The men, and some women, worked in schools, customs, harbour boards, railways, police, post offices and prisons and often were Afro-Caribbeans.[11] They had their leaves in Britain, which they had visited briefly when travelling from the islands to their ancestral motherland when first transferred, or accumulated months of leave in order to recross the Atlantic.[12]

Edith Rita Goring, 'appointed from Barbados', first arrived in the Gold Coast on 7 October 1906 where she taught for a dozen years.[13] Known to have been of African descent, Miss Goring retired to England in 1920.[14] By 1911 the policy of recruitment in the Caribbean for the Gold Coast was flourishing, with H. R. Biltcliffe, Sergeant Major of the Bahamas police, classified as the 'European gaoler'; J. Concannon was another Sergeant Major, but from the police force of St Vincent. The *Gold Coast Report 1911* also noted that R. H. Roberts and T. A. Smith, second class warders of British Guiana, arrived in the colony on 6 April 1911 and were expected to have 'more effective discipline than Native Keepers'.

A passenger list for the Liverpool-Freetown sailing of 7 November 1908 has second class passenger J. Hercules, who was an engine driver and a British colonial citizen. He was probably from Trinidad. Within five years the Colonial Office's index on Nigeria noted 'as all in-struction required can be given locally' it was no longer necessary to have technical scholarships for the railway, marine and public works departments whose staff had been trained in Britain or Sri Lanka (then Ceylon).[15] This must have reduced the number of Africans studying practical engineering and mechanics in Britain, but the West Indian recruits were still employed. R. P. Greaves, a 'tram conductor' on the Nigerian railway, had completed his contract and was 'returning to Barbados' in late 1913.[16] Greaves like the others would have trans-shipped in Britain.

A 'number of men' of the West India Regiment had been on a month long musketry course at Hythe in Kent before they were permitted to visit London. The *West India Committee Circular* of 1 October 1907 also commented 'Their bright and picturesque uniforms, with the scarlet-red headgear, attracted consideration as they wandered about the City.' African soldiers would have trained at Britain's military centres, too.

The men of the colonial police forces might have had some experi-ence of Britain, although the Jamaica constabulary seems to have recruited experienced other ranks from the Royal Irish Constabulary. Which suggests that Black police were less likely to attend courses in Britain than army, railway and marine personnel.

The Jamaica constabulary were asked by the British authorities to investigate the alleged murder of Elizabeth Pollock, who had been pushed into a swamp in 1894 according to the confession of William

Richardson. Richardson, a twenty-nine-year-old blind-maker of Whitechapel Road in London's East End, was held in custody for months. It was confirmed that he was a Jamaican, but nothing could be traced on his alleged victim. The chairman of the Wood Green, London, magistrates was upset and said that Richardson 'deserved a flogging, but unfortunately they could not give it to him'. The clerk of the court told the Jamaican that had he been charged with murder the trial would have been held in Britain. 'I thought I should have been charged out there, that's the reason I gave myself up.'[17] He was released but remained subject to concern by the Colonial Office.[18]

Richardson's dramatic scheme to return to Jamaica had led to a spell in an English prison. Miss Ada Llewelyn, down on her luck, applied to the Chelsea, London offices of the Charity Organisation Society which also contacted the Colonial Office in April 1905. Her claim to be a Jamaican was true, and it was recommended that she was re-patriated.[19] Another London COS committee, that of St Pancras South, reported on Charlotte Arboni on 30 June 1905. These two Jamaican ladies may well have been servants.

The COS dispensed about one third of all money spent on poor relief in Edwardian times.[20] It would not have taken much asking to discover the location of one of the Society's offices.

Joe Clough, a servant who arrived with his doctor master from Jamaica in 1906, was just twenty when he reached England. He remained in Britain when the doctor returned to the Caribbean, and became a driver for the London General Omnibus Company. Motor car drivers had been named chauffeurs because so many of them, like their cars, had been French.[21] No high class car owner drove a vehicle in Edwardian times; this was a new form of employment for workers. Clough drove a number eleven bus from Wormwood Scrubs to Liverpool Street, tough work for the cab was exposed to the weather and there was no power steering. Clough and his bus in 1908 are to be seen in a study of migrants in Bedford.[22] Clough married a London publican's daughter in 1911, drove ambulances in France in the 1914–18 war and then settled in Bedford where he established a taxi business.

Another Black driver in Edwardian London was Lewis Bruce, who must have been a highly skilled and safe driver, for he drove the government inspectors and high-ranking officials on the 21 February 1906 test run of the London United Electric Tramway's new route to Tolworth and Surbiton across the Thames at Kingston. On 1 March the official opening took three trams over the flower-bedecked Kingston bridge; the first was driven by Kingston's mayor, assisted by the company's chief executive Sir Clifton Robinson. Robinson also had his own personal tram, and Bruce was his driver as well as a regular driver of trams numbered 320 and 321. Photographs of the mayor and Robinson in Kingston reveal Bruce standing close to the controls.[23] Nothing else has been traced on this Black worker.

Such workers did not need the assistance of charities or the Colonial Office, so we must guess at the numbers of other Black settlers and residents in Edwardian Britain who worked in industry and transport. Photographs can tease, for the grime of industrial workers, as Ham Mukasa had noted in 1902, made some Whites look like Blacks. One example is a late Victorian photograph of the London, Brighton and South Coast Railway's steam engine *Picardy* taken in Battersea.[24]

Faced with financial failure migrants sought official assistance to return to their natal lands. Whites were classified as destitutes too, including an Australian miner in Sierra Leone in 1907. The Colonial Office's Sierra Leone file for 1911[25] reveals that the colony paid the fares for 'destitute natives' who went from London to Liverpool that year, and the file for 1913 shows that a Sierra Leonean family named Johnson was in Charleroi, in the Belgian coal mining region.

The Black servants, a rank above the destitute of any colour, can be seen in the lists of passengers published in the London weeklies *African World* and *West India Committee Circular*. African servants in Edwardian Britain included the 'native servant' who accompanied the Revd Balmer and his wife on the *Nigeria* which reached Liverpool on 11 March 1905. Balmer was almost certainly the Christian educationalist of the Gold Coast and Sierra Leone.[26] On 20 May that year the same ship brought 'Dr Kumm and one native servant' and the Broadhurst family and two Black servants into Liverpool. Kumm may have been a missionary; the name Broadhurst was associated with Sierra Leone and the Gold Coast, with Robert Broadhurst, a merchant of African descent, having a home in England for decades.[27] On 3 June 1905 a Mrs Jones 'and Native Boy' arrived in the Mersey on the *Burutu*.

Five African servants identified in one year were not exceptional. In February 1906 the *Sekondi* arrived in Liverpool with a 'Native Servant' who had travelled from Calabar with employer Mr W. F. Fraser. These passenger lists are filed at the Public Record Office, and there one can see a man named Pennington travelling first class from Liverpool to Lagos on the *Burutu* in November 1908; his servant was in third class.

The 1905 Aliens Act, which attempted to restrict impoverished immigration from eastern Europe, revealing Britain's class system by applying only to passengers with the cheapest tickets,[28] required citizenship to be stated. Thus when African lawyer J. F. Boston, his wife, son, daughter and maid left Liverpool in November 1908, they were listed as British Colonials. The *Dakar* took S. J. Coker and two men named Nicol to Freetown on 3 October; on 10 October the *Falaba* left Liverpool with W. A. Buckle and W. Taylor for Freetown and C. J. Reindorf and his wife for Lagos; and on 17 October lawyer Claudius Wright, with his children and maid, left for Freetown. They were all British Colonials.[29] So was Sir George Denton's servant (he ruled the Gambia) who sailed with the Senegalese from the Franco-British Exhibition in London.

Liverpool was Britain's major port for ships connecting with western Africa and had developed with the import of slave-grown cotton from the United States. Products for processing in Lancashire and Cheshire came from all over the world, and manufactured goods were exported everywhere. For those who experienced Liverpool life in the late nineteenth and early twentieth centuries, it was the 'greatest seaport in the world' as Pat O'Mara recalled in 1934.[30] He wrote of the Irish communities divided by religion, Hawaiians, Chinese and Blacks. 'Negroes, Chinese, Mulattoes ... most of them boasting white wives and large half-caste families' in Brick Street, with African sailors of the Elder Dempster line living in Gore and Stanhope streets. Black firemen who stoked the boilers and trimmers who kept the furnaces burning were respected because they were better fathers and partners than the drunken and violent (and White) men like O'Mara's father. Local women married these Blacks, O'Mara stated, because they were better off with their wages for a year and their company for three months than being married to a (White) dock worker and 'continually starved and beaten'. 'Half-starved illiterates, desperately anxious to secure economic independence', the White women came from Cardiff, Manchester and London to marry Liverpool's Black sailors.

O'Mara named 'Galley' Johnson who left the sea and established a boarding house for Blacks; Joe Diamond and his wife who opened a 'Negro boarding house' in Cardiff; and that his aunt Janie had married Johnny Murray whose first wife had been 'a coloured woman' and had 'two half-caste children, Anne and Marie' who were sent to live with Black relatives as their White stepmother verbally abused them. Other recollections were a 'coloured bachelor' named 'Charlie the Carpenter' in Bridgewater Street and a sailor who was seen pawning his shirt, as well as Mary Ellen Grant, the 'Connaught Nigger' whose West African father had married an Irish woman. She was a money lender.

The constant movement of men who worked at sea, whose employment kept them abroad for months as they signed on in distant ports for destinations further and further away, seems to have created a transient citizenry. Anyone who has travelled widely, even in the age of jet aircraft, will know how good it is to return to familiar surroundings. Port communities had regular users of lodging houses, shops and pubs, who welcomed continuity although distanced in months from their previous association. During the weeks at sea their wages were

paid to their next of kin by their employers, a working class security
that had considerable advantages.[31]

It was not always necessary for Black Liverpudlians to work in
industries connected to the sea, but the city's reputation for sectarian-
ism forced people to keep to established patterns.[32] Edward James,
who settled in the city from Bermuda in the 1870s, had a son named
Albert who worked in a Liverpool iron moulding factory in the 1900s
and then took a job at the central library. In 1914 he enlisted in the
Royal Field Artillery and survived the war to die in 1962. This Black
presence is known because of his family's interest in history.[33]

Another Black individual from Edwardian Liverpool, traced
through contemporary newspapers, was Frederick Henry Oxley, who
lived at 113 Pitt Street in 1905–6 when he was reported as 'a coloured
man' in Birkenhead. The *Liverpool Weekly Courier* of 27 January 1906
stated that he had been charged under the Vagrant's Act of 1834 when
collecting for 'The Gospel News Mission' at Birkenhead market: 'the
police suspected the mission was not carried on upon a sound basis'.
Their suspicions were justified, but it was not Oxley's fault.

The mission in Price Street, Birkenhead, was run by the Revd Hugh
Lloyd Jones – and run badly. The *Birkenhead News* reported that Oxley
'a man of considerable intelligence' had defended himself, presenting
his story 'very correctly and fluently'. He worked on a 25 per cent commission, had obtained permission from the market authorities, and
had no knowledge how Jones conducted his mission. Jones made a
fool of himself in court, admitting that his accounts had been prepared
just a few days earlier, but it was accepted that the mission was
genuine. Oxley was discharged, to return across the Mersey a wiser
individual no doubt.

Another Black working in Liverpool, studying the timber trade
and therefore working in saw mills, loading, stacking, measuring
wood and carrying out other aspects of an apprenticeship, was
Behresyankee from Upper Axim in the Gold Coast. Relatives had
instructed him to return home. In despair over the reasons for that call
to leave Liverpool, he had tried to kill himself. Suicide was a criminal
act, so the police had to deal with him. In June 1906 he was 'mentally
deranged' and in hospital. The police asked the Colonial Office if they
would be held responsible when the young man got better and was
handed over to his employer 'to be sent to the Coast', where they
believed his life was in danger. This Colonial Office file is cross-
indexed in a chilling way: 'insane native youth at L'pool'.[34]

Jamaicans studying at Liverpool University had been offered reduced price tickets by Sir Alfred Jones so they could visit the island
during the summer holidays, he told the Colonial Office in November
1908. One of the two Jamaicans at the school of engineering had

'worked his passage out to Jamaica and back again in the Engine Room of one of our steamers during the summer vacation'.[35] Was this Jamaican of African descent?

Unofficial sailors reached England: there were '6 Mendi stowaways' on the steamship *Mendi* which arrived in Liverpool on 24 August 1906. The six males had boarded in Freetown, and were probably shipped back home again, labouring on the ship to compensate the owners for their food.[36]

Caribbean and African sailors worked all over the world. Joseph Lamotte from Grenada had fallen on hard times somewhere where contact was made with the Foreign Office, whose 1906 index card noted that the governor of the Windward Islands had been contacted. Lamotte's relatives could not or would not contribute to repatriation expenses, but he solved the problem by getting work on a sailing barque bound for Britain.

Charitable and government assistance was not easy to obtain. Checking claims made by those with origins in the empire took weeks, as mail went by ship. This is clearly seen in the four 'natives of Jamaica' who were being supported by the Shipwrecked Fishermen and Mariners Society in January 1908, when it asked the Colonial Office to take responsibility for them. The matter was still receiving attention in June.[37]

Whatever the motive, those Blacks who turned to crime and were discovered could be confident that their ethnicity would be mentioned in Edwardian newspaper reports. Black criminals were identified through other comments. For example, a 'darkey' named John Frankling was mentioned in the *South London Observer* of 24 October 1906 because of his humour. Tried at Newington sessions for stealing a leather apron, this 'man of colour' pleaded guilty and was asked to explain his conduct. Frankling told the court that witnesses had stated that he had received sixpence for the apron; but it had been fivepence. He was sentenced to one month in prison.

Prison also awaited the young man who arrived in the fishing port of Grimsby on 8 April 1907. Holding a package wrapped in a Berlin newspaper, he registered at the Royal Hotel as Prince Makaroo of Zululand. He telephoned the mayor, who arranged to visit the prince at the hotel. The mayor, in attempting to change the meeting place, had problems for the royal visitor was on the phone to Buckingham Palace. The two men met, and the African presented vouchers from the British consul in Berlin and asked for a loan of forty or fifty shillings (a week's earnings for a working man in 1907). The mayor chatted with the smartly dressed prince and then telephoned the police. Within minutes Prince Makaroo was identified as having been resident in Grimsby around 1901. He agreed that he was the man in a photograph from that time, and was arrested on a charge of trying to obtain money by false pretences. The *Grimsby Daily Telegraph* reported this on 10 April 1907.

Police inspector Baglee stated that the prince was known to him as 'Khaki' Brown, 'who came to Grimsby some years ago, and represented himself as a captain attached to the British Army on a holiday from South Africa'. He believed that the so-called prince had worked as an engineer on steam trawlers out of Grimsby and that 'his name was even now on the books of the local engineers' trade union'.

Makaroo claimed he had an appointment with a Mr Russell of the Natal Agency in Victoria Street, London where his baggage had been sent. Russell would know that he was on an important mission from Zululand (which is in Natal) and that he needed two hundred pounds. The police officer commented on the African's fluency in English, adding 'he says he has been taught nine languages, and his young lady has taught him English'. Baglee remembered that the accused had lived in Grimsby for one or two years. 'I am the rightful heir to Zululand' Makaroo declared: and was remanded in custody for seven days. The *Telegraph* reported that he pulled himself erect 'with a lordly mien'.

The *Grimsby County Times* of 12 April had similar details to the *Grimsby Daily Telegraph* of 9 and 10 April. The prince had established a reputation as 'a regular dandy and "lady killer"' when he had been in the town earlier, and was recalled promenading in uniform during the 1899–1902 war in South Africa. 'A well-dressed dusky personage', he was reported to have admitted that he had been in court before, around 1901.

The magistrates saw Makaroo on 17 April. 'He still retained his majesty of bearing, although his unbrushed clothes and unshaven face detracted from the well-groomed appearance which was noticeable a week ago.' He had talked too much, for the mayor had been surprised when his royal visitor had said he 'was the heir to Abyssinia, being the only nephew of Menelik'. The mayor of Grimsby knew that Ethiopia and Zululand were almost a continent apart. The prince's explanation that he travelled from the continent without servants because he had dismissed his valet for theft was not accepted either. Russell of the Natal Agency had received a letter from Makaroo, but otherwise knew nothing about him. The police informed the magistrates that the man before them was not Prince Makaroo, but Charles Isaac Brown or Isaac Uriah Brown, who had been arrested for impersonating Sergeant Gordon in 1902.

An official of the trade union said he first met Charles Isaac Brown, who he thought was from Cuba, in Grimsby in 1901, when he was wearing army uniform. He had disappeared by 1902 (when he had been sent to prison in London). The court also heard that his passport had been issued in Berlin in November 1906, and that Brown had been to Madrid. The magistrates, perhaps sensing that matters were getting out of hand, decided that Brown should be tried by a higher court, and he was returned to the cells.

Grimsby's quarter sessions were duly reported in the *Grimsby County Times* of 26 April 1907.[38] 'Thomas Makaroo, alias Charles Brown, alias Isaac Uriah Brown, age 23, traveller' admitted that he was the 'Khaki Jim' of the photograph. A detective from nearby Hull advised that Brown had lived in that town's Dock Street in 1902, and said 'he was a native of Ceylon'. Brown told the court that he had left England in 1903 to travel to Africa, where he recruited ten Blacks and taken them to Germany where they worked into 1905. He paid off the troupe, remaining in Germany where he was robbed in the street.

He admitted that he had been in Grimsby as a 'working man, but anyone could see that he did not then mix with the drunken or lower classes'. He had been investigating prospects for his people. He did not explain how the people of Natal and/or Ethiopia could benefit from their future monarch having spent time fishing for cod off Iceland or for herrings in the North Sea.

The court was told of Brown's impersonation of Sergeant Gordon, from which he had obtained money and free tickets to theatres. He had also been sentenced to twelve months in prison, for stealing a bicycle in Hull. The prince explained that the Gordon matter was a case of mistaken identity and that he had been a victim of perjury in Hull, where a man, jealous of his wife's attentions to the Black man, lied to the court. Brown claimed that his mother lived in Australia and that Sergeant Gordon was his cousin. The court decided that he was a liar, and sentenced him to three months with hard labour.

Brown seems to have been Jamaican. In August 1904, when he later claimed to have been in Africa or Germany, clerks at the Colonial Office in London recorded the receipt of a petition to King Edward. Entitled *Condition of People*, it was entered in the index of the file for Jamaica CO 351/19 as submitted by Prince Thomas Makaroo. The document has been destroyed but this entry strongly suggests that the author was writing about conditions in Jamaica, not Zululand, Ethiopia or Grimsby.

The career of Isaac Brown exposes British ignorance and credulity, and their respect for superficialities such as an army uniform or a royal style. It also reveals that at least one Black worker went to sea in the East Coast fishing fleet, and was a member of a trade union.

Other Blacks from Jamaica crossed the Atlantic as Alfred Jones organised the commercial imports of Caribbean bananas, for each banana boat had fifty-eight crewmen. They had a maximum of twelve passengers, but passenger ships also arrived from the West Indies at Avonmouth near Bristol. Colonial citizens, who could be of African, Asian or European descent, were shown on the passenger lists.

In January 1908 a 'domestic' named Miss J. Knight arrived on the *Port Kingston*. In late February when that vessel returned to Avonmouth, the third class passenger C. J. Jump, a 'carpenter', might have been of African descent. When this ship reached England in March it carried six British Colonial passengers. The *Port Henderson* brought Miss Bell and Miss O. Garrett in April 1908, and in June brought thirty-seven colonial citizens – the nurse who accompanied Miss Denny, and J. Baden-Powell's valet were probably Black. Other colonial citizens on this voyage included Miss M. Hutchings, Mrs Lough, and the Revd Sturden from Bermuda, and Jamaicans W. P. Hall and his wife, Dr E. E. Murray, and Mrs D. O. King.

The *Port Kingston* returned to Bristol on 29 July 1908. Mr and Mrs Butterfield and their son and daughter, two sisters named Burke, and the Delgado family were Colonials. In September the *Port Henderson* brought Colonial citizen Miss L. Wylie, a nurse. And when the *Port Royal* arrived at the end of 1908 it had a Mrs Campbell, a cook, travelling from Kingston.[39] Above all these ships had Black crew, stokers and labourers. Their story is very much part of Edwardian working class life, for they – as even Professor Lyde would agree – had an essential role in the daily functioning of the world's largest merchant navy.

They are nameless except in merchant navy records. So too was the 'dusky' worker in London's north Lambeth who was mentioned in Reeves's *Round About a Pound a Week* published in 1913. He was not recalled by Len Bradbrook, a Black Londoner raised in Lambeth from 1903, who remembered that local children 'treated me rough' and tried to see if his skin colour would rub off. His photograph, taken around 1910, accompanied these recollections of being called 'Blackie' and 'Darkie' in *A Century of Childhood* published in 1988.[40]

Another nameless Black Edwardian, probably a London worker on a summer holiday, was in Folkestone on the Channel coast in 1907. London's *Evening Standard* reported on 14 August the following year on the men's beauty show where the competitors

> have to poke their heads through a black velvet screen surrounded by a gold frame, and if there is a funny sight it is that of a grinning face suddenly popping into view. Last year we had a nigger, and his face was so black that it could not be distinguished from the velvet.

Journalists wrote about Black workers, with a piece in the *Pall Mall Gazette* of London copied by the *Blackpool Herald* of 15 September 1908. The subject was the dock area of Low Street in North Shields:

Here is a Kroo boy from West Africa, with blue tattoo marks down the centre of his forehead, who, on the strength of having worked a passage to England by chipping paint and keeping the winches clean, calls himself a fitter, and hopes for employment as such in one of the shipyards.

It also mentioned a Black American sailor with 'a red tie, and a large white collar, ogling the girls from the biscuit factory beside New Quay'.

Some Caribbean sailors were White and some were quite young. In October 1908 two lads from Trinidad, McDonald De Souza and Charles Prudhomme, reached Hamburg, and from there they travelled via Grimsby to London where they booked into the Sailors' Home in the London docks. They had over a pound left, but as they had such little experience of the sea their employment prospects were small. Scruttons, the shipping line to Trinidad, refused to assist as the lads (one White, one Black) would be the company's responsibility when they reached the colony. Resourcefully they got a sailors' charity to pay Scruttons three pounds for the 'lads to be shipped to the West Indies', and left on the *Sargasso* on 29 October.[41] No doubt their stories encouraged others to head for Britain.

This government file also contains documents relating to Theophilus Scott and his wife and thirteen months old child. Scott was prisoner 1040 in Newcastle upon Tyne's gaol, from where he had written to the Colonial Office on 4 August 1908 asking that his sentence be reduced. He had served four months and was not due to be released until November. He had been found guilty of theft, having hired furniture which he sold to settle debts. If his sentence was remitted he could join his wife and child who were waiting to return to Trinidad. He had never been in trouble before, he wrote. Could Scruttons be contacted so that he could work his passage, or would there be some assistance to pay his fare to Port of Spain?

There is no certainty that the Scotts were of African descent, which was also true of the Miss Todd whose uncle was the vicar of St Thomas in Chaguanas, Trinidad. She had experienced difficulties and had made contact with the Church of England Women's Help Society in Westminster. They informed the Colonial Office that she had told them that if she was sent to the workhouse she would commit suicide.

The Trinidad correspondence index of the Colonial Office for 1909–12 starts with an entry on 'a common swindler' named S. Punch whose lack of funds was due to an 'extravagent & reckless mode of living'. A more innocent Black worker in difficulties in London in 1908–9 was 'another Negro, Arthur Herd' or Hird who was introduced to the Charity Organisation Society's Greek Street, Soho, office in

December 1908. He had been employed by another Black, John Semper Bailey, and the pair had travelled from Jamaica to England.

Bailey had taken Herd's money and vanished. The two had called at the Soho charity office and the police were seeking Bailey, as a missing person. On 4 January 1909 Bailey reappeared in Greek Street where he was confronted with Herd's story which he admitted was true. He explained that his father was a clergyman in Barbados and would be able to help.

The police had no idea that Bailey was of African descent; the landlady at 45 Gower Street said he was a 'coloured gentleman' and, according to another letter from the COS to the Colonial Office, dated 8 January, that both men were 'well dressed and had a lot of luggage'. The COS people thought that Bailey was a person of lower standing than Herd, who was now living in a workhouse. They did not have Bailey's address. Arthur Herd, no doubt chastened by his experiences in Edwardian London, worked his passage home to Jamaica on the *Port Royal* in February. Nothing has been traced of the thief, John Semper Bailey.[42]

Trinidad's index had entries on M. and G. Jacob who were receiving charity in April 1909, and on the 'distressed native W. Evans' who was in a sailor's home in June. His old employers would take him to Trinidad if they were relieved of all responsibility for his upkeep there.

William Willis was a Jamaican who had served time in a British prison and was being cared for by the Catholic Prisoners Aid Society in late 1910. Recently released, Willis could not be repatriated unless he was a charge under the Poor Law: without money or valuables. Then he would have to seek aid from a relieving officer, who would state that he had no valid claim on any town or parish in the United Kingdom as he was Jamaican. This 'distressed native' was brought to the attention of the Colonial Office, and letters passed between London and Kingston. During those weeks Willis and other destitutes had to survive. It was possible that his prison sentence had resulted from attempts to obtain money in an alien land.

The COS, which distinguished between the deserving and the undeserving poor, aided a Jamaican sailor named Cumming from February to April 1911, when they informed the Colonial Office that they could no longer keep him.[43] Females seem to have had better treatment, for Mrs E. V. Virtue and her daughter, in Liverpool in late 1910, benefited from the Colonial Office paying half of their fares on the Elder Dempster ship that carried them back to Jamaica.[44]

The Colonial Office wrote to Kingston on 4 December 1911 over H. B. Green, who spent Christmas in the workhouse in Westminster and finally departed for Jamaica on 21 August 1912. Even then two pounds had to be paid to the shipping line and he had to work his passage.[45]

Many must have abandoned hope of repatriation and, to avoid the degradation of the workhouse and continual requests for alms, found a new life somewhere in Britain. Poverty and a loss of self respect were created by the workhouse system in order to keep residents – and costs – to a minimum.

Lilian Macpherson, a Jamaican first recorded in the workhouse at Christchurch in May 1912, had moved on to Poole by September, but what she did that summer and what happened to her has not been reclaimed for the papers have been destroyed and only the index hints at despair. Moving from workhouse to workhouse was part of the system, for able-bodied applicants were refused regular accommodation and they had to move on. This kept local ratepayers happy, but created a mobile and rootless group who could not stay long enough to find steady work. Occasional work or a chance encounter with some generous person might keep these marginal people out of the workhouse. Certainly we must guess that the W. Willis noted as destitute in Vauxhall (London) in November 1912 was the same Jamaican as the Catholic ex-prisoner noted two years earlier. Where had he been working?

A Jamaican named Ramsay was living at the Seaman's Hospital in London in October 1912 when the authorities decided to send him to Tyneside's South Shields where he would be a charge on the local poor law. They could pay his fare to the Caribbean. That a Black sailor in London had links to England's ship-building centre was not a surprise. But what can be made of Mrs A. R. Motley, another Jamaican, who was in the workhouse in Croydon, Surrey, in July 1914?

Croydon's COS had reported in July 1910 that brothers V. and R. Vignale from Trinidad had been suffering and that their case was 'hard'. They were willing 'to go back', the Colonial Office noted in January 1911. The Croydon COS annual report for 1910–11[46] does not name the brothers, but they may have been among the seventy-eight cases referred to the Poor Law Guardians: who would have refused to assist if they had no natal or residential links to that Surrey town.

There is some evidence showing Black participation in Edwardian manufacturing work, mainly in a book published in London in 1930.[47] The author states that he was from Dahomey and had reached Glasgow in 1896. He went to school in Scotland, returned to Africa, reached Liverpool in July 1902, and started work in the paint shop of Humber cars in Coventry where his White colleagues 'did not take kindly to me, and they did everything they knew how to annoy me'.[48] He transferred to the repair shop 'where the men were a little more tolerant'.[49]

Although he named a local innkeeper who has been traced in the city records, his claim to have been Amgoza the celebrated African chief at Coventry's carnival has no other support. Lobagola became a professional entertainer according to his own testimony, and served in the British army, but research by David Killingray has revealed that he was not an African at all. Born in Baltimore in 1887, Joseph Howard Lee's lies and exaggerations are mixed with facts, such as a description of Bewdley in Worcestershire that seems to have been from first-hand knowledge. He states he tried to enter Russia but 'no one was permitted to bring into Russia any black, or any Chinaman'.[50]

There were Black people in Russia, as we will see. The Foreign Office index cards from 1911 note that a request made to the Colonial Office 'to pay cost of sending J. Williams (a negro) from Russia to Sierra Leone' had been refused 'on grounds that he has not been proved to be a native thereof'.

Because Lobagola's story is centred on the lie that he was an African we must question all of it. Nevertheless it was not so remarkable that a Black person had travelled in Britain, across western Europe and to the USA in the 1900s.

Cardiff-born Harriet Vincent's father, son of Caribbean parents in Nova Scotia, Canada, lost his right hand in a sawmill accident. He worked as a cook at sea, settled in Cardiff, selling bread from a cart. He then opened a boarding house with his Welsh wife, also selling tea and soup. He had a dozen lodgers, usually West Indian sailors. Serving a transient community, the Vincents had a decent living from their work. They had two servants, tailored clothes not hand-me-downs, and new shoes. There were fourteen children, six surviving infancy and two boys and two girls reaching adulthood.[51]

She recalled the violence that threatened Bute Town's (known as 'Tiger Bay') mixed and largely seafaring community, and how the 'very dark' workers 'couldn't get a job' when unemployment increased. Her father was a grandmaster of the Oddfellows benevolent society, a staunch churchgoer, and often led mourners at funerals. Harriet's two Welsh aunts were married to West Indians, one keeping a corner shop. Harriet married a sailor from Barbados, who worked in a coal mine for four years and returned to sea.

Her father was recalled in 1988 by Donald John, also Afro-Welsh:[52]

> [He was] the man who always took the lead in every Black funeral procession in Tiger Bay. These were quite spectacular affairs, and something to see. Vincent would be immaculate in black topper and a morning coat, white gloves, spats, and looking quite splendid, as he headed a retinue of similarly dressed black men walking in front of the hearse, which in those days always had a black horse, sometimes two, with black plumes on the heads, and sometimes the funerals were not only those of Black departed, but of white people, late

residents of Tiger Bay, perhaps the white wife of some West Indian or an African, sometimes a well known white resident, but such was the respect accorded to every resident that it made no difference, Tiger Bay being such a well knit society of all its inhabitants, Black or White, but always walking in front would be Mr Vincent. The cortege would start from the home of the deceased, walk through the Bay to St Marys Church for a service, and then continue out of the Bay, into the town for a half mile walk in procession, when everybody would board the carriages for the cemetery about 3 miles distant. I attended some of these affairs, and was always surprised at the attention given by the onlookers of the town, once they saw all those black men walking though town, and all looking so well dressed, with Vincent leading, now wearing his famous topper. Men onlookers would doff their hats, caps, or whatever, and there always seemed to be a respectful silence. Sometimes these funerals would stop the traffic, with a policeman holding back the flow, at intersections, but in those days that would not be much of a problem, as most traffic consisted of horse drawn carts, vans, etc.[53]

John's father was a sailor from Barbuda who deliberately settled outside Bute Town and its Black and other visible minorities. Married to a Welsh woman, by 1911 Elvin John was living in Grangetown working as a labourer. His son recalled, as a small boy, seeing the huge carthorses being led into the building where his father worked. He went to sea on fishing boats, providing another memorable childhood recollection when he came home with a huge cod over his shoulder. At the time of his death in 1924 Elvin John was working in Cardiff docks.

It was at that time that Donald John first made his way to Bute Town where, as he recalled in 1988, there were 'all those black faces and nobody saying "Nigger!"'. Apart from his own brothers and sisters, there were only two or three other Black families in Cardiff outside Bute Town. Even Bute Town's multi-racial community had colour prejudice, as another Black veteran was to note in 1974.[54]

Mrs Edith Bryan was probably Harriet Vincent's sister, for she had been born around 1890 to a Canadian father of African descent who had been a baker, who, with her 'very Welsh mother' ran a boarding house for sailors in Cardiff. They had fourteen children. Mrs Bryan recalled being teased at school because of her colour.

Harret Vincent's family was upwardly mobile, her father moving from being dependent on a weekly wage as a seaman to owning property and having a solid status in the city where he had made his home and raised his children.

Another Black worker who settled in Cardiff after time at sea was John Benjamin Jemmott, who was a merchant navy fireman aged twenty-seven when he married Alice Jones in 1908. Their daughter Lilian Louise Jemmott was born at 15 Bute Terrace on 6 January 1909. Street directories reveal that this was a boarding house and refreshment rooms for the Jemmotts until 1911 when they moved their dining rooms to 49 Bute Street, where they remained until 1927.[55] This was not a poverty striken family: Lilian had piano lessons, passed college examinations, and married a doctor from Nigeria.

Seafaring could be dangerous work. On 9 December 1912 the body of William H. Meyer was found at Southsea beach near Portsmouth during a search for another person. The body had been in the water for some time, but the 'young negro' was identified through photographs in his pockets and letters addressed to him on the schooner *Lux*, Folkestone. This was reported in London's *Daily Chronicle* on the following day.

Joseph Adolphus Bruce from British Guiana was working as a labourer in London's construction industry when, aged thirty, he married Edith Brooks on 22 March 1912, in a ceremony witnessed by a West Indian named Augustus Greenidge. The Bruces lived at 15 Dieppe Street near Earls Court, and their daughter was born there on 29 November. When Josephine Esther Bruce's birth was registered in January 1913 her father was an 'actor'. Greenidge was her godfather. The next person of African descent in her life was her stepmother Jennie Edwards, a child's nurse from Guiana, in the late 1920s.[57]

She recalled her father's sharp retort when called 'boy' in London – 'Where do you think you are? In India or Africa? You're in England and I'm the same as you', and that her teacher was dismissed for telling the class not to talk to coloured people.[58]

Another Black member of London's working class was the 'North African native' reported in the crime and scandal weekly *Illustrated Police News* on 6 July 1912 under the heading 'Marrying a Negro'. Armaar Mohamet and his wife Sophia Gertrude had married in December 1910, and she was seeking a divorce. 'An ebony-black man' aged thirty-seven, Mohamet worked as a photographer. She had left him on four occasions and there had been violence. The court granted a separation.

The *Tonbridge Gazette and Pictorial News* of 9 November 1911 reported that Professor Zodiac, 'a coloured man', had been telling fortunes in central London where he had been arrested for fraud. His accounts showed that this work had gained him £600 in fifteen months. His sentence of six weeks was welcomed by this Kent newspaper. Thirteen months later the *Illustrated Police News* reported that 'a coloured man, known as "Professor Zodiac"' had been in court in Liverpool. Rufus Scott Blair had been telling fortunes which was illegal if a fee was charged. Blair's defence was that he charged for

11. Esther Bruce, born in London in 1912 (Stephen Bourne)

phrenology examinations and that his fortune telling was free. The court heard that ignorant people believed in fortune telling and that Blair was a rogue, taking money from innocents. He was sent to prison for six months.

Working outside the law, as Blair did, justified such newspaper reports and criticism. Edwardian journalists exposed their deep ignorance and prejudices when reporting other incidents involving Blacks, often presuming that a person with a dark skin was guilty. An incident in September 1912, in the east coast fishing and resort town of Yarmouth, provides a fine example.

The *Yarmouth Independent* reported a 'desperate affray on Regent Road' which had ended with three men bleeding from knife wounds. Robert Rody, 'a bloodthirsty creole', of 46 Howard Street North,

Yarmouth, had attacked the men. The magistrate remanded the 'West Indian creole' for a week.

The front page of the *Yarmouth Independent* of 28 September had a court report headed 'accused gives his version'. Rody, 'a coloured man, a native of Jamaica' had arrived in Yarmouth in July 1912 'since when he had been making bangles and taking photographs for a living. He was married, and had one girl, nearly 4 years of age.' Walking with his wife, Ellen, along Regents Road towards midnight, Londoners up for the races insulted her and jostled Rody. She struck out with her umbrella, and he used the knife to protect her from the roughs. The wounds he had inflicted, and Rody's blood-stained knife, were sufficient to keep him in prison until the case could be heard at a more senior court in Norwich.

There, in late October 1912, Rody went on trial on a charge of unlawful wounding. The Yarmouth newspaper stated he was 'a native of the West Indies' and 'an inoffensive man' who had planned to work as a street singer in the seaside resort that summer. Finding that the principal pubs would not permit him to sing, he turned to photography and craft work. He had done no harm to anyone until four London louts set on him.

His companion, Mrs Ellen Banton, had been the victim of offensive remarks and had to listen to Robert Rody being called a black bastard. They had hit him, and he had defended himself. A prison warder informed the court that 'you could not see bruises on a black man so clearly as on a white'. The jury found him not guilty, believing that he had been apprehensive of further violence and had been provoked.

The *Illustrated Police News* reported on Rody's troubles, referring to him both as 'a Creole' and 'a coloured man', whose home was in central London's Shaftesbury Avenue. 'Insulting remarks were made to him and to his wife owing to his colour. He was then knocked down several times' before he drew his knife.

The weeks in prison must have brought their own anxieties, along with the loss of earnings which, at the end of the summer season, would have been precarious anyhow. That a man defending himself and his companion from violence had to be locked up, and that he was needlessly described as 'bloodthirsty', are two aspects of one Black Edwardian's life. No wonder that working as a servant for a reasonable employer had its attractions.

In July 1914 Stewart Gore-Browne returned to England after some years working with the Congo-Rhodesia boundary commission. He was accompanied by two servants, Kakumbi and Bulaya, who were in Surrey by August, working for Gore-Browne's sister. It was decided to sent the Africans home, but Bulaya 'bolted' and worked washing dishes in a London hotel before serving in the British Army under the name Samson Jackson. By 1924 he was an actor in London.[59] Travelling with an employer did not necessarily mean work without prospects for change.

Another Black working for a famous individual was the child's nurse who looked after Tabitha Ransome, daughter of Ivy and Arthur Ransome. He was soon to write *Swallows and Amazons* and other books. In his autobiography he recalled his Jamaican servant as Giggee. His biographer noted that she worked for the Ransomes in Bournemouth and then moved with them to the Lake District in late 1910, and then via London to Hatch near Salisbury. She left that work in September 1911, and disappeared from history.[60]

Another Jamaican servant in Britain arrived on the *Barranca* at Avonmouth in early August 1912, travelling to London where she continued to work for the Judah family at 14 Durley Road, Stamford Hill.[61] Her employers, a wealthy Jamaican family, did not know that their servant Ida (or Indiana) Garvey's brother Marcus would lead an international organisation in the 1920s which scared imperialists and made Black people proud. Marcus Garvey lived and worked in Edwardian Britain, too.

NOTES

1. D. Sullivan, *Navvyman* (London: Coracle Books, 1983), p. 48.
2. N. Longmate, *The Workhouse* (London: Maurice Temple Smith, 1974).
3. F. Dawes, *Not in Front of the Servants: Domestic Service in England 1850–1939* (Newton Abbot: Readers Union, 1975), p. 30.
4. D. Crow, *The Edwardian Woman* (London: Allen & Unwin, 1977), pp. 137, 141.
5. Dawes, *Servants*, p. 30.
6. Harding, *Far Bugles*, pp. 114–15.
7. *Liverpool Courier*, 12 October 1908; *St Albans Post*, 14 October 1908.
8. *African World* (London), 12 December 1908.
9. N. Buzzell, *The Register of the Victoria Cross* (1981; revd edn Cheltenham: This England, 1988), p. 123. Gordon (1864–1922) later had a nominal job at the regiment's headquarters, a grace-and-favour arrangement that was recalled, in the 1980s, by Leslie Thompson who remembered seeing the hero during his years in the band of the West India Regiment.
10. I am indebted to Bernth Lindfors for advising there was a second woman working under this name.
11. A. Nicol, 'West Indians in West Africa' *Sierra Leone Studies* 13 (June 1960), pp 14–23 noted there were 'technicians and train guards' in the 1890s and early 1900s (p. 20).
12. The Barbados-born teacher Edith Goring, whose annual salary was £115, was on leave from 12 October 1909 to 9 March 1910 according to the *Gold Coast Blue Book 1909* and *1910*.
13. *Gold Coast Report 1906*; *West Africa* (London) 24 July 1920, p. 990.
14. Information from her step-daughter Amy Barbour-James; see *Acton Gazette and Express* (London), 8 October 1920, p. 1; ibid 15 October 1920, p. 1; ibid 22 October 1920, p. 3; *Barbados Advocate* 6 February 1939, p. 11.
15. CO 763/1.

16. Ibid, 6 December 1913.
17. *Tottenham, Edmonton, and Wood Green Wednesday Herald* 19 April 1905.
18. CO 351/19 has entries dated 3 April and 2 May 1905.
19. CO 351/19. See C. Mowat, *The Charity Organisation Society 1869–1913* (London: Methuen, 1961).
20. A. Linklater, *An Unhusbanded Life: Charlotte Despard* (London: Hutchinson, 1980), p. 78.
21. E. Turner, *What the Butler Saw: Two Hundred and Fifty Years of the Servant Problem* (London: Michael Joseph, 1962), p. 245.
22. J. Brown, *The Un-Melting Pot: An English Town and its Immigrants* (London: Macmillan, 1970), pp. 23–5, photo 1.
23. G. Watson, *London United Tramways: A History 1894–1933* (London: Allen & Unwin, 1971), pp. 110–11 and three photographs between pp. 128–9. I am indebted to Charles Kay for this information.
24. Photograph in the Charles Kay collection.
25. CO 368/20.
26. *African World* (London) 18 March 1905, p. 276; M. Sampson, *Gold Coast Men of Affairs* (London, 1937; repr. London: Dawsons of Pall Mall, 1969), p. 2.
27. *African World* (London) 27 May 1905, p. 122; information from Amy Barbour-James.
28. T. Roche, *The Key in the Lock: Immigration Control in England from 1066 to the Present Day* (London: John Murray, 1969), pp. 65–71.
29. BT 27/581 for the Bostons; BT 27/580 otherwise.
30. P. O'Mara, *The Autobiography of a Liverpool Irish Slummy* (New York, 1934; repr. Bath: Cedric Chivers, 1968). It is appropriate that I first learned of this book when in Halifax, Nova Scotia, the often forgotten Canadian port with its own magnificent shipping history.
31. I am indebted to Joe Deniz, a Cardiff sailor turned musician, who recounted the contempt he received when visiting the shipping office to collect his father's wages in the late 1920s. He also recalled the sense of community in Bute Town or 'Tiger Bay' in Cardiff in the 1920s and 1930s. He read and then lent my copy of Little's *Negroes in Britain* to a fellow Cardiff-born Black, who agreed that Little had captured the feel of pre-1939–45 war Cardiff but was writing nonsense when he stated that the police blacked up for raids on illegal parties (p. 141; now annotated 'rubbish').
32. Working in Northamptonshire in 1972–5, alerted to 'tribalism' by my years in Uganda and aware that my London accent was alien, I was informed by a Liverpool-raised colleague in his fifties that he had been totally surprised when he was not questioned about his religion when applying for a job in the south Midlands.
33. I am indebted to Ray Costello for this information.
34. CO 343/19.
35. CO 137/669.
36. BT 26/263.
37. CO 351/20 Jamaica register.
38. I have used Makaroo but the Grimsby newspapers had several variants to that name: and of that of police inspector Baglee.
39. PRO BT 26/311.
40. M. Reeves, *Round About a Pound a Week* (London, 1913; repr. London: Virago, 1979); S. Humphries, Joanna Mack & Robert Peter, *A Century of Childhood* (London: Sidgwick & Jackson, 1988), p. 29.
41. CO 351/20 index; CO 295/488.
42. CO 137/676.
43. CO 351/20.

44. CO 351/20; CO 351/21.
45. CO 351/21.
46. My thanks to Croydon library.
47. Lobagola, *An African Savage's Own Story* (London: Knopf, 1930), and published as *Lobagola: An African Savage's Own Story* (New York: Knopf, 1929).
48. Lobagola, *Lobagola*, p. 215.
49. Ibid p. 216.
50. Ibid p. 225.
51. P. Thompson, *The Edwardians: The Remaking of British Society* (London: 1974; repr. London: Weidenfeld & Nicolson, 1984), pp. 114–23.
52. I am grateful to Joe Deniz for this introduction.
53. Undated letter to Jeffrey Green.
54. 'Blacks and Whites in Tiger Bay', *Radio Times* (London) 7 November 1974, courtesy Stephen Bourne.
55. My thanks to Howard Rye for investigating Cardiff street directories.
56. L. Thompson, *Leslie Thompson: An Autobiography* (Crawley: Rabbit Press, 1986), pp. 58, 63.
57. Information from Stephen Bourne. S. Bourne and E. Bruce, *The Sun Shone on Our Side of the Street: Aunt Esther's Story* (London: Hammersmith & Fulham Community History Series No 8, 1991). Obituary in the *Independent* (London) 29 August 1994.
58. Bourne and Bruce, *Aunt Esther's Story*, p. 5.
59. R. Rotberg, *Black Heart: Gore-Browne and the Politics of Multiracial Zambia* (Berkeley CA: University of California Press, 1977), pp. 69–70. I am indebted to Christopher Fyfe for this reference.
60. H. Brogan, *The Life of Arthur Ransome* (London: Cape, 1984), p. 73. My thanks to Joe Standen.
61. Information from Robert Hill, editor of the Marcus Garvey Papers; BT 26/511 *Barranca* passenger list.

— 4 —

In the service of the king

THE uniformed men who had participated in the coronation were
just some of the Black people who served King Edward and his son
George. As in other areas of early twentieth-century life, Black people
were at various levels in the service of the Crown. We have already
noted that the colonial civil service in the Caribbean and tropical
Africa was staffed by Blacks at the bottom, with others in positions of
greater responsibility, and a scattering of doctors and lawyers near the
top, many spending part of their lives in the British Isles. The range of
tasks included the very defence of the realm.

A soldier 'now stationed in Ireland' was reported as 'the only
Soudanese serving in the British Army' by the *Penny Illustrated Paper* of
30 December 1905. In his early twenties, he served in the Durham
Light Infantry. That famous regiment's battle honours included
Ginnis, fought twenty years earlier against the Muslim troops of the
charismatic Sudanese leader known as the Mahdi. The small black boy
found, after the battle, on the banks of the Nile was taken into Egypt by
Sergeant Stuart. Mustapha, renamed Jim Durham, tended the horses
and acted as an interpreter. When the first battalion of the Durham
Light Infantry was scheduled to move to India in 1887 the sergeants
requested that the boy, now their mascot, was allowed to accompany
them, each donating one rupee a month to meet his costs.[1]

The African grew into manhood and, in Mandalay in Burma in
November 1898, was enrolled into the Durham Light Infantry.[2] Named
after Jim Birley and Sergeant Francies Fisher,[3] James Francies Durham
continued to live in India until 1902 when the battalion moved to
Aldershot.

Durham had been trained as a musician, and photographs show
him with a clarinet, as well as on parade in charge of the battalion's
animal mascot, a goat. He had one service stripe on his sleeve.[4] In
October 1905 Durham's battalion moved to Cork. In February 1906 he
visited Nottingham and the now-retired Sergeant Fisher and his wife.
The *Liverpool Echo* reported that Fisher had been one of the adopting
sergeants in Egypt, and that the African was a skilled clarinettist as
well as playing first violin in the regimental string orchestra.[5] Except

12. James Durham of the Durham Light Infantry posed for this
photograph in Cork around 1908 (DLI Museum)

for such leaves the Black infantryman remained in Cork until the
beginning of 1909 when the battalion moved thirty miles north to the
garrison town of Fermoy where the road to Dublin crosses the river
Blackwater.

Jimmy Durham was recalled in 1972 by a veteran who first met the
African soldier when joining the regiment in Cork in 1907. He re-

membered his two service stripes and his lowly rank. Bandsman Durham ran the battalion's branch of the Army Temperance Association. Members were permited to leave the barracks for meetings without being in full dress uniform, a relaxation of the rules to encourage soldiers to abandon alcohol. Innocently the Black bandsman arranged to hold the branch meetings in a room above a pub, and many members went into the bar and not upstairs to hear uplifting tales. When Durham's branch was awarded a prize for having the largest number of members, his colleagues were very amused.[6]

That success took Durham to London in the early summer of 1908. Writing from Cork on 17 April to Stella (probably the daughter of the Fishers of Nottingham) Durham stated that he planned to visit Darlington, in the county of Durham where the regiment drew many of its recruits. Durham had visited Blarney Castle that very day, he told Stella, signing the letter 'your loving brother'.[7] A second letter informed her that he had received the prize from the hands of Field Marshal Lord Roberts himself.

The Times of 15 May reported the temperance meeting at London's Caxton Hall the previous day. Lord Roberts had stressed the need for every barracks to have a branch of the association, for there had been over two hundred courts martial for drunkenness in 1906 (an improvement: there had been 545 in 1901). The officers and men of the Royal Army Temperance Association numbered over 74,000. The Conrad Dillin challenge plate was awarded to the second battalion of the Durham Light Infantry for 'the highest percentage of membership'.

In July 1908 Durham was with the band in Newcastle, the Tyneside depot of the regiment. The African who had seen little of Africa married a Darlington woman named Jane Green, but remained stationed in Ireland. On 8 August 1910 he died in Fermoy, Co. Cork, of pneumonia. Buried with full military honours, his headstone, erected by officers and men of his battalion, recorded that he had been 'specially enlisted' on 23 May 1899, having been adopted by the regiment after the battle of Ginnis.[8] His daughter Frances was born some weeks later.[9]

Back in 1902, in the sole British colony in South America, a thirty-five-year-old post office clerk had left Georgetown for Britain. John Alexander Barbour-James was being transferred from the British Guiana civil service to that of the Gold Coast, but first he had to report to the Colonial Office in London. From Liverpool he took the train to London, where he was invited to watch the coronation parade from the windows of the Colonial Office building. The delays caused by Edward's ill-health forced James to leave for Africa before the ceremony.[10]

Ignorant of Africa other than as the home of his ancestors and from missionary tales of pagans, James, who preferred to be known as Barbour-James, was shocked and stimulated for, when he arrived at Cape Coast, the first aspect of Africa he saw was a group of surplice-clad choir boys walking to the Anglican church.[11] The routine of post office administration, with some minor mishaps,[12] occupied his working hours for fifteen years. During those years Barbour-James benefited from colonial service practice and had spent one quarter of that time on holiday, away from Africa.

At the beginning he tried to have his wife and children in Africa, a wish that his employers rejected. Caroline Barbour-James and the five children moved from Guiana to England where they settled in west London by 1905. He joined them during leaves, and three more children were born to them. These ten pure-African descent Edwardians became known through John Barbour-James's activities in the 1920s, revealed through contacts with his London-born daughter Amy Barbour-James and dozens of mentions in *West Africa* and in the weekly *Acton Gazette*.[13]

Discussions with Caroline Amy Aileen Barbour-James, born on 25 January 1906, suggested mixed motives for the family's activities in Edwardian England. That the wage-earner was a civil servant in British West Africa might explain some aspects; that he and Caroline were firmly Christian gave another perspective on their lives in Britain. That John and Caroline Barbour-James were from a distant and overlooked colony in the British West Indies (or was British Guiana in South America?), and that they were of pure African descent, had influences too.

The children studied music, attended fee-paying schools, sang in the choir of the local parish church, were neatly dressed and took pride in being well-spoken. John Barbour-James favoured spats for decades after that fashion had died. His daughter remembered London street urchins whose boots had metal studs hammered into the soles and heels (giving longer life and providing that now-lost children's delight of skidding in a shower of sparks on the pavement) rushing past the family with a clatter and mass of sparks then turning in the hope of a coin. Seeing the black faces of the Barbour-James family and noting their smart and clean appearance, the remark 'Cor, they must be millionaires' was normal.

The family shared their home in Birkbeck Grove, Acton, with another family with solid links to British Guiana: that of Samuel Spencer Alfred Cambridge. The house was not large; there can be several explanations for this sharing, including Caroline Barbour-James's relative isolation as a Black mother in Edwardian London. Financial restrictions, making sharing attractive, may not have resulted from the family's size but by ambitions to be middle class. Cambridge, a barrister, had an English wife named Lou and three

13. John Barbour-James first visited England in 1902 on his way from British Guiana to work in the postal administration of the Gold Coast (Ghana). His wife Caroline and their five children settled in London

daughters by 1915. His excellent penmanship but poor accent were recalled by a contemporary in the 1980s.[14]

Caroline Barbour-James died, aged forty-four, in 1917 and her husband remarried in 1920. His family's stepmother was Edith Rita Goring, born in Barbados but also a royal servant in the Gold Coast.

Passing through England in 1906, Miss Goring became a teacher at the government girls' school in Cape Coast. The annual reports or *Blue Books* show that she was on leave from 12 October 1909 to 9 March 1910, and again from 15 March to 12 August 1913. Even if she returned to her family in Barbados, the absence of a direct Gold Coast – West Indies shipping service necessitated her being in England.

The fact that she worked at the girls' school could conceal information that came, again in the 1980s, from another Black Edwardian. Richard Savage, the son of a Nigerian doctor[15] and his Scottish wife, attended that school for some time before going to Scotland where he took up medicine like his father. He recalled that Miss Goring was well prepared to use a cane on the bare legs of the children.[16] Her professionalism met with the colonial government's approval, for she became headteacher in 1915 when she had the assistance of 'West Indian teacher' Marie Selina Austin. The *Blue Book* of the previous year had also named Edith Maud Emily Locke, who was dismissed in January 1914.

Serving the king-emperor in the colonies was no sinecure. For Caribbeans, serving in Africa involved lengthy voyages from the West Indies via Britain to the motherland. Until more details are uncovered, John Barbour-James and his second wife Edith Goring must represent those Blacks who served Edward the Seventh in West Africa.

Barbour-James travelled on the *Jebba* into Liverpool just before Christmas, 1906, surely anxious to be reunited with his family and to see his daughter Amy.[17] Still on leave in March 1907, he gave a talk on agriculture in the West Indies in Acton on 5 March, repeated in nearby Ealing on 19 April, noted by the *West India Committee Circular* as by 'Mr. Bertram James'. We can be sure that he had informed that London weekly. He also spoke to the Royal Horticultural Society of London on 19 March.[18] The proceeds were in aid of the earthquake fund for Jamaica.

He had the lecture published in 1908, when he again was on leave (from mid-June to mid-November). He now had three lines in the annual *Colonial Office List*.[19] His wife was now expecting a child, born in 1909 and named Victor.

John Barbour-James was also active during his 1910–11 leave, which started in June. He saw his *The Agricultural and Industrial Possibilities of the Gold Coast* into print. He donated one copy to the Colonial Office and another to the Royal Colonial Institute, where he was one of the few Black members. The African-edited *Gold Coast Leader* of 13 May 1911 noted his return to the colony on the *Burutu*, that he had been ill whilst in England, and praised the 'very interesting book, which adds much credit to himself and to his race' and which had resulted from his 'perservering efforts and splendid ability'.

14. Three of the Barbour-James children, posed in London (Amy Barbour-James)

These public efforts had to be within the expectations of the Colonial Office, for an unguarded remark could terminate his contract and effectively stop further employment in both the African colonial service and that of the Caribbean. It seems unlikely, unless private correspondence is uncovered, that we will ever know what went through the minds of the Black men and women who served in the Edwardian colonial service. That all of them spent time in Britain is seen from the passenger lists: Alfred William Downer of the British

Guiana police, active in the Gold Coast from 1901, travelled to Liverpool on the *Burutu* in May 1905 (by 1911 he was a senior superintendent);[20] Ebenezer Adonis James, also from Guiana, was a superintendent of the Gold Coast police aged forty-two when he reached Southampton in February 1913, travelling from Trinidad to Africa.[21]

Another aspect that can be forgotten in an age of air travel is that the weeks on board enabled contacts to be made: and as the bulk of travellers were White, we could suppose that Black travellers usually got to know each other. That police superintendent Downer travelled into Liverpool in 1905 on the same ship that carried Black author Edward Wilmot Blyden shows the rich possibilities.

The leaves taken away from the colony did nothing to ensure efficiency, and when Barbour-James returned in 1911 the post office was in near chaos. A British postal expert named Ford was seconded to the colony in mid-1911. Barbour-James was appointed district surveyor in the postal department.

African nationalist sentiments, evidenced in the *Gold Coast Leader* newspaper during 1911, would have been known to Barbour-James. The coronation of George the Fifth, Edward's heir, involved no Blacks according to the *Leader* of 15 April, the issue that reported that Dr Savage had been removed from his government post at Cape Coast. On 11 February it noted the retirement of an African postmaster, 'our respected countryman', which took place in June.

There was evidence to support the image of the 'white man's grave', for yellow fever had broken out in Accra in May 1911. Death did not free people from the petty indignities of imperialism, for the cemetery at Sekondi was segregated.[22] There were few schools: the girls' school at Cape Coast where Miss Goring worked had average attendances of 89 and a role of 133 pupils.[23] The entire colony had just nine government schools; the US-Black led AMEZ mission had three schools with 298 pupils.[24]

African lawyer Thomas Hutton Mills, whose children were being educated in Britain, was a member of a commission of enquiry into the chaos in the postal administration, which had two travelling surveyors who moved around the colony administering those of the seventy-plus post offices which had problems. A telegraph training school was reopened at Cape Coast under an instructor sent from Britain, and a new training school opened at Accra.[25] Fifty telegraphists had qualified by 1913; and the new postmaster's suggestion that African women worked as telephone operators was taken up with success.[26]

These administrative problems added to the difficulties of commerce and mining in the colony. The trickle of educated Africans was absorbed by the mines and in business. Penny-pinching continued however: stamps with Edward's image were not replaced by Gold Coast stamps with King George's image until 1913.

The Black imperial servants included Derwent Hutton Ryder Waldron, a Jamaican who had graduated at Edinburgh in 1879.[27] He had first served in St Kitts, then worked in the Gold Coast in 1881 and Lagos in 1882.[28] At the beginning of 1902 he was one of four senior medical officers, working as a health officer at Elmina in the Gold Coast on an annual salary of £640.[29] Dr Waldron had also studied law in London, qualifying as a barrister in 1893. The following year he had become a Fellow of the Royal Meteorological Society.[30] He retired, after eighteen years service, in mid-1908 on an annual pension of £608.[31] He settled in London where his address was listed in the British medical directories into the 1920s, when he moved to Brighton where he seems to have died by 1930. Nothing has been traced of Dr Waldron during these decades in Britain, but it seems unlikely that such an individual would have had a passive retirement.

The Africans who held senior posts, serving the king in West Africa, went to and from Britain on business and holiday. A deputy post-master of the Gold Coast, Robert E. Quartey, was in London in 1907 on a course at the head office of the whole imperial postal system – the General Post Office near St Paul's Cathedral. He had joined the customs in Accra in 1881, and had steadily climbed the promotional ladder to be one of the Gold Coast's five postmasters by 1910: fellow African W. Bannerman, Barbour-James, the yet to be identified F. L. Soper, and a vacant place were also listed in the *Colonial Office List 1910*.

The harbourmaster of Freetown, Sierra Leone, was an African. Emanuel Akita Cole's onerous task is revealed in the *Sierra Leone Blue Book*, which states that nineteen thousand crew from nearly four hundred steamers as well as sailing boats used the harbour in 1908. Cole was paid five pounds a week in the service of King Edward.

In 1908 Cole took his leave in England, and obtained permission to expand his professional knowledge. Through his reports to the Colonial Office we can trace details of his time in Britain.[32] He lodged at 5 Landsdown Place near Brunswick Square in central London. On 17 August Cole reported that he had been to the east coast port of Lowestoft on 27 July, where he had been shown round the lighthouse. He had made other contacts with officials of Trinity House, the organisation responsible for lighthouses, lightships, and other aids to safe navigation. On 3 August Cole had boarded their vessel *Satellite* at Harwich, and visited two lightships in the Thames estuary, returning to London the next day.

Cole visited three docks in the London area, including Tilbury. He arranged with Sir Alfred Jones of the Elder Dempster line to be in

Liverpool for one month from the end of August 1908, and duly reported to the Colonial Office from Mulgrave Street, Liverpool, on 23 September. He had studied modern port management with Captain W. P. Thompson, marine superintendent of Jones's shipping company. Thompson confirmed that Cole had been with him for more than three weeks, and the pair submitted a recommendation for a buoy for Freetown's harbour.

On 29 September Cole was back at Landsdown Place, writing to the Colonial Office. He asked to be booked on the ship due to sail to Sierra Leone on 7 October. He reported that he had spent twenty-three nights of his leave on Sierra Leone government business, and was owed more than seven pounds for costs. It was agreed that this loyal and industrious civil servant should travel first class, and arrangements were made to have Cole back in Freetown on 21 October. He drew twenty pounds for expenses and packed his trunk.

Emanuel Akita Cole never took up his first class berth on the steamer. He was found on the train to Liverpool with his throat cut. The London *Evening News*, copied by the *African World* of 10 October, noted that Cole, 'a coloured gentleman', had been on the 2:00 am King's Cross to Liverpool train, and 'was found lying on the floor of one of the compartments with his throat cut and with a razor in his hand. He was removed to hospital, where he died a few hours later.' There was no easy explanation for this suicide. 'A week ago he went to Liverpool on business, and came back appearing very worried. In his possession was found £30 and a ticket from King's Cross to Liverpool.'

The *African World* noted that Cole, 'a fine figure of a man' who stood over six feet tall, was aged about fifty. He had promised to write an article for the London weekly. The news was published in the *Sierra Leone Weekly News*. On 13 October his nephew wrote to London for more information. The Colonial Office files have no details on why he killed himself. Early in 1909 his widow was awarded a compassionate payment.

As well as spells in Britain for training and holidays, the Black men and women who served in the British Empire were in Britain for medical treatment. Locomotive fitter W. E. Carter from Trinidad, who had been working in the Gold Coast, was on sick leave in Britain during the winter of 1909–10 before returning to the Caribbean.[33]

Another Black railwayman who moved from the New World to Africa, via Britain, was Amos Shackleford. Born in Jamaica in 1887, where he worked on the railway from 1902, Shackleford transferred to Nigeria in 1912. By the time he died, in Accra in 1954, where he was a highly reputable businessman and nationalist, he was listed in the *Who's Who* of both Jamaica and Nigeria.[34]

James Carmichael Smith was the postmaster of Freetown during the early Edwardian years. Born in the Bahamas, he retired to London where he had a daughter, and wrote books and articles.[35] Henry Downing, who had served in the United States consular service in Loanda in the Portuguese colony of Angola, had settled in England by 1900 and remained into the 1910s. He wrote stories and plays. James Weldon Johnson, another American of African descent, served as US consul in Venezuela in 1906 and in Nicaragua from 1908–12.[36]

Johnson had been in London in 1905. His *The Autobiography of an Ex-Coloured Man* of 1912 concerns a light-complexioned individual who had been a servant or valet to a wealthy American of European descent; the pair toured Europe for months. He noted 'London stands for the conservatism, the solidarity, the utilitarianism, and, I might well add, the hypocrisy of the Anglo-Saxon.' He added 'I have seen the black West Indian gentleman in London, and he is in speech and manners a perfect Englishman.'[37]

The men and women who had been in the service of the king may well have been seen in that way by others. Their employment was secure provided they did not offend; their place in the colonial hierarchy was known, being published every year in the *Colonial Office List*; their pensions were guaranteed. It seems unlikely that their conformity was always as solid as their employers expected. Shackleford's encouragement of African nationalism, Smith's association with the *African Times and Orient Review* from 1912 (a Third World-focused radical journal that was to be raided by the police), and Barbour-James's work from 1918 with the African Progress Union, a Black-led protest group in London active into the late 1920s, show another side to these imperial servants.

NOTES

1. B. de Lisle, *Reminiscences of Sport and War* (London: Eyre & Spottiswoode, 1939), p. 29.
2. *The Bugle*, 14 June 1894, p. 49 has 'James Francies Durham'; ibid 28 July 1899 noted his rank as Boy, number 6758; ibid 27 October 1899 carried comments from the now retired sergeants whose human trophy had joined their regiment.
3. His middle name is usually spelled in the orthodox style 'Francis'.
4. My thanks to Stephen Shannon of the DLI Museum & Arts Centre, Durham.
5. *Liverpool Echo*, 7 February 1906, p. 6.
6. C. H. Chester recollections, January 1972, DLI Museum.
7. DLI Museum.
8. *Northern Echo*, (Durham) 20 December 1978; *The Bugle* 28 July 1899 notes Durham's enlistment number.
9. Information from Stephen Shannon, DLI Musuem.
10. Amy Barbour-James to Jeffrey Green.
11. Ibid.

12. When some money went missing at his post office, Barbour-James had to repay the loss.

13. Donald Simpson of the Royal Commonwealth Society led me to Miss Barbour-James; the newspaper library of the British Library had back copies of Acton newspapers, revealing sustained efforts by Barbour-James and his African and Caribbean friends to promote positive images of Blacks as well as a remarkably wide range of contacts in London.

14. Cambridge's link is seen in the *Acton District Post*, 28 May 1915. That funeral report reveals a Mrs R. A. Clarke attending. She must be the London-resident wife of Robert Arthur Clarke, born in British Honduras [Belize] where he worked for the post office from 1893, transferring to the Gold Coast in 1902; see *Colonial Office List 1907*, p. 500. Leslie Brown, son of Jamaica-born Dr J. J. Brown, recalled on 31 May 1987 his first meeting with fellow Afro-British London children; for Cambridge also see *Post Office London Directory 1926*, p. 806; *West Africa* (London) 24 June 1922, p. 660.

15. *Colonial Office List 1902*, p. 186.

16. Information from Richard Savage of Edinburgh.

17. *African World*, 29 December 1906, p. 388; *Gold Coast Blue Book 1906* notes his leave from 4 December 1906; the following volume noted it ended on 2 May 1907.

18. *Journal of the Royal Horticultural Society* (London) vol, 33; extract donation at the library of the Royal Commonwealth Society, London.

19. *African World* (London) 20 May 1905, p. 75; *Colonial Office List 1908*, p. 527.

20. PRO CO 96/406/3408; *Gold Coast Blue Book 1903*; *Colonial Office List 1911*, p. 193; *African World* 20 May 1905, p. 75.

21. BT 26/568 voyage of the *Clyde*; see also CO 343/20/37716 and *Colonial Office List 1911*, p. 193. James retired to Guiana according to CO 343/26/2140 of 1919.

22. J. Casely Hayford, *Ethiopia Unbound* (London, 1911, repr. London, Cass, 1969), p. 84.

23. *Gold Coast Blue Book 1911*.

24. *Colonial Office List 1911*, p. 187.

25. *Gold Coast Report 1912*.

26. *Gold Coast Report 1913*.

27. *E. U. Calender 1880-81* (Edinburgh: James Thin, 1880), p. 181.

28. *Colonial Office List 1902*, p. 531.

29. *Gold Coast Blue Book 1903*.

30. *Gold Coast Civil Service List 1908*, p. 427.

31. *Gold Coast Report 1908* notes that his replacement at Akuse was Dr J. B. H. Davson from Sierra Leone; *Gold Coast Blue Book 1920*.

32. CO 368/19.

33. CO 343/21 11 December 1909; CO 372/16 21 February 1910.

34. R. Okonkwo, *Heroes of West African Nationalism* (Enugu: Delta, 1985), pp. 45–58. My thanks to Hazel King.

35. D. Simpson, 'Mr. Smith of the Colonial Service' *Library Notes* (Royal Commonwealth Society, London), ns 181 (May 1972); R. West, *Back to Africa: A History of Sierra Leone and Liberia* (London: Cape, 1970), photograph 'Hill Station' opp p. 113 shows Smith, seated.

36. E. Levy, *James Weldon Johnson: Black Leader, Black Voice* (Chicago: Chicago University Press, 1973), pp. 109-19.

37. J. Johnson, *The Autobiography of an Ex-Coloured Man* (New York: Knopf, 1912; repr. New York: Garden City Publishing, 1927), p. 153.

— 5 —

Entertaining the multitudes

HUNDREDS of Black people worked in Edwardian Britain's entertainment industry. Urban theatres throughout the kingdom had two – sometimes three – shows, each of two hours, six days a week. Acts toured from town to town, appearing in these new and grand halls seating over one thousand, providing glamour, thrills, music, humour and song. In the cities some acts rushed, by cab, to another theatre and thus could make four appearances nightly. The audiences learned what was on by seeing street posters, sandwich board men, and the local newspaper, by recommendation, and, for the enthusiast, weekly theatrical journals such as *The Era*. These were widely read by management and performers, and from announcements, advertising and publicity puffs in the trade press performers can be traced.

Local newspapers published previews and reviews, as they did of public entertainments that were in assembly rooms and civic halls. Identification of African descent performers needs caution, due to the use and misuse of 'Negro', 'coloured', 'black' and 'African', often describing Whites in burnt cork make-up in the minstrel traditions. Further caution is necessary, for the publicity claims and biographic accounts were aimed to attract attention and audiences to the entertainer, and were not always the truth. As with other activities involving Black Edwardians, the truth and fiction sometimes merged; certainly the credulity of Whites was often an essential part of a Black entertainer's success.

In June 1902 the monthly *Hull Lady* published a photograph of a Black man, along with a brief biography.[1] The man, Duse Mohamed, had established a reputation as an actor in that port town. He claimed to be of Egyptian birth and Nubian descent, educated in England in the 1870s. The so-called Egyptian was entertaining. His fame spread inland, as we can see in the *Beverley Guardian* of 6 December 1902. 'Duse Mohamed Ali, the only English-speaking actor the East has yet produced' was due to appear at that Yorkshire town's assembly rooms to present 'dramatic and humorous recitations assisted by Mrs. Mohamed'. A preview noted that this 'distinguished coloured reciter', who would be 'known to those who have kept themselves posted of events in Hull', was scheduled to appear in Beverley on 10 December.

Three years later his fame was such that when the highly respected Leeds theatrical weekly *The Magnet* published an interview with actress Kitty Lord, it made no comment when she stated that she would return to London to join the actor Duse Mohamed for his sketch '"Getting His Own Back," in which I am to play Kate'.[2]

It was in 1905 too that England's third major theatrical journal, *The Encore*, reported (on 14 September) that 'Mohamed is the only coloured actor and dramatic author in the world. If this fact is realised by managers there can be no question of the success of Mohamed as a novel draw.' These publicity notices suggest that being non-British had advantages in Edwardian public entertainments.

All-Black shows would exploit those advantages, and professional Black groups and individuals were far from rare in Edwardian times. They needed accommodation, spent hours travelling from town to town, and participated in promotional activities as well as making stage appearances, all of which suggests that Black entertainers may have had a considerable impact on perceptions of Blacks in the minds of the majority. News of their successes must have encouraged others to enter that world.

The US-born Belle Davis worked in all-Black shows in America before, aged twenty-seven, she is recorded arriving in Southampton in June 1901 on the *St Paul* with two child entertainers: Irving Williams (aged nine) and Fernandes Jones (aged seven).[3] From 10 June they appeared at Collins's Music Hall in north London's Islington, where they were billed as 'America's Greatest Coon Cantatrice of the Century' with 'her two Piccaninny Actors'.[4] She and the lads also worked at the Middlesex Music Hall and in Brixton. Miss Davis sang; the two boys danced in a very acrobatic style. After this London success they travelled to Brighton, Edinburgh, Glasgow and Newcastle; then returned to London for Christmas.

The two youngsters were referred to as 'Senegambian piccaninies' by *The Stage* in mid-January 1902 when they were in Leeds. They made gramophone records,[5] worked in London music halls into the early autumn, and then toured through Bradford, Sheffield, Hull, Edinburgh, Glasgow and South Shields before returning to London: and then played Dublin through the Christmas week.[6] In June 1903 Belle Davis was still performing in British theatres; the following year she married, in London, Henry Troy – another American entertainer of African descent.[7]

Sometimes with three Black youths, Davis appeared in Swansea, Nottingham, Leicester, Manchester and Hastings before she worked in Berlin in May 1905. She was in Paris in June, the Netherlands in

October, and then at Plymouth's New Palace and Bristol's People's Palace to reach, in December 1905, the Palace Theatre in central London where she was on the same bill as another light-complexioned African-American woman, Abbie Mitchell. Miss Mitchell, the wife of the innovative Black American musician Will Marion Cook, was the mother of a future US ambassador.[8] In 1905 she was touring with her Tennessee Students.

The *Referee*, a London weekly of musical interest, reviewed Belle Davis's act in January 1906. The three expert dancers included the smallest 'ebony youngster' – 'just the sort of little nigger-boy you find in children's picture books'.[9] That was, in 1906, an excellent review and Britain's foremost music hall chain, the Empire group, continued to employ them until they left for the continent in July. There – probably in Germany – two films were made of Belle Davis and 'her picks'.[10]

Miss Davis and her small male dancers reached Russia in 1907, Belgium in 1908, Germany in 1909 and were in Vienna and Prague in 1910. They still kept touring Britain: July 1906 in Walsall, February 1907 in Birmingham, September 1907 in Nottingham, then Manchester and London.[11]

She continued to tour the best British music halls in 1909, 1911, 1912, 1913 and 1914, with excellent reviews in the trade press as well as continental tours. As the small boys grew older and taller they must have been replaced. Sometimes there were four boys. Belle Davis entertained during the war years and then relocated to Paris in 1920.

The act – a stately creole dancer-singer and cavorting children who grimaced and acted the fool – was an excellent entertainment which, fortunately, has survived on film. Much less has been uncovered on Pete and Juno, whose interview in *The Magnet* of 16 September 1905 showed them to be Black. Both claimed to be from America, which they had left eleven years before. Pete lived in Huddersfield and Juno in Newcastle; both were married to English women. We should not put too much trust in this article, for Pete's hometown is named as 'Little Rock, Kansas [sic]'. The Leeds weekly noted the pair were to appear in south London and then in Stoke-on-Trent, touring the provinces for eight weeks with two weeks in the capital. 'Few coloured teams can boast of having remained in England as long as we have, maintaining their success all the time.'

Connie Smith could. She had arrived in England in 1899 at the age of twenty-two. She joined Augustus Smith in a song-and-dance act called Smith and Johnson, which took her round Britain from 1902 into 1905. That year the *Era* noted these 'coloured vocalists' at the Royal Hippodrome in Salford. By 1908 they were touring Holland. Connie Smith settled in England and was living in London in the 1950s.[12]

The boosting if not boasting of entertainers can confuse. George Bohee was another Black entertainer whose act (with brother James, who died in Wales in 1897[13]) was musical. The banjo-playing Bohees were born in Canada. When George Bohee's portrait was published in the *Sketch* on 30 January 1907 it was stated that he had 'taught the king to play the banjo'. The brothers had written music, had a London music school and toured the nation. George Bohee was touring Scotland in 1902 when his one-time pupil was crowned. He was in Newcastle at the beginning of 1904.

Amy Height, who toured with the Bohee Brothers in the late nineteenth century, singing comic songs,[14] also worked in the legitimate or dramatic theatre. She was observed in *Madame Delphine* at Wyndham's Theatre, central London, by *M.A.P.* on 28 July 1900. 'A chocolate complexion, large mouth, and typical negro features' enabled Miss Height to be 'quite in demand for coloured parts'.

Demeaning roles and racist stereotypes were not solely the work of White writers and producers. The all-Black show *In Dahomey*, which opened in central London on 16 May 1903, included lyrics and stage performances that libelled Africa and Africans. The organisers soon added aspects of America that British audiences expected, and made changes that enabled the American accents to be understood.

In Dahomey's first act was set in Massachusetts where a group of Black Americans seek a casket and the fortune it contains. They move to Florida for the second act; and to Africa for the third. Dominating the show were two comedians: George Walker and Bert Williams. *In Dahomey: A Negro Musical Comedy* was basically a minstrel show, being a frame on which singing, dancing, melodrama, music and humour were fitted. 'A really fresh and novel experience' noted the experienced *Era*. The *Daily Mail* noted that:

> those who had come to scoff remained to laugh. And they did laugh. There were moments when the audience literally screamed with merriment over the whimsicalities of a tall low comedian named Williams.

The staid *St James's Gazette* admired 'the wildly inconsequential abruptness' of the ending. *The Times* devoted half a column to it on 18 May. The show was interesting because

> very nearly all concerned in it are negroes or coloured people, and that a kind of ethnological purpose seems to run through the whole undertaking. Ethnology on the stage is not of itself very exhilarating; but there can be no denying the success of the piece.

The fifty African-Americans were not uniform in skin colour: the *Sunday Sun* described their complexions as ranging 'from the slightest trace which the octoroon possesses to the deep purple of the full-blooded negro'. The *Standard* commented on this – 'from ebony to the slightest shade of olive'. The reviewers were also somewhat baffled by Bert Williams, who blacked up in the minstrel style.

One of the female singers was Abbie Mitchell, wife of the orchestra's conductor Will Marion Cook. Their baby son Mercer was with them in London in 1903. She sang 'Brown Skin Baby Mine' and had *The Times* praise her trained voice. Her husband had been trained in Germany, the *Daily News* noted in an interview published on the day the show opened. Cook informed the journalist that the only task that had involved Whites was the painting of the scenery, and that the rest of *In Dahomey* was a Black creation. As the members of Cook's orchestra have not been identified, and reviews paid little attention to his instrumentalists, it is far from certain that the band was Black. If it was then the show involved seventy or more Blacks. The show kept changing, adjusting to the British public and, no doubt, for illness or loss of voice among the performers, but there were songs written by Americans of European descent as well as those with African ancestry.[15]

Cook told the *Daily News* that White Americans at the Cecil Hotel had objected to their Black fellow Americans, and so the management asked the Blacks to find another hotel. The reporter had probably anticipated a story of racial prejudice in the USA, not in London. The *Daily News* also showed its ignorance when its theatre critic, expecting bandanna handkerchief head wear was nonplussed by the Paris fashions of the showgirls – 'the negro who has assimilated what is worst in European civilization'.

The *Star*'s reviewer stated 'It is difficult to accept a chorus of black – or at least dark – ladies with equanimity.' Within weeks a commercial postcard company published a 'Real Coon' series showing many of the performers: in colour, too. The rouge on the Black females must have been quite a shock to the staid British in 1903.

The Sphere ('An Illustrated Newspaper for the Home') regretted that Cook had omitted plantation medlodies. Britain's image of Black Americans was one from minstrel shows and anti-slavery propaganda. The Black presence outside the Old South slave states was hardly known. Cook (from Washington DC) had been educated in Ohio, Berlin and New York. Walker, from Kansas, had met Williams (who probably came from Antigua) in California. Abbie Mitchell had a New York and Baltimore background whilst Hattie McIntosh, whose skills were praised by the *Pall Mall Gazette*, was from Detroit. The story – if a 'plotless' show could be said to have one – was by Jesse Shipp, from Ohio. Shipp was the oldest of the group, and experienced in theatrical and musical productions.[16]

15. A stylish American dancer of the popular *In Dahomey* show in
London, 1903. The show toured the nation

These experienced music hall (vaudeville is the US word)
entertainers swiftly added an outmoded dance to the London
performances, with such success that for decades the introduction of
ragtime to Britain has been dated to 1903. The 1890s cakewalk dance
was so associated with Black Americans that Britons expected it. The
Era noted it had been added, as did the *Weekly Dispatch* of 31 May 1903:
it had 'wonderful vitality'. The *Era* reported on 20 June that the 'cake'
prize was over two metres tall and lit by one hundred electric lights. *In*

Dahomey was a benchmark in Black entertainment, and many entertainers claimed to have participated in it.

The list of passengers arriving at Liverpool on the *Urania* on 7 May 1903 shows some truth in that claim. Fifty-six individuals associated with the show are listed (but not Cook or any instrumentalist). Shipp was aged forty; the youngest was eighteen. There was an equal number of males and females. James Vaughan, L. H. Salisbury, Alex Rogers, Henry Stafford, George Catlin, Dick Connors, James Hill, Lloyd Gibbs, Henry Troy and E. Richardson are some of the males. Peter Hampton, aged thirty-six, settled in London into the 1910s; Norris Smith, aged twenty-four, stayed in London for sixty years, marrying the sister of a member of parliament.[17]

Actresses include Hattie McIntosh, Maggie Davis, Louisa Gaston, Katie Jones, Lizzie Wallace and Laura Bowman. Louisa Gaston and Dick Connors were stars in a truncated performance of *In Dahomey* which was performed at Buckingham Palace on 27 June 1903 for the ninth birthday of Prince David (Edward's grandson, the future King Edward the Eighth, who abdicated and is known to history as the Duke of Windsor). The *Era* reported that the royal children had been excited by 'the prospect of seeing real niggers on stage'. The best pair of dancers in the cakewalk were Gaston and Connors. The *Era* had already reported that George Walker had been giving dancing lessons to the smart set in London.

The show, with its song 'My Dahomian Queen' with a line referring to 'my dusky turtle dove' and 'On Broadway in Dahomey' (written by Alex Rogers) which mentioned a hippopotamus as a justice of the peace, had songs by Black poet Paul Dunbar and by James Weldon Johnson. 'Jonah Man', a song about bad luck, had Williams sing 'They named me after papa and the same day papa died.' He performed it at Buckingham Palace.

In Dahomey played to packed houses, remaining at the Shaftesbury into Christmas. It then toured Britain, appearing in Woolwich at the end of January 1904, then playing Hull, Newcastle, Sheffield, Manchester, Edinburgh and Glasgow. Bert Williams became a member of the Waverley lodge of Scottish freemasons, 597, during 1904.[18]

Laura Bowman settled in suburban London with Peter Hampton. Her biography was published in 1961.[19] Like all theatrical biographies it cannot be relied upon, but it fleshes out the lives of Black Edwardian entertainers. Born in 1881 (but aged twenty according to the passenger list of 1903), her mother was Dutch and her father half European and half African. She recalled crossing the Atlantic and calling at Cork before reaching Liverpool 'on the *Curania* [*sic*]', travelling on 'a funny looking train' to London, and staying at theatrical lodgings.

16. The comic stars of *In Dahomey* were Bert Williams and
(rear) George Walker

After their *In Dahomey* period ended she and Hampton worked with
Will Garland (perhaps he was one of Cook's musicians; certainly he
had worked with veteran Black composer-band leader W. C. Handy
whose autobiography recalls him in Cuba around 1899) and Fred
Douglas, rehearsing near Leicester Square to Garland's piano. Named
the Darktown Entertainers, by 1905 they were in Germany. They had
made recordings, as had Hampton under his own name. Indeed
Hampton was a prolific recording artist in Edwardian Britain.[20]

Hampton and Bowman's advertisement in *The Encore* on 18 July

1907 referred to their 'Down in Kentucky' act, and that they were 'colored Character Duettists'. By mid-1908 Laura Bowman was at the London Hippodrome. It was a successful career in British and continental entertainment that left few traces back in the USA where they are almost forgotten.[21]

She and Hampton, with a Russian servant, made a home at 14 Marlborough Road near Wimbledon Park station in south west London, a house they named Darktown Villa. Bowman, who was from Illinois, worked in the Southerners and the Four Mexican Girls. By 1910 her parents Lois Adelaide and Charles Bradford had moved to Darktown Villa. Her mother is reported to have died in July 1912; the three Black Americans remained in London until Charles Bradford, aged seventy-five, left for America in 1914.

Peter Hampton's recordings contain in text and titles some very unhappy associations. 'Dat Phrenologist Coon' of January 1904; 'Dat's De Way To Spell Chicken' and 'Rufus Rastus Johnson Brown' of 1905 were negative presentations of Blacks. So was his 'Nigger Laughing Song'. Hampton also recorded the *In Dahomey* song 'Jonah Man' in mid-January 1904.

However much these are to be regretted, that Hampton and his partner could earn a steady income as entertainers in Edwardian Britain and that he had several recording contracts show how often Black entertainers appeared before British audiences.

Yet another Black American who earned a living by entertaining Britons and continentals was Billy McClain. Active in music and boxing, McClain kept in contact with the United States by letters to the *Freeman* of Indianapolis, Ohio, which in part encouraged others to cross the Atlantic. His comments included, in a letter from Manchester dated 27 October 1905, that he had seen 'Harry Brown, Tom Brown and Navarro, Charles Johnson of Murray and Johnson . . . all playing the city here'.[22]

A year later, writing from Southampton, he informed the Black-edited paper that 'There are a good many colored performers in England, some doing well and others not.' McClain added:

> There is just as much prejudice here in England as in America and you will find it out if you stay long enough, but I have made my personality win with all by manhood! An Englishman believes in fair play and an American doesn't.[23]

McClain was a self-elected representative of Afro-American entertainers in Edwardian Britain. He and his wife Cordelia were mentioned in *The Entr'Acte* of 10 June 1905, visiting the grave of Bessie Lee Cumminger at Weaste cemetery in Manchester, where they laid flowers. On 15 January 1906 the *Encore* reported that Ben J. Mercer (late of the Jetneys) had died from tuberculosis in Leeds the week before. Twenty-nine years old, this Black entertainer had been interred at Burnham Tofts cemetery. 'His surviving partner, Mr. A. Ray, wishes to thank Mr. Billy McClain for the many kindnesses shown to the deceased during his four months' illness.'

McClain was 'briskly booking his smart colored sextette' which was appearing in Clapham, south London, according to *The Entr'Acte* of 24 August 1906, which added 'This breezy "coon" number is an especial favourite.' McClain continued to be heavily involved in various entertainments, including boxing, around Britain for years.

Sir Alfred Jones was involved with members of a choral society from Jamaica who entertained the British in 1906. Responding to the widespread ignorance of Jamaica that had been noted by a visiting member of the colony's legislative council, and believing that economic and commercial benefits would result from publicity, Jones arranged for ten members of the Kingston Choral Union to sing at the Colonial Products Exhibition in Liverpool in early 1906.[24]

Renamed the Native Choir from Jamaica, they travelled on the *Port Antonio* reaching Avonmouth at the end of January 1906.[25] Adeline McDermot, Marie Lawrence, Connie Coverley, Evelyn Gordon, Henry Nation, T. Ellis Jackson, Louis George Drysdale, J. Packer Ramsey or Ramsay, Carlton Bryan, and J.T. Loncke then went to Liverpool to appear at St George's Hall from 30 January to 8 February 1906. Photographs were published on postcards and in *Smith's Liverpool Weekly* on 27 January, the day they performed at the Compton Hotel after Sir Alfred's speech on the 'value to England of her Jamaican colony'.

> Presently the dusky singers left the tables, mounted the stage, and commenced to sing. . . . Their singing, in good English, is very creditable and most enjoyable, whilst the pianist, Mr. Harry Nation, is an excellent artist and Mr. C. Bryan a most amusing comedian.[26]

Smith's Liverpool Weekly also reported on the choir's impact at the exhibition hall. 'The choir sang in a manner which brought tears to some eyes and a catch to the throat.' It praised their rendition of 'our National Anthem'. Unaware that Jamaica had been a British imperial possession for more than two centuries and that its people spoke English, revealed why Jones was involved in promoting the island. The 'strangers from beyond the seas' who sang 'from their hearts' were ambassadors of Jamaica.

The *Liverpool Echo* reported that so many wanted to attend the concerts that three overflow performances had been arranged. The group's commercial value was soon realised. A telegram from England dated 23 January was published in the weekly *Jamaica Times*: they 'have declined several lucrative offers from Music Halls'. Two

17. The Kingston Choral Union of Jamaica first toured Britain in 1906. Pianist Henry Nation (rear, right); bass Carlton Bryan (front, left, astride chair)

weeks later it reported that their work at the exhibition had been 'a complete success'; and on 3 March it told of Connie Coverley's fame as 'the Queen of the troupe'. On 7 April it quoted from the *Fruit Trader's Journal* music critic's praise of 'their quaint enunciation and strict attention to light and shade'.

The group started touring, with Bryan providing comic relief, and them all wearing 'native costume' as well as evening dress. They avoided the ban on commercial entertainments on Sundays by presenting 'sacred concerts' which relied on collections. This had to be an unreliable source of income. Two poorly attended Sunday concerts in Swansea at the end of April 1906 led the *Daily Post* to scold the town for 'poor patronage at a musical treat'. It praised the choir's 'plantation melodies and choruses, in which the company appears in native costume'.

The entertaining Jamaicans were in Worthing, on the Sussex coast, from 30 July to 5 August. The *Worthing Mercury* noted their concert at the Pier Pavilion, one of ten shows they presented that week. 'Clever songsters ... every item is vociferously applauded'. The choir had bookings to the end of the year, it added.

The *Worthing Observer* of 4 August noted that they were 'well educated and well-trained'. On Sunday 5 August, a public holiday weekend, their sacred concert was 'in Camp Meeting Dress'. The Jamaicans had moved to Whitby for performances on 21 and 22 August. The *Whitby Times* of 24 August was to report that the choir had appeared twice daily for three days, a schedule that included an afternoon appearance at the pavilion and an evening show at the theatre. Their sacred concert included a Madame Ella Russell and their performance was praised: 'Remarkable musicians and vocalists, their whole programme being full of charm and interest'.

They moved south, to Bridlington, where they sang from 25 to 28 August, according to the *Bridlington Chronicle*: along with a report that they were taking bookings into December 1906. They returned to Whitby and Madame Russell. After that repeated success they re-traced their steps to Worthing, where they performed for a week from Monday 10 September. The *Worthing Observer* commented that their earlier visit had been well received, and that they had added new songs but retained favourites including 'Motherland' and 'Climb up ye little children'. The *Mercury* said that 'these talented coloured artistes' provided the real treat.

The *Jamaica Times*, which seems to have been Black-edited, reported on the choir's successful year abroad on 5 January 1907 when the first of the conquerors returned. Bryan, Loncke and Miss Coverley were to be followed by the others.

'Such a hit' at the exhibition, the choir had taken bookings for three months, extending to the end of the year. They had been to Tynemouth, 'the world-famed Crystal Palace', Kent, Norfolk, Suffolk, Yorkshire, Chester, Gloucestershire, Sussex and Essex, as well as Scotland where Bryan had had a great triumph in Dundee. The tour had ended with four weeks in Ireland, appearing in Waterford, Londonderry, Kilkenny, Ennis and Dublin. From this report more details have been traced.

The Jamaican choir was in Wrexham, north Wales, at the public hall from 1 to 3 November 1906, making five appearances. Ennis in the south west of Ireland received them on 28 and 29 November: the editor of that small town's *Saturday Record* noted that they had 'a high reputation'. Bryan told the *Jamaica Times* that Irish audiences 'are something like ours, lively, sympathetic, and very responsive'. He also said 'The English people have not got the American colour prejudice. It does not matter in England if a man is black, white, blue, green or yellow'. Bryan also was reported as saying that 'England is cultivated like a garden' having 'no waste bushland'.

The Jamaican newspaper reported on Henry Nation's success in Whitby where the pianist replaced Madame Russell's accompanist who had become unwell. With no time to rehearse, his contribution led to six curtain calls which the 'world famous singer' insisted on sharing with Nation. Stuffy racists in Jamaica would not have liked that. Nor would they have welcomed the idea that these Black men and women had seen historic sites in Britain which they knew mainly from books.

Bryan's comic routine had included a minstrelsy-based rolled eyes pose which, for financial reasons or a reason that remains impenetrably obscure to the present writer, was published as a postcard which went on sale in Kingston in early 1907.[27] The *Jamaica Times* of 5 January 1907 (page 15) announced that 'postcards of the members of the [Kingston Choral] Union who toured England, and of Mr. Bryan "pulling a face"' were on sale at the store where the newspaper had its offices.

The triumphant choir's musical skills were detailed: McDermot was the prima donna, Ambrosine (Marie) Lawrence was a soprano, Coverley a mezzo-soprano and Gordon a contralto. Loncke and Drysdale were tenors, Ramsay was a bass, and Bryan was 'basso-profundo and humorist'. Nation played the piano and Jackson was the group's musical director. Loncke was from British Guiana and Ramsay was from Barbados: he had lived in Jamaica 'for some fourteen years'. 'All the others, we believe, are natives of Kingston'.

With the choir came:

> Mr. W. J. Masters ... the son of parents who belonged to Jamaica, coming either from Montego Bay or St. Ann's Bay. He was born on ship board. He has been seven years connected with the stage in England. He met with the Union in Wrexham, North Wales.[28]

The documented truth was slightly different.

18. The enlarged Jamaican group posed outside St George's Hall in Liverpool, 1907 (Rainer Lotz)

William Masters was born, according to his birth registration, at 43 Hopwood Street in Liverpool on 5 June 1887. That document stated that his mother was Ann Jane (née Williams) Masters and that his father, a seaman, was William Masters. His career entertaining the multitudes began in 1892 but has been difficult to trace as he took the stage name Gordon Stretton.[29]

Tracing the Jamaican choir in 1907 has been difficult too, for an earthquake struck Kingston in mid-January, causing nearly one thousand casualties including the mayor. Sir Alfred Jones experienced the disaster at first hand, for he was making his second visit to the island. Attention moved away from the singers. The group travelled to Britain on the *Port Royal*, reaching Avonmouth on 27 February 1907 according to a list of passengers in the *West India Committee Circular* of 12 March. William Masters, Bryan, Jackson, McDermot, Nation were members, as was the Miss Welsh: the 'Miss Loirens' named must have been Marie Lawrence.

The group again graced the Colonial Products Exhibition in Liverpool, held from 5 to 9 March 1907. The *West India Committee Circular* commented on 26 March:

> The native choir from Jamaica, in their picturesque costumes, having filed in front of the dais and sung a verse of 'God Save the King', the leader of it, in a well delivered speech, thanked Lord Elgin for attending.

Elgin was the current colonial secretary. Having been thanked by Jackson he visited some 'native workmen' from West Africa whose presence in Britain has otherwise not been documented.

In mid-March 1907 a postcard of five women and ten men in plantation costumes was mailed to Stockton-on-Tees. This 'Jamaica Choir at the Exhibition' was 'very amusing', noted the sender.[30] The same fifteen people, with Nation clearly visible seated on the left, now wearing formal evening dress and also posed outside St George's Hall, Liverpool, appeared on another commercial postcard. One man holds a guitar and another has a metal clarinet or saxophone.

Other than an appearance in Plymouth, nothing else has been uncovered on the Jamaican singers in Britain in 1907. They must have been both a popular and a commercial success, for they were advertised in mid-1908 in the British entertainment press. Their advertisement in the *Era* of 6 June 1908 noted that the 'twelve coloured ladies and gentlemen' were the 'most successful, novel, and smartest combination now before the public'. This was no minstrel group promotion – 'Evening dress, native costumes, or camp dress. Royalty delighted. The public delighted. Managers want return dates. A most

extensive and varied repertoire'. This 1908 group included 'Real coon
singers and dancers'.

In August 1908 the choir returned to Plymouth, where the newspaper reports mentioned their previous visit. The *Western Daily
Mercury* of 18 August also noted their songs: 'Keep Down de Middle of
de Road', 'De Water Melon on de Vine', 'Ma Dark-eyed Venus' and 'If
the Man in the Moon [was a Coon]'; surely far from the concert music
they had performed as the Kingston Choral Union? These were
minstrel or plantation ditties, set in a bogus Deep South in the United
States.

Their Sunday sacred concert included McDermot singing 'Holy
City' which, like 'Twilight Bells', had nothing to do with Jamaica. The
dancing humorist must have been Bryan. Nelson's piano skills were
praised, and Miss Welch sang 'Little Black Me'. The *Mercury* of 24
August named G. Stretton as the singer of 'Dear Homeland'.

The clue that enabled us to uncover this week in Portsmouth was a
postcard of the 1907 Liverpool group which numbered fifteen. The *Era*
had announced there were twelve performers. Further confusion
comes from the *Blackpool Herald* which noted there were thirteen
'coloured ladies and gentlemen. A unique entertainment' in that resort
town on 11 and 12 September 1908. Indeed, the earliest card showing
ten, almost certainly posed in Jamaica in late 1905 or early 1906, was
subtitled 'Native Choir from Jamaica (Twelve Coloured Artistes)' and,
the same photograph, '"The Jamaicans"'.

The recollections of the son of the leader of the choir both clarify and
conflict with other evidence of this popular and long-lasting group of
Black Edwardian entertainers. Ellis Jackson, born in New Jersey in the
United States in 1891, was interviewed in London in the 1970s.[31] His
first time in Britain was with a choir from Jamaica in 1906 or 1907. He
stated that Masters led the choir after the earthquake, that the pianist
was named Barnes, and that there had been a saxophone player
named Sexias. We know from the 1907 list of passengers that Masters
was with the group in Britain from 1907, and that a saxophone was
held by one of the group posed in Liverpool that year. The name Barnes
appears in the passenger list of the *Port Royal*, too. There is a young
male, who might be Ellis Jackson, in the 1907 group photographs.

The 1908 tour lasted from March to November, with the group's
entertaining in Britain ending as it had begun: at a colonial products
exhibition in Liverpool. The *Liverpool Courier* of mid-November 1908
referred to their 'triumphal tour of the United Kingdom' and their
farewell concerts. The choir had opened the exhibition with an
'impressive rendering' of the national anthem and of Elgar's 'Land of
Hope and Glory'. T. Ellis Jackson proposed a vote of thanks to the
Lord Mayor of Liverpool.

The choir was replaced at the exhibition by 'members of the dusky tribes of Dahomey'. We have described the nationwide spread of Dahomey and bogus Dahomey living exhibits earlier.[32] The artistic and genuinely skilled musicians and singers from Kingston had been replaced by African or allegedly African imperial exhibits. We are left to guess at the proportion of Britons who saw, in the Jamaican entertainers 1906–8, just another Black act. We also have to guess what tales were told, back in the Caribbean, by the men and women who had been all over the British Isles. Both Drysdale and Marie Lawrence were based in London in the 1920s, and, as we will see, Bryan was in England in 1913.

Among the songs which were associated with Black singers were the Negro Spirituals, Christian songs of joy and lamentation that had sprung from the Black-led churches of slavery times in the United States. Introduced to Britain in the 1870s by a group of students seeking funding to develop their university in Nashville, their style of presentation – always combined with genteel manners and quiet dignity, for they had been welcomed by Victoria and had entertained prime minister Gladstone – linked Fisk University with Negro Spirituals. From the 1880s, using the Fisk name but quite independent, a choir led by Frederick Loudin toured the world.[33] There also was a splinter group which reached South Africa.[34]

Loudin was based in England in the late 1890s. One of his earliest companions, Thomas Rutling, lived in Dragon Avenue, Harrogate in the Edwardian period, teaching music.[35] Orpheus and Eugene McAdoo, having taken the music to South Africa, were in Sydney, Australia, around 1899. Orpheus McAdoo died in Sydney in mid-1900.[36] Eugene McAdoo toured Edwardian Britain as a member of the Fisk Jubilee Trio, itself apparently the residue of a larger group managed by W. H. Thompson, a veteran of South Africa. Postcards of Thompson's jubilee singers show three men, three women and a boy. McAdoo and both Laura A. Carr and Euna M. Mocara were in that group.[37] McAdoo's two companions were with him in south east London in mid-1908.

Their performance was entertainment, but not on the music hall or theatrical circuits: and thus is not mentioned in the trade press including the *Era* and the *Performer*. The Fisk Trio's appearance at the Central Hall, Plumstead, in mid-June 1908, was located through a postcard. Advertised in the *Kentish Independent* of Friday 5 June and the following week, it was clear the three had been in Plumstead before. They were scheduled to perform on Saturday and Monday at eight o'clock, and on the Sunday at 3:15 for a meeting of the Men's Brotherhood as well as later for an overflow concert, for young people. Tickets were three pence each: except for Sunday when 'liberal

FISK JUBILEE TRIO.

Miss Euna M. Mocara, Mr. Eugene M. McAdoo. Miss Laura A. Carr.

19. Eugene McAdoo had worked in South Africa and Australia, but toured 1900s Britain with Euna Mocara and Laura Carr

collections [were] expected'. They 'have sung before our King and Queen, and practically every living Monarch and Ruler. They have just completed a world tour.'

It was the Whitsun holiday weekend, and the hall was sold out. The advertisement stated 'Miss Euna M. Mocara will sing her famous echo song, the wonder of all musicians. There will also be trios, musical sketches, medleys, secular glees, etc., by this marvellous trio of coloured artists.'

Carr was a contralto, McAdoo a bass, and Mocara a mezzo soprano, according to pencilled annotations on the postcard, which also noted 'Miss Euna dwelt on one note 20 seconds and 32 seconds elapsed between time of breathing calculated by the world critics as a record.'[38] British Sundays were widely known to be dull and stuffy,[39] and these musical tricks, the semi-religious music, and the presence of Black people who knew about slavery explains why their recitals were popular.

Seven weeks later the *Brighton Advertiser* advertised that the Fisk Jubilee Trio would be appearing at the Central Wesleyan Hall in Langney Road, Brighton, on 1 August 1908 'the last concert of the series'. Civic halls had the trio, for one postcard was annotated 'Town Hall Dec 2nd 1909'. Another, mailed in Greenwich, south east London, was dated 18 April 1910. It is extremely likely that McAdoo and his colleagues toured all over Britain.

Yet another entertainer, one whose presence might have escaped attention, was Charles Cornish. He was well known to the theatrical trade and so his obituary was published in the *Performer* on 25 January 1933. It stated that he had worked as a 'coloured vocalist' in the Olympian Quartette in the 1900s before employment in the London office of the Musical Hall Artistes Railway Association. He made ticket and seat reservations for acts and their sometimes considerable luggage, fully aware of problems that would be created if props, clothes and entertainer were separated. Born in the United States in the 1860s, Cornish had lived in Britain since around 1903.

One of the groups Cornish would have known was Rastus and Banks, an 'expert American duo' who appeared in west London in February 1906.[40] By May the pair were in Lancashire, where the *Wigan Observer* of 12 May referred to them as 'coloured American entertainers' at the Hippodrome. David Banks is thought to have arrived in Britain by 1905; certainly the pair were pictured in the *Variety Theatre* of 1 September 1905, with a note that their British career had started in Sheffield in 1904. Bessie Banks died in August 1911, but the act continued into the 1920s.[41]

The Spirituals tradition was found in the performances of the Jalvans, according to the *Variety Theatre* of 6 October 1905 which reported that Jalvan had worked with Orpheus McAdoo in South Africa and in Sydney where he met and married a Miss Marshall, a contralto. The pair, billed as Oriental Entertainers, had worked in Mexico, Cuba, Canada, India and for seventeen weeks at the Liège exhibition of 1904. At the time of this excellent publicity they were appearing at the London Palladium. Jalvan is clearly of African descent in a photograph of the pair – wearing Japanese gowns. When he had reached South Africa in mid-1897 he had been a juggler and humorist (unless that Jose or Joe Jalvan was a different individual).[42]

Robert Cropp, who had worked in Manchester in 1898, also teamed up with a White woman. They worked as Pueblo and Cropp, 'creole star artists' in Edwardian Britain, and were still working (in Denmark) in 1921.[43] Charlie Walker, a comedian, worked with Ida May and they were interviewed in the *Era* of 3 March 1906. Walker was blind. One entertainer known from a stamped postcard was Peter Shannon, 'champion buck and sand Dancer'. His African descent is clear on a card mailed in London one November during Edward the Seventh's reign.[44]

Cropp, Walker and Shannon are almost shadows in the brilliant, gaslight theatres of early twentieth century Britain. The publicity surrounding entertainers is confusing and often inaccurate, but we can

20. Charlie Walker and Ida May appeared at the Palace
Theatre, Davenport in June 1907

be confident that the woman who appeared in Essex in August 1908
was an actress of African descent.

The seaside resort of Southend with its reliable railway links with
the metropolis attracted thousands of Londoners every summer, and it
was in the London *Evening Standard* that the resort's ladies beauty
contest was detailed. Scheduled for 19 August, this relative novelty
attracted widespread attention and the London press was copied by
other newspapers when an African princess asked permission to
enter.

Southend showman P. P. T. Bacon stated that the 'dusky priness
most anxious to show her charms' had cabled him from Yarmouth,
where she had not been allowed to enter a beauty contest 'on account

of colour'. Bacon told the reporters that 'a little nigger' had been entered in the baby show in 1906 and had won.

> For weeks afterwards I was absolutely mobbed whenever I went out. Why couldn't you give the prize to a baby of your own colour? What do you mean by it? How could you dare? was the cry, and all the time it was the audience who decided the winner. Anyway, I am taking no risks this time.

He was prepared to accept the entry of Princess Dinubolu from Senegal provided the decision was made by a committee.

There is nothing in the *Yarmouth Weekly Standard* on a colour bar or indeed any beauty contest, but a Plymouth newspaper had a column headed 'Chocolate Barred from the contest'.[45] The *Evening Standard* of 20 August reported that 'Princess Dinubolo' was twenty, spoke French and Spanish, and had 'left her native country about eighteen months ago' to travel in Europe with a musician 'of inferior caste'.

News of her arrival spread around Southend in fifteen minutes. Bacon had reserved a first class seat for her, but the 'dusky competitor' had travelled third class in an attempt to avoid reporters. 'She was identified by the description she had herself given as "chocolate coloured"'. Bacon's superb publicity included driving her around the town in an open carriage before installing her in the Palace Hotel.

The *Southend Telegraph* had the third spelling of Dinuvolu when it reported backstage gossip on the reason why the Black woman had entered a beauty contest. 'Her great charms in her native country, only needed to be backed up by public recognition of her beauty here, to melt her father's heart', for he had not approved of her lover.

There were forty-nine contestants at the Kursaal; the length and volume of the applause were the deciding factors, and the princess was greeted with sufficient enthusiasm to enter the second round. But the 'Southend public were too patriotic' and Nellie Evans was the winner. The *Evening Standard* reported that 'the chocolate princess was well received, but she by no means proved a formidable opponent'.

The Lancashire resort of Morecambe had several Black entertainers who worked with Alex Day. Day proclaimed his skills as a 'naval and versatile actor vocalist and cornet soloist' on a publicity postcard which had his address as 1, Brunswick Road, Morecambe, in 1910. His group of seven included four Black men. Another Day card had six Whites and one Black male (he appears on the 1910 card too). A third pose, also with a Black male, has survived.[46]

At the other end of England, in Ramsgate on the Channel coast, Ellison's Entertainers also numbered seven and in 1910 also included one Black man. Another Ramsgate Black entertainer was Chief

21. Morecambe, Lancashire in 1910 had splendid beaches and, in Alex Day's group, black entertainers

22. Seaside resort entertainers included Ellison's group in Ramsgate, Kent, 1910 (Maureen Green)

Idilulgo, whose 'native tribe' from Southern Nigeria entertained on the seafront in an act including 'native dances'.[47]

A group of genuine Africans who entertained the British from 1904 into 1909 are nameless. Although there are several different photographic postcards of them only their manager's name has survived. Jason Balmer had taken an 'African Native Choir' from South Africa to America in the 1890s, where he had abandoned it. Adopted by the Black-led churches, these young men and women went to college in the United States, returning to Africa (changing ship in Britain, no doubt), in the 1900s.[48]

Balmer's new venture, his 'Kaffir Boys', appeared at the Edinburgh Castle in London's East End in April 1904. 'Africa in Song and Story' was presented at the large onetime pub, an Edwardian temperance centre. Two seven year olds had expanded by 7 and 8 November 1907 when 'Four African Singing Boys' appeared at the Corn Exchange in Newark, Nottinghamshire, when they were billed as singing in Dutch, English, 'Kaffir and Hottentot'. Balmer would recount 'Thrilling Stories of Life in Africa'. This was a return visit, in aid of a local Sunday school.[49]

On 15 June the following year another card was mailed. The sender identified the Africans as one bushman, one hottentot, and two 'kaffir boys of different tribes'. The 'boys' numbered five on yet another card, which included Balmer. Two days later another card was mailed in London, with the comment that 'these clever Kaffir Boys ... sang their Hymns beautifully' at the 'Orient in London', a reference to a missionary exhibition on Africa and the Orient. This group was on a circuit similar to the Fisk Trio, for standard theatres did not employ them. A card mailed in May 1909 had a note that Balmer's group 'took part in the Missionary Exhibition'.

Black acts appearing on the regular stage were mentioned in the *Era* and other entertainment industry publications. On 5 February 1910, for example, it noted 'Yangar, the West African magician, gives a very smart display of talent' at the Regent Theatre of Varieties in Salford, near Manchester, and that Sadie Foote, 'a real, high-toned lady of colour' was appearing in *The Lady of Colour* at the Standard Theatre in London's Pimlico.

A Black woman entertainer who had considerable publicity in the winter of 1912–13 was Annie Gross. The *Daily Chronicle* of Monday 2 December 1912 had 'Actress shot in Bloomsbury. Murder by Six-Foot Negress. Music Hall party tragedy. Midnight entry to house by trick'. Annie Gross and her husband Harry had worked in New York before touring British music halls. Harry Gross left her for an actress named Jessie Mackintosh, and they were living in theatrical lodgings at 2, Coram Street, in central London. He had been working in a song-and-

23. Jason Balmer's 'Singing Boys' or 'Kaffir Boys' entertained as part of his 'African Song Lectures'. They have been traced in London in 1904, and remained active for years

dance act at the Empire in New Cross, and was preparing to leave for Sheffield after a party to celebrate his success. About midnight on the Saturday night the front door bell was rung, and Miss Mackintosh opened it. There was nobody on the step, but a small girl was running off up the road. She gave chase, but could not catch her, and so returned to the party and told the others of this incident.

Some two hours later she stepped on to the landing or, according to other accounts, into the room she shared with Harry Gross, and came face to face with Annie Gross. She fired a revolver several times; her errant husband rushed out, had the revolver pointed at him, and the trigger pulled. There were no bullets left, so Mrs Gross turned and ran downstairs and into the night. Chased by sobered party-goers, she gave herself up, without a struggle, to a police officer at Russell Square.

The *Illustrated Police News* loved the story, publishing an artist's impression of the shooting on the landing on its front page of 5 December. 'Bloomsbury Tragedy. Alleged Midnight Murder by a Negress in a Boarding House. Jealousy Believed to be the Cause of the Crime'. With sex, race, murder and jealousy combined, it was a widely reported incident. The *Illustrated Police News* carried reports until 16 January 1913.

As usual there were contradictions in the details of various reports. Annie Pohe or Poke Gross was a 'splendidly proportioned negress' aged twenty-nine, who was charged with wilful murder and remanded in custody. The tale of the girl running off was crucial to the evidence, for had Annie Gross waited inside 2, Coram Street, for two hours, it was unlikely that the shooting was an accident. If she had entered later, met her husband's paramour, and shot her with the gun she claimed to carry for her own protection, the lesser verdict of manslaughter would be likely. Certainly a verdict of murder would take her to the gallows.

The Times reported 'Arrest of a coloured woman' on 2 December and named the victim as Mackintosh or Mackenzie. On 3 December it reported that Mrs Gross had entered the building by closely following two or three men. The *Daily Chronicle*, as we have seen, had reported she had entered by a trick.

Number two, Coram Street, was favoured by 'coloured people' and was 'chiefly occupied by negro rag time artists'. Harry Gross had separated from his wife in December 1911; she lived near Shaftesbury Avenue. The revolver had been supplied by a 'man of colour' named Frank Craig, who lived in Old Compton Street, also in Soho. By mid-December Craig had been arrested, and was released when the police could not disprove his statement that the gun had been for her protection as 'she was the only coloured woman in the house'. *The*

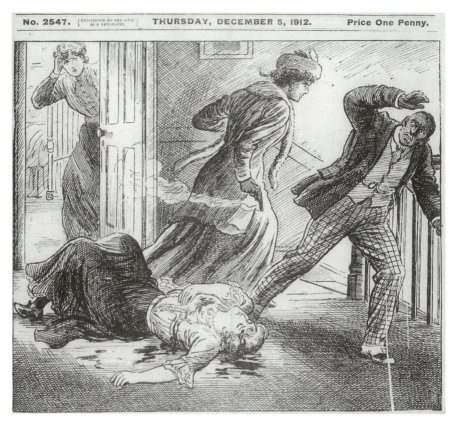

No. 2547. [REGISTERED AT THE G.P.O. AS A NEWSPAPER]   THURSDAY, DECEMBER 5, 1912.   Price One Penny.

4. When entertainers Annie and Harry Gross fell out, Gross's girlfriend was killed and Annie Gross was charged with murder. The *Illustrated Police News* was typically sensational in its reporting (British Library)

Times noted that Craig was a 'coloured pugilist' and that he had mumbled something about getting into trouble as a result of doing people favours.

'For a woman of colour she is strikingly handsome' noted the *Daily Chronicle*, which published a sketch of the accused. *The Times* of 19 December stated that she was 'a married woman of colour' and a British subject; but now was paying more attention to a poisoning case in India.

Annie Gross went on trial for her life at the Old Bailey in January 1913. The court was told that Henry 'Harry' Gross had married the accused in Chicago in 1903, had moved to London in 1908, and was later joined by his wife. He had taken her money, concocted a case in the hope that she would be deported, forced her into prostitution, had twice beaten her with a poker, and then had deserted her for another woman. Gross would have got money 'more easily' from White prostitutes than from his wife 'she being black and not so attractive'. He had 'forced her to go on the streets'.

The landlady stated that there had been seven Black males, one Black female, and one White female in the Coram Street kitchen where the party was held on the night of 30 November 1912. Two pugilists, 'one known as the Coffee Cooler' – this was Craig, who is known to have been in England since the late 1890s[50] – gave evidence. Annie Gross told the court that she had gone in search of her husband, and that he had hit her. She pulled out the gun and fired, not aware that she had hit Jessie Mackintosh.

The judge told the jury that if they believed she had set out to murder her husband, and accidentally killed his mistress, their verdict should be manslaughter. If Gross had hit his wife and she had then killed him, the verdict then should have been manslaughter. But if she had hidden, emerging to kill the mistress hours later, the verdict should be murder.

The jury retired for thirty-five minutes and returned to the court, with their decision that it was manslaughter. The judge disagreed with them and said so. The *Daily Mail* reported the verdict on 11 January under the headline 'Judge and Negress. Strong Comments at Murder Trial' in a case which had involved 'some of the worst aspects of the racial question': the *Mail*'s way of referring to inter-racial sex. The newspaper thought that the judge should not have expressed his disagreement with the jury's decision. *The Times* also reported the verdict that Saturday, from a legal angle. A verdict of manslaughter in a murder trial (instead of 'guilty' or 'not guilty') and that the judge told the jury he thought their decision was wrong, were aspects which interested *The Times*.

Annie Gross was sentenced to prison for five years. She smiled at the jury as she left the dock. Surely the jury had felt that she had suffered enough, with the beatings, humiliation and prostitution. They also probably had no respect for the dead woman who had taken up with a Black entertainer from the United States.

The association of prostitution and show business was not new; and there is other evidence to suggest that Black female prostitutes could earn a living by consorting with White males (as will be shown). Annie Gross's fate is not known.

Other Black entertainers who were in the news, albeit in less startling ways, in England in early 1913 including Carlton Bryan, the rolled-eyes humorist of the Jamaican choir. Bryan appeared at the Empire in north London's Holloway Road from 10 February. The show was *Uncle Tom's Cabin*. The old slave Tom was played by John H. Boehm; Dinah by Mabel Bowman; and Cassy by Stella Harrington.

F. C. ELGER, GREEN BANK STUDIO, FALMOUTH.

HYBERT'S UNCLE TOM'S CABIN CO.
Season 1904-5.

25. Shows based around the 1850s novel *Uncle Tom's Cabin* gave employment to Blacks and Whites, reaching many parts of Britain. This group is in Falmouth in 1904

26. Black actress-dancers such as Ada Cuffy could find work
in *Cabin* shows (Bernth Lindfors)

The *Era* reviewed it on 15 February, and noted there was 'a grand plantation festival by real negroes'. The drama was interrupted by an intermezzo with speciality acts: almost anything could be added to a Cabin show, just as in British Christmas pantomimes. Bryan and 'the Tennesseans, jubilee singers' were speciality acts. Dancer Fred Davis and singer-dancer Dinah Dixie may have been Black.

The *Era* of 8 March noted that this *Uncle Tom's Cabin* show had moved to the Grand Theatre in Southampton, and named Lizzie Allen (who had appeared in a Cabin show in London in 1903). It also noted that the 'Three Cape Girls' were dancing at the Empire in Bradford; on 1 March they were at the Coliseum in Glasgow. The *Era* also reported

'The Eight Rag-time Darkies, American coloured vocalists and dancers' were at the Hippodrome in Belfast.

On 26 February 1913 the *Era* noted 'a team of cultured coloured people known as the Royal Poinciana Quintette' was being employed by Alfred Butt (a highly reputable showman who became a member of parliament and was knighted). These 'artists of the negro race made a highly favourable impression'. Tenor H. J. Sutton and his colleagues were named in the *Wednesday Era* of 19 March 1913. Their manager, a bass, was Charles B. Foster; Walter Hilliard was second tenor; R. M. Cooper was a baritone as was O. A. Hawkes who played the accompaniments. This stylish group had entertained America's ex-president Taft.

The phrasing of these reports needs considerable thought. Did the phrase 'cultured coloured people' mean that others of African birth or descent were automatically perceived to be roughs? There were other complexities, for 'artists of the negro race' could just mean that these five entertainers were genuine Blacks, as opposed to burnt-cork performers whose minstrelsy was usually boisterous and whose language could be vulgar. Certainly the use of 'black', 'negro', 'coloured' and even 'African' in entertainment announcements and reviews could mean Whites in black face. Our confusion is greater than that of the Edwardians, but they were not always certain. Perhaps the use and mis-use of these words and phrases teased the public and drew them to the shows? Whatever the audience's perceptions and experiences, it is certain that there was regular employment for Black entertainers working in Edwardian Britain.

From their British base, as we have already seen with Laura Bowman and Belle Davis, these Black Edwardian entertainers travelled widely on the continent. These tours had their own pitfalls, clearly exhibited in the example of Will Garland's troupe in eastern Europe in the latter half of 1913.

Garland, who had been a British associate of Pete Hampton and Laura Bowman, had toured Germany in 1906–7, and again in 1909, his show becoming *A Journey in Negroland* and performing in France, Russia and Germany in 1910. On 8 May 1913 his *Negro Operetta Troupe* left England, and was in Finland by July 1913. From Berlin and Budapest they moved east, falling on hard times in Russia. One of the dancers was Emma Williams, who wrote from Kiev to an African friend in London.[51] That friend, a Mrs Boucher, wrote on 1 September 1913 to the Foreign Office in London.[52] Two other complaints reached the Foreign Office that month.

The troupe continued to tour Russia, reaching the Ural mountains and thus as far from St Petersburg as the Russian capital was from England. Emma Williams 'a native of British West Africa' had told

Nannette Boucher of 'Mr Boehm, the managing director of the company, who complains that she will not obtain money for him by going with men'. The Foreign Office asked its correspondent in Ekaterinburg (Sverdlovsk) to ascertain who in the group were British. They were duly informed that Garland and his wife were Black Americans, and that there were three 'coloured' British subjects and four 'coloured Americans'. That a 'Negro troupe' had its Black members noted suggests that White officials had difficulties in grasping the concept that Black people were mobile.

Emma Williams was aged twenty-nine (she gave Mrs Boucher's London address); Caroline Coffee was twenty-six and a resident of Bradford; 'John Harris Boehm, 29, native of the Gold Coast, (coloured)' had no British address. The Foreign Office believed it was a typical case of showgirls finding the realities of touring not to their liking, especially when they had run out of money. It was suggested that Scotland Yard looked into Garland when they had struggled back to England.

It was not a bed of roses for male entertainers either. The Black-edited *New York Age* reported in late 1913 that Maxine Elliott had cabled to deny that she had refused to be carried from the stage by two Black men 'in the play in which she is appearing in London'.[53]

We have already noted Duse Mohamed's career in British theatrical drama. In old age he recalled going to Russia in 1905. His experience of theatrical work was practical, for he worked as an electrician preparing the Franco-British Exhibition in London in 1908. When that grand exhibition opened he worked in a sideshow, as an Egyptian. Then he opened a theatrical agency in London, offering advice to would-be playwrights and authors.[54]

One of his contacts was Bermuda-born Ernest A. Trimmingham. His *The Lily of Bermuda* was staged by Mohamed, and opened in Manchester in November 1909. They moved to Middlesbrough by 15 November, where the show was abandoned and the scenery pawned. Mohamed turned to journalism, as we will detail. Trimmingham continued to entertain the multitudes, appearing in two films that were released in October 1912.[55] He was Beetles to Percy Moran's highwayman in *The Adventures of Dick Turpin* and a 'Negro' in *Her Bachelor Guardian*.

Beach entertainers, theatrical troupes, variety turns, instrumentalists, dancers, choral groups, actors and actresses. Edwardians could see such Black acts in small towns such as Ennis and Whitby, in cities from Belfast and Edinburgh to Plymouth and Swansea. With imperial exhibits at exhibitions and on tour, and the appearances of singing groups such as the Fisk singers and Balmer's Africans in halls, was there any part of the British Isles without a Black presence in the Edwardian years?

NOTES

1. I am indebted to Ian Duffield for sight of this photograph.
2. *The Magnet* (Leeds) 23 September 1905, p. 4.
3. R. Lotz, 'Belle Davis and Her Piccaninnies' *ARSC Journal* (Annapolis MD) 25, 2 (Fall 1994), p. 182 [using PRO BT 26/189].
4. Ibid [using *The Referee* (London) 9 June 1901, p. 6].
5. R. Lotz, *German Ragtime and Prehistory of Jazz: Volume 1* (Chigwell: Storyville Publications, 1985), pp. 72–3.
6. Lotz, 'Belle Davis', p. 184.
7. Ibid.
8. 'A diplomat and a Negritrude scholar', obituary, *West Africa*, (London) 23 November 1987, p. 2296.
9. Lotz 'Belle Davis' p. 185 [quoting *The Referee* (London) 7 January 1906, p. 4].
10. *Der Kinematograph*, 17 March 1907, Lotz, *German Ragtime*. I am grateful to Rainer Lotz who showed me these rare moving pictures which revealed the elastic dancing of the small boys and the tasteful composure of Miss Davis.
11. Lotz 'Belle Davis', pp. 190–91.
12. E. Scobie, *Black Britannia* (Chicago: Johnson Publishing, 1972), pp. 176–7.
13. J. Green, 'British Newspapers as Source Material. The Case of James Douglass Bohee (1844–1897)' *Black Music Research Bulletin* (Chicago) 7, 1 (Fall 1986) which led to N. Rosenburg, 'Canadian Newspapers as Source Material: Further Notes on James Douglass Bohee (1844–1897)' *Black Music Research Bulletin* (Chicago) 10, 2 (Fall 1988); see also *Merthyr Express* (Wales), 11 December 1897, p. 5 and R. Lotz, 'The Bohee Brothers (1844–1897/1856–1926[?])' *78 Quarterly* (Key West, FL) 1, 7, pp. 97–111.
14. Lotz, 'Bohee Brothers', pp. 106–7, shows her appearance in Manchester's Free Trade Hall on 6 May 1889.
15. The music library, Buckingham Palace Road, London, has copies of programmes.
16. E. Southern, *Biographical Dictionary of Afro-American and African Musicians* (Westport CT: Greenwood Press, 1982), pp. 81–2, 259, 275–6, 337, 386–7.
17. Scobie, *Black Britannia*, p. 178.
18. W. Spinks, 'Bert Williams: Broken-Hearted Comedian' *Phylon* (USA), 11, 1 (1950), pp. 56–63.
19. L. Antoine, *Achievement: The Life of Laura Bowman* (New York: Pageant Press, 1961).
20. Lotz, *German Ragtime*, pp. 136–7.
21. Southern, *Biographical Dictionary* ignores them.
22. H. Sampson, *Blacks in Blackface: A Source Book on Early Black Musical Shows* (Metuchen NJ: Scarecrow Press, 1980); H. Sampson, *The Ghost Walks: A Chronological History of Blacks in Show Business, 1865–1910* (Metuchen NJ: Scarecrow Press, 1988), pp. 351–2. I am indebted to Rainer Lotz for access to these titles and for happy times at his home in Bonn, Germany.
23. Sampson, *The Ghost Walks*, p. 379.
24. *Daily Gleaner* (Kingston), 7 December 1905; see also J. Green, 'The Jamaica Native Choir in Britain, 1906–1908', *Black Music Research Journal* (Chicago), 13, 1 (Spring 1993), pp. 15–29.
25. PRO BT/26/254 has the passenger list.
26. *Smith's Liverpool Weekly*, 3 February 1906.
27. I am grateful to Maureen Green for obtaining a copy in England (before I knew of the reference in the *Jamaica Times*).
28. *Jamaica Times*, 5 January 1907.
29. Information from Howard Rye and Rainer Lotz. Masters was active in popular

music in Britain in the 1910s and early 1920s, moving eventually to Argentina where he was interviewed in old age.

30. Rainer Lotz collection.

31. Ellis Jackson, a trombonist who was an agile dancer, worked for many years in the showband of Billy Cotton, appearing on British television into the 1960s.

32. P. Greenhalgh, *Ephemeral Vistas: The Expositions Universelles, Great Exhibitions and World's Fairs, 1851–1939* (Manchester University Press, 1988) shows how ethnic displays were far from rare in major British exhibitions in the 1900s.

33. I am indebted to Detroit Public Library for allowing me to handle the 300 pages in scrapbooks of the 1884–90 world tour, largely newspaper previews which repeated information from press releases. There were many concerts in Britain (*The Hastings and St Leonards Observer* 3 May 1884; *Croydon Chronicle* 7 June 1884; *The Northern Whig* [Belfast] 28 December 1885, for example), and across Australia too.

34. J. Marsh, *The Story of the Jubilee Singers and their Songs* (1880) was reprinted into 1903, selling thousands of copies and through the musical examples, bringing Spirituals into the concert music world of amateur musicians across Britain. For South Africa see Willan, *Sol Plaatje* (London: Heinemann, 1984) and V. Erlmann, '"A Feeling of Prejudice": Orpheus M. McAdoo and the Virginia Jubilee Singers in South Africa 1890–1898' *Journal of Southern African Studies* 14, 3 (Apr 1988), pp. 331–50; which is in hardback in V. Erlmann, *African Stars: Studies in Black South African Performance* (Chicago: University Press, 1991), chapter 2.

35. P. Fryer, *Staying Power: The History of Black People in Britain* (London: Pluto Press, 1984), p. 440; T, Rutling, *"Tom": An Autobiography; with revised Negro Melodies* (Torrington: Dyer, ca 1910). My thanks to Peter Fryer for bringing this to my attention.

36. Erlmann, *African Stars*, p. 51 quoting *The Freeman* (Indianapolis, Ohio) 6 October 1900.

37. Jeffrey Green collection.

38. Ibid.

39. I. Maisky, *Journey into the Past* (London: Hutchinson, 1962), pp. 84–5 reports fellow Russian émigré Lenin's experiences of Sundays in London.

40. *Acton Gazette* (London) 16 February 1906, p. 4.

41. Information from Howard Rye.

42. Erlmann, *African Stars*, pp. 36–7.

43. Information from Rainer Lotz.

44. It has a stamp of Edward but the year is unclear. Jeffrey Green collection.

45. *Western Daily Mercury* (Plymouth) 18 August 1908.

46. Jeffrey Green collection.

47. M. Mirams, *Old Ramsgate* (Rainham, Kent: Meresborough Books, 1984; repr. 1989), p. 13.

48. D. Coplan, *In Township Tonight! South Africa's Black City Music and Theatre* (Johannesburg: Ravan Press, 1985), pp. 41–2; Erlmann, 'Feeling of Prejudice'; Geiss, *Pan-African Movement*, p. 463.

49. Photocopy of an unidentified Newark or Grantham newspaper in author's collection, from a now forgotten source but clearly 1907.

50. Information from Howard Rye; *Blackheath Local Guide and District Advertiser* (London) June 1895, courtesy Christopher Fyfe.

51. R. Lotz, 'Will Garland and his Negro Operetta Company' in Lotz and Pegg (eds), *Under the Imperial Carpet*, pp. 130–44.

52. FO 369/617/33073. Mrs Boucher was the daughter of Sierra Leone author, nationalist and medical doctor James Africanus Horton. I am indebted to Christopher Fyfe for this information.

53. *The Crisis* (New York), November 1913, p. 323.
54. Ian Duffield kindly supplied copies of Mohamed's autobiographical column from the *Comet* of Lagos in the late 1930s.
55. Stephen Bourne, whose history of Blacks in British film and television, entitled *Black In The British Frame* is due for publication in 1998, supplied these details; see also *Who's Who in the Theatre*, 12 ed. (1957) which notes Trimmingham's death on 6 February 1942, whereas his death registration has 2 February 1942, aged 61.

— 6 —

A revelation in strange humanity

MAKING an appearance on the stage, from prestigious theatres in Edwardian British cities to the Kursaal at Southend, a public hall in Wrexham, the Corn Exchange in Newark or the pier theatre in Blackpool was work; and reviews, even from such unlikely publications such as the *Fruit Trader's Journal*, were clipped and treasured by entertainers. Fame and fortune could be fickle, and those entertainers who failed to adapt to changes in the public's taste would find work falling off. It must have been with chagrin that Edwardian entertainers noticed the successes of the Congo pygmies during the years 1905 to 1907, for their attraction was merely that they were short adult Africans. In the contemporary comments we can see ignorance and prejudice, curiosity, and show business enterprise. We can also observe governmental impotence, high society's naivety, journalism at its best and worst, and a subtle victory by the six Africans over the hundreds of thousands who paid to look at them.

The Edwardians had difficulty in viewing Africa without prejudice. Not only was there little knowledge of the continent, but whenever informed Whites considered Black people (which must have been very occasionally) they did so through an accumulation of missionary and imperial writings which were themselves a veneer over the centuries of the trans-Atlantic slave trade. Africa was thus a land of 'incessant cannibalism, massacre and torture'.[1] The Black people of Africa were savages, whose fate in New World slavery could be – and was – presented as an improvement.

Those in the West Indies were seen as 'blighted by poverty and ... incapable of self-help' due to 'conditions rooted in an unhappy past, partly to climatic, racial, and other natural features that will persist to the end of time'.[2] In Africa, efforts by colonialist forces, invariably considered as 'bringing civilisation', met with disapproval and resistance by the natives. The Hut Tax wars in 1890s Sierra Leone, a British colony for a century, were, as a contemporary noted, where 'the tribes, in fact, were to pay for their own police .... [and] had no very ardent desire for white protection'.[3]

The people of the central African rain forests had their homes in a region of Africa that had been brought to the attention of Europeans only in the late 1870s, when the Welsh explorer and journalist Henry Stanley crossed equatorial Africa from east to west. His *Through the Dark Continent* of 1878 was followed, after more years in tropical Africa, by the immensely successful *In Darkest Africa* of 1890. This two volume book sold 150,000 copies in English, and had editions in Dutch, French, German, Italian and Spanish.[4] The Congo pygmies – short adult inhabitants of the Ituri forest – were now known, through this book, to thousands in Britain.

In 1905 six Congo pygmies reached Britain. The individual behind their presence in Edwardian Britain was James Jonathan Harrison, a Yorkshire landowner and part-time soldier whose hobbies included global travel and big-game hunting. He had been in South Africa before writing *A Sporting Trip Through India: Home by Japan and America* in 1892.[5] In the second half of 1896 Harrison was in Central Africa, and at the end of 1899 he was in Uganda and Ethiopia. His photograph albums also include a group of five horsemen 'going to visit [the emperor] Menelik' on 5 January 1900, naming one as Percy Powell Cotton. Cotton's *A Sporting Trip Through Abyssinia* was published in London in 1904. Publisher Rowland Ward, whose taxidermists were kept busy preparing Harrison's trophies, also issued *Records of Big Game*. Harrison's name is well indexed in the 1899 edition.

Harrison had a semi-scientific interest in the creatures he slaughtered. A pygmy antelope was named after him, as were a painted or woolly bat *Kerivoula harrisoni* and a finch or lark *Pyrrhulauda harrisoni*.[6] From March to May 1904 Harrison crossed the vastness of the Congo – the river system, imposed on a map of Europe, would reach from St Petersburg to the Bay of Biscay – hoping to shoot a white rhino and also an okapi: the latter antelope-like creature being one inspiration for the unicorn of legend. Harrison shot enough elephants to have 257 kilos of ivory with him when he left from Boma, the Atlantic port of the Congo Free State.[7]

In showing his photographs to friends, Harrison was asked 'why I could not bring some of these pygmies to England, and I was thus first led to think of doing so'.[8] At the end of February 1905 Harrison was back on the eastern, Ugandan, edge of the Ituri rain forest.[9] Harrison's diary differs to the account in his twenty-four page *Life Among the Pygmies* book, but it is clear that a pygmy youth named Mongongu (or Baruti, Mongongo or Mongonga) who spoke Swahili was able to lead Harrison's party into the forests on a quest 'to induce others to visit England with us'.[10] Anxious to leave before the rainy season, Harrison recruited 'enough now for our purposes' and set off on the first day's twenty-eight mile journey. The pygmies rode on donkeys. Out of the forest's shade the equatorial sun knocked them out: they fell off the donkeys. 'They cannot stand the sun' he wrote in his diary on 15 March 1905.

The group travelled nine and ten hours daily, covering twenty-two to twenty-eight miles. One female was thought to have measles, and was escorted back. The four males and two females continued with their escort, porters, donkeys, and Harrison. Harrison, who had served with a socially-elitist yeomanry regiment based in York but had seen no war service despite his rank of major (hence his honorary rank of lieutenant colonel on retiring in 1904), must have had considerable organisational skills to keep such a group provisioned, fit and moving day after day. They arrived at the swamps of the Sudan-Uganda border region and went on board the river boat *Dal* on 1 April, sailing north down the Nile towards Khartoum. They reached the town on 11 April, and the news was telegraphed to Britain.

Whoever was handling the theatrical engagement aspects of Harrison's venture has not been identified, but his or her publicity efforts spread news of the pygmies and Harrison to many newspapers including the *Daily Mail*. One unforeseen result was that the president of the Church Missionary Society contacted Britain's foreign secretary. Sir John Kennaway was a veteran member of parliament ('father of the house') having represented a Devon constituency since the 1870s. Kennaway had written to *The Times* on 19 January 1905 about his society's plan to establish Christian missions in the region between Khartoum and Uganda: the region known as Equatoria. Rescuing its governor Emin Pasha had been the official motive behind Stanley's trans-Africa journey of 1887–9, which in turn had led to the publication of *In Darkest Africa* and thus much of the current knowledge of the pygmies.

When Kennaway's news reached Lord Lansdowne the foreign secretary, he authorised a telegram to the de facto governor of Egypt and the Sudan, Lord Cromer. The noble lord wanted to know on what conditions the pygmies were being brought to England, if they understood those conditions, and would their health be likely to suffer.[11] Three days later Lord Cromer replied. The minutiae of this correspondence surely reveals how the British dominated so many millions around the world, for here was the fifth Marquess of Lansdowne, in his sixth year as Britain's foreign secretary, an ex-governor of both India and Canada, capable of making war when Secretary for War 1895–1900, and of initiating policies that would affect generations unborn, bothering about six small adults from a corner of the globe that was neither in the British empire nor of any known economic value. His correspondent, Lord Cromer, whose Egyptian domains had been under British control for less than a generation, ruled millions whose political and religious allegiances were to the Sultan of Turkey and to religion of Islam, certainly not Edward the Seventh, but through whose land the Suez canal carried millions of pounds of merchandise.

In Cairo, where Harrison and the six Africans were resting, Lord Cromer had 'sent for Colonel Harrison' and had arranged for Dr Cyril Goodman of the Egyptian Sanitary Department to examine the pygmies. Goodman's report survives at the Public Record Office in Kew, for it was sent to Lord Lansdowne in London. In the three days between the despatch of the telegram from London and Cromer's reply of 18 April 1905, as well as providing a medical examination, two men who spoke Swahili had been located in Cairo, brought to meet the Africans, and through Mongonga who knew 'a little of that language', had interviewed them for ninety minutes.[12]

They all 'suffered from slight coughs'; three of the four males were anaemic; three had enlarged spleens; two had enlarged livers; two had irregular hearts. The older woman had a swollen left knee from an arrow wound, was 'greatly emaciated', had a curved spine, clubbed fingers and a 'feeble' pulse. The younger woman, said to be twenty-two but considered by Goodman to be much younger, was well nourished. The doctor thought that Mongonga was younger than eighteen. The six were fairly intelligent and all but the older woman were 'happy'. But he stated that only two were fit enough to continue to England. The malaria which probably had caused the enlarged spleens and livers would be accentuated in Britain, as would any lung disease. The anaemia would decrease.

The two Swahili-speaking Whites concluded that 'if the pygmies had their choice they would return to their forests, though they would only say that they had "come a long way & were tired"'. Lord Cromer read all this, and informed Lansdowne that his personal opinion was that they should be 'returned to their natural home in the forests of the Congo'. He must have made that clear to Harrison, who rushed via Italy to present his case to the foreign secretary.

As he did so, the newspapers continued to print information on the six Africans. The *Daily Mail* of London was copied by the weekly *Beverley Guardian*, printed in the town closest to Brandesburton Hall where Harrison lived when he was not globe trotting. 'Pigmies Coming to England' it reported on 15 April. The following week it had a headline 'Pigmies for England. Foreign Office Witholds Consent', adding that Harrison 'appears to have taken great care of the natives. His idea was to take them to England, and after a brief stay return them to their country, as he promised.'

On that same day, 22 April 1905, the Cairo correspondent of the *Pall Mall Gazette* despatched a report that was published in that London daily on 28 April. 'Forest Pigmies in Hospital. Possible Government Action'. The six

> are all ill and are at present in Kasr-el-Ainy Hospital. It is stated that unless their health improves the Government will insist on their being sent back to their native parts. The general opinion is that they ought never to have been brought away, and great curiosity is expressed as to what is going to be done with them in England.

Lord Lansdowne had met Harrison in London, and accordingly cabled Lord Cromer on 28 April, advising that he had said that having the pygmies 'for the purposes of exhibition would be very undesirable. I have added that it would be most satisfactory to me to learn that he had abandoned the idea.'

The next day another cable was sent to Cairo, for Lansdowne had read the *Pall Mall Gazette*'s report that all six were in hospital. 'Is this true?' he asked Cromer. The belief that Lansdowne could prohibit the entry of the six Africans into Britain and that Lord Cromer could prevent them from leaving Egypt for Europe, which had been held by the press and by Harrison, was false. On 3 May the foreign secretary sent a report to Cairo that Harrison was 'under a misapprehension' that such prohibitions could or would be enforced, and washed his hands of responsibility by stating 'If they are brought here and exhibited, this would be done entirely upon his own responsibility and at his own risk.'

Harrison had been interviewed in London by the *Daily Mail* on 25 April, and that had been copied by the *Beverley Guardian* (and, no doubt, other regional newspapers). Harrison said that the Foreign Office did not have the authority to stop the party:

> He would not, for all the pygmies in the Ituri forest, have taken any steps which might have caused Lord Cromer any trouble. It would have been a poor return after the great kindness experienced from every Government official in the Soudan and Egypt.[13]

Harrison was a dissembler, concealing his motives and failing to mention every fact. He knew that theatrical entrepreneurs were interested in showing the six Africans; indeed, his express journey from Cairo to the Foreign Office looks like the action of a man about to lose heavily on an investment. His local newspaper reported on 6 May that Harrison had stated 'thousands of people will be glad of a chance of seeing what they have read about so much', adding that the Africans would be in Yorkshire 'in the early part of August'.

As the pygmies went on stage within five days of reaching London, and made a visit to Yorkshire in early August, Harrison probably had signed contracts before he went to Africa. Harrison blamed the protests on the human rights group the Aborigines' Protection Society, remarking that 'these little people are free agents, and they volunteered to come with me'. He said that a group, abducted from the rain forests by a German who wanted to take them to France, remained outside the forests and 'will not return to their own people'.[14]

Pygmy people attached themselves to larger, agricultural, Africans, hunting in the forests and supplying meat in exchange for vegetables and fruit.[15] The story of the German was true, for Harry Johnston's autobiography tells of that man's efforts to secure twenty or thirty pygmies for the Paris exhibition of 1900, how he was arrested when crossing Uganda ('and sentenced to a heavy fine, as the imprisonment of Europeans was not, at that time, a convenient thing') and that seven pygmies were placed near Johnston's home at Entebbe where one died. Before taking the survivors back to the Congo, Johnston had the skeleton despatched to the Natural History Museum in London.[16]

Harrison's group left Egypt in May, on the cargo ship *Orestes*, and reached the English Channel on 31 May 1905. A reporter boarded the ship off Portland Bill, and now the publicity became shriller and outrageous. 'These strange ape-like people were discovered by Stanley, and until a few months ago those now in England had never seen a white man.' The thirteen day voyage ended with the pygmies rejoicing and dancing. 'They have come under the civilising influence of soap. During the last fortnight they have been tubbed daily.'

There were remarks that included 'their language consists of strange clicking sounds', that the older woman had been seasick and the Sudanese attendant had prevented her companions from killing her, and that their appearance was 'ape-like in the extreme, with coppercoloured faces, woolly hair, spreading noses, and great gashes for mouths'.[17]

The six, in ill-fitting coats and bare-footed, were photographed on a ship with a White man, and one pose was issued as a commercial postcard. Two others were published in *The Sphere*, an illustrated weekly, which had already alerted its readers to the pygmies on 6 May. The comments included 'the sailors taught the men to bathe and the ladies of the ship instructed the women in the use of soap', that 'they are quick at imitating', that 'pigmies are full-grown at twelve' and that the older woman was '"perhaps the nearest thing to a human monkey Europe has ever seen"', which must have been a quote from a Harrison-inspired publicity sheet.[18]

The decorous *Tatler* published a full-page photograph of the 'much-discussed pigmies from the Congo. The little folk in their Sunday suits',[19] a picture that was also issued as a commercial postcard. Two other poses, also taken in the studio of society photographers W. and D. Downey, had the Africans in their stage costumes, with weapons and drums. These postcards remain far from rare nearly a century afterwards.

The six pygmies went on stage at the London Hippodrome on Monday 5 June 1905. A splendid circus-cum-music hall, seating over one thousand twice daily, it had an immense water tank large enough for animal displays which, the week before the Africans appeared, included seventeen polar bears.[20] The *Era* reviewed their appearance:

> The curtain rose upon a scene which represented a tropical forest, in the midst of which was an opening, containing four wigwams of small dimensions. Outside were the group of little people who will for some time be objects of curiosity to amusement-seeking Londoners. Three of the males are armed with miniature spears, or bows and arrows, while the fourth had charge of a tom-tom. The two women of the party were seated, and, together with their male companions, stolidly regarded the audience, who were informed that the scene represented a fairly exact picture of the pigmies' homes in the Ituri Forest of Central Africa. The chief and two of his male companions were then persuaded by signs to come forward into the ring, and in the same manner invited to perform their native dance, which, when completely given, is divided into three parts. For some time the men made no response; possibly they were shy in the presence of the large audience; but they appeared to gain confidence by taking a long whiff from a cane pipe, and the leader began a low, dirge-like chant, which was an accompaniment to a dancing movement, the tom-tom player also beating time. As the performers warmed to their work, the audience applauded; but the effect was contrary to that intended, for the pigmies at once ceased their dancing, and retired to the rear.[21]

The *Referee* of 11 June 1905 noted that the pygmies were 'drawing big business' to the Hippodrome, and added:

> Ethnologically the exhibition of these dwarf savages from the Ituri Forest is interesting enough. Taken as a mere show the poor little wretches are somewhat repulsive. . . . You behold the Pygmy variety artists squatting around their tiny wattled kraals much in the same manner as bandits' scenes in old-time melodrama.[22]

The Africans were introduced by a statement that the pygmies 'are very uncertain and wayward, and that sometimes it seems doubtful whether they will dance or do anything to oblige'. This reviewer noted that 'after some tom-toming by one of the pygmiest of the Pygmies' assisted by 'some pianissimo tom-toming' by the orchestra, three males danced 'in a strictly decorous variant of a dance which is popular all over the Dark Continent'. The reviewer decided that 'There is something painful about it' and commented that the attenuated legs and thighs of the Africans resulted 'to their lack of walking exercise. They prefer, it seems, to inhabit trees'.[23]

Advertising in that issue had the Africans described as 'The most curious race in the world. Only four explorers have ever seen them. Miniature men and women. Absolute specimens of primitive creation'. The show was twice daily. The Hippodrome group of theatres spent considerable amounts on advertising, and it has to be doubted that thoughts of such financial realities were absent from the reviewers or their editors.

The *Era* and the *Referee* noted the continuing presence of the pygmies at the Hippodrome, from which can be seen a change in comprehension. The former, on 17 June, noted that the males trimmed their eyelashes with sharp arrow-heads; on 1 July it noted that 'those little people . . . are a strong attraction' and on 5 August recommended that 'Everyone in London should see these little people, who are a revelation in strange humanity.'[24] The *Referee* of 17 June noted 'The Pygmies are going strong. I took tea with them on Wednesday afternoon.'

This was within three weeks of their arrival in England as 'savages untouched by European customs and just as in their primeval forests'.[25] These allegedly unwashed savages who preferred to live in trees had transformed into people.

On 18 June five of them travelled by car to Crawley in mid-Sussex. The *Southern Weekly News* reported the visit 'From Africa To Sussex' on 24 June, explaining that 'one of the female members of the party, unfortunately, has had to undergo an operation'. It also said that all were from different tribes.

'Sturdily and substantially built, suggesting to the observer strength, endurance, and activity', they appeared 'more intelligent than most coloured people we are acquainted with'. The males wore 'knickerbocker sailor suits, with blue stockings to match'. There were some fifty people in a 'string of motor cars', which was filmed. They had picked strawberries on the way through Surrey, reaching the George Hotel around 12:30, where they were fed. Little was seen of them, because the car was enclosed, their overcoats were buttoned up, the men had felt hats and the woman wore a veil (against the dust from the road). They dined, with Harrison, in a small but warm room, using knives and forks 'as if to the custom born'.

> The youngest of the company, however, was more lively. He perched himself at the window [of the hotel], and whether he or the crowd outside was the more amused is an open question. At any rate each had a good view of the other, and all seemed perfectly satisfied with the result.

The report ended 'Crawley is wondering what will be the nature of the next Hippodrome visit.'

At the end of June five of them (the older woman being absent) visited parliament where they were photographed with eleven white males and one female, including Harrison and his interpreter William Hoffman.[26]

Other photographs of the pygmies at Westminster were taken by Sir Benjamin Stone, MP and president of the National Photographic Record Association.[27] The group pose has recently been described as a 'careful placing of the MPs in a semicircle around the visitors, their "mental" and political "superiority" emphasized in their visual and physical encapsulation' of the Africans.[28] Sometimes the most obvious explanations escape attention, for the short Africans were in the front of the group because they could not have been seen if the Whites were gathered there.

Consider that the four male Africans were carrying their weapons, thus this was an armed group of 'savages' at the centre of the empire's government. In under one month the pygmies had become completely trusted.

This was seen again within two weeks, when the pygmies went, again armed to the teeth, to Buckingham Palace where they attended the birthday celebrations of Princess Victoria. The *Beverley Guardian* of 22 July reported 'Princess and Pygmies. Little Brown Men at Buckingham Palace'. Two of the males danced, joined by Mongonga who 'tried to kill an old cock sparrow with his spear'. 'The pygmies undoubtedly achieved the triumph of the afternoon' despite the presence of a baby elephant from the Royal Italian Circus. There were 150 guests; and Queen Alexandra was present. The armed Africans were escorted to the palace by Harrison and the Hippodrome's manager Fred Trussell.

The transformation of the six Africans was due to their own humanity, but it must have been aided by the linguistic talents of interpreter William Hoffman. Hoffman was such a bizarre character that, like Harrison, we need to examine him in order to understand Edwardian life. Black visitors and residents came into contact with all manner of Whites from the chambermaids noticed by Ham Mukasa, the instructors at army, railway, and marine centres, stagehands at theatres, and the men, women and children who rode Joe Clough's bus and Lewis Bruce's tram.

Hoffman's life had changed radically when he delivered some luggage to the London home of Henry Stanley in 1884. The apprentice bag-maker, born in Magdeburg, Germany, in 1867 and raised in London in the 1870s,[29] was employed as Stanley's valet during his participation in the Berlin conference 1884–5 which decided how the

27. Promoted as unwashed savages, the Africans earned the trust of the mighty and by late June 1905, with spears and bows and arrows, at parliament, posed for Sir Benjamin Stone. Their exploiter, Colonel Harrison, stands behind Mongonga, the smallest African. Interpreter William Hoffman, their companion for over a year, stands front, right

map of Africa would be divided. Hoffman then went with Stanley to the United States, and in 1887 the pair went to Africa on the Emin Pasha relief expedition which led to the writing of *In Darkest Africa*.

The 1887–9 expedition was the most documented journey by Whites in tropical Africa, with six other books in 1890, four in 1891, and three more by 1898. Hoffman is excluded from most accounts including Stanley's, although he was Stanley's personal servant throughout those months. Hoffman was left behind in Africa by Stanley, working for Francis de Winton as an interpreter at the customs house, Mombasa.[30] 'Ignored in all the other officers' letters, diaries and re-constructed accounts of the expedition', Hoffman must have done or seen something 'to condemn himself to such unpersonhood'.[31]

Stanley, a famous man, member of parliament in 1895, and knighted in 1899, had returned to Africa in 1897–8, with Hoffman as his valet on a visit to Bulawayo on the newly opened railway to Rhodesia.[32] When Stanley died, in 1904, Hoffman was left £300. He started making veiled threats to expose the truth behind Stanley (whose reputation had fallen sufficiently that burial in Westminster Abbey was not permitted[33]), which led to widow Dorothy Stanley confiding in her millionaire friend Henry Wellcome 'I think he means everything that is good – but he writes badly and might unwittingly do ill-service.'[34] She and Wellcome were busy buying off people and buying up materials that could damage Stanley's reputation. Hoffman continued to receive money from them until their deaths (hers in 1926; Wellcome's in 1936).[35]

Hoffman's contacts with Dorothy Stanley and Henry Wellcome would always cause anxiety, but they had influence and money and Hoffman needed both. On 30 May 1905 he wrote to Wellcome, asking if he knew Harrison, who was seeking a person 'who could speak Kiswahili, and know their ways. I should think that as I have lived with them in the Aruwimi forest and know their ways and habits I would have a chance.'[36] With a recommendation from Lady Stanley,[37] Hoffman and his wife Jani were employed by Harrison to look after the pygmies.

They lived at 5 North Crescent off Tottenham Court Road, the 'pygmies quarters' as Hoffman had scrawled on one letter. He allowed august (and no doubt paying) visitors to meet the Africans there: including Lady Stanley by 19 July. Another group included relatives of Edmund Barttelot, who had died on the Emin Pasha expedition.[38]

Although Hoffman had the linguistic skills that Harrison needed, that Lady Stanley recommended him seems odd, for she wrote in mid-August of Hoffman 'They only have to intoxicate him and bribe him, and there is no knowing what he may say, perhaps I am unjust to him, but he is a weak, untruthful man.'[39] It was this man who, with his wife, accompanied the pygmies for over a year. It was a curious association.

The people of Beverley finally got to see the Africans at the end of July 1905. Brandesburton Hall, just off the main road from Beverley to Bridlington, had a fete over a weekend, with a militia band, the Africans on show from 10:00 to 12:30 and 1:30 to 8:00 on the Saturday, with appearances from 11:00 to 1:00 and 1:30 to 7:30 on Sunday. The hall, with its sporting trophies, would be open, weather permitting. There was 'a considerable number of people assembled at the station in the hope of catching a glimpse' of the six Africans when their train arrived on 28 July. Harrison had a private bus which drove off leaving most spectators with a flash of red hats and bows and arrows. Three thousand people went to Brandesburton: by bicycle, on foot, horse-drawn carriages, the railway's steambus, and a few motor cars. Over twelve hundred paid to visit the Hall. By 8:30 'the village was as quiet as though no one had been'.[40]

West of the village, some twenty miles away, lay Market Weighton and the grounds of Londesborough Park, where Lord and Lady Londesborough had one of their five homes.[41] The pygmies attended a garden fete and bazaar in the grounds.

> Despite the somewhat heavy charges, hundreds of people paid them a visit, and many stayed to see them dance. They seem to thoroughly enjoy themselves, mixing with the crowd when not seated on the platform. One smoked a cigarette, others ate chocolate or grapes with evident enjoyment, and from children's toys all of them seemed to gain a great delight.[42]

The pygmies exhibited their skills with weapons, killing running rabbits with bow and arrow.[43] There was also a play, military bands and a military tournament, for Lord Londesborough was the deputy lieutenant of East Yorkshire and owned over 52,000 acres of land.

The remainder of August 1905 saw the pygmies on stage at the London Hippodrome, with a second visit to Yorkshire on 27 August when Lord Londesborough arranged for food to be made available to them on the train, which was delayed nearly one hour and so had caused a reception to be cancelled.[44] Just before that trip the six Africans had gone to the London recording studios of the Gramophone Company. These recordings, made on 25 August 1905, were the first commercial recordings of Africans made in Britain. Yet again there was confusion in the minds of the organisers.

The catalogue for January-February 1906, when the discs were available after being pressed in Germany, states:

> These records of the language and Folk Songs of this remarkable tribe of dwarfs who inhabit the forests of Central Africa are absolutely unique. For many years stories have been told by various travellers of

28. The first commercial recordings, in Britain, of African music and language were on 25 August 1905. Issued at the beginning of 1906, the five shellac discs are rare (Wood End Museum, Scarborough)

the existence of such a tribe, but they have been looked upon almost as fables. Colonel Harrison, the explorer, discovered them, and after the greatest difficulty was successful in bringing six of them to England. Their language is quite unknown, and they have created the greatest interest in anthropological and scientific circles.[45]

One of the recordings is in Swahili. Another is of the two women talking, and two have Matuka and the chief Bokani singing to drums. Two start with a plummy English voice stating the day.

The Africans were taken to the Natural History Museum in London, and photographs were taken there. Undated, identified as being from the 'Belgian Congo', a state which existed only from 1908, the pictures include both the women and Bokani wearing nose sticks, probably porcupine quills. Dr Murray Leslie is identified as 'Doctor in charge of pygmies' and he was recalled in Hoffman's 1938 book, *With Stanley in Africa*, as 'their own specialist' who 'examined them for coughs and colds'.[46]

Hoffman was unreliable, and his niece advised that his book was ghost-written.[47] Its final chapter is on the pygmies, and contains a photograph not located elsewhere, but it ends with Hoffman (misspelled as Hoffmann) stating that he had no further contact with Africa. Actually he worked for Lever Brothers in the French Congo from 1911 to 1913.[48]

The pygmies triumphed at the Natural History Museum, even if they were taken there as living exhibits or to be pushed and measured by so-called scientists. Rosemary Powers, who worked at the museum since 1954, recalled a woman who had been a nurse telling her that she had nursed the younger female pygmy and that later they had become friends. 'The younger women made a second visit to London and sold programmes at one of the great exhibitions',[49] which fits events uncovered for 1907 as will be shown.

The council of the Anthropological Institute, chaired by Harry Johnston, had made 'a full scientific report on the African pygmies' according to the *Beverley Guardian* of 16 September 1905.[50] It has not been traced. The Africans were no longer appearing at the Hippodrome, but were expected to appear in Beverley itself on 14 October. The town's assembly rooms had receptions at 7:15 and an hour later. The Hoffmans were with them, with William described as 'one of the survivors of Stanley's expedition, and was with the celebrated explorer when the pygmies were discovered'. Hoffman spoke on the 'life and habits of these strange nomadic tribes'.[51]

They moved north via Driffield to York, then south to Lincoln where the *Lincolnshire Chronicle* of 13 October advertised their appearance, at the Central Hall, on Wednesday 18 October. They were to make four appearances on that one day. They had 'been honoured by a command to appear before the King and Queen' – their Buckingham Palace appearance had been before the Queen, the King and his sons being absent.

After this the pygmies, accompanied by the Hoffmans, toured major cities in England and Scotland, on the Empire theatre circuit. The newspapers of these cities used publicity supplied by Harrison and announced the group in ways similar to those seen in the first days in London in June 1905. Exposure to the Africans, on stage and backstage, brought the journalists into contact with people, and, as seen in the metropolitan newspapers, changed perceptions. While that transformation was taking place, the audiences saw a few minutes of a bogus Africa with genuine Africans on stage, and the Africans had problems with accommodation, food, warmth, travel, and their healths. Dr Goodman's prognoses were becoming true.

Their work at the Manchester Hippodrome began on Monday 23 October 1905. They had two appearances daily, with a third in the afternoons of Tuesday, Wednesday and Saturday. Upwards of twenty thousand people could have seen their act in one week. As at Beverley, there were five Africans, 'interesting as curiosities, but disappointing as entertainers. . . . Shyness is their principal characteristic, and this is not commendable from the view of the gallery.'[52] The gallery had the cheapest seats and was famed for enthusiastic criticisms.

The first show was reviewed as by 'Five strange little beings . . . a source of great and wondering interest'. 'One of the two women actually giggled like a giddy young English girl, and at the end of their performance three or four of them kissed their hands' and said 'good-bye'.[53]

The following week saw them open at the Empire in Lime Street, Liverpool. They were advertised as 'The Talk of all Europe! The most Curious People ever seen! They are half-way between Anthropoid Apes and Man!'.[54] That newspaper's reviewer was critical. 'The music-hall stage is scarcely the place whence to promulgate the principles of Darwinism.' To the 'battering of a wooden box, a member of the troupe commenced the alleged war song, which was, if anything, less musical than the accompaniment'. The crowds in the cheaper seats were abusive.[55]

They moved north to Scotland, where they were to appear at the Empire Palace at Nicolson Street, Edinburgh, from 6 November. Described as 'something of a novelty calculated to arise an interest not usually associated with the music hall', the five again paused before 'the spirit moved them' and they sang and danced.[56]

They went west to Glasgow, where they were to appear at the Scottish Zoo and Glasgow Hippodrome. The 'anthropoid ape' announcement appeared in the local *Evening News*, with details of their schedule: twice a night and at 3:00 on Wednesday and Saturday at the theatre, and at the zoo for an hour each afternoon on Tuesday, Thursday and Friday. The *Evening Times* review on 14 November referred to them as 'midgets' and 'little folk', that 'by the way, [they] speak very good English', and 'last night they executed a war dance in neat style'. Another newspaper's review appeared the following day: 'They are an interesting spectacle and the opportunity of witnessing these entertaining little folk is one not to be missed.'[57]

Hoffman's book has a comment which may well be true:

> The only difficulty we experienced was in the matter of lodgings. At Glasgow, for instance, we arrived from the station in the 'bus our agent had hired for us, only to be met at the door of the hotel by an irate landlady who declared that she could not possibly have 'blacks' about the place.

Her regular tenants would be annoyed and her custom would be affected. Hoffman says he left the Africans on the bus and searched for accommodation, receiving the same negative response. 'Luckily the landlady's heart had softened at the thought of the six pathetic little natives huddled in the 'bus', and they rushed to the 'roaring fire'. This Mrs Nicholls told Hoffman 'Your pygmies are not very bad. You can stay here a few more days if you wish.'[58]

One has to question the quality of the agent who booked a Black act into racist accommodation; but as Hoffman refers to six Africans, perhaps he was again spinning a tale.

After their time in Glasgow, they moved south to Birmingham to appear at the Empire Palace from 27 November. It had seating for two thousand.[59] With two shows each night and a matinee on Thursday, over twenty-five thousand could have seen them in one week.

> A very large audience greeted the Central Africa Pygmies with mingled awe and amusement at the Empire last night, but when it was found that the dusky little folks were well-formed specimens of humanity, and, so far from being in the least unpleasant to look upon, could give the common or 'garden' nigger many points as to manly beauty, the attitude of the house became entirely friendly.

This review, in the *Birmingham Daily Mail* of 28 November, suggests that there was confusion between minstrels and genuine Africans. It refuted some of the publicity:

> Officially stated to be the missing link between the ape and man, the pygmies, by their appearance, certainly do not suggest the connection; however this may be, the exhibition is an exceedingly interesting one, and during the course of the war-dance which they go through one seems to trace the origins of the cake-walk.

They moved to Shepherds Bush in west London, where the Empire had seats for 1,650.[60] Then they went to Bradford where they were again advertised as 'the talk of all Europe'. The review in the *Bradford Daily Argus* of 12 December included comments on the 'many pleasing features', that there was a 'war dance' and 'a native song' to a drum. 'The turn is both interesting and instructive, and should appeal to ethnological students.' There were only four performers, and Hoffman's talk on 'their habits and their development since their arrival in this country' probably had to be extended. The *Bradford Daily Telegraph* of the same date observed:

> The display is not characterised by much vigour ... the exhibition is of a most interesting nature, and shows what a great work there is for those who have in hand the civilisation of the races of Central Africa.

As Christmas approached, and the Hoffmans went with the Africans to Brandesburton, they left behind audiences that had numbered hundreds of thousands.

They moved off to Germany, where Hoffman's mother tongue

would have been very useful.[61] They were back in England by August 1906. There was a flurry of theatrical activity, with appearances in and around Brandesburton – Withernsea on 27 July, Hornsea on 28 July, at the Grand Pavilion in Bridlington (billed as a 'return visit') on 3 and 4 August, at Brandesburton Hall over the public holiday of 5 and 6 August, and at the King's Hall in Grimsby from 7 to 9 August.[62] They were at The Spa in Whitby, north east Yorkshire, on 13–14 August.[63] Hoffman complained to Wellcome that the pygmies 'are not doing anything at present' and he had no income two days before the Africans appeared at Barmouth's Pavilion.[64]

The following week they appeared at the Pavilion, at the pier at Eastbourne, from 2 to 5 October, with a total of seven receptions. Their supervisor was John Osborne. The handbill that provided this evidence indicates that the Africans were often given presents 'including money, jewellery, feathers, clothes, and beads'.[65]

The six Africans settled down at Brandesburton Hall, where Harrison had extended the building and made a heated summer house for them. They were not prisoners, but walked the short distance from the hall into the village, where they mixed with the local people. A gravel-mining and farming community, Brandesburton retained memories of the Africans into the 1990s. Some recollections were not supported by other evidence, notably the burial place of the younger woman's child. It seems unlikely that anyone in the village had access to Hoffman's 1938 book which also tells of a still-born child.

The pygmies walked about the village, wearing animal skins and always with their bows and arrows. 'They used to run about here like normal and when I were ten they were aboot [*sic*] my size', collecting wild honey and ignoring bee stings. They were seen at Bassingdales the blacksmith's forge, hammering nail ends into arrow heads. 'They knew what they were doing' and were 'very clever'. 'Tough little folk, without a doubt' who 'learned to speak quite a bit of English', they handled money at the local shops and 'were quite brainy, the way they adapted'. They did not go to school or to church. 'There wasn't a tall one amongst them'.[66]

Dr J. E. S. Walker, a general practitioner whose patients told him stories of the pygmies in the 1960s and 1970s, noted these memories and advised that

> the pygmies were certainly made to feel at home at Brandesburton eg they attended one of my patients parents wedding. They used to enjoy (or at least the ladies did) dressing up with the Hall staff. They enjoyed playing football with people their own size – with whom they would have superior strength – but did not like loosing. They were also fond of practical jokes.[67]

29. When the six pygmies were not touring they lived at the Hall in Brandesburton, Yorkshire, where they were recalled with respect for decades by the children who were their companions (Peter Calvert)

Photographs in Harrison's collections show them playing with that Edwardian fad, the diabolo; others show them in front of the Hall as gardeners go about their work. There are undated photographs of huts they had constructed in the grounds, and recollections of rabbits killed by their arrows. Photographs of them and Yorkshire children on a foggy day, with the Africans on donkeys, have been retrieved.[68]

The chief's head, sculpted by leading Welsh artist Goscombe John in late 1905, went on show at the Royal Academy in 1906.[69]

Another set of commercial photographs was issued in 1906 as postcards. This time their heights were stated, along with their names, and a mention of the dead baby. The Africans continued to appear in halls around the country, not the grand theatres seating over a thousand, but to groups at receptions, surely a sign that they could converse in English? They were at the King's Hall in Westcliff-on-Sea, Essex from 25 February to 2 March 1907, a 'farewell appearance before leaving for the forest', under Osborne's supervision. They made two shows daily, for an hour each. On 25 May they were at the Victoria Rooms of the Colston Hall, in Bristol, a return visit which led to no reviews although it was advertised in the *Bristol Evening News*, the *Bristol Echo*, and the *Bristol Guardian* that day.

Slowly the number of British witnesses to the pygmies was approaching one million. Then, in June 1907, came employment at one of the London exhibitions.

The *Era* of 8 June 1907 reported that the Balkan States Exhibition included 'Old Japan' with fishing cormorants, that there were 'Hindoo freaks', a flying machine, two bands, and

> Just across the way are the Pygmies, an interesting and very happy little family which Colonel Harrison brought from the Congo, and which are going back to their native forest at the close of the Exhibition.

Thousands visited this show at Earls Court, and the Africans attracted crowds to the extent that *Punch* had a one-and-a-half page article 'Petting the Pygmies' at the end of August. It ends with:

> The Pygmy Chief appears to be pondering over the excessive susceptibility of the British Public to the charms of his country-women, in whom, though fine women enough in their way, he can see nothing whatever to make all that fuss about. But then these big white folk, though they have their uses in providing him with cigarettes, do seem to him to be rather lacking in intelligence.[70]

The exhibition continued for two more months, and the Africans continued their work there.

They reappeared in the London press at the end of October, for

Osborne had gone with two male pygmies (armed with bows and arrows) to the shop of a trader who had sold 'a trashy watch' to the Africans. The shop keeper brought a court action, charging Osborne with threatening him. The defence pointed out that the Africans were 'about 2ft. 6in. high'. A 'coloured man' named Aaron Martin had witnessed the incident and testified that the jeweller had been very frightened, being sick for two hours. The magistrate adjourned the case as there was no evidence that Osborne had used threats, and the pygmies got their refund.[71]

The exhibition had closed and the Africans had returned to Brandesburton that weekend, in 'excellent health'.[72] With a final set of lectures in Hull, while they waited to board the *Hindoo* for Port Said and on to Mombasa, the Africans and Osborne closed the national touring on 16 November. The *Hull Times* announced the appearance was in aid of the local hospital; and that Osborne had praised the Africans' 'cleanliness and their intelligence', a view far removed from the nonsense published in May and June 1905.[73]

The Africans reached Nairobi on 26 December and were in Entebbe on New Year's Day, 1908. Harrison's diary shows that they were back in the Congo forests and among Bokani's people on 23 January. Eventually from Mombasa the news agencies cabled England, and the *Beverley Guardian* of 7 March 1908 reported that the six had reached their home in the Ituri Forest. It had been three years.

The story of the six pygmies has revealed several aspects of Edwardian Britain. First, that around one million Britons had seen people usually promoted or introduced as savages. Secondly, that the individuality of these people had triumphed in both a short time and often around the nation. Furthermore, the involvement of imperialists such as Hoffman and Osborne (who was in Uganda 1908–9), artists such as Goscombe John, doctors, museum staff, theatrical people from those at the Hippodrome who took the group on a trip to Crawley to orchestral players who 'tom-tommed' to the Africans, journalists, anthropologists, commercial adventurers such as the Gramophone Company and the publishers of Harrison's book, photographers and printers, reveals what a widespread impact Black Edwardians could have.

The Yorkshire farmer who settled in Kenya with the ambition of tracing their tracks half a century later, Lord Londesborough, the frustrated Lords Cromer and Lansdowne, and that strange man James J. Harrison, who returned to the Congo twice, locating one of 'his pygmies' on the second trip in January 1910, must be some of the least likely individuals whose lives were touched by the four men and two women from the heart of Africa. The story could have been produced by the imagination of a novelist.

NOTES

1. A. Sinclair, *The Savage: A History of Misunderstanding* (London: Weidenfeld & Nicolson, 1977), pp. 49–50.
2. S. Jeyes, *Mr Chamberlain: His Life and Public Career* (London: Sands, 1903), p. 556.
3. Ibid. p. 588.
4. *Dictionary of National Biography, Supplement 1901–1911*, p. 392.
5. J. Harrison, *A Sporting Trip Through India* (Beverley, Yorkshire: Hall, 1892). Privately printed and missing from standard biblographies, this was located in Hull Central Library by Bernth Lindfors, who knew of my interest in Harrison after I had examined postcards in his collection. I already knew, from a book in the private library of my good friend Rainer Lotz, that the pygmies had made gramophone recordings in London in 1905. When David Killingray told me about his arrangements for a conference on 'The African Presence in the United Kingdom' for the Royal African Society, and asked if I had a contribution, I suggested the pygmies. My material, delivered on 14 December 1991, was also presented to the anthropology department of University College London in May 1993. Revised, it was presented on my behalf by Killingray at the African Studies Association of America annual conference in Seattle in late 1992. Peter Calvert of Beverley, Yorkshire, whose assistance and encouragement were crucial, continues, with my blessing, to present talks to local history societies in that area where the pygmies lived in 1905–7.
6. O. Thomas, *Annals and Magazine of Natural History for 1906*, 7, 18, p. 149; *Ibis*, April 1901.
7. FO 123/436.
8. J. Harrison, *Life Among the Pygmies of the Ituri Forest, Congo Free State* (London: Hutchinson, 1905), pp. 5–6.
9. Diaries and photograph albums courtesy Ian Massey, Wood End, Museum of Natural History, Scarborough.
10. Harrison, *Pygmies*, p. 8.
11. FO 141/390.
12. Ibid. One was Captain Owen, the Acting Director of Intelligence, Cairo; the other was 'Mr Wilson' of the Uganda Civil Service: possibly George Wilson, an Australian music hall entertainer who had become a missionary then a district commissioner; and if he was, did he advise the six on aspects of entertainment? See I. Beckett, *Johnnie Gough, V.C.* (London: Donovan Publishing, 1989), p. 125, which quotes from Gough's papers when he was in the Kings African Rifles.
13. *Beverley Guardian*, 29 April 1905.
14. Ibid. 6 May 1905.
15. H. Stanley, *In Darkest Africa* (London: Colonial edition, Sampson Low, 1890), pp. 363–4; P. Schebesta, *Among Congo Pigmies* (London: Hutchinson, 1933).
16. Johnston, *The Story of My Life*, pp. 344–7. The skeleton remains at the museum.
17. *Beverley Guardian*, 3 June 1905.
18. *The Sphere* (London), 10 June 1905, p. 236.
19. *The Tatler* (London), 26 July 1905, p. 121.
20. J. Read, *Empires, Hippodromes and Palaces* (London: Alderman Press, 1985), pp. 151–3; W. Macqueen Pope, *The Melodies Linger On: The Story of Music Hall* (London: W. H. Allen, 1950), pp. 241–3.
21. *Era* (London), 10 June 1905, p. 19.
22. *Referee* (London), 11 June 1905, p. 4.
23. Ibid.
24. *Era* (London), 17 June 1905, p. 18; ibid., 1 July 1905, p. 19; ibid. 5 August 1905, p. 19.

25. *Daily Telegraph* (London), 7 June 1905.
26. National Portrait Gallery, London, photograph 22270. My thanks to Diana Parsons, whose 'The Pygmies of Yorkshire', *Country Life* (London), 10 November 1977, p. 1361, was located by Bernth Lindfors in Hull Central Library.
27. C. Cook, *Sources in British Political History 1900–1951* (London: Macmillan, 1977), 4, p. 187; *Who Was Who 1897–1916*, p. 682. My thanks to the National Portrait Gallery.
28. B. Stone, 'British Popular Anthropology: Exhibiting and Photographing the Other' in E. Edwards (ed.), *Anthropology & Photography 1860–1920* (New Haven: Yale University Press, 1992), p. 123.
29. Alfred Sharpe to Royal Geographical Society, London, 22 April 1920; Western Papers 6010, Wellcome Library, London, Hoffman ms 19 pp on his 1887–1889 travels, apparently written some years later, p. 1 'Oct 10 being my birthday'.
30. Hoffman ms, Wellcome Library 6011, p. 33.
31. J. Bierman, *Dark Safari: The Life Behind the Legend of Henry Morton Stanley* (London, 1991), pp. 329–30.
32. R. Hall, *Stanley: An Adventurer Explored* (London: Collins, 1974), pp. 348, 351–2.
33. Ibid. p. 353.
34. Dorothy Stanley, letter 20 August 1904 to Henry Wellcome, RGS.
35. Hall, *Stanley*, pp. 354–7; Wellcome Library, Wellcome Papers, Box 43, 4.
36. Stanley file, RGS.
37. Ibid. Hoffman to Wellcome, 10 July 1905.
38. *Dictionary of National Biography, Supplement 1901–1911*, p. 393 notes Barttelot's brother's book as 'written in a spirit of virulent animosity against Stanley'; Stanley file, RGS, undated but certainly after 2 August 1905 as Hoffman had been to Lord Londesborough's 'place' (see *Scarborough Post*, 1 August 1905).
39. Dorothy Stanley to Henry Wellcome, 15 August 1905.
40. *Beverley Guardian*, 29 July 1905; ibid. 5 August 1905.
41. *Who Was Who 1916–1928*, p. 641.
42. *Scarborough Post* 1 August 1905, p. 3.
43. *Era* 2 September 1905, p. 20.
44. Ibid.
45. My thanks to Lucy Duran of the National Sound Archive, London.
46. W. Hoffmann [*sic*], *With Stanley in Africa* (London: Cassell, 1938), p. 278.
47. Interview with Jeffrey Green, London, 3 February 1994. She did not want her name published.
48. RGS, Lever Brothers to Burroughs, Wellcome, 13 July 1911; Hoffman to Wellcome, 5 December 1913.
49. Dr Robert Kriszynski of the Natural History Museum, London, letter to Jeffrey Green, 26 March 1991.
50. *Beverley Guardian*, 16 September 1905, p. 6; *African World* (London), 16 September 1905, p. 247.
51. *Beverley Guardian*, 14 October 1905; ibid. 21 October 1905, p. 5.
52. *Manchester City News*, 28 October 1905, p. 7.
53. *Manchester Evening News* 24 October 1905, p. 6.
54. *Smith's Liverpool Weekly*, 27 October 1905, p. 11.
55. Ibid. 3 November 1905, p. 4.
56. *Edinburgh Evening News* 7 November 1905, p. 2.
57. *Daily Record and Mail* (Glasgow) 13 November 1905, p. 4.
58. Hoffman, *With Stanley*, pp. 274–5.
59. Read, *Empires*, p. 40.
60. Ibid. p. 108.
61. *Beverley Guardian*, 14 July 1906, p. 5 states they were in Berlin; *Grimsby News*, 27 July 1906, states they were coming direct from Berlin.

62. *Beverley Guardian* 14 July 1906, p. 5; *Bridlington Chronicle* 27 July 1906.

63. *Whitby Times* 10 August 1906, p. 4.

64. Hoffman to Wellcome, 25 September 1906, RGS; *Barmouth and County Advertiser* 27 September 1906, p. 3. 'Six men and two women' were advertised. Ibid. 4 October 1906, p. 6 'There were good audiences and every one seemed to be both amused and instructed at the same time.'

65. My thanks to Bernth Lindfors for sight of this document.

66. G. Winter, 'The Pygmies of East Riding', unidentified cutting c. 1983; telephone conversation between Grace Watson [aged 90] and Jeffrey Green, 12 February 1991.

67. Letter dated 20 July 1991.

68. My thanks to Peter Calvert.

69. F. Pearson, *Goscombe John at the National Museum of Wales* (Cardiff: 1979), p. 41. A copy of this bust is in the Royal Anthropological Institute, London.

70. *Punch* (London), 28 August 1907, p. 149.

71. *Illustrated Police News* (London) 26 October 1907, p. 14; *Beverley Guardian* 9 November 1907, p. 8.

72. *Beverley Guardian* 26 October 1907, p. 5.

73. *Beverley Guardian* 16 November 1907, p. 5; *Hull Times*, 16 November 1907, p. 10; *Yorkshire Post* (Leeds), 15 November 1907, p. 9 states the last appearances were at the Albion Lecture Hall on 15 and 16 November.

7

Children, the young and students

BERMUDA-BORN actor Ernest Trimmingham's films included *Jack, Sam and Pete*, released in 1919. This was based on a highly popular and influential series of children's stories which had first appeared in the Edwardian weekly comic *The Marvel*.[1] The adventures of the three boys set a standard that was to be copied in other publications aimed at children. Pete was a Black ventriloquist whose skills got his companions out of trouble. From 1905 their adventures were reprinted in the *Boys' Friend Library*, and were copied by their author in the war years as Dan, Bob and Darkey. An ethnic member of a boys' trio became essential in Edwardian comics: the comic and faithful Chinese, Eskimo or Negro thus reached millions of readers over the decades.

Genuine children of African descent can be traced in Edwardian Britain, through school and group photographs, family papers, and by their fame as adults. That most publicised of groups, the entertainers, can have their Edwardian childhood origins revealed. The groups of Black dancers who toured Denmark in 1926 and in 1930 with Philadelphia-born choreographer Louis Douglas (himself a veteran of years in Edwardian Britain with Belle Davis) had to obtain work permits from the Danish authorities, and in the Copenhagen files Morten Clausen located their applications. Their passport details had been recorded, from which we can see that the Black dancers included Hilda Grace Brown who had been born in London in February 1902, Ellen Smith who had been born in Manchester in July 1894, Hilda Dawson who had been born in London in late 1892, and Phoebe Zausa Williams who was born in Liverpool in April 1899. Annie Solomon was born in October 1914, Josephina Wood in May 1912, and Olive C. Mendez in 1906: all in London. Rona Glasspool was born in Cardiff in May 1914, Natalie Stoici in January 1913, and the youngest of the 1930 group, Annie Thomas, also in Cardiff, in January 1915. Beatrice Bernard was born in Manchester in October 1911.[2]

A 1940 group in Copenhagen included 'Miss Louise – Negro Singer' who had worked with Paris-based jazz musicians. Clausen's investigations revealed that her work permit file states she was Louise Hamilton, born in Manchester on 10 February 1910. We know no more: she and the others had families, educations, friends, ambitions and achievements, which all remain to be traced.[3]

There are young African students buried in Colwyn Bay in North Wales in the 1900s, because of William Hughes who had been a pioneer Baptist missionary in the Congo. Hughes wrote *Dark Africa: and the Way Out* in 1892, proposing that a school for Africans in Britain would be a more practical way to spread Christianity in Africa. Instead of a foreign missionary who knew little of local people and less of their language, who struggled against illness and the problems of working in isolation and then effectively abandoned his or her mission to take lengthy breaks in Britain, Hughes wanted promising converts to travel to Britain. There, surrounded by convinced Christians, they would learn practical skills such as pharmacy, carpentry, medicine and printing from local practitioners. They would also be distant from any temptation to return to traditional beliefs. His Congo Institute expanded recruitment and changed its name to the African Institute. On its board was Sir Samuel Lewis of Sierra Leone.[4]

It soon reached out to South Carolina and to the West Indies, and had students from southern Africa by the mid-1900s. Alfred Jones authorised free tickets on his steamers; both Henry Stanley and King Leopold of the Belgians (the Congo was his personal empire) gave it verbal support. One of its students was Ashaker, the thief and alleged fraudster. Another was Ernestina Francis, the daughter of a Dutch merchant at Banana (where the river Congo pours into the Atlantic ocean). George Fraser, the Congo-born son of a Scot, was also an early student at the Institute.

Lulu Coote, also from the Congo, was studying nursing locally by 1904. Eight students from Sierra Leone, one from the Gold Coast, Peter Nyambo from Zambia, and Davidson Don Jabavu from South Africa were also students there. Jabavu moved on to Birmingham University. An earlier student, Akinsanya Oluwale from Nigera, had gone to Liverpool University, and Ayodeji Oyejola studied medicine at Edinburgh where he qualified in 1906 (as we have noted when the Alake of Abeokuta visited Scotland).

Cecil B. Conton from St Albans in Bermuda left Colwyn Bay in 1904 and travelled with his mother to Lagos, where they worked as practical missionaries. With them was Joseph Morford, an American who had spent months in Liverpool and London as well as three years in the coal mines in south Wales before attending the institute. Conton married Ernestina Francis in Nigeria in 1906; she returned to Wales to have their baby. Mother and baby died and are buried in Colwyn Bay, as are two earlier students from west Africa.[5]

Blacks with assets, both Caribbeans and Africans such as Sir Samuel Lewis, Kagwa, Lewanika and Dr Richard Savage could afford to send their children to boarding schools in Britain. The colony with the longest tradition of having African children attend British schools and universities was Sierra Leone. The first Africans to qualify as professional doctors were from Sierra Leone in the 1850s. Its pioneer medical student was James Africanus Horton, who died in 1883.[6] His British connections survived through his daughter Nannette, the Mrs Boucher who had pressed the Foreign Office for action over the plight of the Garland troupe in Russia in 1913.

Nannette Boucher's daughters were born in Britain; her son James has not been traced in the British birth records so a Sierra Leone birth might be presumed, for Nannette met and married W. H. Boucher there after her education in England and Germany in the 1890s.[7] They moved to England with Dr Horton's widow, and the Boucher children were brought up in south London. The widow, the African grandmother of the now English Bouchers, died in Dover in 1910.[8]

They had links with other Black Britons, notably the singer Mabel Mercer whose career in between-the-wars Paris and post-war America led to interviews, recordings, and a biography. Born near Burton upon Trent on 3 February 1900, there is no father named on the registration, which states that her mother was a 'musical artiste' named Emily Wadham.[9] Her father is believed to have been an American of African descent. Her mother toured abroad, leaving Mabel in the care of her theatrical grandmother in or near Liverpool. By 1908 she was boarding at a convent school named Blakely near Manchester.

> At school all the kids thought I was rather odd. They'd never seen anything like me. I was the only one, you see. They christened me Golliwog, which was an affectionate term, because the 'golliwogs' the children had were little black dolls, with black woolen hair. I was always envious of the girls with long hair.[10]

Her education, which ended in 1914, was excellent, but she was bound up in a theatrical family and so joined her aunt's group, moving on to join what must have been a Will Garland show, *Coloured Society*, which had an African bass singer.[11] Nannette Boucher got her to move from risky theatrical lodgings, and thus Ena and Madeleine Boucher became life-long friends of Mabel Mercer. All three Black Edwardian children eventually settled in America. Mabel Wadham, known internationally as Mabel Mercer, died in New York in April 1984. One thousand five hundred people attended her town hall memorial.[12] Her voice, which never lost an English accent,[13] was the instrument of her success. It was her British years that gave her an education which included a Christmas carol 'The Twelve Days of Christmas', now a classic song, revived solely through her recording.[14]

One Sierra Leone family with considerable links to Britain were the

Smiths. Adelaide Smith was raised in Jersey from the 1870s. Her half-brother Francis Smith had qualified as a lawyer at that time, and worked as a judge in the Gold Coast, retiring to London in the 1900s. Her sister married, in Jersey, Dr John Farrell Easmon, another Sierra Leonean medical man. Their son Charlie (M. C. F. Easmon) was educated in Britain, at Collet Court School in Hammersmith, then qualifying as a doctor in 1912. His sister Kathleen had her education in Edwardian Britain, too, at the Royal College of Art.

The Easmons lived at 5, Melrose Terrace in west London's Shepherds Bush by 1900 while the adult males worked in Africa. Adelaide Smith was courted, in London, by Joseph Casely Hayford. He had been born in the Gold Coast in 1866, but educated in Sierra Leone and at Peterhouse (Cambridge), to be called to the Bar in 1896. His son Archie, by his first wife Beatrice, was educated entirely in Britain (he became Minister of Communications in the first, 1957, independent government of the Gold Coast). Adelaide Smith married the lawyer in London in September 1903. The honeymoon was spent at Stratford upon Avon. Their daughter Gladys was born in 1904.

The London home of the four Easmon and Casely Hayford children was visited by Elizabeth Dawson and Mrs Coussey, whose children were being educated in Britain too. By 1907 Adelaide and Emma Smith's half-sister Laura Davies had married Claude Wright, another Sierra Leone lawyer who was as much at home in Britain as he was in Africa.[15]

Those Black children who were born in Britain, like Mabel Mercer and those showgirls of Denmark, have had an obscure childhood. Some details have been recovered, notably on Olive Harleston who was born in Wigan on 10 November 1906.

Remaining in that mill and mining Lancashire town until she had completed her basic education in 1920, Olive Harleston then went to New York to join her parents. Her father was Daniel Joseph Jenkins, a Baptist minister and leading Black citizen of Charleston, South Carolina. Her mother, Eloise Harleston, had been his secretary and became his second wife. The father had founded an orphanage in 1891, and in 1895 had brought a band of children to London to gather donations. In 1906 he, his future wife, and another Afro-American woman were in Britain. Olive was entrusted to midwife Alice Layland and the adults returned to the United States where the orphanage had been managed by Paul Gabasie Daniels, who had been educated at Colwyn Bay until mid-1899.[16]

Miss Layland rejected the Native American name suggested by the baby's mother, and registered the birth without naming a father. The baby grew up at 20, Lower St Stephens Street. When she made a visit to England in 1983 Olive retained traces of a Lancashire accent. She recalled her 'aunt' Alice Layland out and about day and night, how she had made a dress that she had proudly worn aged four, and her attendance at the local church school. Piano lessons, visits to relatives in Plumstead (south east London) and in Lancashire, and eating fish and chips were remembered. She had no recollection of seeing any other Black person until she was taken by Miss Layland to New York and handed over to the now Mrs Jenkins in 1920.

She remembered being called 'Blackie' by a boy who was scolded by the teacher. Her school friends, in 1983, recalled that she had pulled faces at someone who had teased her because she was Black. Olive said that her Wigan school was superior to the segregated school she first attended in the United States, but had no memory of the face pulling incident. Olive Harleston was planning a second reunion with the survivors of All Saints' School, Wigan, when she was killed by a car in New York in August 1987.[17]

A second girl, identified through the chance survival of a photograph, is known in far less detail. The photographic postcard was mailed in Croydon on 15 October 1906 to a Revd A. G. Edwards of Elmwood Road, in that Surrey town. It showed some two dozen children, eight young women, and some severe adults of the St Jude's Home for Girls in nearby Selhurst. The home was absorbed by the Church of England's Children's Society at that time, and their *Waifs and Strays* (November 1906) published the photograph: with three people removed. The three were wearing dark uniforms, and appeared to be teenage workers at the home. One is obviously of African descent. Who was she?

The Children's Society advised that their files stated that the youngest salaried employee at that orphanage was thirty-six, so the Black girl was an inmate.[18] The laws on education then required all in England to remain at school until they were thirteen; and the Selhurst home kept the youths for a further two years. During that time they looked after the infants and smaller children, and were taught cooking and sewing, all part of a preparation for a life in domestic service. Known as House Girls, they were permitted to work in local homes for several hours a day. By the time they reached fifteen they had a broad experience and, it was hoped, sufficient skills to fend for themselves. The Black girl, born around 1895, was just one of some forty inmates of the right age in 1906. The society's records are quite rightly confidential and so details of the origins, parentage, and future of the inmates are not available.

Two children and their Black mother were living in Surrey at this time. The African who said he was the son of 'a chief in Zanzibar' had married in Croydon in 1870. Known as John Springfield, he had been an itinerant Christian preacher when he met his wife Eliza. From 1880 his name is to be found in the street directories of Guildford, where he made and repaired shoes. He died in February 1891. His daughter Miriam, 'a coffee-coloured beauty', who had been 'abused because of her colour', married a tailor named William Twort and had two children.

Zilah Twort, born in 1898, recalled in 1985 that she and her brother were 'not hurt by our colour. We fought it out if anybody said anything to us.' She lived in Dorking and Reigate, was reunited with her father in 1951, and by the time she was interviewed by Jeremy Seabrook in 1980, was a grandmother. She had been in domestic service. Her mother had died in the 1910s, an isolated and proud Black Edwardian whose only moment of happiness was 'when the minstrels used to come to the town'.[19]

The following year a small African boy travelled to Scotland with the Dundee millhand-turned-missionary Mary Slessor. Aged six, and (re)named Dan McArthur Slessor, the Nigerian was 'a help to fetch and carry' as her best-selling biography was to state.[20] The boy returned clad in 'English clothes' with a toy watch and train.[21] Mary Slessor was commemorated in the parish church of High Wycombe in 1933, one of seventeen women who had made a mark in history. An African child is at her feet. As we have seen with Gambia and her companions in semi-slavery with the Willoughby Osbornes in nearby St Albans, there was no official challenge to the removing of Black children from Africa.

Such young individuals seem to have left little documentation other than their presence in school photographs, as with the children of John and Caroline Barbour-James in Acton. But information on children has been reclaimed.

On 28 May 1907 Reginald Foresythe was born in Hetley Road, west London.[22] His father, Charles Albert Foresythe, was a lawyer of Sierra Leone origin, and his mother was Charlotte Annie née Falk. Their son had a decent education, studied music, became an innovator in orchestral music by the 1930s, and then served in the Royal Air Force. But for his fame in the world of entertainment we would probably know nothing of him.

The obituary of another Black musician, Ray Ellington, stated that he was born in south London in 1916, his father being an 'American negro' and his mother a White Russian, and that he had originally studied to be a cabinet maker.[23] A study of bandleaders published in 1950 said he had two sisters and one brother, and was the youngest.[24] But for their baby brother's fame in later life we would have no knowledge of these Black children of the 1910s.

Another child whose adult fame has drawn attention to her origins was Ida Shepley, who sang on the radio in the 1940s, and has an entry in *Radio and Television Who's Who of 1950–1951*.[25] Born Ida Mary

Humphrey in Nantwich, Cheshire, in December 1908, her father was a West African herbalist and her mother from Canada.

The rather unlikely figure of the Foreign Minister of China in 1927 was the father of a Black family educated in Edwardian Britain. Eugene Chen, who spoke no Chinese, was born in Trinidad and had married Alphonsine Agatha Gantaume, who had African features and a French West Indies birth. From 1906 Chen, a lawyer, took his holidays in Britain, settling in Earls Court (London) in 1908. His son Percy went to school in Bath.

The Chens returned to Trinidad but in 1911, following the revolution in China, Eugene Chen went to China from where he cabled his wife to take their children to London. As Percy Chen was to recall,[26] they first lived in Paddington, and then settled at 11, Clifton Hill. Percy Chen went to Loudon House School where he was named 'Inky' because of his complexion. 'There were not many colored people in London' he wrote. He studied for a scholarship to one of London's prestigious secondary schools whilst at Collet Court School, winning one to University College School in Hampstead. He left Collet Court in a blaze of glory after several prizes fell to him at their sports day in June 1914.

His father had returned from China in 1913, and his mother studied drama and dancing in London; daughter Sylvia went to the same dancing school. Their house rang with music, for an adopted aunt, Germaine Julien from Barbados, played the piano. Jack Chen was to take up law also, whilst Yolanda became a teacher in Trinidad. Sylvia Chen was in China and the Soviet Union in the 1930s, settling in New York. Percy Chen and his father spent the 1930s in China, and in 1982 was living in Hong Kong when he told the author that his father, knowing of the consequences for China of the poorly armed Boxer uprising against White imperialists, argued for a struggle that would defeat imperialism but not a military fight when the Chinese would be certain of defeat by superior weaponry.

There were other Trinidadian children in London when Percy Chen was at school, whose memoirs recall the 'Isles' whose funding came from their father's taxi and motor business in Port of Spain. The oldest boy was studying for the Bar and the second, perhaps Bruce Iles, was Percy Chen's junior at University College School. 'His sisters [Rita and Vera] were pretty brown-skinned girls who were studying the piano'.

Chen recalled 'as a boy in Trinidad I was supposed to be one of the governed, not one of the governors'; his British schooling had inculcated respect for the letter of the law and for the impartiality of justice. In 1982 he said that London had been 'a happy place' and that his mother had been 'bringing up a brood of talented children' in London in the 1910s.[27]

Yet another Trinidadian youth in Edwardian London was Hubert Julian, whose autobiography[28] states that he was born in 1897 and first arrived in England 'in the care of one of the family servants'[29] in 1912. His father owned a shoe factory and planted cocoa, and wanted his son to study medicine in Britain. Julian became fascinated by aeroplanes, and from his London lodgings at 46, Museum Street, went to air displays where 'the gangly young darkie was a familiar sight to all the pilots and staff'.[30] Julian sailed to Canada in late 1914 where 'as in England, I met none of that racial prejudice which so mars my adopted country, America'.[31]

A slightly younger schoolboy in London at that time was Randall Lockhart, who was from Dominica but whose education in Martinique made him bi-lingual.[32] He attended school in south London's Clapham and later returned to Britain where he was called to the Bar in 1922. There is an intriguing possible connection to two Black undergraduates at Oxford, the Zulu Pixley Seme and his American friend Alain Locke, who visited Clapham School for Boys at 71, High Street, Clapham, on 19 October 1908.[33] We will detail the undergraduates later.

Arnold Sheppard was born in South Wales in 1908. His boxing career (when he was known as Kid Sheppard) involved nearly three hundred fights, usually as a welterweight, between 1926 and 1939. He became blind, and died in Claybury Hospital for mental cases.[34]

Alamu Ojo Olaribigbe was a Gambian medical student in Edwardian Britain. He qualified LRCP, LRCS at Edinburgh and LRPS, Glasgow in 1915. He had a medical practice in London into the 1920s according to the *Medical Register*. By the time he became the first African doctor (in the European tradition) in Ibadan, Nigeria, in 1925, he had been in Britain for twenty years.[35]

Another Scotland-trained doctor was Hopetoun Edward Bond, who qualified in 1910. He returned to Jamaica where he worked at the mental asylum in Kingston, publishing an article on pellagra (vitamin deficiency leading to insanity) in the *Journal of Tropical Medicine*.[36] By the 1930s he was working in north London, having resigned himself to being constantly refused promotion at the asylum.[37]

Moses Da Rocha, a Nigerian, studied medicine at Edinburgh from 1902 to 1911. Writing to ex-slave journalist John Bruce in New York he complained of 'various troubles with beastly landladies . . . and vulgar Europeanized Negroes'.[38] Scotland trained H. R. Bankole Bright, whose 1906 correspondence with Keir Hardie, the leading socialist member of parliament, led to questions on imperialism in Africa being raised in the House of Commons.[39]

Francis 'Frans' Dove had studied at Lincoln's Inn from 1886 to 1891, and returned to Sierra Leone where he practised law before moving to

Accra in 1897. In London in December 1896 he married Augusta Winchester of Tooting, and their address was still 23, Upper Baker Street, London, when their son Francis Thomas 'Frank' Dove was born in September 1897. He was to study law at Oxford after medal-winning bravery in the British tank corps in France in 1917. His sister Evelyn, born in London in January 1902, studied music in London, and in the 1920s worked with Mrs Boucher's son and daughter in shows on the continent. The African father of this Black Edwardian family died, aged eighty, in London a few days after greeting King George the Sixth at the Colonial Month in 1949.[40]

Wendell Bruce-James, born in Antigua in 1891, was brought up in British Guiana and went to Keble College, Oxford from 1910 to 1912 when he took a third in Classical Moderations. He served in the University and Public Schools corps of the Royal Fusiliers in the war of 1914–18, surviving to be active as a pianist in Britain into the 1930s.[41]

The Goffe family of Jamaica included Dr Ernest Goffe, born in 1867, who worked at the North Eastern Fever Hospital in Tottenham in 1907. His son Alan was a student at University College Hospital in London.[42] The *Who's Who of Jamaica* (1940) has other Goffes, including the doctor's brother John Vincent Goffe, born 1896, who was educated in England. The family's income came from shipping. A Mrs Goffe arrived at Avonmouth on the *Port Henderson* on 1 July 1908 and a Mr Goffe on the *Port Royal* on 8 October 1908.[43]

The Manley family of Jamaica had their children educated in Britain despite the deaths of the parents by 1909. Vera Manley had won a scholarship and was studying music in London where her success was praised by the Prince of Wales (the future King George the Fifth) in the summer of 1909.[44] 'Unmistakably coloured' Vera Manley was joined by her siblings Roy and Muriel by 1912, and they attended West Cornwall College.[45] Muriel Manley later attended medical school in London and Roy went to Felstead public school. In the early autumn of 1914 they were joined by brother Norman, who had won a Rhodes Scholarship to Oxford.[46] In 1915 the brothers enlisted in the army, in the field artillery made up of east Londoners who called them 'Darkie' until they were made aware it was disliked. Roy was killed serving in Belgium.[47] Norman went to Jesus College, Oxford, qualified as a lawyer in London, and returned to the Caribbean where he was one of the architects of independent Jamaica.[48] Vera Manley returned to Jamaica where she married the London-educated Dr Ludlow Moody and busied herself in concert music.[49] Muriel Manley qualified as a doctor and continued to live in London into the 1930s.[50]

The fruit shipping business of the Manleys and of the Goffes had paid for education in Jamaica and England; and the Union drugstore in West Parade, Kingston, of Charles Ernest Moody financed his sons to an English professional education as we will see.[51] Scholarships could only assist those whose families had been able to pay school fees, but less fortunate Blacks did have opportunities for training in Edwardian Britain. The *Port Antonio* which carried the Jamaican choir into Bristol in early 1906 also had thirty-eight British soldiers and '2 boys WIR' on the passenger list. Neither was over fifteen. Probably West India Regiment musicians, they would have been destined for tuition at the British Army's school of music, Kneller Hall, in Twickenham in west London.

The colonial officials in London recorded the information that came their way on the activities of Black students in Edwardian Britain: and not always when there had been expressions of anti-imperial views. One example is C. E. Reindorf, a medical graduate at Durham, whose alleged sexual behaviour was noted in 1912.[52] Reindorf and his cousin Frederick Victor Nanka-Bruce visited the Colonial Office together in November 1907.[53] Nanka-Bruce, born in Accra in 1878, had studied medicine in Scotland from 1901 and qualified MB, BCh in 1907. Reindorf had joined him at Edinburgh.[54] Following his studies in Durham Reindorf worked at the Royal Infirmary, and in 1914 married Emma Evans and returned to Africa.[55]

When Nanka-Bruce returned to Africa he was the third African doctor in the Gold Coast. Benjamin Quartey-Papafio, born in Accra in 1859, had studied in Durham, London and Edinburgh, became a doctor in the colonial service in 1888. He retired in 1905. In 1911 he was a member of a protesting delegation to London over the Forest Bill. His son and five daughters were educated in Britain: Mercy, Ruby and Grace become teachers in the Gold Coast.[56] The other African doctor in the Gold Coast in 1907 was Ernest James Hayford, who had studied at St Thomas's in London where he qualified as a surgeon and in Dublin where he studied gynaecology. He later took a degree in Brussels. Dr Hayford moved to Edwardian London where he studied law in the 1910s, qualifying as a barrister in June 1913. He died, in London, on 6 August that year.[57]

One student whose activities greatly interested the Colonial Office was Bandele Omoniyi. Born in Lagos in 1884, his parents sold land to finance his studies in Edwardian Britain. He started reading law at Edinburgh University in 1906, then turned to anti-imperial journalism in socialist, Scottish and Nigerian publications. He wrote *A Defence of the Ethiopian Movement*, published in 1908. He died, aged twenty-eight, in Brazil in 1912.[58]

Another African student in Edwardian Britain was Isaac Pixley Seme from southern Africa. Born in 1881, Seme joined his cousin John L. Dube in New York in 1898. Seme was aided by missionaries and evangelicals who enabled him to attend college in Massachusetts until

1902 when he started at Columbia University in New York. He graduated in 1906 and went to England where he enrolled at Jesus College, Oxford. He gained his BCL in June 1909 and moved to London where he studied and, in 1910, was called to the Bar; he then left for the Africa he had quit when a herdboy.[59]

One of his Oxford contacts was A. E. Maxwell Gibson, the son of an African solicitor in the Gambia. Gibson had read law at Wadham College from 1894 to 1897 and then had been active in Nigeria and the Gold Coast. He married in Lagos, and contributed to the *Sierra Leone Times* and the *Journal of the African Society*.[60] He was back in Oxford in 1908–9 preparing for the largely ceremonial award of BCL and an MA. Gibson had been a pupil of F. E. Smith, the brilliant maverick politician who later became Lord Birkenhead. Smith is supposed to have saved Gibson from death by drowning.[61]

Gibson was recalled by a contemporary as one of 'about a dozen coloured undergraduates' at Oxford, most of whom studied at Balliol. 'He read Law and learned the piano. He contemplated practising at the Bar [in England] and giving piano lessons to augment his income.' This recollection noted that there was a strong evangelical Christian urge to undertake foreign missionary work but it had not struck any of these students that individuals like Gibson 'here among us were the products of foreign Missions'.[62]

Some thirty letters from Seme have been preserved in the papers of yet another Black Edwardian student at Oxford.[63] Alain Leroy Locke, a Harvard graduate from Philadelphia, was awarded a Rhodes Scholarship, duly mentioned in the British press in early 1907. Seme saw this and wrote to Locke to congratulate him 'for what you have done for our race by taking so high a rank among American scholars'.[64]

Assured by Seme that 'others of your race who have carried first class honours' would be at Oxford, along with 'the best blood of India, Japan and of the world', Locke prepared for years of study in England. Seme warned him that 'Rhodes Scholars are simply a drop in the ocean here. They have no influence whatever.'[65] From Brussels, at the end of August 1907, Seme recommended that Locke visited 'the great Negro author' Theophilus Scholes when he passed through London. 'Simply introduce yourself properly to him and tell him that I asked you to go to him. He already knows about you.'[66] This letter, along with one dated 28 October 1907 from Dr Scholes at 11, Mornington Crescent, London, thanking Locke for visiting him in London and for Seme's suggestion, reveals that an informal network existed and that apparently dissimilar individuals met. Seme, the herdboy-turned-lawyer; Locke, the aesthete scholar; and the Jamaican doctor-turned-author shared African descent and a deep interest in the development of African peoples at home and abroad.

Arriving at Plymouth on 30 September Locke had travelled by train to London, where he spent ten days in October 1907 before beginning his Oxford years at Hertford College. Many of his letters and telegrams to his mother have survived. Of London he wrote 'I never saw such a city – enormous, and the crowds of people and vehicles far outdoes New York.'[67]

Fellow Americans spurned Locke at Oxford, but his colour led to Britons expecting him to be informed on the 'colour question' as he wrote to his mother – he had a role as a 'self ordained authority' on US racism. 'Everyone who meets me wants to know about the Negro problem.'

He admired the refinement of Asian students. He went to the theatre. 'Every afternoon except Sunday rain or shine I am out with my crew' on the river. The scholarships bequeathed by Cecil Rhodes required both athletic and academic skills, and Locke – a slight man[68] – was no athlete. His letter, postmarked December 1907, also informed his mother that he had coxed successfully and had won his cap (representing the university at sport) which 'gives the black eye to those people who said I did not qualify athletically for the Rhodes scholarship'.

He went to London, the Scilly Isles and Jersey before crossing to Dieppe to spend Christmas 1907 in France. His letters to his mother also reveal that he took piano lessons and duetted with 'a most lovable Englishman (a sort of contradiction in terms)' who played the clarinet. Locke joined the French Club where conversation was only in that language, and the Cosmopolitan Club: by May 1908 he was its secretary; Seme was the treasurer. The first issue of *The Oxford Cosmopolitan* was published that month.

Locke informed his mother that he had entertained at twenty-five lunches, and had been entertained at twelve, which left just five on his own in his first term at Hertford. He found his musical feet, according to a letter postmarked Oxford 24 January 1908. He had purchased some music by Edward McDowell (whose 'To a Wild Rose' remains in print nearly a century later) and of the London-born composer Samuel Coleridge-Taylor who was 'very popular in England it seems – I shall get round to seeing him bye and bye'. Coleridge-Taylor was the London-born son of a Sierra Leone-born African doctor, and this composer's African descent was quite visible. Coleridge-Taylor had already made two trips to the United States, and there could be few Blacks in Edwardian Britain who did not know of this composer and his *The Song of Hiawatha*. We shall return to him in detail later.

Seme 'is blossoming out in African exuberance into everything', Locke told his mother at the end of October 1908. The two students

11 Mornington Crescent
London N.W.
Oct. 28' 1907

Dear Mr Locke

I am obliged
to you for your letter which I
received about a week or so ago.
I am gratified to have heard
of your successful education
at Oxford, & of the cordial
reception which you from you
have had received.
I wish that your academic
career should be proper to
prosperous.
It was very agreeable to me
to have had your company
on the Sunday that you
were here, & for this I am

grateful to Mrs Verna, who
suggested to me that you
should be invited, & also
& twisted & you & the
invitation.

Yours very sincerely
Theo Elmund Wolla

30. Theophilus Scholes, a Jamaican doctor who had worked in Africa, lived in Edwardian London and wrote several books. The African Pixley Seme suggested that Locke, an American, contacted the Jamaican. This is one of just two letters showing that contact (Moorland-Spingarn Research Center)

went riding, took French lessons, and talked – 'Seme is here often, almost every day'.

A month later Locke wrote:

> Seme and I and a Gold Coast Negro by the name of Gibson who returned to Oxford to take his MA and BCL (think of that you Afro-Americans!) went to a wonderful performance of Coleridge-Taylor's Hiawatha – I had never heard it before – it stunned me. . . . I shall not stop long in London next time but I must look him up. Strange too that he is of African extraction.[69]

Locke's programme is annotated 'Heard with Seme and Gibson'.

These Black associations, which must have been rich and may have taken up considerable time, are known to us because of Locke's letters. What took place that was not conveyed to his mother? In Seme's case, his letters to Locke reveal the fun and problems for one African student in Edwardian Britain.

Seme is thought to have had no financial support from home, due to cattle disease; and, unlike America, he was unable to find work during the lengthy vacations. He contacted liberal White South Africans, but the lack of certainty over money must have been painful.[70] Locke, after all, had the Rhodes grants.

Seme moved to lodgings in London where he started to meet the requirements to be admitted to the Bar. He attended parliamentary debates in March 1908, sent several joking letters to Locke about his creditors, moved through various accommodations (24, South Park Gardens in Hampstead; 149, Ledbury Road in Bayswater; and 24, Charlotte Street in central London), and then in Fitzroy Square with other South Africans including Alfred Mangena who was called to the Bar at Lincoln's Inn in 1909.[71] Mangena, who had been living in London at 2, Rochester Square (a short walk from Mornington Crescent) in the autumn of 1903 when his name was listed as a member in the *Journal of the African Society*, had been involved in English legal work for Africans since 1907. After Seme also became a barrister on 8 June 1909 the two African lawyers represented their kin who were protesting against the South Africa Bill in Britain.[72]

Seme expressed his opinions on the need for the African people of South Africa to unite in the face of European settler oppression. He had admired the representatives of Black America he had seen in New York, and probably from contacts with Scholes, Gibson, Locke, and others during his Oxford years, he saw that unity among people of African birth and descent was both desirable and possible.

Certainly Seme and Locke founded the African Unity Society when at Oxford. The constitution states it was 'open to all men of African or Negro extraction who are interested in the general welfare of the Race

31. The first Black Rhodes Scholar Alain Locke went riding with Seme in the lanes around Oxford in 1908. Locke was in England for three years before returning to the United States (Moorland-Spingarn Research Center)

both in Africa and in other parts of the world'.[73] Seme had written to the leading Black American in April 1908 that 'I am trying to urge the African students here in England to form a club or society for the interchange of ideas' for in Britain (or did Seme mean Oxford?) 'are to be found the future leaders of African nations temporarily thrown together and yet coming from widely different sections of that great and unhappy continent'. On returning to Africa, fired by the contacts that Seme was largely imagining at this time, they could influence public opinion and help regenerate Africa.[74]

Seme received some encouragement from the American, who was the educator Booker T. Washington. Washington's 1901 auto-biography *Up From Slavery* had been a widely published work, translated into many European languages (and Braille) in the next few

32. Pixley Seme, a Zulu herdboy educated in New York, studied law at Oxford from 1907. He had links with many Black people in Britain (Moorland-Spingarn Research Center)

years.[75] Washington had been in England in 1899, and returned in 1910 when he met Seme in London as we will see. *Up From Slavery* was in the hand baggage of the bogus Prince Makaroo when he arrived in Grimsby, and it is inconceivable that Seme and Locke had not read it.

Seme had contacts with the Berlin-educated sociologist W. E. B. Du Bois, who was teaching in Atlanta. Du Bois, who was to take over Washington's role as the leading American of African descent, replied in June 1908.[76]

No list of members of the African Union Society has been traced. Locke and Seme arrived in Oxford too late to have known James Hutton Mills (who died in 1906)[77], whose father was to investigate the near collapse of the postal service in the Gold Coast, but his brother Alexander was at Keble at this time.[78] Another student, thought to have been a Jamaican named John Thomas, was an undergraduate in April 1908.[79] A 'J. Williams' made reference to his membership of the society when writing to Locke from London in October 1909.[80] Maxwell Gibson would have been involved, of course. As Seme knew Dr Scholes within a few months of his arrival in England, we can be sure that he had contacts with other Blacks too.

Seme left England for Amsterdam where he studied Dutch, and then, without returning to England it seems, he went to Africa. He wrote to Locke from Johannesburg on 6 March 1911. Mangena had returned before him, and established the right for Africans to practise law in South Africa. Seme had been admitted into the Transvaal legal establishment in late 1910, and went into partnership with Mangena.[81] Seme issued the clarion call for unity and, after meetings in his offices, founded what became the African National Congress. It was just eighteen months after the Whites of South Africa had benefited from the formation of the Union of South Africa – the result of the legislation that Seme and Mangena had challenged when in England.

Locke's experiences with day-to-day Britons did not get much mention in his letters to his mother. His observations on fellow Americans were passed across the Atlantic, but he must have been unaware that those at Oxford looked on him slightly differently: one noted in his diary that 'Locke seems so much darker over here'.[82] Indeed, his Oxford years forced Locke to consider his position as a person of African descent. The opinions of Jeffrey Stewart are that Locke, knowing that his natal land would not welcome him back 'with applause and open arms' because he was Black, found out at Oxford that the British were also racist. The British were more subtle, avoiding US-style segregation, apparently welcoming the 'best and brightest of the colonial subjects' to Britain where they were 'indoctrinated with the imperial ideal, and sent back to their countries to carry out what were essentially British colonial policies'.[83] This interpretation is of Locke's Oxford experience, for Locke travelled widely in Europe and spent much time in London. Locke also missed his mother (his father had died when he was very young) and lacked Afro-American contacts in Britain. Of his contacts with students from Africa (including Egypt) and British India, Locke's growing friendship with Seme was the most important. Seme had lived in New York and so shared Locke's experience of being Black in the United States. He also had a positive attitude to Africa and Africans that inspired Locke, who left England without an Oxford degree in 1910. He wrote from the *Mauretania* in March 1910, to Booker T. Washington, that he was returning to get in touch with 'race affairs'. He had written to his mother that Oxford 'is a training-school for the governing classes – and has taught your son its lesson'. He joined the faculty of Howard

University, a Black institution in Washington, DC and became an intellectual whose comments on Afro-America, notably in *The New Negro* (1925), were admired.

A slightly earlier grouping of Black Edwardian students and friends is known to us because its constitution remains in the papers of W. E. B. Du Bois, whose *The Souls of Black Folk* had been published in 1903.[84] The Ethiopian Progressive Association had been formed in Liverpool on 19 November 1904. It planned to discuss 'matters of vital importance concerning Africa in particular, and the Negro race in general'. The thirteen founding members had been increased to nineteen by 6 March 1905 when the amended constitution was sent to Du Bois.

The five officers were I. A. Johnson from Freetown, Dr D. Hamilton and Jonathan Knight from Jamaica, Kwesi Ewusi from the Gold Coast, and secretary R. Betton whose origins are not stated. Their committee included S. N. Kinson from Fernando Po (a Spanish colony but with considerable British and West Indies associations from the 1840s), Dr H. B. Gabashane from South Africa, J. A. Abraham from the Gold Coast, and C. Bartels-Kodwo who lived in Cornwall and therefore may have been involved in the mining industry.

Associated with them were J. M. Whitfield from Sierra Leone, A. W. Neizer from the Gold Coast, J. A. Caulcrick from Nigeria and R. R. Miranda from Cuba. There were two ministers from Sierra Leone (J. P. Richards and E. D. L. Thompson) and four others from the Gold Coast: I. Minnow, the Revd T. E. Ward, K. S. E. Insadoo and James Hutton Mills (who was a student at Oxford as we have noted).

When the constitution was amended there were three new names that suggest southern Caribbean links: La Fontaine, C. De Sousa and Clarke. This association has been claimed as a student one, and there is a reference to 'West African and West Indian natives, students at the various colleges',[85] but the presence of three ordained ministers and two doctors strongly hints that the group included some mature members. A claim that it was short-lived[86] seems undeserved as it was formally founded in November 1904 and two of its officials (Ewusi and Johnson) were writing to Booker T. Washington for support on 14 February 1906.[87] The group also published *The Ethiopian Review*.[88]

It is certain that the number of Black students in Edwardian Britain is as unknown as the number of Blacks in other walks of life. Their studies included art, medicine, law, engineering, commerce, languages (notably Greek and Latin by undergraduate law students, but also French as with Seme and Locke) and various apprenticeships in practical subjects. Many who had come to the British Isles without contacts must have made connections of the sort that Seme made in 1907.

It is tempting to see students only as recipients, but Pixley Seme's contacts were of such value that veterans met through him. A letter to Locke, apparently dated 30 September 1907 (which was when Locke first put foot on English soil) and thus probably from 1909,[89] explained that Seme had been requested to introduce Dr William Awuner Renner to Dr T. E. S. Scholes in London. Scholes had published several books in London (as we will detail) whilst Renner, a Sierra Leonean who had medical qualifications from Liverpool, London and Brussels, had headed the Sierra Leone Medical Department in 1902, and was still serving in the colony's medical service.[90] Dr Renner was no stranger to Edwardian Britain. But he needed the South African student to make the connection to Scholes.

Seme's letter is amusing. Scholes was to meet them at the 'mighty columns of the British Museum' and then they went to the Trocadero restaurant for lunch. The two veteran doctors 'tucked in', having brought 'mighty appetites with them', ignorant of the fact that Seme only had a borrowed 7s 6d (£0.37) in his pocket. With a 'chill down my back' he escaped to the toilet and gave the waiter sixpence, instructing him to present the bill to Dr Renner. 'Locke you have heard of English Bull-dogs and their determination – This is nothing compared to the tenacity of an English waiter once he gets an idea into his unfrequented brain.' 'Dr Scholes could scarcely move' because of the quantity of food he had eaten.

An American youngster who was briefly in England in 1912 was Norris Herndon, whose father had started life in slavery in Georgia in 1858. Without formal education, Alonzo Herndon had moved from peasant farming to hairdressing, eventually owning three barbershops in Atlanta. He invested in property, and in 1905 merged several benefit or insurance enterprises to form what became the Atlanta Life Insurance Corporation and the largest Black-owned insurance company in America.

He and his wife had moved to a new home in Atlanta when she died. Remarried to Jessie Gillespie, he took his new wife and Norris to Europe for three months in 1912. The last eight days were spent in England, and young Norris Herndon's diary reveals they left Calais on 15 August, travelled by train to London where they saw Piccadilly, parliament and the abbey at Westminster, Buckingham Palace and the museums. They ate in various restaurants including Slater's and Lipton's. On 23 August they reached Liverpool, rested at the Lime Street Station Hotel, and boarded the *Campania* for home.[91] They had probably seen more of the world than most Georgians. Norris Herndon travelled widely as an adult after his education at Atlanta and Harvard, served the insurance company through the years, and died in 1977.

Alfred Adderley was from the Bahamas. He studied law at

St Catharine's, Cambridge, from 1912 and became a barrister. His son followed him there, and there is an Adderley Prize which celebrates their presence. Another Black Cambridge undergraduate was Thomas Hutton Mills, junior. He was also at St Catharine's and may have been the individual Adderley mentioned in a speech in London in 1918, when he said:

> I have been some time in this country; and I have mixed with different classes. For the first time I have had the opportunity of mixing with Africans, my own brothers. I can tell you they have left an abiding impression upon my mind. When I went to Cambridge in 1912 there was not a single son of Africa there. I was sorry. But when the first one came I was the first to go and grip his hand, and say, 'While you are here, you are with me.'[92]

Cambridge had not been welcoming in 1910, members of the African Society were told in April 1913 at a 'Conference with Africans'. Harry Johnston reported that 'one or two negroes, received rather unkind treatment, discourteous treatment' at the university around 1910.[93] This London meeting had discussed how to improve the lot of African students in Britain, who, 'with no one to take any interest in them', would 'get into bad ways and fall into bad society, and get bad companions'.

The actor-turned-journalist Duse Mohamed reported on the meeting in his *African Times and Orient Review*. He remarked that 'he thought it wise that every encouragement should be given to the African visiting England for education'. A. B. C. Merriman Labor, a Sierra Leonean author and journalist who will be detailed later, commented that he had the 'hope that those present at that meeting would not go away with the idea that the generality of Africans held the opinion that London was not the proper place for the education of Africans'.[95]

James Carmichael Smith, the retired postmaster of Freetown, said that Africans 'spoke of going to England as going home'.[96] Another New World Black who was to spend years in West Africa, C. E. M. Abbensetts, commented 'It was very painful to many men of colour when they took a voyage to be placed in one part of the vessel while the white men occupied another part.'[97]

The meeting agreed that a committee, which would include four Africans, was to investigate the possibilities of establishing a hostel in London.[98]

These students shared only their African origin or descent with William Johnson, a working man whose British-born children had a minimal education and lived in a world that was literally a class apart.

William Benker Johnson was a Sierra Leonean who worked for the

Elder Dempster shipping company at sea and at their Liverpool works. When he married Margaret Maher in Chorlton, south Manchester, in 1902 he gave his occupation as 'mechanical engineer'.[99] Their son Leonard Benker Johnson was born in October 1902 in Barnabas Street, in east Manchester's Clayton. Albert was born in July 1904, Billy in October 1905, and a sister named Dora completed the family. They had moved to Leeds where their African father lived when he was not touring in a boxing booth show. In 1912 he worked as a waiter at the Prince Albert Hotel in Hunslet, Leeds; and his sons went to elementary schools. They were to follow their father into boxing, with Len becoming a famous middleweight: touring to Australia with his father, and to the USA. He was not allowed to fight for British titles because of his colour. In the 1930s he ran a touring boxing booth with his brothers and employed other British Blacks, including 'Darkie' Ellis from Bridlington. He died in Oldham in 1974: when Adderley's son, a post-war law graduate at Cambridge, was practising in Nassau.[100]

NOTES

1. E. Turner, *Boys Will Be Boys* (London: Michael Joseph, 1948), pp. 108–9, 178. Their tales were 'unending' and 'interminable'.
2. I am indebted to Morten Clausen for this fascinating information which needs to be followed up in British birth registrations and street directories.
3. Don Johnson, born Cardiff in 1913, recalled Annie Thomas. Stephen Bourne interviewed Miss Wood in 1997, who recalled how Belle Davis had recruited in London's East End for Black dancers and employed her and her brother.
4. University of North Wales, Bangor, for the Institute's *annual reports*. Others are at the National Library of Wales. I am indebted to Ivor Wynne Jones and Hazel King for details: 87 studied at Colwyn Bay between 1889 and 1912.
5. King, 'Agbebi', pp. 99, 104; information from Hazel King.
6. C. Fyfe, *Africanus Horton 1835–1883, West African Scientist and Patriot* (New York: Oxford University Press, 1972).
7. Ibid. pp. 152–3.
8. Ibid. p. 153. There are direct descendants in England in the 1990s.
9. H. Rye, 'The Southern Syncopated Orchestra, part 2', *Storyville* (Chigwell, Essex) 143 (September 1990), p. 174.
10. W. Livingstone, 'Mabel Mercer', *Stero Review*, February 1975, pp. 60–65.
11. R. Wild, 'She Never Looked Back', *Park East* (March 1953), pp. 16–21; J. Haskins, *Mabel Mercer: A Life* (New York: Atheneum, 1987), pp. 10–15.
12. *New York Times*, 12 June 1984.
13. Livingstone, 'Mercer'; Josephine Harreld Love to Jeffrey Green, 30 January 1987.
14. *The Times* (London), 23 April 1984, obituary.
15. A. Cromwell *An African Victorian Feminist: The Life and Times of Adelaide Smith Casely Hayford 1868–1960* (London: Cass, 1986).
16. *African Times* (London) 5 June 1899, p. 87; Green, *Edmund Thornton Jenkins*, pp. 12–17, 21, 23; J. Green '"Beef Pie with a Suet Crust": A Black Childhood in Wigan (1906–1920)' *New Community* (London) 11, 3 (Spring 1984), pp. 291–8.

17. John Chilton, jazz historian, spoke with her in New York in the late 1970s. From information supplied by her the present writer sought out Wigan veterans. This process involved writing to every Layland and Leyland in the local telephone directories, and to the parish church with a request to place a notice on their church hall board or in the parish magazine. The minister expressed his surprise to helpers in the church. One had been in Olive's class – the link had been made.

18. I am indebted to Christopher Jackson of the Childrens' Society, London.

19. J. Seabrook, 'The Story of Jumbaloowalee', *New Society* (London) 19 June 1980, pp. 301–2 courtesy Christopher Fyfe; *Surrey Advertiser* (Guildford) 25 January 1985, p. 1; Anne Johns of Surrey Local Studies Library, letter 10 April 1992.

20. W. Livingstone, *Mary Slessor of Calabar: Pioneer Missionary* (London: Hodder & Stoughton, 1917), p. 239.

21. Ibid. p. 245.

22. My thanks to Howard Rye; *African World* 7 June 1913, p. 277 names Mrs C A Foresythe, Master Foresythe and baby on the *Akabar* which left Liverpool for Lagos on 4 June 1913.

23. *The Times* (London) 2 March 1985.

24. J. Vedet, *Band Leaders* (London: Rockliff, 1950), p. 176.

25. My thanks to Stephen Bourne.

26. P. Chen, *China Called Me: My Life Inside the Chinese Revolution* (Boston: Little, Brown, 1979), pp. 9, 11–17.

27. Telephone conversation with Percy Chen, Hong Kong, 1982; interview with Marjorie Leekam (widow of a Trinidad-born doctor), Sussex, 1982.

28. H. Julian, *Black Eagle* (London: Jarrolds, 1964).

29. Ibid. p. 28.

30. Ibid. p. 29.

31. Ibid. p. 30.

32. Information from Randall Lockhart. Lockhart was recalled as a 'young man from Martinique' who enthused over Karl Marx; see Chen, *China Called Me*, p. 16.

33. Seme correspondence, Locke Papers. The motive for their visit has not been determined.

34. I am indebted to Afro-Welsh entertainer and one-time boxer Don Johnson for these details.

35. *West Africa* (London) 24 October 1925, p. 1404; ibid. 5 December 1925, p. 1635.

36. *Medical Register*, 1915.

37. Leslie Brown, London-born son of Jamaica-born Dr J. J. Brown, recalled Dr Bond and his complaints that newly-qualified British doctors were put in charge despite their lack of experience of insanity and of Jamaica. The Jamaica indexes to the files of the Colonial Office reveal Bond's name through the 1910s and 1920s, supporting Brown's information.

38. John Edward Bruce Papers, Schomburg Library, New York.

39. H. Adi, 'West African Students in Britain, 1900–60' in David Killingray (ed.), *Africans in Britain* (London: Cass, 1994), pp. 108–9.

40. Information from Stephen Bourne, including copies of 1896 marriage and 1897 birth registrations, and obituaries from the *Daily Echo* (Accra) 25 August 1949 and *African Morning Post* (Accra) 7 September 1949.

41. Rye, 'The Southern Syncopated Orchestra, part 2', *Storyville* (Chigwell, Essex) 143 (September 1990), p. 173.

42. N. File and C. Power *Black Settlers in Britain 1555–1958* (London: Heinemann, 1981).

43. PRO BT 26/311.

44. *West India Committee Circular* (London) 15 September 1909, p. 436; W. Brown, *Edna Manley: The Private Years 1900–1938* (London: Deutsch, 1975), p. 37.

45. Brown, *Manley*, pp. 37–9.
46. Ibid. pp. 41–3, 63–4.
47. Ibid. pp. 63–8.
48. P. Sherlock, *Norman Manley: A Biography* (London: Macmillan, 1980), pp. 60–63.
49. Brown, *Manley*, p. 147; information from Leslie Thompson, professional musician in Jamaica in the 1920s before he migrated to England in 1929.
50. Ibid. p. 230.
51. D. Vaughan, *Negro Victory* (London: Independent Press, 1950), pp. 39–41; Leslie Thompson, *Leslie Thompson: An Autobiography* (Crawley, Sussex: Rabbit Press, 1985), pp. 4, 64–5. The Moody children became doctors and a dentist-turned-sculptor, and just one returned to Jamaica.
52. David Killingray's introduction to Killingray (ed.), *Africans in Britain*, p. 9.
53. PRO CO 96/492/13624.
54. M. Sampson, *Gold Coast Men of Affairs* (London, 1937; repr. London: Dawsons, 1969), pp. 178–80.
55. Ibid. p. 179.
56. Ibid. pp. 203–4.
57. Ibid. pp. 155–9.
58. H. Adi, 'Bandele Omoniyi: A Neglected Nigerian Socialist Nationalist', typescript 1990, courtesy David Killingray.
59. R. Rive and T. Couzens, *Seme: The Founder of the ANC* (Trenton, NJ: Africa World Press, 1993), pp. 13–22. My thanks to Bernth Lindfors for supplying a copy of this book, first published in South Africa in 1991, and a useful review by C. Saunders in *South African Historical Journal*, 25 (1991), pp. 196–217.
60. *Sierra Leone Weekly News* (Freetown), 20 July 1901; ibid. 27 July 1927; *Sierra Leone Times* (Freetown) 13 February 1904; ibid. 20 February 1904. My thanks to Christopher Fyfe.
61. An Oxford MA converts a BA after four years and the payment of a nominal fee. Wadham College files note Gibson's return for this ceremony in October 1908. I am indebted to Clifford Davies, Keeper of the Archives at Wadham College, for clarification and for sight of Gibson's obituary in the *Wadham College Gazette for 1927*, pp. 313, 329: 'who came to us from West Africa 30 years ago, and did his best to take part in all College activities. He was a loyal member of the College to the last, and maintained Wadham's legal reputation at the West African Bar. It was not for nothing that he had been a pupil of Lord Birkenhead, who not only instructed him in Law, but also saved him from drowning.'
62. T. W. L. Casperz typescript memoir, p. 15, Wadham College Muniments 11/10B.
63. Locke papers at Howard University, Washington DC.
64. Locke Papers, Howard University; Seme to Locke, 4 March 1907. C. Saunders, 'Pixley Seme: Towards a Biography' *South African Historical Journal* 25 (1991), pp. 202–6 uses the letters. Jeffrey Stewart, Locke's biographer, aware of Saunders's article, devotes less than one page to Seme in his 'A Black Aesthete at Oxford', *The Massachusetts Review*, pp. 411–28.
65. Seme to Locke 21 July 1907.
66. Ibid. 28 August 1907. John Bruce of New York had written about Scholes in *The Voice of the Negro* 4, 7 (March 1907), pp. 114–5, but this was published after Seme left the USA.
67. Locke Papers, Howard University. I am indebted to Esme Bhan for her assistance and advice, and for her introduction to Jeffrey Stewart.
68. Locke's passports show him to have been officially 5ft 2in in 1918 and 5ft 4in in 1926.
69. Locke to Mary Locke, letter postmarked 26 November 1908.

70. Saunders, 'Seme', pp. 203–4.
71. Ibid. p. 204.
72. Ibid.
73. Locke Papers.
74. L. Harlan, 'Booker T. Washington and the White Man's Burden' *American Historical Review*, 71, 2 (January 1966), pp. 441–67; repr. Okon Edet Uya [ed.], *Black Brotherhood: Afro-Americans and Africa* (Lexington, Mass: Heath, 1971), pp. 150–1; L. Harlan and R. Smock [eds], *The Booker T. Washington Papers, Vol 9: 1906–1907* (Urbana: University of Illinois Press, 1980), pp. 500–1.
75. L. Harlan, *Booker T. Washington: The Making of a Black Leader, 1856–1901* (New York: Oxford University Press, 1972), pp. 245–52.
76. Du Bois correspondence microfilm 3, 1 June 1908.
77. Sampson *Gold Coast Men*, p. 153.
78. A. MacMillan, *The Red Book of West Africa* (London: Colingridge, 1920), p. 225; Violet Hutton Mills studied in Brighton from 1912 (ibid.).
79. Mathurin, *Henry Sylvester Williams*, p. 151.
80. Locke Papers, letter dated 8 October 1909 from 9, Minehead House, Sackville Street, London.
81. Saunders, 'Seme', p. 206.
82. Stewart, 'Black Aesthete', p. 423.
83. Ibid. pp. 421–2.
84. Du Bois Papers (microfilm I, 886–90); Harlan 'White Man's Burden' in Uya (ed.), *Black Brotherhood*, p. 151.
85. Adi, 'Students', p. 109; see also Harlan, 'White Man's Burden', p. 151.
86. Adi, 'Students', p. 109.
87. Harlan, 'White Man's Burden', p. 151.
88. Adi, 'Students', p. 110.
89. It is on Middle Temple, London, paper so it must be 1909.
90. Fyfe *Sierra Leone*, pp. 423, 615.
91. My thanks to Marva Griffin Carter, and the Herndon Home, Atlanta.
92. *West Africa* (London), 25 January 1919, p. 902.
93. *Anti-Slavery Reporter* (London) July 1913, p. 55; *African World* 10 May 1913, p. 49.
94. *Anti-Slavery Reporter* April 1913, p. 2.
95. Ibid. July 1913, p. 57.
96. Ibid. p. 59.
97. Ibid. p. 60.
98. Ibid. October 1913, p. 173.
99. M. Herbert, *Never Counted Out!* (Manchester: Dropped Aitches Press, 1992); Christopher Fyfe confirmed that this 'West African' had a name common in Sierra Leone.
100. Archivist, St Catharine's College, Cambridge, letter 22 July 1980 to Jeffrey Green.

8

Sports: the challenge between equals

DISCRIMINATION against Manchester-born boxer Len Johnson because his skin was dark sorely affected his professional career. The larger society must have been ill at ease to restrict free competition in sports. That individuals could compete, on the same terms, at a sport, challenging others in contests arranged within agreed rules and regulations, was a basic egalitarian concept. When people were excluded or penalised, solely because they were of African descent, what was exposed was the bogus nature of imperialism. What divine or genetic gifts enabled Whites to rule humankind if they went in fear of combat on equal and controlled terms? In their discrimination against Blacks in sports the British revealed their insecurity and their ignorance.

Nevertheless, individuals of African birth or descent were involved in British sports and, yet again, achieved in ways that would have astonished racists who tried to exclude them. Playing the game was just one aspect; representing 'the race' was another. And there was the sheer pleasure in playing games. Some had enjoyed games at school and college, and continued into maturity. Others played for relaxation, and some, like William Benker Johnson and his sons, for the money. There were Blacks whose successes inflamed White opinion and others whose sporting activities were seldom noted and have been ignored. Black Edwardians in sports were as varied as they were in other areas of social life: except for the almost complete invisibility of females.

Individuals who played games as a pastime but who had public recognition in other fields included composer Samuel Coleridge-Taylor who played an occasional game of tennis in Surrey. Medical practitioner John Alcindor played cricket in Edwardian London, as did the Jamaica-born Dr James Jackson Brown, who represented the London Hospital. Locke on the river at Oxford, Seme and Locke horse-riding, and the British Guiana-born children of Caroline and John Barbour-James in school sports are examples of how sport was part of a lifestyle. The *Acton Gazette* of 2 August 1907 noted that one of the Barbour-James boys (probably Joseph) had come third in the senior

Springfield College. F. T.
1908. 9

33. Black children participated in everyday activities in Edwardian Britain. Joseph Barbour-James was in his school soccer team in Ealing, west London, 1908 (Amy Barbour-James)

egg and spoon race at Springfield College's sports day on 26 July. He won the 440 yards walking handicap race. He was in that Acton Hill school's soccer team, and was photographed with his colleagues.

In south west England, at the navy base of Plymouth, James Peters played rugby. Born in Salford, the 'classic slum' of Manchester, in 1880, Peters worked and played rugby in London before moving to Bristol where he played for Knowle in 1900–2. He relocated to Plymouth, working in the dockyards at Devonport and playing for Plymouth. His skills were such that he was picked for the county team, and 'did so much towards securing Devon the County Championship last Saturday', as the *Sportsman* commented on 14 March 1907.

Peters 'gave such an admirable exposition of half-back play' against Durham, at Exeter, that 'he could not well have been left out of the side' that was picked to represent England. The front page of the *Western Independent* of 11 March announced 'Peters gets his cap'. Another Plymouth newspaper, the *Western Morning News*, named the England side that was to meet Scotland on 17 March. It commented 'the choice of Peters to partner his county colleague Jago will give general satisfaction to the West of England'. A short biography followed, making no reference to his African descent. The *Sportsman* of London had a readership outside Devon which may explain why it referred to 'the dusky Plymouth man' when reporting on the England v. Scotland match. England's team photograph[1] clearly shows that Peters was Black.

The *Western Morning News* had noted, on 17 March, that Peters's 'claims for international honours have been repeatedly put forward, but he has been overlooked' for the last two seasons. Was there prejudice among the selectors? Peters

> is a player of amiable temperament, and his play has always been marked with unusual cleaness. At the present time he is the vice-captain of the Plymouth Club. On and off the field he is respected by his colleagues, and by his excellent personal character has won the regard of a host of friends.[2]

England was expected to be defeated by the Scots, who had already beaten Ireland, but, aided by Peters, England scored nine points to Scotland's three. The *Sportsman* noted 'For a first international the dusky Plymouth man did many good things, especially in passing'. On 22 March it reported that the England team, including James Peters, had gone to Paris to play France, and that the British ambassador was expected to attend the match. Devonians were disappointed that Jago was unwell, so Peters's half-back partner was Adrian Stoop of Harlequins and Middlesex.

Following an ambassadorial reception England beat France before a

34. James Peters (front, right) born in Manchester, played rugby football for Devon and, in 1907, for England (Tim Auty)

'record' crowd of 5,500. James Peters continued to play for Plymouth, for Devon, and his country. The *Western Daily Mercury* noted that Peters had helped Plymouth defeat Torquay on 4 January 1908. On 18 January Peters was in the England side that lost to Wales 28:18 in Bristol. The *Mercury* of 20 January reported that 'Peters may not earn the unanimous praise of the critics, because he missed a couple of passes'. On 29 January, playing for Plymouth against the Royal Navy, Peters failed to convert a try.

He and Jago were in the county side against Cornwall, but Peters was dropped from the England team for the match against Ireland on 8 February 1908. The *Western Daily Mercury* noted this had caused 'a grumble' in the city of Plymouth. *The Times* of 10 February observed that in dropping Peters England's selectors had made 'no material improvement'. Ireland lost by ten points.

James Peters, the international rugby player of Plymouth, has not been located in any street directories, which suggests that he lived in lodgings. In 1910 he lost three fingers in a dockyard accident, which suggests that he was a working man. He had been paid by Devon County, which the Rugby Football Union found offensive, so he was suspended in 1912. Peters then tried to introduce the professional game (Rugby League) into Devon, and then signed for Barrow-in-Furness – another massive shipyard and navy town, which suggests Peters continued to work in the docks. James Peters died in 1954.[3]

A Black sportsman whose fame took him from America to Europe and Australia was Marshall 'Major' Taylor, who was born in Indianapolis in 1878. An errand boy, his employer thrust Taylor into a cycle race 'to inject a laugh' in 1892: Taylor won.[4] Faced with massive hostility, which led White competitors to cooperate and to attempt to block him, Taylor developed a simple technique – he raced to the front and stayed there. He was the sprint champion of the United States in 1899 and 1900. In 1901 he raced against the champions of Europe in Berlin and Paris, beating the French champion. He also raced against England's sprint champion, Charles Gascoyne, in 1901. He cycled in races in Australia, New Zealand and Canada, travelling with his wife and child. He retired as world champion in 1904; returned in 1907, and was back in France in 1908. He gave up sprint racing in 1910.

Taylor appeared in England around 1902, and seems to have challenged Britain's Sid Jenkins. His successes would have been known to British cycling devotees and to Black Edwardians. Bicycle handlebars named after Taylor were sold in Britain into the 1930s. Taylor died in Chicago in 1932.

Veterans recalled Black sporting achievers of the 1900s. One England-born son of a Jamaican, interviewed in 1987, named Gerald Foster, a Jamaican who participated in the Olympic or Empire Games before the First World War.[5] In 1940 the Black-led League of Coloured Peoples recalled Walter Daniel Tull. Tull's story has been traced by Phil Vasili.

Walter and Edward Tull were born of a Barbados father who worked as a joiner. Their mother died in the 1890s and the boys grew up in a children's home in London. Edward was adopted by the Warnock family in Scotland, and took the name Tull-Warnock. He worked as a dentist in Aberdeen and Glasgow from 1912. Walter Tull, born in Folkestone in April 1888, was playing soccer in an orphanage team when a talent scout picked him to play for Clapton. He transferred to Tottenham Hotspur in 1908, but refused to become a professional footballer until he had completed his apprenticeship in printing.

Walter Tull's first match for Spurs was at their first division debut in 1909. The London team had crowds that numbered thirty thousand, and they thrilled to Tull's skills. He was an inside forward, with the role of supplying the winger with good passes. The *Daily Chronicle* observed that Tull was a class above many of his team mates. It was felt that had Spurs obtained a decent winger then the combination would have been the best in England. Newspaper reports of Spurs matches refer to Tull as 'West Indian' and 'darkie'.[6]

The 1910–11 team photograph has Tull with twenty-four colleagues, four men whose roles may have included fitness, two trainers, the club secretary and four men who have 'Esq' after their names – a reminder of the importance of class in Edwardian Britain.

In 1911 Tull transferred to Northampton Town. He volunteered for the army in 1915, and was enlisted in one of the divisions of the Middlesex Regiment that was made up of soccer players. During the war years he appeared as a guest player for Fulham. He was commissioned in May 1917, despite military regulations forbidding 'any negro or person of colour' being an officer. Lieutenant Tull was killed in action in France in March 1918. His body was never identified and his name is on the massive memorial to the missing at Arras in northern France.[7]

Another professional sportsman was Charles Augustus Ollivierre, who had been in the West Indies cricket team which toured Britain in the summer of 1900. Ollivierre, from St Vincent, scored 883 runs in that tour, and was 'far and away the best batsman'.[8] He remained in Britain, playing for Derbyshire until 1907. He batted more than two hundred times, scoring a brilliant 229 against Essex in 1904, enabling his team to win the three day match. Eye trouble took him out of the professional game, but he played for Yorkshire club sides and later coached. He died in 1950, and has an enduring status as the first West Indian cricketer to have a sporting home in England.

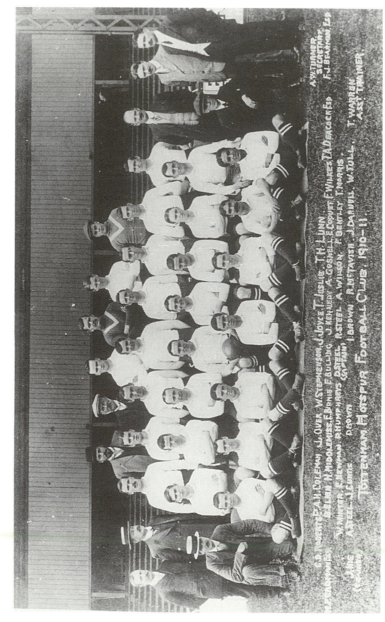

35. Folkestone-born Walter Tull (front, right) played for Tottenham Hotspur in the 1910s before transferring to Northampton

J. HUMPHRIES   A. WARREN   W. BESTWICK   G. CURGENVEN   L. G. WRIGHT   S. NEEDHAM
W. STORER   C. A. OLLIVIERRE   S. M. ASHCROFT   S. CADMAN   H. F. WRIGHT
(CAPTAIN)

DERBYSHIRE

36. Charles Ollivierre was the first West Indian professional cricketer to play for a county. Derbyshire in the mid-1900s

In 1906 he had to play against his brother Richard, an all-rounder whose bowling was the best in the West Indies team that toured Britain that summer. The other African-descent members were Lebrun Constantine, W. Burton, O. H. Layne and C. P. Cumberbatch. The fourteen-strong side reached Southampton on the *Trent* on 3 June 1906. They booked in at the Manchester Hotel in Aldersgate Street, London, and had a celebration dinner at the Imperial Restaurant in Regent Street.[9] Burton was from British Guiana, Layne was a professional from Barbados, whilst Constantine and Cumberbatch were from Trinidad.[10] Constantine and Burton had toured Britain in 1900.

Their first match was against a scratch side led by veteran W. G. Grace, in south London, and they were soundly defeated. Constantine's eighty-nine was the best from the visitors. The *West India Committee Circular* said he had been 'brilliant'. Constantine also won an award from the *Daily Mail*. Layne bowled six for seventy-four.[11]

The Caribbean team lost again, to Essex, despite Layne's century. They lost their third match, against Lord Brackley's team at Lord's, but three days later, in part due to Constantine and to left-hander Sidney Smith of Trinidad (who took nine wickets and scored ninety-three), they won in Ealing against a Minor Counties side.[12]

The touring side lost against Surrey, Wiltshire and Hampshire. The visitors showed no skill apart from Smith, who enabled the West Indies to beat South Wales at Cardiff. They lost against Kent at Catford, too. They returned to the centre of English cricket, and both George Challenor and Cumberbatch batted well against the MCC; the Black professional from Barbados was not out.

They travelled north to Derby, where Charles Ollivierre's sixty-four aided the home team's victory over the West Indies – and his brother. They continued north to Scotland, winning in Edinburgh. No doubt Caribbean students from the university were in the crowd.

Playing an 'England' side in Blackpoool the West Indies drew because of rain, although the visitors looked like winning. Constantine's batting and Richard Ollivierre's bowling were excellent. Moving on to Sunderland the Caribbean team played a combined Durham and Northumberland side, and won.

On 3–5 August 1906 the West Indies team met the mighty Yorkshire at Harrogate. Constantine and Layne were the top scorers; Ollivierre and Smith bowled well – Ollivierre's fast bowling took seven wickets for twenty-three. Following this unexpected victory the West Indies met defeat against Leicestershire despite Constantine's batting. This was followed by an easy victory at Norwich, a draw against Nottinghamshire, and victory over Northamptonshire.

The West Indies team had won seven and lost ten of the nineteen matches, with their successes being in the later stages of their tour. They had taken time to adjust to local conditions, for too many were run out, taking risks that were not necessary in the three day matches. The home sides took advantage of the slackness in fielding, which was 'especially noticeable with the black members of the team'.[13] The *West India Committee Circular* also noted the 'dark deeds' of the visitors and scoffed at the Black player who would 'not budge from the emergency exit of a music hall, owing to an overwhelming dread of premature cremation'. One team member was reported to have halted an express train in order to send a telegram. The tour was reported in the local and national press, as well as in the *Sportsman*.

Less attention was paid to a young man who won medals in international athletics in 1912. The sole reference to his African descent is in the New York *The Crisis*, a monthly devoted to Black activities, edited by W. E. B. Du Bois. In September 1912 he wrote:

> Jackson, a coloured student at Oxford University, won the 1,500 metre race at the Olympic Games. The credit for this victory goes to England and the Negro race has scarcely been mentioned.[14]

Du Bois had earlier named sprinter Howard Drew of Virginia who was in the US Olympic team in Stockholm, and as he had been in England in 1911 (as will be detailed) Du Bois may have made Black contacts in Oxford. No other contemporary reference to Jackson's ethnicity has been located but Du Bois did not publish a retraction. A photograph of Jackson hints at an ancestor of African descent.[15]

Jackson beat US-title holder Abel Kiviat, who was called 'the New York Jew boy' by the *Athletic News and Cyclists' Journal* of 8 July 1912. It named 'A. Howerd. The coloured Canadian sprinter, at the Olympic Games' but its photograph is so poor that an African ancestor has to be guessed. Its photograph of Jackson, published on 15 July, is equally indistinct. The *Sportsman* reported on Jackson's tactics and that he had won his gold medal but had not beaten Kiviat's world record. The *Athletic News* referred to his uncle C. N. Jackson. Who was Jackson?

Melvyn Watman's *History of British Athletics* (1968) stated that Jackson's battle to the tape was one of the most thrilling in Olympic history, that he was born in 1891, and that his uncle was the hurdles pioneer Clement Jackson. Du Bois may have been informed (or misinformed?) by a Black student at Oxford or by Jackson himself, for Arnold Nugent Strode Jackson had been in America with a combined universities athletics team. Jackson had been born in Surrey: which is the eastern part of Jamaica as well as the county south of London.

Supporting a conspiracy theory, his old school, Malvern College, could produce no photograph although Jackson, who was there from 1905 to 1910, had been head of his house, a cadet officer, head of the athletics team, a prefect and a successful cross-country runner. College records made no mention of his Olympic gold medal, which can be explained by the lack of importance of that event in the early twentieth century. Arnold Jackson had a private education (but so had Lewanika's sons, the Chens, and the Goffes), had participated in school sports (as had Percy Chen and young Barbour-James), had been in the cadet corps (Chen again), and had entered Oxford university (was there any year without a Black undergraduate at Oxford? – Gibson, Seme, Locke, Bruce-James, Manley) where he read law at Brasenose.

Jackson served in the British army in the 1914–18 war (so did Len Johnson's father, Lobagula, Albert James, Walter Tull, Joe Clough and the Zambian servant of Gore-Booth) but Jackson was a rarer individual for he was awarded the Distinguished Service Order four times: one of about a dozen officers with that remarkable record.[16] His photograph is not on file although he was a Brigadier-General at the age of twenty-seven, probably the youngest of that rank. A. N. S. Jackson participated in the peace treaty negotiations in 1919, and was awarded a CBE. He completed his studies and was called to the Bar at the Middle Temple. These military and civic achievements led to entries in *Who's Who* but editions of 1926 and 1971 reveal nothing that challenges or supports Du Bois's statement.

What would Jackson gain from public knowledge of an African ancestor? Mentioning a concealed African ancestry to a colleague at Oxford or to the Harvard-educated Du Bois also made little sense: but that was what William Albert Aldridge was to do in a letter to Du Bois in May 1921. That Manchester resident, a retired insurance salesman, said he had been born in New Orleans in 1849, and that his mother was a 'quadroon' by which he meant one of her grandparents was Black.[17]

The individual sports personality whose success threw Whites into a fluster was the flamboyant Texas-born Arthur John 'Jack' Johnson. Heavyweight boxing champion of the world, Johnson was to meet the English champion in London in 1911. A campaign to prevent the fight was led by the Revd F. B. Meyer, an individual whose biographer says was 'noble and generous' and a champion of the underdog.[18]

Frederick Brotherton Meyer was the leading nonconformist Christian minister in Edwardian Britain. At first glance Meyer seems to have been an unlikely agitator against Black endeavours, for he had aided the Pan-African conference in London in 1900,[19] was the vice president of the League of Universal Brotherhood and as such had assisted Gold Coast delegations in 1906[20] as well as Nigerians in 1913, as we have noted. Was Meyer's opposition, which could not have been totally racist in view of his Black associations, due to class and social pretensions? Boxing had such support among gamblers and the lower classes that opposition to Johnson had its own momentum. Of course the race card was played in what became a 'victory gained for decency and good behaviour'.[21]

Jack Johnson was in England in 1908, seeking a match against Tommy Burns, the Canadian world title holder. Burns 'drew the colour line' and refused. Johnson fought Ben Taylor in Plymouth instead.[22] He followed Burns to Australia where, on 26 December 1908, he became the world champion. His career was now a very public one, with reports of womanising, drinking, driving fast cars, and gambling.

Angered by this audacity various White Hopes rushed to challenge Johnson. All were defeated. Stung by racial pride, the retired champion James 'Jim' Jeffries returned to the ring and, described as the undefeated world champion, met Johnson in July 1910 in Nevada. He was crushed by the Black champion. Cities across America saw inter-racial clashes and at least a dozen deaths. The *Daily Mirror* of London pictured the pair on 18 July 1910, and reported that Johnson's victory had led to race riots. Many upright communities banned the film of the fight, and Johnson's stage appearances were cancelled by nervous theatre owners.

British theatrical entrepreneurs realised that Johnson would attract crowds, and so booked the champion to sing, dance, and play the string bass. Without any income from fights Johnson accepted these invitations, and so made his second visit to England in June 1911. Arriving at Plymouth, he signed a contract with James White to meet England's heavyweight champion over twenty rounds at Earls Court, west London. Johnson was fêted so much that some have commented that his presence in London made the coronation of King George the Fifth seem very tame.

Johnson met the ex-king of Portugal, noted *The Times* on 25 August. Johnson left to train near Paris, breaking his music hall contracts. His opponent, William 'Bombardier Billy' Wells, started training near Putney. Posters advertised the forthcoming championship match; there were reports that the prize money would be eight thousand pounds, a huge sum for the era. A poster caught the eye of Meyer and his protests eventually led him to the London headquarters of boxing, the National Sporting Club. There he admitted that he had not been aware that Blacks and Whites had boxed in England before.

At least six Black boxers had some fame in England in 1911. Sam Langford, billed as the 'American Black Marvel' although he was from Canada, was on his third tour of Britain when he defeated Australia's Bill Lang in London on 16 February 1911. The prize money was over three thousand pounds. Langford's camp (the group gathered around a boxer when he is training) pictured in *Boxing* that month included Bob Armstrong who had fought Jeffries and was now Johnson's sparring partner, 'Liver' Davis, and Andrew Jeptha from South Africa. Jeptha had been the United Kingdom welterweight champion for seven months until he was defeated by Curley Watson at the National Sporting Club in November 1907. The *Sporting Times* had referred to Jeptha as 'the black'.[23] *Boxing* of 18 March 1911 showed him, with his wife and three children, and stated that the ex-champion was blind.[24]

Noting comments on Langford's victory two weeks before, *Boxing* had commented 'the old colour-line is once more being advocated' in British boxing. It believed that to refuse to meet challenges from Blacks would show that the White race was 'ready to confess its inferiority'. The classic example of the colour line in boxing was US champion John L. Sullivan's refusal to meet Peter Jackson, a St Croix-born boxer who had become Australian champion. In England, in 1911, it seemed to be ineffective for Aaron 'Dixie Kid' Brown, the world welterweight champion, had a match in England on 3 July.[25] The National Sporting Club saw 'Darkey' Haley meet 'Seaman' Hayes in March 1911, whilst Billy McClain's British school of Black boxers included Joe Gans and Sam McVey. McVey had at least two matches in London in 1911. *Boxing* described his manager McClain as a comedian and boxing promoter.[26]

Indeed the cover of *Boxing* on 12 August 1911 pictured McVey,[27] Langford, Jack Johnson, and a fourth Black boxer Joe Jeannette. McVey had fought Johnson in 1903.[28] Gans was also American,[29] and Jeannette had fought Johnson in 1905 and 1908.[30] Elsewhere the magazine named Bob Scanlon, who was to defeat Petty Officer Curran at Plymouth in September 1911.

Black boxers fought differently to Whites, because of the racist nature of the larger society. White boxers believed that possession of the ring was important, and that aggressive action was essential. Certainly spectators expected that from White boxers. Black Americans came from a culture, as Randy Roberts explains, that had a capacity to retort and defend, notably in trading verbal insults. By controlling anger the Black population of late nineteenth-century America had a survival technique. In the ring, against Whites, Blacks yielded space and made their opponents tired; then they would gain the upper hand. This theory is evidenced by records for knockouts by the leading Black and White American boxers.[31]

There were enough appearances by Blacks in the boxing rings of Edwardian Britain to influence audience expectations on the lines of those in America. As Roberts noted 'Culture had conditioned boxing spectators every bit as much as black and white fighters.'[32] What is clear from the conflict that Wells and Johnson had with Meyer is that the respectable classes of Edwardian Britain had considerable influence.

No daily newspaper could be more stuffy and respectable than *The Times*, but it reported on Jack Johnson as a sporting personality with skills. *The Times* of 12 September reported from Paris and wrote of Johnson 'It is astonishing how often his counter gets in before his opponent's lead.' Two days later it published a letter from Edward White, chairman of the London County Council. Stimulated by a London gathering headed by Meyer, he reminded the august readers of *The Times* that on 10 July 1910 his council had warned theatres against exhibiting the film of Johnson's victory over Jeffries as it was 'undesirable'. As the LCC was responsible for checking and licensing places of public entertainment in the metropolis, this letter suggested that the management of the Empire Hall, Earls Court, were risking their licence by presenting the Wells v. Johnson fight.

On 15 September the *Sportsman* noted 'L. C. C. Chairman Interferes' and advised its surely largely unpolitical readers that the Wells v. Johnson fight contract had been signed on 19 July. Until the Methodists had reminded chairman White of the council's resolution of 1910, officials had been silent. The *Sportsman* indicated that the hall's management should regard White's letter as one from an individual, not reflecting an official decision by the council.

Within a week people of influence gave vent to their opinions: *The Times* reported on 18 September that the head of the Church Army had expressed his support for Meyer's campaign to prohibit the match.

37. Texas-born Jack Johnson lost a legal battle to meet British champion Billy Wells, but the campaign exposed ignorance and the uncertain status of boxing in 1911 (Black Cultural Archives, London)

The next day a letter, which *The Times* headed 'The Colour Problem', stated that that White-officered police in the West Indies had experienced difficulties after news of Johnson's victory over Jeffries reached the Caribbean. That Monday's issue of the *Sportsman* commented that the campaign was nonconformist in origin and support, and that Meyer's supporters objections were that boxing was brutal and demoralising, and that 'racial trouble' might result. Other inter-racial matches had taken place in Britain without fuss – the crusade was 'mere piffle'. The champions would meet in a match under the Marquis of Queensberry's rules, for this was not a prize fight.

Six thousand tickets had been sold, some at five guineas (£5.25 – two weeks' income for a labouring man). A peer of the realm had set the rules. The inter-racial aspect was not at all new, for there never had been any problems from Black-White encounters or from showing the film of Jeffries's defeat apart from in America and the Caribbean.

Meyer pressed on. His biographer recounts that he had the Bishop of London contact the Home Secretary: and that 'Resolutions poured into Mr. Meyer's room in shoals (on one morning there were no fewer than 260)'.[33] The *Sportsman* began to get nervous, with three columns dedicated to the matter of 19 September. The anti-gambling aspect of the campaign had led a vicar in Ealing to ban whist drives. The *Daily Mail* published the views of a retired alderman. The *Pall Mall Gazette* was quoted as stating that the official view should be that boxing should be permitted unless it was brutal. The following day the editor of the *Sportsman* noted that Meyer's campaign was stronger than ever and that he 'must be wasting a good deal of time in letter-writing'; and published a picture of both '"brutal" boxers'.

> The racial question is only involved simply and solely to strengthen a weak case, for white and black have met in opposition ever since the days of Fig and Broughton, and are, in fact, boxing in the ring every day of the week.[34]

It also published a letter suggesting that if Meyer disliked cruel sports he should agitate against the hunting of otters and hares.

'Are the Whites Afraid of the Negro' asked the *Sportsman* on 21 September. It commented on Meyer:

> The Nonconformist makes a boast of his desire for equality in all races and conditions of man, and yet he is now holding up a possible black victory as something not to be tolerated, even in a boxing ring.

A Cape Town newspaper stated that the match should be banned, and that if it took place no pictures should be shown in South Africa.

The whole racist ethic was exposed. A huge empire would come close to collapse if a British soldier met a Texan labourer in west London. The empire was indeed a confidence trick.

Meyer had said that 'the present conflict is not wholly one of skill' for Johnson had the advantage of 'the instinctive passion of the negro race'.[35] Meyer's biographer was unable to identify why he took the decision to fight against the tournament.[36] He had been unware of inter-racial boxing, and had refused to see film of the Johnson v. Jeffries fight on the grounds that it had been edited. We know that Meyer worked with Blacks in London before and after this campaign, and have to consider that his enthusiasm to prevent a prize fight and brutality (Jeptha's blindness was due to his batterings) led him to add the racial arguments.

In suggesting that instinctive passions and the 'immense animal development' of Blacks, who are 'so differently constituted' to Whites, plus the prospect of 'the great financial gain',[37] would fire Johnson, Meyer totally ignored the passions and instincts of Billy Wells, who had punched and smashed his way to the top, gaining money and prizes on the way. The instinctive racism of the larger society made Meyer overlook the simple fact that eight thousand pounds would stimulate lots of people.

The *Church Times*, the printed voice of the majority Christian group in England, stated on 22 September that 'the importation of colour prejudice into the discussion is deplorable' and regretted that the Anglican church's leader (the Archbishop of Canterbury, who was in Italy) was claimed by Meyer's camp.

Bishops, headteachers, university masters, the former chairman of Edinburgh University, leading Labour Party member of parliament Ramsay MacDonald, Field Marshall Lord Roberts and war hero and Boy Scouts founder General Baden-Powell were among those named as supporters of Meyer's campaign.[38] There were letters to the newspapers revealing that both Fiji and Nigeria had experienced unrest when they received news that Jack Johnson was the world champion. Fair play, equal rights, justice and other virtues claimed by the British and usually represented by such personages were jettisoned as intolerance, class snobbery and Negrophobia were exposed.

Reality was ignored. W. G. Barker, who had paid for world rights to the film of the match, commented that no army corps had been sent to any part of the empire to suppress Black people as a result of them seeing the film of Langford beating Lang – which had been shown all over the world.[39]

There were good reasons to dislike boxing, including its commercial status, but to ban the match made no sense to *The Times*. 'There have been large numbers of contests between white and black men and there had never been an attempt to get a licence of the premises where they were held revoked as a consequence.' On 27 September promoter James White and the two champions had to appear before a magistrate at Bow Street, to convince him that the fight would not lead to a breach of the peace.[40] The sole witness, a police superintendent, had never seen a boxing match. Meyer's petition to have the fight banned on the grounds of public order had been delivered to Winston Churchill, the Home Secretary, who is stated to have said 'what is contemplated is illegal'.[41]

If Wells met Johnson in the ring there could be no certainty that there would not be public unrest: so the magistrate banned the fight. Wells and Johnson agreed in court never to fight anywhere in Britain. Frederick Meyer had won.

The *Sportsman* devoted four columns to the matter on 28 September, and *Boxing* commented on 30 September 'As the rivals are of separate colours, our coloured fellow-subjects throughout the Empire might be incited to rebellion by the possible victory of a black man over a white rival'. Thus the sport had been reduced to a challenge between races. But the empire had not exploded when Jackson fought Slavin, when Johnson beat Burns, when Langford beat Lang, or when Scanlon fought Curran 'or in any one of hundreds of the other occasions when black and white boxers have met in rivalry. Nor did any terrible uprising of our colonial subjects take place in any one of these cases.'

Two White boxers were prevented from boxing in Birmingham a few weeks later, again on the grounds that there was no guarantee that everything would be peaceful,[42] so the judicial view was not a totally racist one. In using race Meyer had presented a view of Blacks that was negative. Nevertheless, Jack Johnson returned to England.

Johnson's fame was widespread. When the Jamaican Robert Rody was attacked in the streets of Yarmouth in September 1912, one of the louts had said something about 'Jack Johnson's cat's meat' and 'You dirty dog, Jack Johnson'. British newspapers had carried the news from Chicago that Johnson's wife had committed suicide, reminding people that Etta Terry Johnson was White. In October 1912 the champion was arrested in the United States, charged with abduction under the Mann Act which had made it illegal to cross a state line with a female companion not one's wife, for sexual purposes. Freed on bail, Johnson married Lucille Cameron, the White woman who had been with him when he crossed a state line. She now could not testify against him.

White America was outraged: half of the twenty states that permitted inter-racial marriages saw bills against such 'miscegenation'; Congress saw twenty-one such bills.[43] Johnson attempted to purchase a home in a select and lily-white area of Chicago, which inflamed Whites. In 1913 Johnson was charged and went on trial for alleged Mann Act offences. These matters were mentioned in the British press in May and June, with further details as Johnson fled the United States to Canada at the end of June, taking a ship to France.

British theatrical entrepreneurs again saw profits in a public show of Jack Johnson, and the champion arrived in England on Sunday 24 August 1913. The *Folkestone Express* reported that ex-queen Amelia of Portugal and Cardinal Bourne were recent 'notabilities at Folkestone'.

> The third distinguished personage was Jack Johnson, the prizefighter, who came from Paris on his way to London. When the steamer came alongside [the dock] the darkey was seen seated in a handsome motor car which stood on the main deck. His white wife was with him.[44]

The violent animosity that surrounded Johnson in his native land was absent. 'The couple created a great deal of curiosity, but there was no demonstration, hostile or otherwise.' 'No doubt she [Lucille Cameron Johnson] feels the ostracism with which other women treat her. One who was very sick, to whom she spoke consolingly, turned sharply away.' With his agent and chauffeur, the champion was driven off to London.

Theatrical appearances of notorious people had upset the Variety Artists' Federation, which had successfully campaigned against the appearance of a person closely associated with a recent murder trial. Faced with the escaped champion, who had served time in prison and was widely considered to be a white-slaver, Johnson's twenty minutes, twice a night, was regarded as a threat to public decency. *The Times* carried details on 22 August, before Johnson reached Britain. One of the protestors was Meyer: Johnson invited the minister to meet him.

The Federation's threats and the possibility of their licences being withdrawn made theatre owners cancel Johnson's bookings. He still appeared, but in the auditorium, no doubt getting some payment. But he needed more money, and put on exhibitions of boxing, including one in Gravesend, Kent. In the first week of September his car collided with a London taxi, and he wrenched his back. He returned to France, where he broke his arm in a match.

The French boxing authorities declared that a convicted criminal should not be permitted to hold a world title, and while the International Boxing Union investigated, Johnson could not box. Having the French view rejected, he was free to box again and remained in France into 1914. *The Times* suggested on 30 January that Johnson might be meeting Sam Langford for a purse of three thousand pounds. *Punch* suggested on 29 April 1914 that Johnson was contemplating becoming a French citizen.

Three days after a long and boring fight with Frank Moran in Paris on 27 June 1914, Johnson returned to England where he recorded 'Physical Culture' for Edison Bell records at their Peckham, south London, studio. Only one known copy existed until 1986 when a second was located in Scotland.[45] It was issued in September when much of Europe and all the British Empire was at war.

Johnson lost his title in Cuba in 1915, and returned to England where he was expelled under the Aliens Restriction Act in 1916, by which time the six inch shells of Germany's artillery were known as 'Jack Johnsons' to British soldiers in France and Belgium – probably because they moved fast, were black, and hit with considerable power. Denied a championship match in Britain, the American had still made a lasting impact on the British.

Johnson went back to the United States where he served his prison sentence in 1920. He continued a very public life, and died in a car

38. John Alcindor played cricket for relaxation, for his Paddington, west London, medical practice was busy (Frank and Evelyn Alcindor)

crash in 1946. Neither blind like Jeptha or destitute like Langford, Johnson was still too powerful for many. Not one boxer or a floral tribute from colleagues in that sport were at his funeral.[46]

Distant from Jack Johnson in wealth and fame was the Black man who was photographed at Aintree racecourse in Liverpool in 1902.[47] Anonymous, this racing tipster wears wooden clogs, a cast-off police uniform coat and helmet, and looks generally unkempt. No doubt this exotic, like gypsies, was thought to have special powers and thus could sell tips to gamblers. A later and well-known racing tipster was 'Prince' Ras Monolulu from the 1930s.[48]

There is no doubt that a close scrutiny of Edwardian sports team photographs, including women players, will reveal other Blacks who participated in games. One such picture appears in *British Sports and Sportsmen: Cricket and Football* which, published in 1917, shows John Alcindor, a wicket keeper who played for London teams in the 1900s and 1910s.[49] A graduate of Edinburgh University, a busy medical practitioner in west London's Paddington, Trinidad-born Dr Alcindor was distanced by education and occupation from Jack Johnson. He was a member of the Black bourgeoisie whose lives were lived distant from the public fame of Tull, Ollivierre and Peters.

NOTES

1. My thanks to Tim Auty.
2. *Western Morning News* (Plymouth), 17 March 1907.
3. D. Hands, 'Peters broke fresh ground for England', *The Times* (London) 17 February 1988, p. 48; General Register Office for birth and death registrations.
4. A. Ritchie, *Major Taylor: The Extraordinary Career of a Champion Bicycle Racer* (San Francisco: Bicycle Books, 1988).
5. Interview with Leslie Brown.
6. My thanks to Phil Vasili and David Killingray.
7. See 'Hero of the pitch died forgotten in the trenches', *Daily Express* (London) 19 February 1997, p. 16. Jack Leslie deserves investigation as he is reputed to have been selected to play for England in the 1930s before the selectors discovered he was coloured, and withdrew their invitation. My thanks to Charlie Frost.
8. C. Nicole, *West Indian Cricket* (London: Phoenix House; repr. London: Sportsmans Book Club, 1960), pp. 17, 39.
9. *West India Committee Circular* (London) 6 June 1906.
10. Nicole, *Cricket*, p. 47.
11. Ibid. *West India Committee Circular* 13 June 1906.
12. Nicole, *Cricket*, p 48; *West India Committee Circular* (London) 29 August 1906 has a summary.
13. *West India Committee Circular* 29 August 1906.
14. *The Crisis* (New York) September 1912, p. 221.
15. I am indebted to Di Napier for sight of K. Rolley and C. Aish, *Fashion in Photographs: 1900–1920* (London: Batsford, 1992), p. 144.
16. I am indebted to the Imperial War Museum for clarification.
17. Du Bois correspondence, microfilm.
18. W. Fullerton, *F. B. Meyer: A Biography* (London: Marshall, Morgan & Scott, c. 1930).
19. Mathurin, *Williams*, p. 78.
20. Ibid. pp. 133–4.
21. Fullerton, *Meyer*, p. 121. Approached by Duse Mohamed, the radical Black editor of the new *African Times and Orient Review*, Meyer's recommendation was published in its first, July 1912, issue (p. 13): he believed that 'ordinary newspapers' were suitable and a Black-focused London publication was not needed. If Meyer was racist why did Mohamed contact him and why did he respond?
22. F. Farr, *Black Champion: The Life and Times of Jack Johnson* (London: Macmillan, 1964); R. Roberts, *Papa Jack: Jack Johnson and the Era of White Hopes* (London: Robson, 1986), p. 52. I follow Roberts in Johnson's forenames.

23. *Sporting Times* (London) 16 November 1907, p. 4.
24. *Boxing* (London) 18 February 1911, p. 397; ibid. 18 March 1911, pp. 493–4. Research into Jack Johnson led me to learn of Jeptha. It was instructive to observe, in Atlanta, a street near the Black colleges had been named in his honour; see also M. Golesworthy, *Encyclopaedia of Boxing*, 7th edn (London: Robert Hall, 1983), p. 61.
25. *Boxing* (London) 15 July 1911; ibid. 23 September 1911, p. 503.
26. *Boxing* 15 July 1911.
27. Sometimes spelled McVea.
28. Roberts, *Papa Jack*, p. 30.
29. Ibid. p. 91.
30. Ibid. pp. 45, 51, 102.
31. Ibid. pp. 25–6.
32. Ibid. p. 26.
33. Fullerton, *Meyer*, p. 121.
34. P. Fryer, *Staying Power*, pp 445–54 lists many inter-racial prize fights from 1791. An early (1810) bout took place close to East Grinstead where this book is being written. Prize-fighting made it ideal to have sites very close to county boundaries and thus confuse local law enforcement personnel.
35. *The Sportsman* (London) 22 September 1911, front page.
36. Fullerton, *Meyer*, p. 118.
37. *The Sportsman* 22 September 1911, front page.
38. *The Times* (London) 26 September 1911; *Boxing* (London) 7 October 1911.
39. *Boxing* 23 September 1911.
40. Farr, *Black Champion* devotes less than a page to Johnson in England in 1911 but his photograph 11 shows Johnson emerging from a taxi at Bow Street 'in answer to a summons for creating a disturbance and impeding traffic'. Roberts, *Papa Jack*, pp. 127–9 uses the *New York Times* and *The Times* (London) but gets to grip with Meyer through S. Mews 'Puritanicalism, Sport and Race: A Symbolic Crusade of 1911' in O. Cuming and D. Baker [eds], *Studies in Church History* (Cambridge) 1, 8 (1972), pp. 303–31.
41. *The Sportsman* (London) 25 September 1911, p. 8; *Annual Register 1911* (London: Longmans Green, 1912), p. 220.
42. Disquietened that 10,000 people were expected in Sparkbrook, Birmingham, to see Jim Driscoll meet Owen Moran, local people sought the legal remedy that Meyer had obtained. The boxers were represented by a lawyer whose fees were paid by the National Sporting Club; but he lost; see *The Times* (London) 6 November 1911, p. 8, and G. Deghy, *Noble and Manly: The History of the National Sporting Club* (London: Hutchinson, 1956), p. 159. Expecting a 'protest against such brutal exhibitions in public places' in 1911, showman Charles Cochran hired 'a clergyman in full canonicals to announce the bouts', C. Cochran, *Cock-A-Doodle-Do* (London: Dent, 1941), p. 200.
43. Roberts, *Papa Jack*, p. 159.
44. *Folkestone Express* 27 August 1913, p. 5.
45. National Sound Archive (London). My thanks to Bruce Bastin.
46. Roberts, *Papa Jack*, p. 227.
47. My thanks to John Joseph.
48. Of Caribbean origin, his fame led to a central London pub becoming The Prince Monolulu in the 1980s.
49. *Acton District Post* (London) 25 June 1915, p. 3; ibid. 20 August 1915, p. 3.

9

The black bourgeoisie

THE African elite sought education in and professional qualifications from British institutions. Opportunities in Africa were extremely limited. Fourah Bay College in Sierra Leone attracted students from British West Africa; and Afro-American institutions attracted both Africans and Caribbeans, with some Black students at liberal White colleges, including South Africans such as Seme, one of the 'considerable number of youths to go to America and England'.[1]

The elite of the British West Indies also sent their sons and daughters to the United Kingdom for their education. For those aspiring to become doctors and lawyers it was essential to have British qualifications. There had been Sierra Leonean medical students in Britain from the mid-nineteenth century and it was the London-born son of a Sierra Leonean doctor who was the most widely known member of Edwardian Britain's Black middle class.[2]

Samuel Coleridge-Taylor's father was Daniel Peter Hughes Taylor, who qualified in London in 1874 and had returned to Sierra Leone months before Alice Hare Martin had their son in August 1875.[3] Raised by his mother in Croydon with the man he was to call grandfather, and then with his step-father George Evans and his mother's three children by Evans, the Black child's early years were not middle class. Evans had a steady job on the railway, and his Black stepson sang in a church choir and there was enough cash for a violin and formal lessons locally. In 1890 he was accepted by the Royal College of Music, London, where he soon won a scholarship, turned to composing, and met Jessie Fleetwood Walmisley, his future wife.[4]

Between 1898 and 1900 his name was often in the musical press, for a student production had led to a commission by the Three Choirs Festival, from which had come another commission to write for a highly regarded choral society. Using Longfellow's Native American poem *Hiawatha*, Coleridge-Taylor created *The Song of Hiawatha*, which was first performed in its entirety in 1900. It had a tremendous reception. It entered the repertoire of choral groups and, rewritten for instrumentalists, was played all over Britain during the Edwardian

MR COLERIDGE TAYLOR   USSELL

39. London-born Samuel Coleridge-Taylor's compositions were well regarded
when he sat for this photograph around 1904

years. *The Song of Hiawatha* made its creator's name and his African
descent known to thousands.

He married Jessie and had two children, continuing to live in
Croydon where he worked as a professional concert music composer.
It was an uncertain living, but the fact that he had two servants and
that his wife did not have to work showed he had become middle
class. Like other musicians before and since, he taught locally and in
London, directed local music makers, wrote for the theatre, and
conducted his works and pieces by others around the nation. His fame

40. Coleridge-Taylor in the garden at Dagnell Park in Selhurst, near Croydon. His family did not understand why he wore his gardening hat (Marjorie Evans)

had spread abroad, and he was invited to the United States by Americans of African descent. He made the first of three visits in 1904.

An Afro-American connection made in England was with the pioneer jubilee singer Frederick Loudin. Introduced to Negro Spirituals through the veteran choir manager, Coleridge-Taylor used the theme of 'Nobody Knows the Trouble I See, Lord' in the overture to *The Song of Hiawatha*. Orchestrating Negro Spirituals was not unexpected for late Victorian composers searched for melodies and inspiration in folk music. The massive sales of *The Story of the Jubilee Singers with their*

Songs had made them available all over Britain: and 'Nobody Knows' was on the book's first page.

Coleridge-Taylor's links with other Black people in Britain can be dated to 1896,[5] and his concern for the race led him to participate in an international conference in London in 1900. That Pan-African Conference had been organised by Henry Sylvester Williams and involved Loudin and others who will be detailed later.

Financing the conference were Americans associated with W. E. B. Du Bois, who was in Europe for the Exposition Universelle in Paris where there was an American Negro exhibit.[6] In his autobiography Du Bois states he was in the audience with Jessie and Samuel Coleridge-Taylor for a performance of *The Song of Hiawatha*. The composer was widely respected by other middle class Blacks in Britain and abroad. In 1904 he completed *Twenty-four Negro Melodies Arranged for the Piano*, which was published in America the following year. The introduction was written by Booker T. Washington in Alabama the day before the composer's ship left England. He described the composer as 'the foremost musician of his race' who 'was an inspiration to the Negro, since he himself, the child of a Negro father, is an embodiment of what are the possibilities of the Negro under favorable environment'.[7]

His arrangements of the two dozen melodies included sixteen songs from Black America, a Caribbean theme collected by a New York music critic, six from a collection of Mozambique music published in 1897, and one from West Africa. Its bass line was a 'West African Drum-Call (?) in the Author's Possession'. 'O lo ba' had Yoruba words and had reached the London composer through 'Mrs Victoria Randall'.[8] She was the wife of Dr John Randle, a Sierra Leonean medical practitioner trained in Edinburgh in the 1880s.[9] Her father James Davies (an African sea captain) had married a woman from Dahomey who had been adopted by Queen Victoria. Their daughter Victoria Davies became the British monarch's god-daughter.[10]

Victoria Davies, who was no stranger to Windsor Castle, stayed with the Smith sisters in London, and from Adelaide Smith Casely Hayford's biography it is obvious their friend was a leading member of London's West African middle class. The composer knew them all, of course. He set the *Fairy Ballads* poems by youthful Kathleen Easmon to music, and had them published in 1909. She dressed as an African princess when attending the first performance of his *A Tale of Old Japan, opus 76* in late 1911.[11] It will be recalled that her brother qualified as a doctor the following year.

In the summer of 1905 James Weldon Johnson, who was to be a US consul in Nicaragua, was in London with his brother Rosamond and Bob Cole, a successful song-writing partnership based in New York but now appearing at the Palace theatre. With him at their first night were 'the colored English composer, and his wife; they sat with me'.[12] Johnson 'grew aware of the beauty in the ruggedness of London' through aimlessly riding on the tops of motor buses. But he felt free from American racism, failing to observe that British Negrophobia was merely less honest.

Coleridge-Taylor had duetted with a violinist of African descent named White during his 1904 visit to the United States. From his home at 30, Dagnall Park,[13] in north Croydon's Selhurst he wrote to Clarence Cameron White on 23 September 1905, responding to White's request for advice on musical training in Britain. White, born in 1880 and now living in Washington DC, wanted to expand from music teaching into composition. Coleridge-Taylor taught at the Crystal Palace School of Art, Music and Literature and at the Croydon Conservatoire of Music, a local school which, he confessed to the American, 'is not a very good one'. He recommended both the Royal College of Music and the Royal Academy of Music in central London. He explained 'I do not teach the violin now, but I shall be pleased to give you composition lessons should you come' at Crystal Palace, at Trinity College of Music, 'or by correspondence'.[14]

Clarence and Beatrice White arrived in London in 1906. From 10, Upper Grove, Norwood (still in the Croydon area near his mother), on 27 July Jessie Coleridge-Taylor invited White to perform at their new home on 16 August 1906. White may also have attended the Croydon String Players Club concert of 27 October, for the programme is in his papers. That group of local amateur musicians spent hours under the composer's baton, and that honed his skills as an orchestral conductor.

On 10 October Jessie wrote to White, to tell him that her son Hiawatha was to give his first recital on 21 November: 'I daren't tell his father, so please don't *you* name it!' This and other friendships with musical Londoners brought the Whites back to England in 1909, now with their two small children.

It was at this time that Alain Locke was indicating to his mother that he would visit the Croydon composer when next in London. If he did he would have seen that Coleridge-Taylor had a copy of Du Bois's *The Souls of Black Folk* of 1903, which had been sent to him by friends in Washington, and that *Credo*, received from Du Bois himself in early 1905, 'hangs in a most conspicuous position in our Dining-room, where everyone can see it'.[15]

It was in 1908 too that we can see a clear example of Coleridge-Taylor taking a public stance as a person of African descent. An article on 'the negro problem in America' in London's *Reynold's Newspaper*, by a Virginia judge named Kelly was a real Southern view. On

2 August Coleridge-Taylor's 'In Defence of the Negro' was published by *Reynold's Newspaper*. He commented that being

> English, and not American, seemed to do away with the race prejudice that does understandably exist [in America], and I was welcomed [by the President] precisely as if I had been entirely, instead of only partly, white.

His two trips to America had led him to observe that class for class, Black and White Americans had similar modes of living.

> In conclusion, let me say that I know too many beautiful coloured homes, both in England and elsewhere, too many beautiful families, to despair of some ultimate and definite place for the negro in the world's history.

The piece reached Africa and there it was republished in the *Gold Coast Leader*.[16]

In November 1904 the all-Black choral society named for the composer had him conduct them, accompanied by the orchestra of the US Marine Corps, in Washington DC. The baritone soloist was Harry T. Burleigh of New York, and in 1908 he and his wife were in England.[17] Information on their contacts has been located in the Black-edited *New York Age* and in letters Burleigh wrote to Locke in Oxford.[18]

The Burleighs were on the fringes of an elitist circle in Edwardian England. The trip had been funded by John Pierpont Morgan, the son of a multi-millionaire, who had settled in England in 1902. Another American supporter was the wife of Lewis Harcourt, who was to be Britain's Colonial Secretary from 1910. A famous London hostess, her father W. H. Burns was Morgan's partner and brother-in-law. The Duchess of Marlborough, who had been Consuelo Vanderbilt, yet another daughter of an American millionaire, was involved with the Burleighs too. The *New York Age* said the Burleighs were mixing with 'the best people of London'.[19]

The Burleighs stayed at 46, Gower Street, from where the singer travelled to appointments in stately homes in London and the country. One appointment was at ten in the evening on a Sunday in late June 1908, at Broughton Castle near Banbury. This after-dinner song recital was at the home of Lord Bernard Gordon-Lennox (son of the Duke of Richmond and Gordon) and his wife (daughter of Sir Henry, later Lord, Loch, Britain's high commissioner in South Africa 1889–95). Their young sons were to become an admiral and a general. This was an aristocratic British family who would not have employed minstrels. Burleigh was to stay overnight in Banbury. The changes to his schedule made it impossible to meet Locke in nearby Oxford.

On 16 July 1908 the *New York Age* reported that Burleigh had performed for 'many of the crowned heads of Europe'. He sang before King Edward the Seventh on 3 July. The Burleighs were so impressed with Britain that their son Alston, born in 1899, was sent to school in England in the early 1910s. Clarence Cameron White wrote to the *Age* towards the end of 1908 claiming that Burleigh's reception by royalty 'goes to show that it is here more a question of fitness than of color'.

As White had been in Britain for months, and had got to know Coleridge-Taylor, his comment seems to have been genuine. By aspiration White was middle class, and his associations were certainly not with prize fighters, the female waif in Selhurst, Joe Clough, Lewis Bruce and others of the working class. Towards the end of 1908 Coleridge-Taylor wrote to his Washington friends Andrew and Mamie Hilyer

> Mr. White and I see quite a deal of each other; he is studying with Zacharewitsch, a very fine player and one of my best friends. . . . It seems that quite a lot of Washingtonians and others have been over to England this season. I suppose the [Franco-British] Exhibition has had a great deal to do with it. Some I've seen and some I haven't.[20]

These visitors must have been a nuisance from time to time. One slightly earlier comment from an American contact remarked on the 'pleasure of lending impoverished Americans some of your English pounds'.[21]

Burleigh was a visitor, in 1908 (perhaps earlier too) and when he returned to Britain the following year. The two appeared on the concert platform together. Another was Booker T. Washington's daughter Portia, who studied music in Germany and told her father 'I shall visit Mr. Taylor'.[22]

So was Emma Azalia Hackley, a Detroit resident who graduated in music in Denver in 1899. In England in 1909 she had planned to 'meet and talk with persons of note' including the Coleridge-Taylors. She gave some song recitals, but she was ill for much of her time and was in hospital. She wrote to her husband Edwin that 'the English certainly are an eccentric people . . . a solid people, but dull and stolid, not much given to smiling'. The men were 'cold and dictatorial' and the women 'cheery, bright, and witty, a great contrast in appearance to the French women'. She regarded British open coal fires as inferior to the stoves she knew in France and Germany.

She had met the Fisk singers (no longer led by Loudin who had died in Ohio in 1904), who told her that they planned to 'refuse to look at ham and eggs on their return to America, we get them every morning for breakfast'. Mrs Hackley organised three choral groups in Britain in 1909, possibly connected to Toynbee Hall, a London charity arts centre on the edge of the slums of the East End: she taught there for a spell.[23]

Mrs Hackley had given five hundred dollars so that White and his family could be in Britain in 1909. On 17 April 1909 White wrote from London to the *Chicago Defender*, acknowledging a donation of eight dollars which had been handed to him by Hackley.[24] His letter was from Talbot Road, Paddington. 31, Talbot Road appeared on a post-card dated 28 May 1909 which he received from Coleridge-Taylor in Southport ('Kind regards to *all* at 31').[25] It also is on an undated post-card written to Burleigh by the composer.[26] It was the London home of John Alcindor, the Edinburgh-trained doctor from Trinidad.[27] This association continued into 1910, for when Jessie wrote to White at the end of March that year, her note ended 'Kind regards & to Dr Alcindor'.[28] We will examine the doctor after we have detailed his composer friend.

As Coleridge-Taylor's friend and biographer recalled, while some incidents 'caused him more amusement than irritation, more un-pleasant experiences were not infrequent'.[29] A clergyman in Kent around 1905 assumed the Anglo-African composer was Japanese.[30] When a lawyer addressed a local debating society and suggested that 'the black man was even nearer the ape than the white',[31] Coleridge-Taylor exploded with a letter to the *Croydon Guardian* which stated that 'there is an appalling amount of ignorance amongst English people regarding the negro and his doings'.[32] When this led to criticism, Coleridge-Taylor wrote, on 1 March 1912, to the *Croydon Guardian* making the following comments: 'there is no reason for adopting an aggressive tone when discussing the coloured people of America … they did not go to that country of their own accord'; and 'As for South Africa, after all, the blacks were born there, and Africa is their country in many ways.'[33]

Coleridge-Taylor's musical skills had been observed, when a student, by August Jaeger, who encouraged and developed them from the late 1890s.[34] Jaeger worked for music publishers Novello and as a critic for the *Musical Times*. His letters to Coleridge-Taylor have not been traced, but as both men met in London 'several times a week'[35] it seems unlikely any correspondence would reveal much. In his com-ments to Elgar, who lived far from London, there was one aside which reveals Jaeger's sense of disillusionment with Coleridge-Taylor, expressed in a way that exposes Edwardian racial prejudice.

Elgar referred to Coleridge-Taylor as 'a clever man' in April 1898; in May Jaeger described him as 'wonderfully gifted'; and in September 1899 Elgar wrote that he was 'a dear chap'. In 1898 Jaeger had made a crucial recommendation about 'the coming man'[36] but by January 1900 both Elgar and Jaeger thought he was not achieving, using the words

41. Coleridge-Taylor (lower, left) in command of choir and orchestra, probably at Crystal Palace (Marjorie Evans)

'rot' and 'uninteresting'. By September 1903 Elgar wrote that 'Taylor's work was a disgrace to any civilised country'. These comments are not unreasonable given the composer's work during these years.

However, Jaeger dismissed Coleridge-Taylor as 'the young Blackie' who had limited 'depth & poetic imagination' in March 1901.[37] There was no reason to call him Blackie. This insult could not have been known to the Croydon composer, for Coleridge-Taylor conducted his own *Ballade in A Minor* at the memorial concert for Jaeger, who died from tuberculosis, in January 1910.[38]

Within three years 'the young Blackie' had died: aged thirty-seven. The musical world mourned, as did neighbours and friends in Croydon, and informed Blacks in Britain, the United States, the Caribbean and in mother Africa. News of the composer's death, from pneumonia, on 1 September 1912, was spread by the news agencies and reached many parts of the world within days. *The Song of Hiawatha* had made Coleridge-Taylor's other works attract attention, and entered the concert music repertoire of many instrumentalists and singers. He had written incidental music for four plays produced at His Majesty's Theatre in central London; he tried and failed with opera; was an adjudicator at music festivals; a teacher and a conductor; and poured out symphonic works, choral works both sacred and secular, rhapsodies, piano pieces and cantatas. The March 1909 edition of *Musical Times* had had a ten page article about him; his photograph portrait was sold; he had visited America three times; children struggled over and adults enjoyed his piano arrangements of orchestral works; his music was in print and performed across the nation.

His funeral drew Black people to Croydon, and from newspaper reports and cards taken from wreaths, surviving at the Royal College of Music, we can see that there were some thirty West Africans present, including Emma and Frans Smith, Mrs Easmon with Kathleen and Charles, three members of the Renner family, John Eldred Taylor (a Sierra Leone businessman based in London), Frederick W. Dove (another Sierra Leonean family much at home in Britain), Samuel Hughes from Lagos, and Cornelius May, editor of the *Sierra Leone Weekly News*, who reported the funeral in due course. May had been in England for most of that summer.[39] From the Gold Coast region came K. Afa-Amonu and from South Africa the student Davidson Don Jabavu. Also present were the Downings, Dr Alcindor and at least one American.[40] Africa, missing from his childhood, was present at his death, for his widow was to write that her husband had died 'in the presence of his mother, a West African friend, two nurses and myself'.[41]

His sale of the copyright in *Hiawatha* had meant that the composer

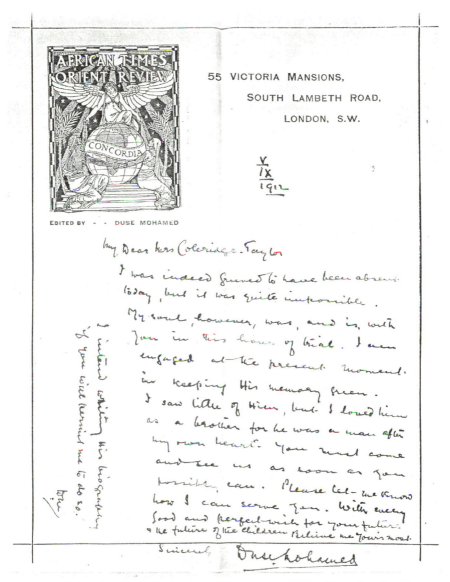

42. Coleridge-Taylor's death on 1 September 1912 led to national and international grief. The Black-rights journalist Duse Mohamed, unable to attend the funeral in Croydon, wrote to the widow (Royal College of Music)

had never had financial security, although few contemporaries had realised that *Hiawatha*'s success earned its creator nothing. His widow was awarded a Civil List pension of one hundred pounds, announced in *The Times* and copied from that by Du Bois in his *The Crisis*.[42]

Dr Alcindor, known to young Gladys Casely Hayford as 'Dr

Cinders', also knew the Coussey family, Dr Renner (who Alcindor named in his will), and the Easmons. These African families in London often had the senior male at work in West Africa, and the 'Black doctor of Paddington' became a reliable friend to Africans in London.

Born in Trinidad in 1873, educated at St Mary's College and awarded an Island Scholarship, he studied medicine in Scotland, graduating MB, BCh in mid-1899. He moved to London where he worked in several hospitals including Plaistow, Hampstead and Camberwell, with a spell in Acton where he joined the Mill Hill cricket club, before establishing his own medical practice in Paddington around 1907.[43]

He carried out research, and had articles published in professional journals. A piece on influenza appeared in the *General Practitioner* in 1907 and one on cancer in the *British Medical Journal*. A third paper, on tuberculosis, was to appear in the *Practitioner* in January 1913. He noted that 'lowered vitality' and 'unhealthy surroundings', insufficient and low quality food, having large families and unbalanced diets had played a part. He recommended injections of trypsin for inoperable cancers. He noted poor hygiene among working class Londoners.

John Alcindor was thirty-eight when he married Minnie Martin in 1911. They had three sons: John Francis 'Frank' Alcindor was born in September 1912, Cyril in February 1914, and Roland 'Bob' in mid-1917. His medical practice and home were both at 37, Westbourne Park Road, until he relocated his surgery to the Harrow Road across the bridge over the railway. The mass of his patients were poor people who, from mid-1912, had some state support through the new National Health Insurance Act. From 1917 he also worked as a Medical Officer of Health for the Paddington Poor Law Guardians.

Minnie Alcindor was a free thinker, and her parents cut her off when she married the Black doctor. He remained true to the faith that had been part of his school days at St Mary's College in Port of Spain, and attended the local Catholic church. His first two sons went to Cardinal Vaughan's School, the eldest going on to Mount St Mary's Catholic boarding school.[44]

On the other side of London lived another Afro-Caribbean medical man. James Jackson Brown, born in Jamaica in October 1882, had family wealth from land, which enabled him to study in Canada in the early 1900s. Disliking the style of tuition and suffering from snow blindness, Brown made his way to London where, in September 1905, he presented his Canadian and Jamaican credentials and was accepted by the London Hospital.[45] With plans to become a surgeon, Brown mixed his studies with practical work and assisted the future Lord Dawson of Penn (King George the Fifth's doctor) and surgeon Jonathan Hutchinson.

He married Millie Green, the daughter of his landlord, members of a

43. James Jackson Brown (rear, right) with his wife Amelia 'Milly' (front, right), Mother-in-law Elizabeth Green (centre) and cousin Marie Hart posed with unknown friend in Scarborough in 1906. Brown's medical studies were lengthened by his love of cricket and work at the London Hospital (Leslie Brown)

long-established Jewish family in east London's Hackney. Sometime in 1906 Brown and his wife, her mother, a cousin, and an unidentified Black male friend, posed for a group photograph in Scarborough.[46] At the end of that year Gerald was born; and in 1909 the family was completed by Leslie. Interviewed in 1984–5, Leslie Brown recalled 'the first coloured children we had ever seen' when Lou and Alfred Cambridge visited them, with their three daughters, before 1915. The Cambridges lived across London in Acton, where they had shared with the Barbour-James family, as we have noted.

Brown qualified in 1914, the delay partly due to his family responsibilities and also through his love of cricket. He played for the London Hospital and for an 'all coloured' team which included Asians. By the 1920s his 'Africs' team included Archie Casely Hayford, who took Leslie Brown to Africa in 1934. The Browns lived at 63, Lauriston Road into the 1940s. Gerald Brown also became a doctor. Dr J. J. Brown died in 1953, and his practice was run into the 1990s by Barbados-born Colin Franklin whose daughter also became a doctor. When she went to work in Jamaica, seventy years of one Black medical practice in London ended.

Homes such as those of Cambridge, the Smiths and Easmons,

Dr Alcindor and Barbour-James may have been in Coleridge-Taylor's mind when he had written to *Reynold's Newspaper*. One 'coloured home' that must have been well known to him was 2, Bedford Gardens, off Kensington Church Street, where there lived the widow and two daughters of a New York-born actor who had died in 1867.

Ira Aldridge had spent decades touring provincial theatres around the British Isles, with London appearances, but he died during a tour of imperial Russia.[47] His mistress Amanda Brandt, who had recently become his wife, continued to live in London with their two daughters Luranah and Amanda, who had been born in 1860 and 1866. Both had an education in Belgium; Luranah then studied in London, Paris and Berlin, and became a concert music singer with international praise. The younger daughter was a student at the Royal College of Music from 1883 to 1887, one of the first students at that London institution. She sang and accompanied her sister at the piano, and from the Edwardian years almost to her death in the 1950s taught vocal technique and the piano.

Her pupils included members of London's Black middle class, including Frank Alcindor and Amy Barbour-James, as well as Alice Evans (Coleridge-Taylor's half-sister). From 1901 into 1932 she lived at 2, Bedford Gardens.[48] It was from there that she or her sister wrote to Beatrice and Clarence White on 16 July 1906 'It was such a pleasure to see you both' and that his violin playing had been delightful.[49] White later recalled his visits to the Aldridges's London home: 'Colored Americans who have visited England during the past ten years have felt their trips incomplete without a visit to the London home of the late Ira Aldridge', he wrote, disregarding the fact that the actor had never lived in that house. 'It has been the good fortune of a number of us to be welcomed in the home at 2 Bedford Gardens.' This 'modest little home' was run by Ritchie, the maid he was sure old American visitors would recall.[50]

With Sir Charles Villiers Stanford, head of the Royal College of Music, living a short walk away, and the Royal Albert Hall, Trinity and Royal colleges of music within a twenty minute walk, the Aldridge sisters and their visitors helped make the district a musical one. Next door lived Frank Bridge, a composer and teacher whose works were performed in London (in 1905, and at the 1907 and 1913 Promenade Concerts, for example[51]) although it was his pupil, Benjamin Britten, whose fame from the 1930s has drawn modern attention to Bridge.

The sisters gave recitals as well as attending concerts and arranging musical 'at homes'. *The Times* of 5 June 1905 reported on a recital at the Steinway Hall; the Amanda Aldridge Papers[52] also contain details of Luranah's recital at the Queen's Small Hall on 16 December that year, as well as an event in the Pump Room in Bath on 4 April 1908, and a return to the Queen's Small Hall on 17 June 1911 when Amanda also gave a piano recital; Coleridge-Taylor's songs to the texts by Kathleen Easmon featured in the sisters' programme. Both sisters were at that central London recital room on 29 June 1912 and 7 June 1913. There was another Queen's Small Hall recital on 23 May 1914. These events were not reported in *Hazell's Annual* and we have to conclude that the sisters were not major figures in Edwardian concert music-making.[53]

The home life of the three Aldridge women was not without stress despite the attentions of Ritchie. Their mother was bedridden and died in 1915, aged eighty-one.[54] Luranah took to her bed, ending a fine musical career and forcing her younger sister to stay close to home. Amanda developed a career as a composer, writing under the name Montagu Ring, and teaching. Frank Alcindor recalled, in 1984, that his doctor father had believed that Luranah had no physical illness.

Amanda Aldridge had met a group of Black American singers at the Steinway Hall, and had fallen in love with Dr David Phillips, a Jamaican who had recently qualified.[55] That would seem to be 1902 but the obituary clipping from the *Daily Gleaner* of Jamaica in Miss Aldridge's papers indicates that Dr Phillips, who had studied in Philadelphia, Montreal and London, had been an assistant at a south London hospital, so it might be a little later. This highly qualified medical man was another member of the Black middle class of Edwardian Britain. His association with the American singers remains unclear. His death in the 1930s led to Miss Aldridge keeping the clipping.

Another poignant aspect of her pride in her African descent is that she kept the copy of the *Musical Times* that, in 1908, detailed the career of George Bridgetower, a Black violinist born in Poland, associate of Beethoven, who died in Peckham, London, on the last day of February 1860.[56]

As Montagu Ring Miss Aldridge wrote music with African themes: 'Luleta's Dance' had West African elements according to 'an African' who reviewed its performance at the Queen's Hall on 23 May 1913 for the Black-edited *African Times and Orient Review* of July, apparently Togo and Fanti themes. She also had written the music to 'Where the Paw-Paw Grows (African Serenade)' which had words by Henry Downing.

Henry and Margarita Downing were another Black household known to Coleridge-Taylor.[57] They had participated in the 1900 Pan-African Conference in London (as had Alcindor) and served with the Coleridge-Taylors on its committee. Earlier, after service as a US consul in Luanda, Portuguese Angola, Downing had presided over the United States African News Agency in New York.[58] That news service group represented leading Americans of African descent.

The Downings were also friends with the Aldridge sisters, with their correspondence continuing into the 1940s, when Mrs Downing was informed by Amanda Aldridge that she had taught Dr Charles Easmon's wife and was in contact with Mrs [Adelaide] Casely Hayford.[59] Azalia Hackley from Detroit had wanted to visit the Aldridges in 1906; no doubt Burleigh called during his time in London 1908–9.[60] These were genteel music makers, not minstrels, ragtime performers or song-and-dance acts that entertained the multitudes. Not that Coleridge-Taylor dismissed all such acts, for his half-sister recalled that he spoke without scorn of Bert Williams and George Walker of *In Dahomey*.[61]

Those who settled in Britain, through such associations and connections, could be brought up to date on the state of their natal lands, and those like the Aldridge sisters and Coleridge-Taylor could have first-hand information on the lands their forbears had left.

The example of James Alexander George 'Jags' Smith suggests that Black British contacts helped him become a major figure in pre-1950s Jamaica. Privately educated in England where he was called to the Bar at Lincoln's Inn in 1910, he practised law in London for nine months and then returned to Jamaica. He seems to have been a frequent visitor to Britain on legal matters. He was elected to the legislative council of Jamaica and was a thorn in the side of the petty tyrants who ran Jamaica, until his death in 1943. Dr Brown nursed him back to health 'for several weeks' after he collapsed on the doorstep at Lauriston Road, and at that and other times Smith was updated with the wider world of Black people.[62]

Smith is hardly known outside Jamaica. Few know of James Hutton Brew, a resident of London from 1888.[63] Educated in Britain in the 1850s, he was a licensed attorney in the Gold Coast which allowed him to represent clients in court. Active in Fanti politics and journalism, he founded the *Western Echo* and then the *Gold Coast Echo* (edited by his nephew Casely Hayford) and challenged Britain's colonial claims of the 1870s. Brew suggested a local parliament selected by all classes and urged that Africans should take their arguments directly to Britain. He worked with Samuel Lewis in London in 1888 and apparently never returned to Africa.

Brew was associated with delegations in 1895 and 1898, and kept in close touch with other West Africans, especially lawyers, but his Edwardian years remain unresearched. He had business interests and bought and sold companies. He died at 14, Paulet Road, in the Brixton district of south London, in April 1915. His death registration states his occupation was 'land company promoter'. Family legends in Africa, as Peggy Priestley has revealed, suggest that his ambition was to be the first Gold Coast member of the British parliament.

For the Black middle class of Edwardian times, Brew's ambition was not fantasy. There had been Asian members of parliament and there were Black and Asian knights. The universities had honoured Black students, Black lawyers had won legal battles in the highest courts, and there were other men and women of national distinction: Coleridge-Taylor, Victoria Randle and Sergeant Gordon spring to mind. As a Londoner Brew would have had opportunities to learn of the successes of another Black lawyer who had taken up a political career in London.

Henry Sylvester Williams was born in Trinidad and educated there and in Canada before reaching England in the 1890s, as we have noted when detailing the Pan-African Conference of 1900. He qualified as a barrister, married, settled in London, travelled to South and West Africa, assisted African delegations, and was elected to Marylebone council in 1906. The *Marylebone Mercury* of 17 November 1906 made no mention of his ethnicity but when he resigned, in a letter mailed from Trinidad, the *Mercury* of 23 January 1909 referred to him as 'the Negro member'. Williams, who died in the Caribbean in 1911, had achieved little as a councillor, due to his African wanderings.[64]

Another Black lawyer, who was active in local politics until his death in 1940, remained invisible to historians until 1983.[65] Edward Theophilus Nelson, the son of a British Guiana builder, was born in Georgetown in 1878. Twenty years later he started studies at St John's College, Oxford, graduating in the summer of 1902. In March 1900 he had been elected secretary of the Oxford Union debating society, and became its treasurer by the beginning of his third year. Back home John Barbour-James noted this success, cabled congratulations, and announced the triumph in the colony's newspaper.[66]

Another Union officer was Raymond Asquith, whose father was to be Britain's prime minister. He described Nelson to his father as 'a West African Nigger, called Nelson for some reason, black as pitch', adding that his voice was 'a most magnificent organ, like the sound of heavy guns at sea'.[67] Nelson took up a career in law where that voice must have been a wonderful asset in his court appearances.

Graduating in 1902, Nelson moved to London where he was called to the Bar at Lincoln's Inn in November 1904.[68] From 1906 the street directories of Manchester listed him at Stamford Road, Bowdon in Cheshire until 1909 when his address changed to Cecil Road in the bosky suburb of Hale. He lived there until his death in 1940. His legal practice was at 78, King Street, in central Manchester, and he was registered to appear before the county courts of both Cheshire and Lancashire.

Marriage, the birth of a daughter, daily activities with professional colleagues and clients, a suburban home with domestic servants – all met the expectations of an Oxford-educated lawyer; blameless lives of comfort, a quintessential middle class existence in Edwardian Britain. But Edward Nelson was to achieve fame through a man he may never have met.

George Harry Storrs had inherited a cotton spinning business in Stalybridge, to the east of Manchester, and developed interests in bricks, timber and building.[69] Following his marriage in 1891 he lived at Gorse Hall, and there he was murdered on 1 November 1909. An intruder, armed with a revolver, inflicted fifteen stab wounds and Storrs died within an hour. There were four witnesses, including Mrs Storrs who had grabbed the gun.

Cornelius Howard, a petty criminal and cousin of Storrs, was charged with murder. His defence was that he had been in Huddersfield on the night of 1 November, to which he added that he had not possessed a gun since leaving the army after eight years service. Howard was represented at his trial by Percy Macbeth and Edward Nelson, who would have benefited from the publicity (Howard had no money) for the crime offended two aspects of the essence of Edwardian middle class life: a solid citizen had been murdered and private property invaded.

Nelson assembled witnesses, and the coroner's court heard from four of them that the man who had testified that Howard had not been at the lodgings in Huddersfield had, himself, been absent. A fifth witness stated he had been with Howard in that town about the time of the murder. Nevertheless Howard was sent to Strangeways prison, and from there he went on trial for his life at Chester Castle in March 1910. The jury accepted the testimony from Nelson's five witnesses, and took twenty minutes to decide that Howard had not murdered Storrs and that the Gorse Hall witnesses had been confused. Nelson's enquiries in Huddersfield had saved Howard from the gallows.

Three months later a courting couple were attacked by a knife-wielding stranger near Gorse Hall. Mark Wilde looked like the description of the man at Gorse Hall. He was an ex-soldier too, having served five years in Jamaica and Bermuda. He had also owned two revolvers, which he had thrown away as soon as he had heard about Storrs's death. In July 1910 Wilde was found guilty of the attempted murder of the courting couple, and sentenced to a mere two months.

There seems to have been an understanding between the police and the judge, but the public had no knowledge that Wilde was suspected of killing Storrs. Wilde had told the police he had returned home on the night of 1 November 1909 with blood on his face and clothes. The case against Wilde was assembled as he served his sentence, with old army colleagues identifying the gun, and three of the Gorse Hall witnesses agreeing that Wilde looked like the murderer. So, when

Wilde walked free from Knutsford prison on 30 August 1910 he was arrested and charged with murder.

Edward Nelson was solely responsible for the defence of Mark Wilde. At Chester Castle in the final days of October the jury heard the prosecution present arguments similar to those used against Howard. Nelson stressed that his client was the second individual to be prosecuted on the same charge of murder: a very rare event in British legal experience. But for the sensational murder trial of Dr Crippen in London, the trial in Chester would have been reported in greater detail by the nation's press.[70]

A mass of evidence was presented about the gun although death had been caused by stabbing. The prosecution introduced James Bolton, who had been stabbed by Wilde when walking home with his girlfriend. Nelson made an error when questioning Bolton, for he indicated that Wilde had been violent. Nelson and the judge argued, but the jury now knew that Nelson's client, who stood charged with murder, had been violent to a complete stranger.

Nelson also failed to gain the most from the testimony of a Home Office analyst who had said that there was no blood on Wilde's trousers or knife. Another witness told the court that Storrs's fourteen wounds were such that the murderer would not be splashed with blood.

Nelson brought in Wilde's mother, whose testimony was to her son's advantage. He further upset the prosecution with a brilliant move. He asked for Cornelius Howard to come into the courtroom. Howard testified that he too had been accused of murdering Storrs, and then was made to stand next to Wilde in the well of the court. Nelson asked for the gas lights to be turned up, for dusk was gathering. That ploy left the two men in view of the jury for longer. The jury would be unlikely to remember that Wilde had been on a prison diet since June; Howard was quite plump. There was little similarity between the pair.

Nelson seems to have spent hours with Wilde, coaching him how to respond to his questions. Wilde denied owning the five-chambered revolver, and said he had never been in or near Gorse Hall. He had never met James Bolton until he attacked him with a knife, but that was not mentioned.

The fourth day of the trial brought embarrassment to the police, for they had mislaid, then found, and then lost the screw which a soldier witness said enabled the Gorse Hall revolver to be fired as he had seen Wilde do in Malta. The prosecution scored when asking Wilde why he had thrown away his guns after the murder, when taking them to the police would have removed any suspicion or doubt. Wilde's response was vague and unhelpful, which suggests that either he was flustered or Nelson had not given him guidance on how to answer such an obvious question. Wilde also said he had not stabbed James Bolton, which did not help him for it was known that he had served a term in prison for that offence. Wilde testified that his scratched face on the night of 1 November 1909 had resulted from a brawl, but he could not identify the other man.

Nelson came to the rescue of his client, but made an error when questioning Wilde's girlfriend. Her brother was then questioned by Nelson, who got him to state that he had seen Wilde's two guns at his house after 1 November 1909. The summary by Edward Nelson, on the fifth day of the trial of Mark Wilde for the murder of George Harry Storrs, took two hours. He stressed mistaken identity, both of the revolver and of the man seen struggling with Storrs. The jury retired and took less than one hour to decide that the case against Wilde was not strong enough. Mark Wilde joined Cornelius Howard for an evening meal and Edward Nelson packed his papers and returned to Cecil Road.[71]

Nelson's local fame, through the Stalybridge murder of 1909, continued until he died in Manchester in April 1940.[72] He stood for and was elected to Hale Urban District Council in March 1913, winning with 224 votes against 91.[73] The local newspaper reports do not mention his ethnicity, but his African descent was clear in the photograph published on 28 March. The *Altrincham, Bowdon and Hale Guardian* commented on 11 April 'His success is naturally the source of a good deal of elation among his supporters, who feel that in Mr. Nelson they have a representative who is well able to protect their interests.'

In July 1913 Nelson became the chairman of the lighting committee,[74] and later became active in affairs relating to the borough's library. The electors of Hale returned Nelson to the council until 1940. A colleague stated in 1984 that 'Nobody ever objected to the professional blacks.'[75]

In 1919 Nelson defended Africans accused of rioting in Liverpool (his fees coming partly from a London-based Black group that included John Barbour-James and which was soon to be headed by Dr Alcindor) and we have already seen that Liverpool had working class Black residents. It had middle class Black residents too.

George William Christian, his two brothers and sister Octavia are four examples of Liverpool's Black bourgeoisie. Their father, Jacob Christian, had been born in Antigua and had first arrived in Liverpool as a fifteen-year-old sailor. He married Octavia Caulfield. By the time his son George was born in November 1872 he was a ship steward. In 1874, when the family lived at 14, Robertson Road, Toxteth, he was listed as a mariner. He gave up the sea and became a timber merchant.

His children went to school in Aigburth, and then George and his brother Alexander worked for John Holt. Holt was a pioneer trader in western Africa, with commercial interests and ships, developed with his brothers from the 1860s.[76]

Working for Holt was an excellent apprenticeship (Sir Alfred Jones had started there, too) and the Christian brothers went to Nigeria after training at the Liverpool headquarters. George Christian was running his own business by 1904, largely in the German Cameroons. His African descent was so obvious that the Germans, believing him to be a British West African 'native', charged him seventy-five pounds for failing to register his title to land; and then expelled him. Christian protested to his member of parliament who, in turn, wrote to the Foreign Secretary. Eventually Britain's ambassador in Berlin dealt with the matter and sought compensation, in 1906.[77]

Christian relocated his business to Nigeria by 1904. His head office at 12, Canning Place, Liverpool, was managed by his brother Alexander. He had been active with their father in the timber trade, in Hill Street, but by the time George Christian married Isabella Callow Stanbury in April 1911, Jacob Christian had died.[78]

Isabella Stanbury was not of the class that, O'Mara indicates, married Elder Dempster stokers for financial security. A nurse, and trained midwife, at the Hope Street, Liverpool, hospital where she had met her husband, her family had business and civic associations in Liverpool and across the Mersey in Birkenhead and Wallasey. Her husband's occupation according to their wedding registration was African merchant; he lived at 20 or 26, Sudley Road, Aigburth.

Just one year before his business had been described by Alfred Calvert in *Nigeria and its Tin Fields*, which included his portrait photograph and two photographs of his stores. These reveal corrugated iron roofs on square buildings, on flood-avoiding supports, but the romance of the trade is captured by his telegraph address: IVORY LIVERPOOL. His company owned six stores in Nigeria, and Calvert stated that Christian had 'exceptional qualifications for the trade' which was both cash and barter, and that his business met the 'requirements of both Europeans and natives'. There was no reference to his African descent.

G. W. Christian and Co. Ltd was incorporated in 1911, and the business expanded. His wife went with him to Africa, and they were photographed in Onitsha, seated in a motor car behind an African driver.[79] She returned to England to have their three children. When they were not in Africa they lived in a substantial house in Wallasey; and Isabella's unmarried sister looked after her children, who had private educations.

Less is known of Arthur and Octavia Christian, except that they also

44. Liverpool-born George Christian and his brothers ran
a tropical products trading enterprise in Nigeria (Margaret Othick)

married Liverpool people and that the Antigua sailor's African descent was visible in their complexions. The death of George Christian
in the Cameroons saw his widow leave Africa, to take over the daily
care of her family. Alexander Christian continued the business, which
was purchased by one of the giants: which kept his brother's name
into the 1930s, such was the reputation George Christian had established in Africa and in Britain.[80]

The Black bourgeoisie was mentioned in the fiction of Arthur Conan

Doyle, creator of the Sherlock Holmes detective stories. His *The Memoirs of Sherlock Holmes* involves an English woman who, having lived in Georgia, returned to England a widow, and then remarried. She lived in a cottage between Croydon and south London's Streatham, and there she had hidden the daughter of her first marriage to John Hebron of Atlanta. The daughter showed her African-American father's colour. Having discovered this, the fictional detective assured the new husband that his wife's eccentric behaviour was not the result of blackmail. He assured Holmes that his Black step-daughter would be welcomed into the family.

In *The Case-book of Sherlock Holmes*, set in Edwardian Harrow, Conan Doyle details a 'huge Negro ... dressed in a very loud grey check suit with a flowing salmon-coloured tie' who asked for 'Masser Holmes'. He was Steve Dixie 'the bruiser', who, with others of the Spencer John gang, intimidated and assaulted for profit. The gang had been employed to steal a manuscript which detailed the relationship between a young man and a woman of a higher class. The heiress, about to marry a duke, would have been blackmailed or a victim of scandal.

In *The Black Doctor*, published in 1908, Conan Doyle (himself a doctor, trained at Edinburgh University where he would have seen Blacks, as well as during his spell as a ship's doctor on the West Africa run) detailed Dr Aloysius Lane, who had settled in a Lancashire village in the 1870s. He had qualified in Scotland, and 'he came undoubtedly of a tropical race'. His title 'the black doctor' was a joke but, when his skills became better known, it was 'a title of honour'. The doctor was described as being from Argentina. A British-trained professional, Dr Lane was disparaged solely because he had a darker skin than the majority.

Where professionals – the Black middle class – have been researched inspiration often came from the need to detail Black anti-colonial efforts at the centre of the empire. Those whose achievements were outside that single but important area of work have included some remarkable people. Discussions with the son and the nephew of Dr J. J. Brown revealed that Risien Russell was an Afro-Caribbean medical man. The *Post Office London Directory, 1938* (p. 3274) confirmed that he had a medical practice at 44, Wimpole Street, in the Harley Street doctors' neighbourhood of central London. Dr Russell was named in a diary entry of 1913.

Mrs Humphry Ward, a highly popular novelist and leader of the campaign to keep voting rights for men only, was unwell. A relative, Dr Henry Huxley,[81] recommended to her husband that she consulted a 'very good nerve man, Risien Russell'.[82] Ward was a respected *Times* journalist; his wife was rich and internationally known. Dr Russell was at the top of his profession.

The men and women whose aspirations and achievements made them members of the middle class were not distanced from petty slights and racism. No matter how successful when training, no matter what their professional experience, the larger society viewed their African descent as a negative quality. Newspaper reports strongly suggest that journalists did not understand that it was possible to be cultured, neatly-dressed (no salmon-coloured ties), quiet, polite, respectable – and Black. This is clear from reports in the London press in September 1903.

The *Daily News* of 9 September 1903 reported that 'a coloured man of gentlemanly appearance, and speaking in a cultured manner' had informed magistrate George Denman, of Great Marlborough Street court in central London 'that he and some friends had been refused refreshment by a publican simply because of their colour. Their behaviour had been quiet and proper, and the only excuse was the one mentioned.' Denman was asked if the licence that had to be possessed by a publican obliged the licence holder to serve customers. The magistate said 'I cannot compel the publican to serve you.' The Black stated that he had looked up the law and had concluded that a publican was obliged to serve anyone unless they were a bad character or were behaving in a disorderly manner. 'We from different parts of the British dominions wish to know whether we are to be treated little better than beasts.' The matter was reduced to a basic question: 'what is the status of coloured men in the heart of the British Empire?'. Denman prevaricated, saying 'I think his rights are those of others.'

He avoided responsibility by stating that he could take the matter no further. 'So we have no rights in the heart of the Empire?' received his answer 'You have the same rights as others.' But as central London publicans had not refused to serve White people this was a 'very serious' matter. The Black man who had sought an informed view on English law was deeply disappointed. His 'gentlemanly appearance' and 'cultured manner' afforded no protection. 'We shall soon be in the same position as our ancestors if such a precedent is established' he warned. Denman was stung, and responded that Black people could not have greater rights than others: which over-looked that they could have fewer rights, which was why the questions had been asked.

The names of the man and his friends were not mentioned in these press reports, but, indignant that American-style racial bigotry had been exposed right in the centre of London, a journalist looked further. The *Daily News* of 10 September noted the 'negro' was 'clearly an educated man', whilst the *Westminster Gazette* of 9 September, refer-ring to the matter under a headline 'A Colour Line in London? Publicans and "Nigger" Customers', stated that the 'gentleman of culture and refinement' was 'well known at the American embassy'. It was W. E. B. Du Bois.

Certainly Du Bois was in England in the summer of 1903 and he was also 'an authority' on 'sociological conditions'.[83] The journalist contacted a friend who is quoted as saying that Du Bois had come 'to England with a high opinion of its wide tolerance and impatience of the prejudices which exist against his race in America, and the experience of yesterday was his first rude awakening to the fact that a "colour line" existed here'. But the man who had sought clarification from Denman had been reported as stating that he was from the British dominions.

He must have been a professional and thus a respectable person, whose public utterances should not result in publicity. Was he a doctor, or a lawyer? Being 'from different parts of the British dominions' excluded the professor from Atlanta. It could not have been Coleridge-Taylor, who had a wide fame. Edwardian gentlemen frequented clubs, not pubs, and Coleridge-Taylor, Casely Hayford, Alcindor and their friends would surely have met the sociologist in a restaurant or hotel if their own homes were not available.

In stepping away from normal bourgeois social patterns these Black people had been confronted with a colour bar. Not that the *Westminster Gazette* saw it like that. Its reporter had traced the pub where the gentlemen had been refused service. It was close to where the *In Dahomey* show was playing to packed audiences. The pub

> has for some time been frequented by a number of undesirable nigger loafers who have been attracted to the neighbourhood by the presence of the coloured theatrical company now appearing at the Shaftesbury theatre. Their presence is peculiarly obnoxious to the members of that company

because they were rowdy, 'fighting and using bad language'.

After a brawl the pub manager refused to serve them. 'It has nothing to do with their colour. It's just that they won't behave themselves.' The reporter asked if the ban applied to all Black people 'no matter how they are dressed, or what their appearance is?', and was informed that the undesirable Black customers were neatly dressed and quiet when they arrived, but got noisy after a few drinks. 'After the row we had the other day' the manager had ruled that 'no more niggers were to be served in this house'.

The ban was widespread in the area. 'The best dressed amongst them are the worst. We serve anybody, no matter whether their colour is green or blue so long as they behave themselves and pay for that they have.' The liberal logic of the *Westminster Gazette* failed to comprehend that bias is often emotional and thus prejudice does not have to be supported by facts or first-hand experience. Economic realities could be ignored, too. 'What does surprise us is that a publican should be willing to turn away a customer solely on account of his colour.' That was not a surprise to Du Bois and his friends. What had stunned them was that it was so blatant and in the very centre of London.

Since the 1890s the United States had seen Southern states enact legislation that formalised discrimination. Britain had no such laws, yet Black people were not respected and their rights were not protected. Myths of White cultural and social superiority, which justified the tropical empire and were linked with class and gender, did not require laws to define Black inferiority. Segregation, anti-Black laws and practices, and lynching were reported in the British press as aspects of the United States of America. When they were exposed in central London in the late summer of 1903 the liberal newspapers can be seen, ninety and more years later, as innocents and dupes.

The 'Racial Question in the West End' as the *Weekly Dispatch* headed a report in 13 September, added nothing for it, like the *Daily News* and the *Westminster Gazette*, failed to comprehend that a ban on Black people was as reasonable as the ban on women voting in parliamentary elections, the role of imperial overlords in the empire, and the way in which vast lands had been taken from their inhabitants and renamed Australia, New Zealand, and, more recently, Nigeria, Rhodesia and British East Africa. The imperial system was in no major way different to the peonage and segregated system of the United States. Did no journalist consider the experiences of the Lozi, the Sotho, Ndebele and other Black groups who had seen their traditional lands controlled by foreigners? The colour line was essential for the empire. And in August and September 1903 it had been exposed in the centre of London.

What of the rowdies? The district had Black residents: Annie Gross, Robert Rody and Frank Craig, albeit later; but it seems unlikely that the rowdies lived locally. Whoever they were, the success of the *In Dahomey* show had drawn them to the district. Their boisterous fun had spoiled the visit of Du Bois and his British friends. They had walked into a central London pub and had been rejected solely because the colour of their skin was similar to a group which had upset the manager. Education, accent, wardrobe, style, manners, social status, income and achievements stood for naught when the colour line was drawn.

Nevertheless, Britain's institutions found places for Blacks. Its concert halls echoed with applause when Coleridge-Taylor's music was performed; church and civic halls were packed when the Fisk groups presented Spirituals; soccer and rugby players and supporters admired the skills of Tull and Peters. Londoners supported Johnson against Wells.[84] There were few unsold seats when *In Dahomey* played in London. Burleigh, Hackley and the Aldridge sisters presented refined entertainments, and Garland his less highbrow entertainments, to appreciative audiences. Universities and the courts of law found places for Blacks, as did private and public schools, medical institutions, and local councils. Yet, as Raymond Asquith's ignorant and racist letter to his father shows, this acceptance could be superficial. In the case of Coleridge-Taylor, a creative artist of international stature whose very appearance showed his African descent, the ambivalent nature of his colleagues has been revealed in that most informative of sources: private correspondence from Jaeger.

It was in *Crisis* that another Edwardian achiever was reported. The selection of John Richard Archer to be mayor of the borough of Battersea in London was reported in the British press in November 1913, largely as a novelty for Archer displayed his Barbados father's African descent. Born in Liverpool in June 1863, he travelled widely and must be assumed to have been in the merchant navy like his father. He had married a Canadian of African descent, settled in London, and worked as a photographer with a shop/studio in Battersea Park Road. On the left wing in municipal politics, in a slum-land inner suburb, Archer, who was named in reports of Coleridge-Taylor's funeral, supported feminist campaigner Charlotte Despard and, in the 1920s, the district's communist member of parliament. But he was a householder, a businessman, and a rate payer – middle class responsibilites in Edwardian London.[85]

He was not elected but chosen by the councillors, but his victory owed a great deal to his earlier work on the council, where he had been diligent during his first spell as councillor in 1906–9. He had supported John Burns and opposed spiritualism, showing his independence of mind. Returned in 1912, he became mayor a year later. The Black press in the USA, where mayors are usually directly elected, welcomed this honour to the race, as did Archer who said Battersea had shown 'that it has no racial prejudice'.[86] Archer has caught the attention of historians because he was involved with left wing and radical movements in the post war years, organising the Labour candidate's success in 1929 parliamentary elections, as well as for his efforts for Black rights as the first president of the African Progress Union. It was that Black group, founded in 1918, which paid some of the fees of that other Black councillor, barrister Edward Nelson, when defending fifteen 'coloured men' accused of rioting in Liverpool in 1919.[87]

Archer's work in municipal affairs included being on the Wandsworth Board of Guardians and the finance committee of Battersea council. There he obtained minimum wage levels for both council and Board of Guardians workers (of thirty-two and thirty shillings a week – £1.50).

Archer's correspondence with New York-based journalist John

45. Margaret Archer, born in Canada, was the wife of the
Mayor of Battersea in 1913 (New York Public Library)

Edward Bruce[88] shows that Archer responded to the American's
congratulations, writing from Battersea town hall on 26 November
1913. Noting that Bruce presided over the Negro Society for Historical
Research, Archer requested a copy of George Washington Williams's
History of the Negro Race which he knew from reading at the British
Museum.[89] On 17 January 1914 Archer thanked Bruce for the book,
and advised that he had received congratulations from other African
Americans, naming Robert Abbott (founder-editor of the *Chicago
Defender*), Robert H. Terrell (one of the few Black judges in America)
and Professor John Cromwell of Washington, DC. He had also heard
from people in Pittsburgh, Atlanta and Ohio.

46. John Archer, Liverpool-born Mayor of Battersea. Published
in the New York monthly *The Crisis*, 1913 (New York Public Library)

Archer's letter advised Bruce that a Mrs Roberts had died on
9 January 1914, aged ninety-five. The old lady had lived with John and
Margaret Archer for many years. 'She was very dear to us, and we feel
her loss very acutely.' That Mrs Roberts shared their home had been
mentioned in 1906 when Harry Johnston (the one-time governor of
Uganda) wrote his *Liberia*. For Mrs Roberts had been the wife of
that Black African republic's first president back in the 1840s. 'This
wonderful old lady still lives (in full possession of her faculties) in a
quiet street off Battersea Park.'

Archer told his new friend in America that she had wanted to be
buried back in Liberia, where she had gone as a child in the 1820s. She

47. Jane Roberts, born in slavery in the United States, had been a pioneer
migrant to Liberia. She lived in south London, in the Edwardian years, in the
home of John and Margaret Archer (Royal Commonwealth Society)

had changed her mind and wanted to be buried in England. Archer
planned to mark the grave so that 'all those members of the race who
visit this capital' would be able to pay their respects to 'one who did
honour to her Race'.

Plot 252 class H block F in Streatham cemetery, Garratt Lane, south
west London, contains the remains of Jane Rose Roberts. The grave's
owner was Margaret Archer. There is no memorial; there never has
been, for the Archers were far from rich.[90]

Along with photographs of the Archers, *Crisis* of March 1914
published the mayor's comment:

> I have learned of one man here, an African, who did not think that I
> ought to hold, as a man of color, my present position. . . . I would like

to meet him because as a member of the board of guardians I have a great deal to do with imbeciles.

Archer's humour had been seen in his acceptance speech, reported in the local *Wandsworth Borough News* on 14 November 1913:

> I am the son of a man who was born in the West Indian islands. I was born in England, in a little obscure village, that probably never was known until this evening, the City of Liverpool. I am a Lancastrian born and bred, and my mother – well she was my mother. She was not born in Rangoon and she was not Burmese. She belonged to one of the greatest races on the face of the earth. My mother was an Irishwoman, so there is not much of the foreigner about me after all.

With Archer, Williams and Nelson being elected to councils, the parliamentary aspirations of James Hutton Brew seem reasonable. Historians will identify other Blacks in municipal politics in Britain in the 1900s and 1910s.[91] Like the doctors Brown, Goffe, Alcindor, Russell, and Easmon, and lawyers Smith and Nelson, these were middle class roles. That so little is known about John Archer's wife, and, until now, that Jane Roberts found a home with that Black couple in Edwardian London, strongly suggests that the Black middle class deserves more investigation.

The aspirations, achievements and educations of Britain's Black middle class did not protect these men and women from British racism. Dr Alcindor's wife had been shunned by her family for marrying a Black man, which must have deeply hurt her husband (whose own family was far away in Trinidad). Institutions were also bigoted, with the Colonial Office's rules showing several examples of anti-Black beliefs.[92] Its 1902 rejection of Black doctors being employed on the same terms as Whites became public in 1909.[93] There were questions in parliament in October 1912, for Dr Easmon had been refused employment in the Gold Coast.[94] It must have been galling for the England-educated doctor, whose London qualifications (MB, BC, MRCS, LRCP) had been followed by work in a hospital in Huntingdon.

Social bigotry could become public at almost any time: the high class London Palladium saw a disturbance in 1914 when a woman objected to Blacks in the audience.[95] Earlier that year a London club, apparently appealing to less refined individuals, had a disturbance resulting 'from objections made by American women to the presence of Negroes in the club. The women threw glasses and bottles around and had to be put out of the club.'[96] The evidence, as usual, has contradictions. Whilst Alcindor's photograph in a book on cricketers suggests acceptance, J. J. Brown was stung into recruiting an all-coloured cricket team by a well-spoken fool who asked at a London Hospital match 'Tell me, Brown, why don't you find more than one or two Niggers together?' – he had responded 'Eleven will come and play you.'[97]

Black doctors were employed in British hospitals and all who qualified in Britain had walked the wards as students. Dr Ogontula Sapara, who had studied in London in the 1890s, was recalled as saying that 'patients, who had never seen a black man, were too frightened to let him minister to them. He didn't mind, because he knew that it was an innocent fear.'[98] Over the years the doctors must have met innocent and foolish ignorance, as well as official and personal racism. This did not prevent Dr Sapara returning to London in 1912–13.[99]

It seems that individuals could be widely respected within their neighbourhoods, which created a 'passport', a word used by Leslie Brown to describe his childhood where his father was an established medical man. There were taunts at school and unforgiven rudeness by one of his teachers. The part Black, part Jewish young Londoner had a stutter and, through some private education, had acquired a 'posh' accent. All four were mocked by one teacher. Brown's sports skills enabled him to make friends and the stutter ceased.[100]

His father had faced bias and racism in the medical staff at the London Hospital. People who had studied for years and had passed the stringent examinations of the professions could be treated with contempt, because they were Black, by responsible persons. In 1913, as Du Bois reported in *Crisis*:

> The Camberwell poor-law guardians of London, England, refused to appoint a colored physician whose qualifications were above those of the other candidates, on the grounds that the fastidious poor would refuse to be attended by a Negro.[101]

Their victim was Harold Moody, a Jamaican of the same age as Brown. Qualified in London in 1912, Dr Moody established his own practice in south east London. He married a nurse named Olive Tranter in May 1913. His brother Ludlow, who arrived on the *Trent* at Southampton on 30 April 1913, aged twenty-one, also studied medicine in London. He won the Huxley Prize for physiology at King's College. He married Vera Manley and both returned to the Caribbean.

Another Black doctor was Ismael Cummings from Sierra Leone, who was working at the Royal Victoria Infirmary in Newcastle in 1913. Joanna Archer, a junior matron, bore his son, Ivor Gustavus Cummings, who was born in West Hartlepool in December 1913.[102] When Dr Cummings went to Africa his family moved to Surrey where they associated with Coleridge-Taylor's widow and children.

With contacts in Britain, America and in the empire, the Black middle classes were well placed to assist new arrivals and to press for Black perspectives to be considered. There can be little doubt that Downing was a source for much of the England-related material that was published in *Crisis* in New York by Du Bois. For Edwardian residents and visitors, associations forged by colour led to a greater understanding of the Black world.

NOTES

1. D. Jabavu, *The Black Problem* (Fort Hare, 1920; repr. New York: Negro Universities Press, 1969), p. 41. Jabavu spent 1903–13 in Britain, visiting America.
2. Middle class is used to mean servant-run homes, schooling beyond the age of fifteen, an occupation that earned fees not wages, children at private schools, and also that so-difficult concept, 'respectability'.
3. CO 368/9 Sierra Leone index of correspondence with London includes a note of despatch 33 of 18 February 1875 from the Acting Governor, being D. P. H(?). Taylor's application for an appointment. The *Sierra Leone Blue Book*, 1876, notes his employment started on 11 November 1875. Taylor's obituary in the *Sierra Leone Weekly News* (Freetown) 27 August 1904 says he returned to Africa in 1875 'and practised for a short time, when in November he received the appointment'. The *Gambia Blue Book*, 1904 and the grave in Banjul cemetery confirm he died on 25 August 1904. The gravestone was erected by Taylor's daughter. My thanks to Christopher Fyfe.
4. W. Sayers, *Samuel Coleridge-Taylor, Musician: His Life and Letters* (London: Cassell, 1915) can be relied on apart from the untruths of his father's time as a doctor in England, for there was no time between qualifying and returning to Freetown to set up on his own in Croydon. The mother's identity was obscured, for she lived until 1953. His wife, whose uncle had been a professor of music at Oxford, is described 'In her schooldays, Miss Walmisley had worked her lessons side by side with coloured girls' (p. 70) remains a mysterious statement, and reappears in the 1927 revised edition of this book.
5. Sayers, *Coleridge-Taylor*, pp. 48–9, 79.
6. D. Lewis, *W. E. B. Du Bois: Biography of a Race, 1869–1919* (New York: Holt, 1993), pp. 246–7. The Du Bois papers contain a receipt for the London conference subsidy.
7. Preface to S. Coleridge-Taylor, *Twenty-four Negro Melodies* (Boston: Oliver Ditson, 1905), p. ix.
8. Ibid. p. 30; see also P. Richards 'Africa in the Music of Samuel Coleridge-Taylor', *Africa* (London) 57, 4 (1987), pp. 566–71.
9. Fyfe, *Sierra Leone*, p. 537.
10. Ibid. p. 318.
11. Richards, 'Africa in the Music', p. 569, quoting from J. Coleridge-Taylor, *A Memory Sketch or Personal Reminiscences of my Husband, Genius and Musician, S. Coleridge-Taylor 1875–1912* (Bognor: Crowther, 1943), p. 51.
12. J. Johnson, *Along This Way* (New York, 1933; repr. New York: Viking, 1990), p. 213.
13. This had been rented by his mother and step-father in the 1890s and thus was where *The Song of Hiawatha* was created. One hundred years after the composer's birth one of London's famous blue plaques was placed on the house. The composer lived in many houses in Edwardian Croydon, as a study of Sayers, *Coleridge-Taylor*, will reveal.

14. White papers, Schomburg Library, New York, Box 2, folder 4. The year is suggested by its contents.
15. Hilyer Papers, Howard University: Samuel Coleridge-Taylor letter 3 January 1904; Coleridge-Taylor to Du Bois, 31 January 1905 (Du Bois Papers, reel I, frame 621).
16. *Gold Coast Leader*, 29 August 1908, pp. 2–3. My thanks to Ray Jenkins.
17. J. Green, '"The Foremost Musician of his Race"' *Black Music Research Journal* (Chicago) 10, 2 (Fall 1990), p. 245 shows the programme cover.
18. Locke Papers. I am also indebted to Anne Simpson who sent me details from the *New York Age* when she was working on her *Hard Trials: The Life and Music of Harry T. Burleigh* (Metuchen NJ: Scarecrow, 1990).
19. Lady Evans was the former Marie Stevens of New York, now the wife of Francis Evans who once had been MP for Maidstone; and Mrs Bradley Morton, once Cornelia Sherman, lived in London's Mayfair with her New York lawyer husband; see Carol Kennedy, *Mayfair: A Social History* (London: Hutchinson, 1986).
20. Sayers, *Coleridge-Taylor*, pp. 221–2.
21. Ibid. p. 206.
22. L. Harlan (ed.), *The Booker T. Washington Papers, Vol 9* (Urbana: University of Illinois Press, 1980), p. 37.
23. M. Davenport, *Azalia: The Life of Madame E. Azalia Hackley* (Boston: Chapman and Grimes, 1947).
24. V. Edwards and M. Mark 'Clarence Cameron White', *The Black Perspective in Music* (New York) 9, 1 (Spring 1981), pp. 55–6.
25. White Papers, New York.
26. Coleridge-Taylor papers, Royal College of Music, London.
27. *Post Office London Directory*, 1909, p. 1763; ibid. 1911, p. 1763. Ibid. 1912, pp. 686, 711 lists Alcindor at 37, Westbourne Park Road, and ibid. 1913, pp. 397, 1816 with his surgery at 201, Harrow Road; ibid. 1916, p. 674 notes a change to 23, Westbourne Park Road.
28. White Papers.
29. Sayers, *Coleridge-Taylor*, p. 262.
30. Ibid. p. 261.
31. Ibid. p. 272.
32. Ibid. pp. 273–4.
33. Ibid. p. 277.
34. Sayers, *Coleridge-Taylor*, pp. 55, 63; P. Young, *Letters to Nimrod: Edward Elgar to August Jaeger 1897–1908* (London: Dobson, 1965), pp. 4, 11–12, 22–3, 61, 74, 279; L. Foreman, *From Parry to Britten: British Music in Letters 1900–1945* (London: Batsford, 1987), pp. 9–10.
35. Sayers, *Coleridge-Taylor*, p. 63 (1927 edition, p. 64).
36. A. Brewer, *Memories of Choirs and Cloisters* (London: John Lane, 1931), p. 94.
37. Foreman, *From Parry*, pp. 9–10.
38. Young, *Letters to Nimrod*, pp. 4, 279.
39. *Sierra Leone Weekly News*, 23 November 1912 reported May's return on 20 November 'after an absence of about five months'; *Anti-Slavery Reporter*, October 1912, p. 214, noted May's visit to their London office, for May was on their Sierra Leone committee.
40. J. Green, 'Perceptions of Coleridge-Taylor on his Death (September 1912)', *New Community* (London) 12, 2 (1985), pp. 321–5.
41. J. Coleridge-Taylor, *My Husband*, p. 60.
42. *Crisis* (New York) September 1913, p. 219; *Annual Register 1913* part II, p. 22.
43. J. Green, 'John Alcindor (1873–1924): A Migrant's Biography' *Immigrants and Minorities* (London) 6, 2 (July 1987), pp. 174–89 has full sources.

44. I am indebted to Frank Alcindor for his recollections of his childhood, and to his wife Evelyn who, although she never met her husband's father (who died in 1924), had spent the 1939–45 war years with his mother, from whom she learned many details of the Edwardian years. This contact was made via the grave records at St Mary's Catholic Cemetery, Paddington, and the telephone book. I thank Ziggi Alexander for her advice, back in 1981. Prying into the Alcindor family story made it possible to place Dr Alcindor in history (see Lewis, *Du Bois*, pp. 249, 452) and to reunite Frank Alcindor with his nephew, whose army officer father had died in 1945. My entry on Dr Alcindor has been accepted by the *New Dictionary of National Biography* (Oxford University Press).

45. Full sources are in J. Green 'West Indian Doctors in London', *Journal of Caribbean History* 20, 1 (June 1986), pp. 49–77; and also J. Green 'Dr J. J. Brown of Hackney (1882–1953)' in Lotz and Pegg (eds) *Under the Imperial Carpet*, pp. 259–77. I am grateful to Dr Brown's son Leslie and nephew Ronald Green for interviews during 1984–5, and acknowledge the stimulus received from both Leslie Thompson and Brian Willan, and the assistance of the *Jewish Chronicle*, *Hackney Gazette*, the London Hospital and Dr Colin Franklin. This mix of veterans, documentation and newspapers was extremely fruitful.

46. Identified by Leslie Brown.

47. H. Marshall and M. Stock, *Ira Aldridge: The Negro Tragedian* (London: Rockcliff, 1958; repr. Carbondale: University of Southern Illinois Press, 1968) remains an excellent study despite its age. The steady research of Bernth Lindfors, leading to what promises to be the final word on the actor, is to be seen in his 'Ira Aldridge, "The African Roscius"', *South African Theatre Journal* (Johannesburg) 10, 1 (May 1996), pp. 71–84.

48. *Post Office London Directory*, 1901, p. 873 lists Amanda Ira Aldridge as professor of singing.

49. White Papers.

50. Ibid. press cutting *c.* 1921.

51. Foreman, *Music in England*, pp. 74, 78, 90.

52. Northwestern University, Evanston (Illinois). My thanks to Bernth Lindfors and the University's special collections library.

53. Foreman, *Music in England* which is *Hazell's Annual* reprinted, does not mention them. Its index gives more space to Coleridge-Taylor than to Bach, Gounod or Debussy. Sayers, *Coleridge-Taylor* does not mention the sisters.

54. Marshall and Stock, *Aldridge*, p. 297.

55. Ibid. p. 304.

56. *Musical Times* (London) 1 May 1908, pp. 302–8.

57. Marjorie Evans recalled them vividly seventy years later, in discussions with the author in the 1980s. Lewis, *Du Bois*, pp. 454, 457, detailing Nina Du Bois's time in London 1914–16 when their daughter was at school in England, does not mention the Downings although their friendship was welcomed by Mrs Du Bois and is documented in the Du Bois Papers. Lewis does not note that Coleridge-Taylor died in 1912 although his family were friends of the very isolated Nina Du Bois in London.

58. L. Harlan (ed.), *The Booker T. Washington Papers, Vol 3 1889–95* (Urbana: University of Illinois Press, 1974), p. 84.

59. Marshall and Stock, *Aldridge*, pp. 304–6.

60. Hilyer Papers, Howard University: Jessie Coleridge-Taylor to Mamie Hilyer, 15 June 1903, suggests that Burleigh was in London at that time 'We are looking forward to meeting Mr. Burleigh'.

61. Marjorie Evans to Jeffrey Green.

62. I am grateful to Ronald Green (interview July 1984) for this and other insights into his doctor uncle. *Who's Who, 1940* (London: A & C Black, 1940), p. 2955 for Smith.

63. M. Priestley, *West African Trade and Coast Society* (London: Oxford University Press, 1969), pp. 158–73.

64. Hooker, *Williams*; Mathurin, *Williams*.

65. J. Goodman, *The Stabbing of George Harry Storrs* (London: Allison and Busby, 1983) was reviewed in the *Times Literary Supplement* the week that my article was accepted by *New Community*; see J. Green, 'Edward T. Nelson' *New Community* (London) 12, 1 (Winter 1984–5), pp. 149–54.

66. *The Argosy* (Georgetown) 31 March 1900; ibid. 21 July 1900. When completing my article for *New Community* I had been wrongly informed that Nelson's year of birth was 1874. Christopher Hollis, *The Oxford Union* (London: Evans Bros, 1965), p. 256.

67. J. Joliffe, *Raymond Asquith: His Life and Letters* (London: Collins, 1980), p. 64; photograph including Nelson opposite, p. 112. My thanks to Richard Symonds.

68. Records Officer, Senate of the Inns of Court and the Bar (London) to Jeffrey Green, October 1981.

69. Goodman, *Stabbing*.

70. Crippen had fled with his mistress, dressed as a boy. Taking a faster ship and using the telegraph, detectives from Britain met Crippen when he reached America.

71. Goodman, *Stabbing* concludes that had Wilde been charged first, he would have deserved to have been found guilty. But there was nothing to connect Wilde to the murder until he stabbed James Bolton, unless the police had ascertained that Wilde had owned an American five-chambered revolver of the type seized during the struggle at Gorse Hall.

72. *Altrincham, Bowdon and Hale Guardian* 9 August 1940 has a two-and-a-half column obituary with photograph; the *Manchester Guardian* 5 August 1940 has a far shorter obituary.

73. *Altrincham, Bowdon and Hale Guardian* 21 March 1913; ibid. 28 March 1913. By contrast, the North ward voters were split 289 – 219.

74. Ibid. 22 July 1913.

75. Francis Sealey, telephone conversation with Jeffrey Green, 10 March 1984.

76. *Merchant Adventure* (Liverpool: John Hope & Co, nd *c*. 1953).

77. PRO FO 367/12/24751. 'I am constantly being pressed for settlement by Mr G W Christian'; 'a mulatto, but a British subject'.

78. Family documents and information courtesy Margaret Othick, daughter of George William Christian.

79. J. Green, 'George William Christian (1872–1924): Liverpool Mercant' in Lotz and Pegg (eds), *Under the Imperial Carpet*, pp. 69–77; photographs between pp. 142–3.

80. I am indebted to the United Africa Company, London, for access to their files.

81. Mrs Ward's daughter had married Leonard Huxley: their sons were Aldous and Julian, both important 1930s writers.

82. J. Sutherland, *Mrs Humphry Ward* (Oxford: Clarendon Press, 1990), p. 331 quotes from Dorothy Ward's diary entry 14 June 1913 [diary at University College London].

83. E. Rudwick, 'W. E. B. Du Bois as Sociologist' in A. Meier and E. Rudwick, *Along the Colour Line: Explorations in the Black Experience* (Urbana: University of Illinois Press, 1976), pp. 28–55.

84. C. Rolph, *London Particulars* (London: Oxford University Press, 1980).

85. This reading is not one that is found in my friend Peter Fryer's *Staying Power*, pp. 290–4.

86. Ibid. p. 291.

87. Green 'Nelson', p. 151; *Liverpool Daily Post* 8 November 1919; J. Green, 'The African

Progress Union of London, 1918–1925. A Black Pressure Group', typescript paper presented at London University Institute of Commonwealth Studies, 5 February 1991, p. 8; *Sierra Leone Weekly News* (Freetown) 28 February 1920, p. 5.

88. Microfilm; typescript courtesy Ian Duffield.
89. J. Franklin, *George Washington Williams: A Biography* (University of Chicago Press, 1985). Williams, not to be confused with the English George Williams, founder of the YMCA and benefactor to several Blacks in Britain, saw his *History* published in 1882. Williams died aged 41, after a long trip to Africa, in Blackpool in 1891: he was engaged to an English woman.
90. Cemetery records. The US-Black historian George Williams's grave in Blackpool was unmarked for more than eighty years; see Franklin, *Williams*, pp. xxiii-xxiv.
91. The author was the first to detail Nelson's career. Nelson's municipal career in Cheshire and Black connections were not known to crime historian Jonathan Goodman, who presciently commented in his *The Stabbing of George Harry Storrs* (p. 222) that had Nelson 'been born fifty years later, he would have become either a leader of the militants in his native country or a spokesman for the civil rights movement in the United Kingdom'.
92. The presence of Black Caribbeans in the colonial Gold Coast needs considerable investigation, with the social groups, clubs and associations used by civil servants examined as it would seem likely that a colour line was drawn. As there is still a lack of awareness of this Black presence, the matter has not been considered. David Kimble's pioneering *A Political History of Ghana* (Oxford: Clarendon Press, 1963), pp. 99–101 suggests an easy recruitment of Europeans and a racial demarcation between administrative and clerical posts but disregards the West Indian presence in the colony.
93. Fyfe, *Sierra Leone*, pp. 614–15,
94. *Anti-Slavery Reporter* (London) January 1913, p. 290.
95. *Crisis* (New York) 8, 3 (July 1914), p. 115.
96. Ibid. 8, 1 (May 1914), p. 12.
97. Green, 'West Indian Doctors', pp. 62–3.
98. A. Duster (ed.), *Crusade for Justice: The Autobiography of Ida B. Wells* (University of Chicago Press, 1970), p. 214.
99. *Anti-Slavery Reporter*, October 1912, p. 214; ibid. January 1913, p. 263.
100. Leslie Brown to Jeffrey Green.
101. *Crisis*, (New York), November 1913, p. 323. Dr J. C. Buttachargi was the medical officer at the workhouse in Lutterworth (south of Leicester) and the victim of a petition raised by the pauper inmates in 1909, who wanted a doctor of 'their own race and colour'. Reported in the *Lancet* (London) 4 September 1909, p. 76, and thus widely known to the British medical profession, that it was rejected was small consolation to Britain's doctors of African or Asian descent.
102. Val Wilmer, 'Ivor Cummings' obituary, *The Independent* (London) 4 December 1992, p. 15.

10

In the service of their Lord

INFORMATION produced to promote the activities of Christian missions to Africa was often shameless propaganda which demeaned Africans, presented negative stereotypes of savage and pagan societies awaiting a White missionary, and used Black artistic creations to encourage criticism of idolatry.[1] There were some Whites, notably the Hungarian Emile Torday, who supplied artefacts from the Congo to the British Museum where they were first displayed in 1909, who understood something of African artistic expression.[2]

Exhibitions promoted by missionary societies, which included grand affairs in Manchester in 1907, Bradford in 1908, Leeds and London in 1909 and Nottingham in 1912,[3] could be local and almost domestic. Other images came in biographies of Livingstone the missionary-explorer and, later, Mary Slessor, which were published time and time again as already noted. These were not exceptions.

The Story of the Life of Mackay of Uganda by his sister had reached twenty-six thousand sales by its seventh edition in 1898. There was an edition for boys too. Anderson-Morshead's *The History of the Universities' Mission to Central Africa 1859–1898* was in its fourth edition by 1905. Holman Bentley, whose *Life on the Congo* was published in 1887, had his two volume *Pioneering on the Congo* in print by 1898. His widow Margo saw her biography into print in 1907. Published by the Religious Tract Society, over four hundred pages long, it carried advertising for *By the Rivers of Africa; or, From Cape Town to Uganda. A Story of Missionary Enterprise in Africa* as well as John Bell's *A Miracle of Modern Missions, the Story of Matula, a Congo Convert*.

John Brown Myers's *The Congo For Christ: The Story of the Congo Mission* was first published in 1895 and its second edition, of the Edwardian years, increased sales to nine thousand. It carried advertising for *Uncle Tom's Cabin*, a biography of Frederick Brotherton Meyer, and *From Kafir Kraal to Pulpit* 'the story of Tiyo Soga, first ordained preacher of the Kafir Race'.[4]

There were missionary magazines, reports and other publications as well as meetings where tales were told by returned missionaries and by their friends who corresponded with them. The impression was

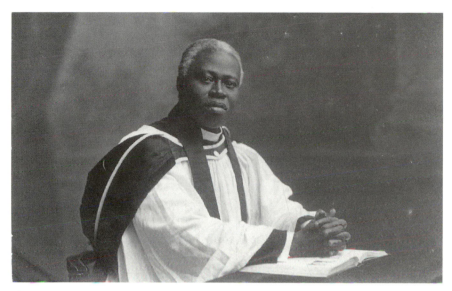

48. One of several Christian workers active in Edwardian Britain, this individual remains unknown although this card suggests he visited Wheatley, Oxfordshire, in September 1907 where he preached at the church

that Blacks needed White guidance to start a 'civilising' process. The truth was quite different.

Black men and women carried Christianity to others: Black Christian missionaries from America, en route to Africa, were far from unusual in Liverpool. When a Liverpool friend attempted to book forty American missionaries and their families under Bishop William Taylor into a hotel in 1884 'the hotel keeper bristled up and said he wouldn't allow a lot of niggers to come into his house at all'.[5] These were Whites.

Amanda Smith[6] had gone from America, via England, to take the Christian message to Africa and India, and Peter Thomas Stanford had been so long in Britain that he was known as England's Coloured Preacher. Stanford seems to have been active in the Baptist church in Birmingham from 1888, and returned from the USA in October 1902 – for his membership certificate of Masonic Lodge 1551 (Birmingham New Street) was reproduced in his *The Tragedy of the Negro in America*.[7]

Caribbeans went to Africa too. Joseph Jackson Fuller left Jamaica in 1844, aged nineteen. With his father and a brother the Fullers were members of the Baptist community on Fernando Po island which, when it was claimed by Spain, moved in a mini-exodus to the mainland. Their 1858 Cameroons settlement was named Victoria.

In 1878 four African-Americans reached Victoria: Calvin Harris Richardson and his wife, her sister Henrietta, and Henrietta's husband

Thomas Lewis Johnson. The Richardsons worked inland into the 1880s, but Henrietta Johnson died and her husband was invalided back to London within months of landing. In March 1900 Thomas Johnson, who had spent twenty-eight years in slavery in Virginia, became a British citizen.[8]

By that time Joseph Fuller was also living in England, having administered the handing over of Baptist Missionary Society property to the Basle Mission when the Cameroons became German in the 1880s.[9] Living at 2, Salisbury Villa, Cleveland Road in Barnes,[10] Fuller attended Baptist meetings around Britain. He was recalled:

> In England, pleading the cause of his African brother, nobody had a better reception from English audiences than this noble negro orator. Who among those who heard him will ever forget his story of the 'Burial of Slavery' and the midnight scene at Kingston, Jamaica, when the vast crowd of liberated slaves sang the Doxology. I never met a negro so full of humour, and he enjoyed saying witty things against himself and his people.[11]

He had married Charlotte Diboll, a missionary from East Anglia, in 1861. Their son J. J. A. Fuller worked for the Baptists in the Congo from 1890 into 1895, resigning in 1896.[12] His parents had moved to 36, Sydner Road in north London's Stoke Newington by 1899.[13]

The Jamaican who had been born in slavery times and served his people and his faith in Africa for over forty years was registered to vote in British elections.[14] He and Charlotte maintained their Baptist connections.[15] Indeed, their move to Stoke Newington was because the Devonshire Square Baptist Church in Stoke Newington Road was that faith's main place of worship, relocated from the original 1638 site in central London to Stoke Newington in 1870.[16] The Fullers were visited by many Baptists, probably including delegates to the 1905 Baptist Congress in London.

Joseph Fuller died in Sydner Road, on 11 December 1908.[17] He was eighty-four years old. He was buried in plot 4699 K 10 in nearby Abney Park Cemetery. A memorial service at Devonshire Square church involved Revd John Brown Myers, of the Baptist Missionary Society and author of *The Congo for Christ*, who was granted probate and handled the veteran's estate: value £137. Charlotte Fuller is not listed in later street directory entries for Sydner Road, and she and her son remain unresearched.

Thomas Johnson, who had first met Fuller in Africa, had settled in Bournemouth in the 1890s, with his second wife Sarah or Sara. There, in 1908, his autobiography went into its eighth edition. The first version, published in Liverpool in 1882, had been reprinted. Newspaper publishers W. Mate of Bournemouth seem to have printed the

1908 version as a commercial venture for Johnson. Over 260 pages, with many photographs, its purple covers soon fading, *Twenty-Eight Years a Slave* was sold at meetings and by mail from Johnson's home at 'Liberia', 66, Paisley Road, Boscombe. It was promoted by a picture postcard. The views of Africa and Africans presented by Johnson are hardly sympathetic. This account of his years in slavery in America, how he got to England and to Africa, and his mission work in the United States, Britain and Ireland has numerous quotations. When they have been checked, they have been found to be true although excisions are not indicated.

Johnson had many friends in the Baptist and evangelical church circles of Britain, and a Miss Bluett promoted the idea of a pension for him, for his lectures, sales of his publications (which included 'The Consecrated Will', a hymn published in 1897 and again in 1903, and *Consecration Thoughts for the New Year* of 1903[18]) and the auto-biographies and postcard, provided an uncertain income. The *English Churchman*, the *Baptist*, the *Christian* and *The Sword and the Trowel* published details of the appeal in 1901. The latter, in July 1901, included a photograph of 'the happy face of Brother Thomas L. Johnson [which] must be familiar to a large number of our readers'. The income when invested gave the Johnsons thirty pounds a year.

Johnson, the ex-missionary, had become an exemplar to the British. He spoke about his faith to soldiers in Winchester, and was present when army commander Lord Roberts visited the Soldiers Home there in 1902.[19] He spoke in Belfast, Reading, Folkestone, Bristol, Haywards Heath and in London.[20] In October 1903 he attended the London funeral of the widow of Charles Spurgeon, the major Baptist preacher. Johnson, who had attended Spurgeon's College in the 1870s, had been at the minister's funeral in 1892. The *Baptist* of 30 October 1903 reported on Johnson's presence at the funeral, and that a 'jet black' college student had been in the parade. This was William Forde, whose studies had started at Spurgeon's College that autumn. College records reveal that he left for Costa Rica in 1907, and that he died there decades later. Forde corresponded with John Bruce and Du Bois in America, but nothing else of his years in Edwardian Britain is known apart from his work for his Lord.

Johnson's somewhat rambling autobiography, which makes no mention of Forde, states that he was involved in a mission in Emsworth in late 1906 and another in Bishop Auckland in the autumn of 1907.[21] In late 1909 he presented a copy of his autobiography to Bournemouth's member of parliament.[22] He was well known in Bournemouth, seen in the streets, chapels, churches and, from the 1910s, in a wheelchair. For many in that town he was the first Black person they had seen close to. His remark 'Shake hands – the black won't come off', the slave chains and whips that decorated the walls of his home, and his Christian faith were recalled into the 1980s. He died in 1921 and his widow's name vanished from local street directories after 1923.

Both Johnson and Fuller had served their Lord in tropical Africa before the White empires had expanded there. Britain's Christians had long been involved with missionary efforts in the tropics, with Methodists active in Jamaica as early as 1789, but it was the Baptists who, in 1813, started a sustained campaign there. They had been stimulated by ex-slave Baptists from the United States who worked in Jamaica from the 1780s.[23] One legacy of the British Baptist link with Jamaica is the image of a Black man on the town crest of the Northampton town of Kettering.[24] Another is the movement of Jamaicans to Africa.

The Jamaican-descent community in the Cameroons included Rose Patience Edgerley. She married an England-born Baptist missionary named Grenfell who had first reached Africa in 1875. George Grenfell severed his links with the mission, trading and travelling, until news reached Europe of the massive river system that had carried Stanley half way across Africa. Fired by stories of the Congo, and by Stanley's reports on the inhabitants, the Baptist Missionary Society asked Grenfell to head their activities in this new mission field. Grenfell was a missionary-explorer in the Congo from 1878 until his death there in 1906. There are three biographies, such was his fame.[25] Examination of these hundreds of pages has uncovered evidence of the presence, in Edwardian Britain, of Rose Edgerley and her children. The limited amount of information retrieved on Black women in Edwardian Britain justifies the fullest details of Rose Grenfell and her daughters.

Mrs Grenfell was described as 'an African bride'[26], and shown as a dark person in *The Christ of the Congo River*.[27] Her ethnicity was detailed by Harry Johnston, the first biographer, who also published a photograph.[28] Johnston's own autobiography states:

> She was a remarkable woman, a West Indian Negress (Miss Edgerley) who had come to the Cameroons with her parents and brother to work for the Baptist Missionary Society. Her brother was long afterwards a builder and carpenter at Victoria, Cameroons, and assisted to put up my Consulate on Modole Island. The Edgerleys were a remarkable family. They were well-educated West Indian Negroes, but probably with white intermixture.[29]

Johnston, who was a linguist, recalled that in 1883 she spoke excellent French and 'also Portuguese, Ki-shi-kongo and Duala'.[30]

By the beginning of the twentieth century Rose and George Grenfell's three daughters were in England. They were at Walthamstow Hall in

Sevenoaks, Kent, a school for missionaries' daughters. The oldest of the daughters, Patience or Pattie, born in 1880, had gone from that school to Belgium, returning to her parents in the Congo where she died in 1899.[31] Carrie and Gertrude Grenfell remained in England, and were joined at Sevenoaks by the youngest, Grace Isabel, by 1903.[32] She had made her journey from Africa to England, with both parents, in April 1900.[33]

Exactly where the Black mother and her daughter Grace were in 1900 is not clear, but George Grenfell was in Belgium, Glasgow, and Birmingham before taking a holiday with his wife in Boscombe (where surely they made contact with Thomas Johnson?). He and Rose remained in Bournemouth at the beginning of 1901 and left for Africa in September.[34]

The third biography's extracts from letters to and about the Grenfell children have provided this information.[35] The school's records indicate that all three Grenfell sisters remained in Sevenoaks until 1907, the year after their father died in Africa. Carrie, who was born in October 1883,[36] was teaching there.

Eighty years later two of her pupils recalled this Black teacher and her sisters. Ethleen Scott's parents were missionaries in India but she had never been there, and so the Grenfell sisters were 'the first coloured people I had seen'. Many of the pupils had lived abroad so 'coloured children were not therefore entirely unknown'. She had no recollection of any difference in treatment, a view supported by a photograph of the sisters and others with the headmistress.

Miss K. M. Claxton also had known the Grenfells in Sevenoaks:

> I remember Carrie Grenfell. In January 1902 I went as a boarder to Walthamstow Hall ... Carrie was then a pupil-teacher. I well remember her sitting on the opposite side of the table helping us with our 'three r's'.

Carrie Grenfell, the twenty-year-old, was recalled 'in the teacher's place and giving us other lessons ... Carrie was a lovely person with a lovely expression. I should say she was a born teacher.'[37]

These years in Britain must have been lonely, despite holiday time spent with the sister of Walthamstow Hall's head teacher, and a visit from Alfred Baynes of the missionary society.[38] Earlier they had been in the care of Joseph Hawkes of Birmingham, whose sister Mary had been Grenfell's first wife.[39] It was normal for the boarders at Walthamstow Hall to have their parents far away, and the teachers would be sympathetic. The Grenfell children were expected to take up missionary work, and Carrie went to Belgium in 1904 to improve her French. She was part of a network that, for example, saw her in Oxford in mid-1905 at a service dedicating a boat for mission use.

Carrie Grenfell loaned letters from her father to biographer George

Hawker and they include one from 1894 (when she was eleven) when he gently scolded her for poor marks in French and music, subjects which were 'the most important ones for you, considering your future'.[40] One to Gertrude in 1897 suggested that Carrie marked a string to show her height, and that Gertrude did the same, and then send the suitably cut strings to their parents in the Congo.[41] In September 1902 Carrie was sent a letter in which her father attempted to deal with her 'blues' which he thought resulted from 'too much introspection'. In October 1903 he was praising Carrie for writing 'at such length though you have had so little in reply'.[42]

In February 1904 Carrie, who was in Brussels, was told to write to her sisters, and that 'As the daughter of a Protestant missionary you may have to share in some of the obloquy that Belgians are just now pouring out on Protestant missionaries on the Congo.'[43] Although the Congo was the personal empire of Leopold, King of the Belgians, many Belgians felt it to be their 'place in the sun'; and Belgian business interests also disliked the humanitarian agitation against exploitation in the Congo Free State – agitation that was seen to be British and Protestant. Carrie Grenfell's African descent was not important in this.

George Hawker, Grenfell's biographer, was the minister of a Baptist church in north London, and he noted that he had taken tea 'with Mr. and Mrs. Fuller in their home in Stoke Newington. Mrs. and Miss Grenfell were also their guests.'[44] No other information has been traced on Rose Patience Grenfell and her three daughters. Marriage to fellow Baptists or a home together in England seem likely.

There were Africans active in the service of the Lord who spent time in Britain. The steam-powered boats that enabled the Fullers and Grenfells to travel the broad waters of the Congo river system had African crew: including Bungudi or Bongudi who spent nearly a year in west London's Chiswick in 1893.[45] Another was Don Zwau Nlemvo, who was in England in 1884, and again in 1892–3 when he spent months in Edgware, translating parts of the bible with Holman Bentley.[46]

His third visit to England was in 1905. He arrived on the *Philippeville* at Southampton on 14 May,[47] and worked on the translation project as well as attending the Baptist World Congress in London. Other Black delegates included two Americans, one female, whose photographs appeared in *The Tatler*.[48] Nlemvo 'spoke a few well-chosen words'.[49] Nlemvo remained in England for months, working with Bentley and living with the Bentleys in Bristol into 1906. Bentley died at the end of 1905, with Nlemvo at his side.[50] The widow's biography has Nlemvo's portrait photograph: he wears a three piece suit. Under it she states 'One of Dr. Bentley's earliest boys, afterwards his assistant translator (during his last visit to England the cold affected his eyes, and he is now entirely blind).'[51] Nlemvo died in Africa in 1938.[52]

Margo Bentley saw nothing odd that her husband had encouraged two mission-schooled Africans to exhibit their printing skills at an imperial exhibition in Antwerp in the 1890s or that the mission's boat was used for imperial and commercial ventures as well as Christian purposes, being taken by Stanley in 1887.[53]

The newspaper-reading British public in 1906 could learn of a 'street preacher' who had been at the House of Commons on 25 September. From his seat in the Strangers' Gallery he had shouted that 'he had come from Almighty God'. The 'man of colour' was seized by four attendants and led away, protesting that he was a British subject. Joseph Emmanuel gave an address in Blackfriars Road, London. He was from Trinidad and his 'real name' was Warner. News of this incident reached the borders of Wales, being reported in the *North Wales Guardian* of Wrexham. This eccentric behaviour has exposed one Black individual whose presence in Edwardian Britain would otherwise never have been known to history.

Two years later there were many Black Christians in and around Westminster. June 1908 saw the Pan-Anglican Congress meet at Caxton Hall, where the opening service was performed by Bishop James Johnson 'a native African'.[54] There were many other Black delegates.

The Anglican church was the major Christian group in Britain, being the official or state religion. Its work abroad was through the Church Missionary Society (CMS), which had links with recent British imperial interference in Uganda and the Sudan. Earlier CMS efforts had placed churches, schools and hospitals in west Africa.[55] A majority of its local leaders were Africans, who undertook many of the daily tasks and much of the vernacular teaching. Bishop James 'Holy' Johnson, the Revd James Okuseinde from Ibadan, the Revd E. W. George 'a native African from Abeokuta', Canon Wilson 'an African native' and Bishop Isaac Oluwale were noted by the London press.[56]

Racist theories of White superiority had become part of the baggage of most Whites who went to Africa from the 1880s, and Africans – inside and outside the church – were treated with contempt. The CMS, like the Baptists, needed active workers and so promoted Black people. James Okuseinde had worked for the church in Ibadan for twenty years, but the most important Black Edwardian Christian was 'Holy' Johnson.

Born and educated in Sierra Leone, Johnson moved to Nigeria in 1874 and there laboured for his Lord.[57] In 1893 he rejected an invitation to be an Assistant Bishop, aware that the CMS no longer promoted Blacks on merit.[58] Isaac Oluwole and Charles Phillips accepted.[59] Johnson moved from Lagos to Benin, and his Lagos church struck out for independence, in the spirit of Johnson's teachings that Africans did not require Whites to show them Christianity. To their dismay Johnson raised his voice against the breakaway: he was not the first revolutionary to dislike the result of his inspiration.[60] His biographer suggests that the veteran minister was less anti-White because of his decent treatment in Britain in 1899 and 1900.[61]

These experiences included an honorary degree and becoming Vice President of the CMS – which invited him to preach at their annual gathering in London in April 1900. He was received by Queen Victoria, of course.[62]

Johnson, whose wife had been educated in England for five years,[63] had been in Britain in 1873 and 1886 too, but his 1908 congress visit was the last. Pious, sincere, and deeply Christian, this son of liberated slaves told the London congress 'Christianity is intended to be the religion not of one particular race of people only, but of the whole world.'[64] He advised the delegates that polygamy was not a moral question and that the Anglican church and CMS were wrong to ignore the social basis of and advantages in African marriage practices. He was acutely aware that polygamists who wanted to join the church had to abandon partners of many years.

The bishop had encouraged the expansion of African missionary efforts into the interior, where local social practices and languages survived vigorously. The coastal communities had been exposed to Christianity for decades, and its peoples were to some extent Europeanised. The names of some seemed very British, so it was excellent that the *Church Times* reported, on 19 June 1908, that forty of the Anglican clergy of West Africa were Black. It noted Canon Wilkinson from Sierra Leone and Canon C. W. Farquhar of the West Indian-led Rio Ponga Mission near Sierra Leone, as well as layman J. F. Buckle from Freetown.

On 17 July the *Church Times* noted that layman and magistrate S. A. Buckle, also from Sierra Leone, was in the group that was to spend the weekend of 18–19 July in Portsmouth. Plans included lunch at the town hall. Delegates moved around Britain for some time. Bishop Oluwole and his wife sailed from Liverpool, bound for Lagos, on 21 November.[65] Ten days earlier Canon Farquhar had left on the *Prasilu* bound for Conakry in French Guinea.[66]

For many months after the congress Bishop James Johnson visited congregations all over Britain. He told of his life and of Africa. In Newry, County Down, Irish audiences suggested that his story should be published and later in the year Johnson's *A Brief Outline of the Story of My Life* was published in London. It sold out and a second edition was soon printed.[67]

Johnson was deceived by Bishop Tugwell and other Anglican church officials in London, whose plans excluded any African-run section of their church.[68] Johnson visited the Colonial Office in London in December 1908, and discussed education in Nigeria. He disliked the secular nature of the colony's education policy (ignoring other faiths), justly criticised the wishy-washy attitude to the training of teachers, claimed that schoolbooks were unsuitable, and recommended that teaching in vernacular languages should be more prominent.[69]

These meetings with senior church and government personnel were pleasant and polite, which made the bishop's homeward-bound voyage extremely unpleasant. The sole Black passenger on the *Aro*, his attempt to hold a Sunday service was fruitless and, scorned by White passengers who refused to sit at breakfast with him, this bishop who had been greeted by Queen Victoria was ostracised and treated as a leper.[70] It was a colour-line which ignored education and achievement.

That colour line was firmly in place in the United States, where Christians of African descent had long ago run their own church organisations. There were other Black institutions, including schools, colleges and hospitals. The intellectual centre of Black America in the Edwardian era was Atlanta – which was where Du Bois taught. His and other colleges attracted Black students from abroad, and also sent missionaries to Africa, many passing through Britain.

Spelman College in Atlanta had trained Nora Gordon who worked for her Lord in Africa from 1888. In 1895 she married a Jamaican missionary who had trained at Spurgeon's College in London. Simeon Cunningham Gordon and his wife then worked for the Baptists in the Congo. Their two children died in infancy and she returned to Spelman where she died in 1901. His second wife Ada Jackson went via Britain to the Congo; and their two daughters were sent to be educated in Jamaica. She visited them there in 1909, and died shortly afterwards, whereupon the girls were sent to Virginia.[71] When and how often Gordon and members of his family changed ships in Britain is not yet known.

Gordon continued to labour for the Baptists in the Congo into 1926.[72] For many years he was at Matadi, where ocean steamers docked and passengers took the railway into the interior. 'It is the meeting-place of many races and nationalities' noted *The Baptist* magazine in 1902. Gordon 'a missionary from Jamaica, for years adopted the work as his own, and not withstanding the aloofness of Europeans from negroes, was held in universal esteem because of his sterling qualities'.[73]

Nora Gordon's impact in 1880s Africa so impressed Joseph Clarke from Scotland that he sent two African women to Spelman College in 1891. Lena Vuna Clarke went from Atlanta to Scotland for two years, and then, with the Gordons, returned to the Congo in 1895. About seven years later, in her thirties, she went to study in Scotland, returning to Africa in 1903. This American-trained African who was in

Edwardian Britain married a Scottish missionary named C. L. Whitman. The pair went to work for their Lord in Nigeria for the United Soudan Mission. Her three sons were in Britain from the 1910s and she died in Britain in 1920; her husband returned to Africa. Nothing else has been traced on these Afro-Scottish lads whose mother had been trained in a woman's college in Georgia.[74]

Even less is known of the second of these African women at Spelman, other than that she took the Scottish name Maggie Rattray, that she stayed in Atlanta into 1902, that she returned to the Congo via England, and that she worked at Lake Ntomba into the 1920s.[75]

Other Africa-Britain-USA connections included Emma DeLany's move from Spelman College to British Central Africa [later Nyasaland; now, Malawi] around 1902.[76] She joined Mississippi-born Landon Cheek, who returned to the United States with two African brothers.[77] Miss DeLany inspired Daniel Malekebu to travel thousands of miles to the Cape, where he obtained her help to make his way to America in 1907, where he qualified as a doctor.[78] Transportation routes strongly suggest that DeLany, Cheek, the Njilima brothers and Malekebu spent time in Edwardian Britain.

The African whose enthusiasm in the service of his Lord reveals more apparently unlikely connections was Salim Wilson. He had experienced war and slavery in Africa before committing himself to Christianity. He travelled widely, wrote his autobiography which was sold around Britain, and then became an evangelist to the unChristian British and a property owner in Lincolnshire.

Hatashil Macar Kathish was a Dinka from the Sudan-Ethiopia region who reached England in 1880 with CMS missionary Charles Wilson: as a servant, of course. Between 1882 and 1886 he attended Hume Cliff College in Derbyshire, and was taken by the college principal on a lecture tour of northern England: as an African exhibit. He went to Africa, apparently seeking his homeland, spending 1887–8 in the Congo with a White missionary before returning to England. Now known as Salim Wilson, he worked for the CMS, and went to north Africa. He settled in Yorkshire, living in Wakefield and in Barnsley.[79]

His *Life Story* appeared in 1889 and a second edition was published in Birmingham in 1901. Around 1906 the same publisher issued his *The Ethiopian Valley*, which was an account of Dinka life from his recollections of thirty years earlier. By these mid-Edwardian years Wilson was active spreading Christianity to the English, from a base in Heckington near Boston, Lincolnshire. He suggested to the CMS that he could work as a teacher among his people in the Sudan, but this was rejected.

Preaching in Anglican churches in Lincolnshire, Barnsley and other places in Yorkshire, Wilson slowly moved to the Methodists and by 1911 he was associated with the Bethel Free Mission. With that organisation he reached Scunthorpe in north Lincolnshire. He settled there, and in April 1913 he married Mrs Eliza Alice Holden, his landlady. This wedding was detailed in the Hull and Grimsby newspapers, and even filmed. 'Black Mates White' and 'Black Prince Marries White Woman' were the headlines. There was 'much good natured cheering' from the crowd. An active member of the Frodingham Road primitive Methodist chapel, he built four terraced houses in that street. He died near Scunthorpe in 1946 and was buried next to Eliza, who had died in 1942.

Rather like John Springfield, the shoe repairer in late Victorian Guildford, Salim Wilson's presence in Britain does not fit the general British view of their history. There were other African preachers in Britain, and Black people were active in religious gatherings all over the British Isles in Edwardian times.

Mark Christian Hayford, born in the Gold Coast in 1864, was the brother of Ernest (the doctor) and Casely (barrister and author). By the age of thirty he was active in the Baptist church and began to aspire to a fine building for his congregation. He travelled to Britain where he was befriended by Alfred Jones, whose assistance took him to Canada by 1899. After months in the United States he returned to Britain, placed orders for building materials, and sailed for Africa in mid-1902.[80]

Promised donations did not materialise and the builders refused to continue until they were paid. So Hayford retraced his path to England in late 1902, where he borrowed from Jones's Bank of British West Africa. He remained in Britain for much of 1903, but was in Africa to greet more materials that had left Liverpool in February 1904. In June 1906 his church at Cape Coast was opened.

Mark Hayford had been begging, in a good cause and in the service of his Lord, for six years, and he resumed these efforts in order to pay for the upkeep of the church, touring the coast of western Africa from Calabar to the Gambia.

In 1910 he was in Edinburgh for the World Missionary Conference, and remained in Britain, largely in Liverpool, for two years. His ambitions now embraced a school and a college at Cape Coast. In 1912 he crossed the Atlantic and attended a conference in Alabama arranged by Booker T. Washington. He returned to Britain in May, where he remained into 1913.

Between 1898 and 1913 Mark Hayford collected up to five hundred pounds a year, in small donations except for one gift of a thousand pounds from cotton-thread magnate Thomas Glen-Coates of Paisley in Scotland. British supporters were more generous than those in

America, but funds were insufficient to keep his school open. The begging activities of Hayford had another dimension, for he presented the view that Africa could be developed by Africans. He spent more time in Edwardian Britain than he did in Africa, had a wide circle of associates, and married White women. In 1926 he claimed to have met King George the Fifth.

When a Scot accused him of false accounts, Hayford sued, and lost. By 1927 he had obtained £22,000 but had almost nothing to show for it. He had been close to being arrested as an impostor. He died in the workhouse in Bath in 1935. Was he a cheat? He is an enigma, but his sophisticated begging in Edwardian Britain had brought him into contact with thousands and they had parted with cash.

Another African churchman who was no stranger to Britain was Mojola Agbebi, whose first visit had been in 1895. He stopped off in 1903, en route to New York, but spent four months in Britain the following year, between New York and Lagos.[81] His independent church had been founded in Lagos in 1888, following no single European concept of Christian worship. His sense of Nigerian or Yoruba identity led him to renounce European clothing styles by 1894 and to change his name to an African one.

In 1904 Agbebi had strong links with William Hughes at the Colwyn Bay institute for Black students. He visited and also preached in churches elsewhere in Britain. He is named in newspaper accounts of the funeral of Henry Stanley in May 1904. He became a member of the London-based African Society. When he sailed to Africa in the autumn his companions included the Contons from Bermuda and Joseph Morford from America, contacts made when at Colwyn Bay.

Crowds greeted the *Akabo* when it reached Lagos in October 1904. The support he had gathered for his Lord when in America and Britain was on his terms; from people who recognised that he wanted an independent church that paid allegiance to Christianity as a moral force, not as a belief system that required White interpretation and practice. Those who met him in Britain in 1904 met a proud, independent, African nationalist Christian. No doubt many would have found Mark Hayford to be an easier companion. Both Africans served their Lord in their own way.

In presenting their appeals and pushing their sincere beliefs the fact that both Thomas Johnson and Salim Wilson had been enslaved would have created sympathy. Agbebi and Hayford presented images of pagan and semi-destitute Africa. Bishop Johnson had changed from being cantankerous to being stuffy and old-fashioned whilst expressing radical opinions on polygamy and colonial education. All these efforts led to some financial support: which explains why the trickster of 1902 had claimed to be the Revd Claude Bevington Wilson.

Whilst we can be sure that Ashaker was not a minister, we cannot be so certain that the Black Edwardians who were so public in their efforts in the service of their Lord were truly welcome in Britain. It does seem that once these Black Christians were involved with a local church or chapel, social contacts developed and a network opened up. Agbebi and the school at Colwyn Bay, Thomas Johnson and the Spurgeon's College group, and Salim Wilson and the Methodists of Humberside seem to have shared faiths and experiences.

Sincere Christians were active in challenging some of the excesses of imperialism, which was why the Bishop of London had greeted Henry Sylvester Williams's Pan-African Conference in London in 1900 and why Frederick Meyer aided Nigerian and southern African protestors. The Anti-Slavery Society had a strong Quaker element whose friendships included Black people. There were Black delegates at Christian conferences – Anglican, Baptist, Methodist and missionary. Books by Black Christians and about Black Christians were on the shelves of pious homes all over the British Isles. And so were the missionary tales of violent and pagan savages, with illustrations of fetish idols and tribal weaponry. Fuller's eyewitness account of the ending of slavery in Jamaica and Johnson's tales of slavery in Virginia were important testimonies which reminded Edwardians that Whites, within living memory, had denied any rights to Black people, and had used violence to enforce their domination.

The impressions left by these Black people in the service of their Lord may well have outlasted the foolishness in White missionary books. The Black lecturers could move congregations and conference audiences in profound ways.

Published works may have had less influence in Edwardian times than the quantities of surviving books first suggest. The printed word in a now majority-literate nation had growing importance, and Black people had their works published in Edwardian Britain. Fiction, drama, history, biography, humour, economics, imperial politics, poetry, and profound studies of Black culture have been traced. There were editors and journalists too.

NOTES

1. J. Pieterse, *White on Black: Images of Africa and Blacks in Western Popular Culture* (New Haven: Yale University Press, 1992), pp. 64–75.
2. 'Images of Africa: Emil Torday and the Art of the Congo 1900–1909' at the Museum of Mankind (London) in 1994 explored this; see also J. Vansina, 'Photographs of the Sankuru and Kasai River Basin Undertaken by Emil Torday (1876–1931) and M. W. Hilton Simpson (1881–1936)' in Edwards *Anthropology*, pp. 193–205. Torday was 'able to exploit Kuba political divisions to acquire precious objects' (ibid. p. 197) and was in search of the 'noble savage'.

3. K. Harman 'A List of World Exhibitions' part 3, *Exhibition Study Group Journal* (West Wickham, Kent) 39 (Winter 1995), pp. 63–4. All these issued postcards.
4. Jeffrey Green collection.
5. W. Taylor, *William Taylor of California, Bishop of Africa: an Autobiography* (London: Hodder & Stoughton, 1897), p. 387. This group published *Illustrated Africa* monthly. For Afro-Americans passing through Liverpool see E. Redkey, *Black Exodus: Black Nationalist and Back-to-Africa Movements, 1890–1910* (New Haven: Yale University Press, 1969), pp. 168, 179, 239–40, 275.
6. C. Moore, *Amanda Smith: an Autobiography* (London: 1906). Moore had revised Bishop Taylor's *Autobiography* (1897).
7. Stanford, *The Tragedy of the Negro in America* (North Cambridge, Mass: 1897; repr. *c.* 1903) p. xi. This book notes that the *Daily Graphic* (London) 3 February 1890 said he had lived in England for some fifteen years, that the *Daily Gazette* (Birmingham) 6 August 1897 said he was 'known as England's Coloured Minister' and that Frederick Brotherton Meyer had written from London on 18 February 1903 that 'I shall be glad to see you when you come to London' (p. xvii). Meyer's campaign against boxing champion Jack Johnson was not based on Negrophobia.
8. T. Johnson, *Twenty-Eight Years a Slave* (Bournemouth: W. Mate & Co, 1908), pp. 254–5. I am grateful to Barbara Ponton who examined the naturalisation papers.
9. Baptist Missionary Society (London) microfilm 72, letter 24 April 1887 on the Richardsons leaving for America.
10. Baptist Missionary Society (London) microfilm 31, Baynes box H 24.
11. T. Lewis, *These Seventy Years: An Autobiography* (London: Carey Press, 1930), p. 91.
12. R. Glennie, *An African Christian Missionary* (London: Carey Press, 1933); E. Payne, *Freedom in Jamaica* (London: Carey Press, 1933), pp. 83–4; *Missionary Herald* (London) May 1890, p. 150; ibid. May 1896, p. 197.
13. *Kelly's Street Directories* as advised by Library Services, London Borough of Hackney, London N16 0JS.
14. Ibid *Electoral Register 1901–2*
15. *The Baptist* (London) 10 May 1889, pp. 291–4; ibid. 11 October 1889, pp. 233–4.
16. *North London Recorder* 13 May 1938.
17. Street directories list the Fullers at number 36 but the documentation concerning Fuller's death has 38; see *North London Guardian* 25 December 1908, p. 9; *Calendar of Wills and Grants of Probate 1909*.
18. *British Museum General Catalogue*, 1964 'T L Johnson'.
19. Johnson, *Twenty-Eight Years*, p. 233.
20. Ibid. pp. 234–5.
21. Ibid. pp. 260–61, 264.
22. My thanks to the Anti-Slavery Society, London; see J. Green 'Thomas Lewis Johnson (1836–1921): The Bournemouth Evangelist' in Lotz and Pegg *Imperial Carpet*, pp. 55–68, photograph 12.
23. Payne, *Freedom in Jamaica*, pp. 18–19.
24. William Knibb of Kettering, Baptist missionary and victim of slave plantation owner rule in Jamaica, had been arrested and had his chapel destroyed. Members of his church were flogged for attending services. Escaping to England in 1832, Knibb spread details of Jamaican planter society's violence and thus aided in the abolition of slavery by Britain's parliament in 1833. Knibb proposed that Jamaicans should go, via Britain, to Africa as Baptist missionaries, and Alexander Fuller was in the first party.
25. H. Johnston, *George Grenfell and the Congo* (London: Hutchinson, 1908); G. Hawker, *The Life of George Grenfell, Congo Missionary and Explorer* (London: Religious Tract Society, 1909); H. Hemmens, *George Grenfell: Pioneer in Congo* (London: Student Christian Movement, 1927).

26. Hemmens, *Grenfell*, p. 74.
27. Myers, *Congo*, p. 80.
28. Johnston, *Grenfell*.
29. H. Johnston, *The Story of My Life* (Garden City NY: Garden City Publishing, 1923), p. 100.
30. Ibid.
31. Hawker, *Grenfell*, pp. 340, 421–2, 477. Grenfell refers to his wife as Patience and to his daughter as Pattie. E. Pike, *The Story of Walthamstow Hall 1838–1970* (Otford, Kent: Longmore Press, revd edn 1973).
32. Walthamstow Hall, Sevenoaks, files.
33. Hawker, *Grenfell*, pp. 454–5.
34. Ibid. pp. 464–9.
35. Ibid. pp. 483, 517, 540 for example.
36. Ibid. p. 340.
37. I am grateful to Walthamstow Hall for these contacts, and for the correspondence with the veterans.
38. Hawker, *Grenfell*, pp. 540–41.
39. Johnston, *Grenfell* p. 9.
40. Hawker, *Grenfell*, p. 473.
41. Ibid. p. 479.
42. Ibid. pp. 476–83.
43. Ibid. p. 489.
44. Ibid. p. 89.
45. Johnston, *Grenfell*, pp. 186, 261; Fullerton, *Christ of the Congo*, pp. 74–5.
46. H. Bentley, *W. Holman Bentley* (London: Religious Tract Society, 1907), pp. 150, 363, 365; *Dictionary of African Biography: Sierra Leone – Zaire*, pp. 256–7.
47. *African World* (London) 20 May 1905, p. 75.
48. *The Tatler* (London), 26 July 1905, p. 122.
49. Bentley, *Bentley*, p. 403.
50. *The Christian* (London) 21 April 1938.
51. Bentley, *Bentley*, facing p. 343.
52. *The Christian*, 21 April 1938; *Dictionary of African Biography: Vol II: Sierra Leone – Zaire*, pp. 256–7 notes Mantauru Duudula also known as Nlemvo lived 1865–1938 and was 'a major African literary expert'.
53. Bentley, *Bentley*, pp. 196–7, 204, 368.
54. *African World*, 20 June 1908, p. 280.
55. J. Ajayi, *Christian Missions in Nigeria 1841–1891* (London: Longmans, 1965); E. Ayandele, *The Missionary Impact on Modern Nigeria 1842–1914* (London: Longmans, 1966).
56. Named by the *African World*; see also *Daily Mirror* (London) 15 June 1908, p. 3; ibid. 18 June, p. 3; ibid. 19 June 1908, p. 5.
57. E. Ayandele, *Holy Johnson: Pioneer of African Nationalism 1836–1917* (London: Cass, 1970), p. 85.
58. Ibid. pp. 260–61.
59. Ibid. pp. 249, 259.
60. Ibid. pp. 254–6, 260–63, 325.
61. Ibid. pp. 264–6.
62. Ibid. p. 265.
63. Ibid. p. 251.
64. Ibid. p. 342.
65. BT 27/581.
66. Ibid.
67. Ayandele, *Holy Johnson*, p. 342.

68. Ibid. pp. 332–3.
69. Ibid. p. 343.
70. Ibid p. 344.
71. B. Guy-Sheftall and J. Moore Stewart, *Spelman: A Centennial Celebration 1881–1981* (Atlanta GA: 1981); F. Read, *The Story of Spelman College* (Atlanta GA: 1961). My thanks to Spelman graduate Josephine Harreld Love of Detroit, for access to these histories of Spelman College.
72. Fullerton, *Christ of the Congo River*, p. 204 noted his years in the Congo as 1890 to 1926.
73. Ibid. pp. 96, 98. Fullerton had been the home secretary of the BMS from 1912 to 1927, and would have known missionaries of all backgrounds. Matadi was the base for the field secretary of the BMS, too, another source for Fullerton. The experience of Gordon with Whites in Africa explains why his children were educated in Jamaica and Virginia.
74. Guy-Sheftall and Stewart, *Spelman*; Read, *Spelman*.
75. Ibid.
76. G. Shepperson and T. Price, *Independent African: John Chilembwe and the Origins, Setting and Significance of the Nyasaland Native Rising of 1915* (Edinburgh University Press, 1958), p. 138.
77. Ibid. pp. 136, 142.
78. Ibid. pp. 142, 391.
79. D. Johnson, 'Salim Wilson: The Black Evangelist of the North', *Journal of Religion in Africa*, 21, 1 (1991), pp. 26–41. My thanks to David Killingray.
80. G. Haliburton, 'Mark Christian Hayford: A Non-Success Story', *Journal of Religion in Africa*, 12, 1 (1981), pp. 20–37. My thanks to Robert Hill.
81. H. King, 'Mojola Agbebi (1860–1917): Nigerian Church Leader' in Lotz and Pegg *Imperial Carpet*, pp. 84–108.

— 11 —

Writers

THE JAMAICAN poet Matthew Joseph, overlooked by modern scholars, had been published in Victorian times, as had African writers including Blyden and Dr Horton. Slavery narratives, sometimes sold to gather financial support in the war against slavery, had been authored by Black men and women of the United States, Africa and the islands of the Caribbean. The books of ex-slave Frederick Douglass, no stranger to Victorian Britain, were widely known. Some Black authors wrote for the British: Stanford's *From Bondage to Liberty*, published in Smethwick in 1889, and Johnson's *Twenty-Eight Years a Slave*, for example.

Others sought a global audience. Henry Sylvester Williams's *The Pan-African* first appeared in London in October 1901, with the ambition to be 'the mouthpiece of the millions of Africans and their descendants [and] to chronicle facts relative to the race's progress and welfare'. It was largely aimed at the British for 'little or nothing is known of the educated British Negro'. There were other issues, known through reviews in the Trinidad press.[1] Williams, who was called to the Bar in June 1902, had made a return visit to Trinidad in 1901, and went to Cape Town where, in October 1903, he became registered as a local advocate. He appears to have written *The British Negro* in 1902, of which there is no known copy.[2]

Edward Wilmot Blyden was another New World Black with experience of Africa and Edwardian Britain. Born in the Danish West Indies in 1832, he had settled in Liberia by 1850. He travelled widely in Europe and made many visits to Britain where his *Christianity, Islam and the Negro* was published in the 1880s. His *African Life and Customs* was published in London in 1908. Blyden, a dark person in a Liberia where the elite was of Euro-African descent, studied many subjects including the roles of Blacks in ancient Egypt and the egalitarian nature of Islam.

Blyden addressed public meetings in Sierra Leone and England in the 1900s, no longer resident in Liberia. These talks were sometimes printed. *West Africa Before Europe and Other Addresses* (1905),*The Three Needs of Liberia* (1908), *The Problems Before Liberia* (1909) and articles in the *Journal of the African Society* in 1902 and 1905 were published in London.

Blyden believed that races were permanently divided from each other, from which he challenged White racists who believed that all good qualities were found in Whites, never in Blacks. 'The African must advance by methods of his own', Blyden declared, proposing that Black people should study the classics of ancient Greece and Rome, non-racial societies, rather than those of a racially conscious Britain.[3]

Blyden was in London in 1903, when he was a guest of honour at a dinner given by 'West Africans residing in London'.[4] He was in Britain in 1905, when he made contacts with Muslims in Liverpool, and in 1906 he spent 'a few weeks' at the Sussex resort of Crowborough where he probably met fellow author Sir Arthur Conan Doyle and other sympathetic Britons. He then resided in Hampstead, north London, where he wrote to arch imperialist Frederick Lugard.[5] The *African World* noted on 6 June 1908 that Blyden had travelled from Africa on the *Salaga* and was currently in London. In the summer of 1909 he spent fifteen weeks at the Royal Southern Hospital in Liverpool following a knee operation.[6] He eventually received a pension from the British government, and died in Sierra Leone in 1912.

Booker T. Washington had written from London in 1899 'Nowhere can one get such a good idea of what is transpiring in all parts of the world as in London' because 'the English colonial system brings every year hundreds of representatives of all races and colors from every part of the world to London.'[7] His autobiography *The Story of My Life* was published in 1900, and *Up From Slavery* in 1901. Washington made a second visit to Britain in 1910.

An educator working among poverty-striken Blacks in Alabama and the Old South, Washington's tour of Europe in 1910 examined the conditions of the poor. Assisted by Robert E. Park, a close friend and ghost writer (later a famed sociologist), Washington left America on the *Carmania* in late August 1910. Volume ten of the Washington collected *Papers* shows his contacts with John Harris of the Anti-Slavery Society, with whom he went to the largely immigrant Jewish street traders of Petticoat Lane in east London. He had lunch with Sir Thomas Fowell Buxton of that society, and at the beginning of September travelled to Scotland where he was the guest of tycoon-turned-philanthropist Andrew Carnegie.

Washington and Park travelled to eastern Europe where Christian and Muslim oppression was forcing many Jewish people to move to the United States. They visited Turkey, Sicily, and Naples; moved to France, Germany, and Denmark where Washington was the guest of the king. Squalid farms in Russia and Hungary, beggars and appalling working conditions in Italy, and filth everywhere except Copenhagen led Washington to conclude that African-Americans were better off than Europeans. Park considered Washington to be a thorough American, not seeing Europe but remembering the wonders of the United States where the mass of his people were forbidden to rise.[8] Washington's name appeared as the author of *The Man Farthest Down: A Record of Observation and Study in Europe*, published in New York in 1912.

The news that Booker T. Washington, famed author and associate of presidents and monarchs, was to be in Britain was known to Black Edwardians. The founder of Tuskegee and author of *Up From Slavery* was a highly respected individual even though his accommodation to racist Whites had questioned the respect that had previously been unchallenged. On 6 October 1910 the Black educator-author was the guest at a lunch in London attended by two hundred and fifty people. Details appeared in the *Anti-Slavery Reporter*, which named Conan Doyle and his wife, and Harry Johnston. A vote of thanks was proposed by P. Awooner Renner, a law student from Sierra Leone. He was also named in the *Gold Coast Nation*'s report of 12 November, which also identified Ernest James Hayford.

Another African at the lunch was Kwamina F. Tandoh. Active in tropical produce trading, a friend of John Barbour-James, and at home in the Gold Coast and England, Tandoh was to marry Sarah Wilson in London the following winter. Their daughter Hagar was raised in England.[9]

It was at this time that Pixley Seme met with Washington, but by early 1911 they agreed that nothing had developed.[10] One individual who refused to meet Washington in London was John Milholland, a successful businessman and civil libertarian who was closely associated with W. E. B. Du Bois.[11] Du Bois, as we have noted, was no stranger to Edwardian Britain where his *The Souls of Black Folk* had circulated since 1903.

Harry Johnston, ex-governor of Uganda, associate of Rhodes and Stanley, biographer of Grenfell, and author of *Liberia*, had visited Tuskegee in 1908, and wrote an article about it in *The Times* in January 1909. His *The Negro in the New World* was published in London in 1910, and Booker T. Washington's review of it appeared in the *Journal of the African Society* in early 1911.

Johnston mentioned 'the desire to marry a Zulu prince or an Ashanti noble on the part of young women of the [British] lower classes' and White women's behaviour 'towards the black contingents that have visited London within the past twenty-five years, and the crop of subsequent police court or Divorce Court cases'.

Other legal matters attracted John Mensah Sarbah after his education at Coleridge-Taylor's father's old school in Taunton. Called to the Bar in 1887, he was probably the first Gold Coast African barrister; certainly Sarbah was a pioneer African author. His *Fanti Customary Law* was published in England in 1897, and a second edition appeared in 1904. Sarbah had been in London in 1903, seeing the revisions into proof – and thus he might have been the questioner over the (lack of) rights of a Black customer in that London pub. Sarbah's travelling companion was William Edward Sam, whose Mfantsipim School was to become famous. Sarbah met Blyden in Britain.[12]

Sarbah's *Fanti National Constitution* was published in London in 1906.[13] He had articles published in the *Journal of the African Society* in 1904 and 1910; and in Liverpool's *West African Mail* in 1905. An African historian whose use of ancient documentary sources and oral history made his books used in Africa and by imperialists, Sarbah protected local African interests in land and taxation; thus influencing the ways in which colonial rule was imposed. He died, aged forty-six, in 1910.

A. B. C. Merriman-Labor, who reached London from Sierra Leone, duly reported in the *Anglo-African Argus and Gold Coast Echo* of 9 April 1904, had the ambition to be the Mark Twain of West Africa. He had already authored *The Sierra Leone Handbook*. He settled down to working in an office: in the summer of 1905 he was the manager of the West African Information Bureau at 60, East Dulwich Grove, in south east London, a new venture publicised in the *African World* (5 August) and in the *West African Mail* of Liverpool one week before. Later he worked in Holborn, in central London, where he dealt with 'over one hundred white lady clerks', as he noted in his *Britons Through Negro Spectacles, or A Negro on Britons, with a Description of London* published in London in 1909. In it he also wrote that he attended St Paul's Cathedral on his first Sunday in London 'five years ago' and, in 1908, had visited the Franco-British exhibition.[14]

The preface is dated London, August 1909. His story, of two Africans in Edwardian Britain, comments on 'the individual in a London street who wants to know how well or how badly he can converse in English', that 'Credulous people...still believe that every Negro with a decent overcoat and a clean collar is an African prince', and that the British knew nothing about West Africa: their minds being 'a perfect blank'.[15]

Merriman-Labor had worked with school children in the Gambia, and he continued these connections in Edwardian Britain by working as a Sunday School teacher. He wrote that this had lasted 'a long time, with nearly two hundred white boys' of the Railway Orphanage in south London.[16] On page 175 he wrote 'I am still here, suffering from some people's dislike of my colour, especially when I visit a low class suburb in Britain.'

Another West African author was Samuel Richard Brew Attoh-

Ahuma whose *Memoirs of West African Celebrities* was published in Liverpool in 1905. It is three hundred pages long. Attoh-Ahuma, editor of the *Gold Coast Nation* newspaper, also wrote *The Gold Coast Nation and National Consciousness* (1911). He was in Britain several times.

The most prolific Black Edwardian author was Theophilus Scholes, who we have already noted as a Jamaica-born, Scotland-qualified doctor who associated with Thomas Lewis Johnson in Britain and Africa in the 1880s, the school for Africans at Colwyn Bay in the 1890s, and both Seme and Locke in London in the mid-1900s. Scholes's first substantial book, *The British Empire and Alliances: Britain's Duty to her Colonies and Subject Races*, had been published in London in 1899. He quoted from Black writers including Sarbah, Henry Carr of Lagos, and D. E. Tobias of North Carolina. Scholes expressed the view that colour prejudice was based on a delusion.

In August 1901 Scholes was observed at the entrance hall of the House of Commons by a peppery colonial police officer named Herbert Thomas. Thomas, who was to spend nearly half a century in the Jamaica police, wrote in his 1927 autobiography that Scholes 'had found the amenities of London, centre of the world's civilization, so much to his taste, that he never returned to his native land'.[17] Unaware that Scholes had practised in Africa, Thomas's comment that he practised in London must be discounted as Scholes's name does not appear in the British medicial reference books after 1887.[18] Thomas stated that the Jamaican doctor 'was a man of truly superb physique'.

In February 1902 Thomas gave a lecture at the Society of Arts in London, which Scholes attended. The doctor had 'with him a little English parson and his wife . . . evidently pleased and proud to have him under their wing'. Scholes challenged Thomas's statement that Black Jamaicans were 'contented and happy', quoting from *The Times* that there was 'widespread poverty' in the island. As Blacks paid taxes they had the right to make requests, and if these requests were ignored they 'were entitled to make a protest without being regarded as seditious'.

Logical and informed, the Black doctor's comments were seen by Thomas as trouble-making. He wrote in his autobiography of Scholes's 'cryptic, incoherent, disingenuous and plausible utterances' which were not understood, and that Scholes was 'the worst example of unreasoning race hatred that I have ever come into contact with'. Thomas would have been wise to have read Scholes's *Glimpses of the Ages; Or, the 'Superior' and 'Inferior' Races, so-called, discussed in the Light of Science and History*. Published in 1905 with a second volume in 1908, these are far from cryptic. They are not incoherent or disingenuous either. Scholes states his facts and comments on them, leaving the reader to judge them. Imanuel Geiss was to write in his *The Pan-African Movement* (1974):

> Scholes belongs unmistakably to the twentieth century, for his arguments are quite modern; there is no further mention of the Bible. Although he scarcely ever identifies his sources, he must have been familiar with the preceding literature. After Blyden he was the first West Indian author to make an important contribution to the emergence of Pan-Africanism. Residing as he did in the capital city of the British Empire, he accepted the latter as a fact of life, and although critical of many details of colonial rule did not want to destroy it. His objective was to transform the Empire into a free association of equals drawn from all races.[19]

Of the *Glimpses of the Ages* volumes, Geiss commented they had 'a wholly modern approach and are still readable today' for Scholes was predicting 'that war and revolution would be the motive force of social change in the near future.'[20]

The first of Scholes's Edwardian publications was *Chamberlain and Chamberlainism; his Fiscal Proposals and Colonial Policy*, which appeared in London in 1903. Using the pen-name Bartholomew Smith, Scholes criticised the policies of Colonial Secretary Joseph Chamberlain. Chamberlain believed that the empire was for settlement by Whites, and his policies ignored the majority. Chamberlain proposed to erect tariff barriers to encourage the sale to Britain of the produce of White imperial lands, placing non-White producers outside that protection and subsidy. Scholes (or rather, Smith) stated that a wise and humane imperial policy would be to pay proper wages to all people in the empire and favour no group over others. The result of such equitable treatment would be increased incomes, which in turn would cause demand to rise, and commerce to flourish. Scholes believed that Chamberlain ignored the millions of Black people in the empire other than to encourage the use of force to keep them in their place.

Scholes was not writing in isolation; he was in the very centre of the empire, attending meetings as we know from the sour recollections of Thomas, as well as meeting others with recent news of imperial developments. In September 1903, for example, Scholes (then living at 17, Rochester Square in north London) was elected a member of the African Society according to their *Journal*. As well as Seme, Locke and Renner, one Black individual who is known to have met with the doctor in Edwardian London was William Wellesley Campbell. Campbell, who qualified MRCS, LRCP in London in 1903, was to practise medicine in Georgetown, British Guiana, but he held posts in two London hospitals according to the *Medical Registers*: a junior assistant demonstrator in anatomy at King's College and as a clinical assistant at the Royal Eye Hospital. He and Scholes discussed aspects of the problems that were tackled in the first, 1905, volume of *Glimpses of the Ages*.[21]

His preface also stated that this was the first of two volumes. When the second volume appeared in 1908, Scholes noted the reviewer of the earlier book who commented on his thanks for Campbell's 'very valuable suggestions. Why did Mr. Campbell omit the obvious suggestion "Don't"?' The two doctors consulted until Campbell left for Georgetown. Scholes wrote the second volume – its preface stating that the plan was now for six volumes 'to inquire scientifically and historically into the circumstances in which the colourless people designate themselves the "superior race," and in which they designate the coloured races as "inferior races" '.[22]

What marks Scholes's writings is his belief that civilisation is a process, to which the coloured peoples would greatly contribute when artificial restraints were removed. He knew the historic reality – glimpses through the ages – that civilisations develop, expand, and decay. Scholes (like Blyden, who, it should be remembered, was often in Britain in Edwardian times and whose books were available at the British Museum) stated that Julius Caesar would never have believed that the people of England, that damp frontier of the glorious Roman empire, would one day dominate much of the globe. Scholes believed that the British would decline in the future – and that was as certain as her imperial rise had been unforeseen.

Scholes was critical of double standards, such as that of the London *Daily News* which had concluded that it was his African ancestry which led author Alexandre Dumas to have lax morals. Nothing on the far from saintly Oliver Goldsmith, Byron or Burns.[23] The often-stated comment that African descent indicated weak morals was not supported by a mulatto-dominated criminal class in America.[24]

Scholes was alert to events in the United States; and certainly to British press reports of Black activities there. He refers to the *Weekly Scotsman* of 29 October 1904 which had listed the contributions made by Blacks to the US economy.[25]

His observations of British national leaders, such as that time in August 1901 he had been seen at parliament by Thomas, included Chamberlain whose speech had quoted from an article by Harry Johnston. Scholes wrote that he had met Johnston in Africa (which would have been around 1886) and had admired his subsequent career and achievements, but deeply regretted his description of Africa as the 'dirty continent'.[26]

Scholes wrote that Whites disliked Africa so much that they had spent millions trying to get to the centre of that dirt, building a railway. Chamberlain had supported taxing Africans in order to drive them off the land and into the mines of South Africa. Complaints that Blacks would not work ignored the facts: Africans were self-sufficient farmers with herds of livestock. Not that Whites were spotless examples of hard work, as Scholes mischievously shows, by quoting a London newspaper report of May 1904 about a London beggar who had worked just three days in twenty-five years.[27]

The view that Jamaicans were idle was challenged by fact-supported evidence of the migrations of labourers to the banana plantations of Honduras and Panama, as well as in the construction of the ocean-to-ocean canal in Panama and a railway in Ecuador. Scholes's evidence pointed to maladministration by colonial Whites. He also noted that intemperate remarks against Blacks were not consistent, with Whites in the USA justifying their racist views because of Black 'viciousness'; in West Africa the Blacks were insolent; and in the West Indies they were lazy. 'Were these accusations true, their variety would suggest, as their cause, local peculiarity, rather than racial idiosyncrasy.'[28] Twenty-three pages later, the first volume of *Glimpses of the Ages* ends on page 396.

Volume two has nearly five hundred pages. Scholes listed some of the wars involving British forces between 1895 and 1898 when, because of Chamberlain's colonial expansion and in response to European nations's ambitions, Britain had been active in the scramble for Africa. Scholes had resented the use of 'our subjects' during the months leading up to Edward's coronation, and made the point that Blacks were not subjects of the inhabitants of the British Isles; everyone in Britain and its empire were subjects of the king-emperor.[29] Yet again, there was a double standard in the metropole's view of empire.

Scholes noted that the Colonial Office prohibited African doctors with British professional qualifications from having the same status as White doctors in West Africa, despite forty-three years of African doctors in the colonial service. Thus 'His Majesty's coloured subjects have been summarily repressed in their legitimate aspiration and lawful ambition'.[30]

Scholes must have clipped newspapers or made copious notes from them. He had noted the London press comments on the Peter Lobengula marriage; and he quoted the January 1907 newspaper reports on Henry Sylvester Williams and the Sotho delegation.[31] Scholes and his friend Dr Campbell had met Williams in London on 12 October 1905, at a formal London gathering arranged by the barrister in honour of Sapara Williams from Lagos. This was reported in the *African World* on 28 October. Individuals such as Scholes, a Black Edwardian with contacts in three continents, must have been known to other members of the Black middle class, the imperial visitors, students, and their friends. His global view of Blacks included South Africa.

Scholes wrote, at length, on the uprising in Natal of 1906 and that the local authorities planned to execute twelve Africans accused of murdering two Whites.[32] The imperial government prohibited this; the Natal government resigned; and the British gave in to the White settler regime of South Africa – the twelve men were shot in April 1906. Scholes, detailing this and other injustices, noted that journalists had been forbidden to ride with the punitive columns. Martial law had been declared throughout Natal yet that province's London representative had stated that no more than fifty Africans had been involved in incidents. The official view was that there had been a little local difficulty in Natal in March and April of 1906.

The reality was smashed homes and destroyed crops, ruined churches, and the deaths of two Africans without trial. The local authorities had censored telegrams, approved the shelling of villages, and had imposed heavy fines. Seven Africans had been flogged. Scholes told his readers that it was a scheme to make Africans 'untrustworthy'. Redefined in this way, they could be expelled from their lands, which were then liable to be seized by the authorities. By June 1906 that had been accomplished. The undemocratic military had made these rules and then leased the stolen lands to Whites. Scholes agreed that there had been unrest: a poll tax of one pound had been imposed (for Africans could not vote in Natal). This tax was an attempt to force Africans off the land and into the mines, to work at the low wages set by the owners. The poll tax sham was clear, for the period for payment had not expired when the expeditionary forces had set off to extort and provoke.

Whites in Natal thus clearly demonstrated that self-government in the empire would result in unfit Whites being in command. Scholes noted that the settlers were 'grossly intolerant, cruel, and incompetent'. Faced with the results of these actions, the British imperial government had capitulated. This was not the first time that a vocal White minority had forced it policies on the imperial government: 'The rights of the coloured section of the Empire are constantly being sacrificed by the parent state, in order to conciliate the colourless section.'

Coercion – a nation of forty-one million holding down three-hundred-and-fifty million people by force – was impractical and bound to fail, as it had failed ancient Rome and, more recently, Spain. Conciliation to the minority settler groups would lead to further injustice.[33] And of course there was a double standard fully documented by Scholes, who detailed a group of White raiders in the Cape who had killed a police officer whilst trying to start a revolt in late 1906. None of the five was executed: 'a dual standard of justice'.[34]

There were three wrongs in the empire, Scholes concluded. First, the peoples in the empire had been forced into it. Secondly, having had their possessions stolen, these people were required to labour without any opportunity to advance. Thirdly, having broken pledges on equality, the coloured peoples were degraded, humiliated, and deceived. Surely it was not possible that Black people could have behaved more dishonourably to the Whites?[35]

Dr Scholes indicated that his third volume would deal with the United States. It never appeared. Scholes continued with his re-searches, and continued to be known to younger Black people into the 1930s.[36]

Scholes is a fascinating individual for several reasons. He had lived in tropical Africa before the imperialists had divided the map of those lands. Based in Britain at the height of imperialism, Scholes observed the myths of imperial rule being developed. He noted how the press reported incidents such as the alake's hat being dislodged and the breach of promise case against Dr Nurse. He visited parliament, attended public meetings, advised others, and kept studying at the British Museum. It seems likely that Scholes, both as a person and an author, was known to many if not most middle-class and student Black Edwardians.

That Seme had made contact with Scholes within ten months of reaching England from America suggests how accessible the author was. This is supported by a comment made at an international gather-ing in London in 1911: one which included other Blacks, notably Du Bois.

Du Bois, who had moved from Atlanta to New York where he edited the monthly *Crisis* from late 1910, wrote in its very first issue that this Universal Races Congress 'promises to be one of the most influential of our time'.[37] Meeting from 26 to 29 July 1911, the congress was proclaimed in *The Times* on 24 July as 'an assemblage of members of all the races of the world'. It noted that Du Bois was to speak on 'the Negro Race' in America and that 'Pastor Mojolo Agbebi, a native of West Africa, will deal with the West African problem'.

Two days later *The Times* reported that three hundred delegates were attending. Exhibits, including photographs, showed 'the extent to which our European civilization has been adapted and assimilated by aboriginal Americans, Asiatics, and Africans'. There were African bishops in gowns, Black students and professors 'in cap and gown', 'the black lady doctors, the highly educated Sioux and Apache, and the Westernized Japanese'.

Du Bois, the Harvard- and Berlin-educated sociologist-turned-editor, welcomed this elitist global parliament. He came to believe that only the outbreak of the First World War, which cancelled a conference scheduled for 1915, prevented the world being changed by these men and women who were, to an extent, a United Nations organisation forty years too soon.[38]

Scared by Du Bois's threat to his reputation, Booker T. Washington sent his assistant Robert Moton to counter Du Bois's impact.[39] The activities of Black people in Edwardian Britain certainly could concern its representatives globally.

The congress's main organiser was Gustave (or Gustav[40]) Spiller of Britain's Ethical Culture movement. His *Papers on Inter-Racial Problems* were the published papers of the conference; which has led some to conclude that Agbebi was present when no other evidence supports that. The book lists nearly thirty honorary secretaries including Du Bois and an A. F. Palmer in St Lucia. The executive council included Harry Johnston (whose autobiography is silent on the conference: he was ill and Du Bois spoke in his place[41]) who represented the Royal Geographical Society. Another was William T. Stead, editor of *The Review of Reviews*.

Spiller's book has pages of names of supporters, some of whom have vanished from history and others, notably Tomas Masaryk, a 1911 member of parliament in Vienna but later president of Czechoslovakia, and Johannesburg lawyer M. K. Gandhi, who had distinguished careers ahead of them. Dr Abdul Abdurahman of Cape Town had been in England in 1906; John Mensah Sarbah died in November 1910; his Gold Coast colleague Joseph Peter Brown lived to 1932 and was an active nationalist throughout the 1920s. Blyden, Bishop 'Holy' Johnson, South African lawyer Alfred Mangena who had trained in London, and the Revd J. R. Fredericks of the Wesleyan church of Sierra Leone are also named.

Whites, who numbered Du Bois's friend and patron Milholland, included radical dissenters such as Edmond Dene Morel whose Congo reform agitation had removed those lands from Leopold in 1908; and Sir Roger Casement, who had assisted in that work and who was to be executed by the British for treason in 1916. Felix Moscheles of the International Peace Bureau had been involved in the 1900 Pan-African conference in London (he was also a leading Esperanto speaker) where he would have met Du Bois; the American visited Moscheles at home in 1911.[42] Mrs Saul Solomon, widow of a liberal Cape Colony politician, was to be imprisoned, with her daughter, in the English campaign for women's votes. Two very radical women named by Spiller, although their connection to the races congress is not known, were Annie Besant (socialist, pioneer birth control publicist, strike leader, and Indian nationalist) and Charlotte Despard, slumland reformer and women's rights campaigner, and a political associate of John Archer in Battersea. That her brother Sir John French commanded the British army in 1914 had no effect on her support for Irish independence.

Photographs published in the *Crisis* reveal at least ten Black or dark people. As Du Bois wrote:

> And more and more the streets of London are showing this fact. I seldom step into the streets without meeting a half dozen East Indians, a Chinaman, a Japanese or a Malay, and here and there a Negro. There must be thousands of colored people in the city.[43]

He added 'there is color prejudice and aloofness undoubtedly here, but it does not parade its shame like New York or its barbarity like New Orleans'.

Scholes was known to some of the delegates, for his work was mentioned in a footnote on page 31 of Spiller's *Papers*: 'A West Indian of immaculate Negro descent, Dr. Th. Scholes, has issued two excellent treatises on the race question.'

The Times reported that Professor Earl Finch of Wilberforce University had spoken on racial mixing and, on the next day, 28 July, noted that he was 'a negro'. This was in a report that observed that 'the Congress lacks unity of purpose'. On 29 July it recorded the presence of both Du Bois and Walter Rubusana 'the first native member of the South African parliament'. Another comment was that journalists seldom reported 'the native's case'; equal opportunity, not special favours, was required.

Professor William Sanders Scarborough, from the African-American Wilberforce University, had been in London in 1899 and knew lawyer Williams and his Pan-African conference colleagues then. He told the 1911 congress that Black Americans were worse off than forty years before. Two Black women might have included that 'black lady doctor', for Dr. S. Maria Stewart, physician to Wilberforce University, attended with her sister Mrs Sarah J. Garnett. They celebrated the latter's eightieth birthday in London on 31 August; she died on 17 September.[44]

Du Bois spoke at social meetings: the Anti-Slavery Society's *Reporter* had announced his planned visit as early as January 1911 (stating that he was available for lectures when in Britain). On 26 June he spoke at the Lyceum Club where his audience included Milholland, Johnston, Casement, novelist H. G. Wells, and the wife of sociologist Havelock Ellis. This was the company he had been educated to mix in, and was largely denied him in the United States. Du Bois also met socialist member of parliament Ramsay MacDonald at the House of Commons. Through that connection and the congress, the Scottish future prime minister recommended that Du Bois's daughter went to school in England in 1914.[45]

The American renewed his links with Coleridge-Taylor, for a typed letter from the composer, dated 1 June, noted his schedule and commented 'We shall expect you to call on us FIRST'.[46] Du Bois may well have visited 10, Upper Grove, in Croydon, for the composer's half-sister Marjorie Evans, aged fourteen in 1911, when interviewed in the 1980s, recalled the name Du Bois in its non-British pronunciation, and added that he had visited her half-brother.

Du Bois lodged at 23, Kildare Terrace, in Bayswater, no great distance from Dr Alcindor. Du Bois watched the coronation of King George the Fifth on 22 June 1911, from seat 65 at 24, Pall Mall.[47] Milholland, staying at 4, Prince of Wales Terrace, was minutes from the Aldridge ladies' home. If they had time to read the newspapers they would have read of the arrest of Lobagola, the bogus African, charged with stealing money from a Black American teacher in east London.[48] They would have seen comments on Billy Wells's challenge to Jack Johnson. But the congress was the central and exciting reason for their presence in London in the summer of 1911, and Du Bois wrote about it at length.

It was mentioned in the Anti-Slavery Society's journal in October 1911, when practical aspects were revealed. There were poor acoustics and so 'few of the speakers were properly heard'; 'no discussion or debate was possible'. Outside the formal gatherings contacts were made: Du Bois met a South African named John Tengo Jabavu.

Olive Schreiner was connected with Spiller before the congress. She was a novelist whose husband (a politician in South Africa) had visited London with Jabavu and Rubusana in 1909, (where they met with Seme and Mangena[49]). They were attempting to prevent the abolition of votes for Africans in Cape Colony.[50] Rubusana, who had been described as 'a full-blooded kaffir' in the *Daily Chronicle* of 26 August 1905 during an earlier visit to England, was to lose his seat because of Jabavu in 1914. Jabavu, founder and editor of *Imvo Zabantsundu* (Native Opinion), had sent his son Davidson Don Tengo Jabavu to Colwyn Bay in 1903, from where he had gone to Birmingham and London Universities. He returned to South Africa after ten years in Britain. Whatever pan-African ideals and friendships he had cherished were not strong enough to overcome his father's decision to challenge Rubusana in the elections of 1914. Tembuland constituency had a split vote between these two Black candidates and a White won.[51]

The British-educated son successfully pressed the South African government to establish a college for Africans. His father spoke on this dream at the Race Congress.[52] He wrote his father's biography which includes a photograph of the two, in Edwardian London.[53]

Another author associated with the 1911 Races Congress was Duse

Mohamed, the actor and dramatist. Stimulated by anti-Egyptian remarks made in London by ex-US president Theodore Roosevelt, he set to work in the British Museum library and produced *In the Land of the Pharaohs* in fourteen weeks. Delivering a chapter at a time, the haste is exhibited throughout the book: which also had sections lifted from other books. Published in London in 1911, it was seen as the first history of Egypt by an Egyptian. Spiller knew Mohamed, who was employed to arrange dignified entertainments for the delegates. He presented the third act of *Othello*. Milholland was impressed and suggested that Mohamed toured the States, lecturing on Egypt.[54]

The great and the good, as listed in Spiller's 1911 book, would not have included people whose later activities deserve attention, so we are left to guess who attended the London conference. Those Blacks who were at home in Edwardian London may well have met with delegates, attended lectures, and discussed important matters outside the formal congress. John Alcindor would surely have made contact with his friend Du Bois,[55] as would those Sierra Leoneans who were as much at home in London as Freetown.

Black visitors would have made contact with Coleridge-Taylor: after all, his *Nero Suite* had been part of King George's coronation festivities at the Drury Lane theatre that May, and the Royal Concert at the Albert Hall had included two of his works (one other composer had more than one work at that concert – Richard Wagner).[56] In the month of the congress he conducted at the Festival of Empire at the Crystal Palace arts centre,[57] but he did not officially attend the congress although he was often in central London preparing to conduct at the Guildhall.[58]

The congress has been regarded as important because, as we will see, it led Mohamed to establish the *African Times and Orient Review*, a London monthly dedicated to the world of coloured peoples. It also has been claimed to have been the stimulus to the formation of the African National Congress in South Africa in 1912.[59] The former is a valid view, but in the light of the ANC's treasurer Pixley Seme's contacts and cosmopolitanism, vice president Walter Rubusana's political experience, and president John Dube's knowledge of America and Booker T. Washington's achievements,[60] the South African concept is false.

Black people in different areas of the globe realised they could not rely on Whites. Scholes had voiced the reality. Stimulated by contacts with Black folk, often in Edwardian Britain or through their writings, they were proud of achievers and aware of White intolerance and insincerity, and made various efforts to have their opinions known to the dominating group. The importance of Black authors was well known, as is seen in the Negro Society for Historical Research.

This Society's constitution, drawn up by John Edward Bruce of New York,[61] includes the requirement that members 'must have had some reading in race literature' and that its librarian was to prepare a journal for distribution to members. The list of members shows the international links of some Black Edwardians. The president was Lewanika of Barotseland (who had been King Edward's guest in 1902) and the members included James Dossen (vice-president of Liberia), Blyden, Casely Hayford, Agbebi, Scholes, the Edinburgh student Moses Da Rocha who returned to Nigeria in 1911, James Smith of Jersey and London (the Bahamas-born retired postmaster of Freetown), Du Bois, E. D. L. Thompson of Sierra Leone (a member of the Ethiopian Progressive Association of Liverpool in 1904), Alain Locke and his family friend W. C. Bolivar among the many Americans, and the Gold Coast-born journalist of Cape Town, F. Z. S. Peregrino (who had lived in both Britain and the USA before 1900[62]). Also on the membership list were the Revd William Forde of 'Port Limon, Costa Rica' whom we last observed as a student of Spurgeon's College in London in 1903, and 'Duse Mohamed, Effendi, London, England'.

These people had been exposed to the British and would have known their hypocrisy. James Weldon Johnson, who had been in London in 1905 with his brother J. Rosamond Johnson, commenced a semi-autobiographical novel *The Autobiography of an Ex-Coloured Man* in 1906.[63] Published in 1912, Johnson wrote of a light-complexioned pianist who is taken to Europe by a White millionaire. London, 'the world's metropolis' stood for 'the conservatism, the solidarity, the utilitarianism, and, I might well add, the hypocrisy of the Anglo-Saxon'.[64] Johnson's brother left America for England in 1913, according to Du Bois in the *Crisis*.[65]

Merriman-Labor, who was probably working on his amusing novel, wrote to *The Times* on 13 March 1907 seeking contacts with other Black people in Britain. He was the secretary of a committee making arrangements to celebrate the anniversary of the abolition of the slave trade by Britain in 1807. Writing from the Birkbeck Bank Chambers in Holborn, he stated that the celebrations were planned for 25 March.

> Our programme will be duly announced. Meanwhile we would welcome names and addresses of persons whose ancestors were connected with Wilberforce and Buxton in their anti-slavery campaign, of English friends who are interested in Africa from an evangelical standpoint, and of Africans, Afro-Americans, and black West Indians now in the United Kingdom.

In his *Britons Through Negro Spectacles* of 1909 he wrote that with a dozen other Black people from Africa and America he had placed wreaths on the tombs, statues and memorials of the abolitionists at Westminster Abbey.

He suggested that Black people in London numbered around one hundred, a figure that seems far too low. He had been in England for three years when he wrote to *The Times* seeking contacts, but he does not seem to have crossed class lines or found contacts among long-established residents. Did he know Joe Clough the bus driver or Lewis Bruce the tram driver? Caroline Barbour-James and her family or their friends the Cambridges? Brown at the London Hospital, Reindorf at Barts, lawyer Williams of St Marylebone council, Dr Scholes in Camden Town, the Easmons, Casely Hayfords, Smiths and other Sierra Leoneans, John Alcindor in Paddington, Laura Bowman and Peter Hampton in Wimbledon, the Boucher family in Tooting and the Aldridges in Kensington, the Archers and their Liberian guest, the boxers, entertainers, children and students: who did the Sierra Leonean author know in Edwardian Britain?

Temporary residents must have had a sense of isolation, which is clearly evidenced from Norman Manley's comment 'I have been an alien first and last. . . . The case is different when I met any of the many West Indians that I know – I feel with them an altogether different person.'[66] Nina Du Bois's letters to her husband in 1914–15 when their daughter was at an English boarding school and she lived alone in London, show that her only contacts were the Spillers and Henry and Margarita Downing.[67]

The Downings had lived in London since the 1890s, participating in the 1900 Pan-African Conference and being good friends of the Coleridge-Taylors. The composer's half-sister Marjorie Evans recalled visiting their Kensington home, and taking care of their parrot when they departed for America around 1917.[68] By 1913 Downing had published eight works, and two with his wife, as well as *Lord Eldred's Other Daughter: An Original Comedy in Four Acts.*[69]

This play has eight male and five female characters in a two set drama centred on theatrical life. Double identities, a stage Irishman whose dialogue is full of 'be jabers', a French maid who says 'ziz' and 'zat', mistaken identity, a lost document, and characters overhearing important information when hidden are all stage clichés. There is a mention that the heroine had been listening to *Hiawatha* at the Albert Hall, and the heiress might be of African descent – 'To have the spending of an income such as her's will be I'd marry a Hottentot'. Her origins in Africa were 'north-west of Sierra Leone' and so there might be 'a very slight strain of the African in her . . . a royal strain'.

Yet another Black writer in Edwardian Britain was J. Edmestone Barnes, who had been born in Jamaica in 1857.[70] His *Signs of the Times: Touching the Final Supremacy of Nations* was published in London in

1903. A trained surveyor who had worked in South America, Liberia, and Cape Town in the 1900s, he had been a member of the boundary commission that settled the frontier of Sierra Leone and Liberia. He then ran a diamond and gold syndicate, possibly in the Gold Coast, for he knew both Edith Goring and John Barbour-James well enough to attend their wedding in London in 1920. Barnes was in New York in 1914 – a true traveller.

His *The Economic Value of the Native Races of Africa in Relation to the Development of the Resources of that Continent* of 1908 was only a dozen pages, but its four page introduction by Charles Garnett raises several questions about links and friendships in Edwardian Britain, for Garnett was a member of the League of Universal Brotherhood and Native Races Association. He had been involved with the Sotho delegation and Sylvester Williams in 1907, accompanying the Africans to meet Lord Elgin and preaching at Arundel Square Congregational Church in Islington in support of their protests.[71] He wrote that Barnes had shown that Black South Africans should be treated 'with every consideration and kindness'.

Barnes wrote that Africa had interested the west since Stanley's travels; the so-called Dark Continent and White Man's Grave was to be a future home for migrants from Europe. The laws of economics had 'snatched away from the blacks' the old order, but the victorious Whites should recognise that Africans 'have contributed their proper share of hard labour'. In early contacts travellers and missionaries from Europe had been greeted as friends by Africans, who 'lavished their hospitalities upon them'.

Africans had tilled the land, raised cattle, and been active in agriculture generally. Europeans had constructed railways from Cape Town beyond the Zambezi. Barnes quoted a railway engineer who believed that this railway would enable cotton to be exported from western Rhodesia. Barnes ignored the Asian-built railway from the Indian Ocean to Lake Victoria which was bringing Ugandan cotton to mills in Britain, for his view (and experience of Africa?) was South African. He complained that although the railway to Katanga in the southern Congo had been built by African labourers, a workforce had been imported from China to dig for gold on the Rand. Before them Africans had laboured for diamonds and gold. Those people, essential in Victorian times, were now 'lazy'.

It had been suggested that African workers had been paid too much; if that was true, Barnes wrote, it was a result of their diligence, and thus they could not be lazy. Chinese miners had been imported because South Africa's Whites had no sympathy for Africans. The Whites insisted that they had to go about armed as they were surrounded by Blacks, yet when it came to employment the Blacks did not exist. Barnes was convinced that the exploitation of the natural resources of Africa would be done with the labour of Africans.

Barnes saw his *The Economy of Life* published in 1920. Sidney Campion, who published it, had a remarkable life according to his entry in *Who's Who*, which again raises questions about those who associated with Blacks in Britain. This book revealed that Barnes had been in Cape Town in 1909 and 1910, where he had addressed a meeting chaired by the mayor and attended by thousands. In *The Economy of Life* Barnes devoted 120 pages discussing why African people lacked the respect of others. He concluded that it was simply a lack of power: which had followed the Negro's 'political and national death'. Although the race had been 'a great and mighty nation' and had 'accomplished great things' in the past. Barnes was in England in 1922 when the *West India Committee Circular* of June noted something of his quite remarkable career.

Blacks featured in Edwardian novels written by Whites as well as the ventriloquist Pete in those children's stories. Notably in John Buchan's *Prester John* of 1910 when an uprising in South Africa was led by the US-educated Revd John Laputa. Art copied nature in Henry Hesketh Bell's African trickster 'Prince Kwakoo' in *Love in Black* of 1911, and the need for financial support which took several Black Edwardians on to the theatrical stage was the culmination of Cullen Gouldsbury's *The Tree of Bitter Fruit*, published in London in 1910.

Gouldsbury, who had worked in Northern Rhodesia (which he referred to in his *Circe's Garden* of 1907 as that 'most unromantic and unspeakably bourgeois territory'), wrote of a colonial official who took an African lad to be educated in Britain in the 1890s, in the belief that 'a day might dawn when colour would have become a question of the past'. The presence of Black people in London, as noted with such enthusiasm by Du Bois in 1911, enabled Gouldsbury to write:

> To the average Londoner there is nothing extra-ordinary in the sight of a well-dressed man escorting a little black boy. Passers-by cast a curious glance at the couple now and again – and, two turnings later had forgotten all about them.

In the great public schools 'Colour is hardly more of a disadvantage to its possessor than red hair or a squint'.

By the 1900s the fictional Mkonto 'save for his colour . . . might, now, have been a member of a London club'. Tricked by a journalist, spurned by his people when he returned to Africa, where he was arrested for assaulting a Scottish merchant, Mkonto returns to England and drifts into show business and falls in love. The final pages of the novel have the African on stage at the Diadem Theatre in Hackney, east London. The crowd anticipated a local 'masquerading in a disguise of burnt cork' but Mkonto performed a genuine war dance, restraining himself from throwing the spear at the 'gaping mouths and upturned eyes' of the crowd. He planned to lead his people against the Whites who laughed and scorned him.

Joseph Casely Hayford's *Gold Coast Native Institutions* was published in London in 1903, with its preface written at the Inner Temple that summer. It was a busy time for him, with his courting of Adelaide Smith in west London and being elected to the African Society in September.[72] In his book he made it clear that he believed that the colonial administration of the Gold Coast was 'doomed to failure' unless it became 'based on sound moral principles'. He described the Colonial Office as 'generally dormant and lethargic, occasionally erratic and irrepressible, if not irresponsible'. Staff, still occasionally appointed by patronage, regarding their early postings to Africa as stepping stones 'to another in some better clime' which meant that any junior who questioned the system would be likely to be removed to an unhealthy area, for the better places would be awarded to lickspittles. The colonial world was one where 'the Native does the hard work, and the European draws the hard cash'.

In 1911 Casely Hayford's *Ethiopia Unbound* was published in London. Inspired by his first wife Beatrice (mother of Archie, who was being raised in London by his second wife Adelaide Smith Casely Hayford) this novel was dedicated 'to the sons of Ethiopia the world wide over'. It begins in Edwardian London when 'three continents were ringing with the names of men like Du Bois, Booker T. Washington, Blyden, Dunbar [the US poet], Coleridge-Taylor, and others' and when 'it was by no means an uncommon thing to meet in the universities of Europe and America the sons of Ethiopia in quest of the golden tree of knowledge'.

Kwamankra, another student named Tandor-Kuma and his partner Ekuba who was 'a nurse-maid', a 'dark man' Kwow Ayensu, who had been a medical student in central London for 'several years', and Kwamankra's old flame Mansa who was 'visiting Europe for the first time to put the finishing touches to her education' with her father are shown to be at home in Edwardian Britain.

Kwamankra, a poorly disguised Casely Hayford, married Mansa who died giving birth to their second child. By 1907 Kwamankra is in the USA where he speaks on the 'universal' appeal of Blyden whereas Du Bois and Washington are 'exclusive and provincial'. The novel moves into the future, into 1925, when Kwamankra's moral force and intellectual arguments had brought profound changes in Africa.

The book is charming. It is famed largely because of its author's later political career and because it was a pioneer novel by an African.[73] No matter why *Ethiopia Unbound* is read, that its African characters argue, in Edwardian London, about which restaurant to favour shows that the Black Edwardian middle class had different concerns to those of their brothers and sisters in the United States where lynch law, other violence, segregation, and demeaning roles were major realities. That also shows the shock which the 1903 pub ban on serving Blacks in central London must have created among its middle class victims.

Casely Hayford's *Gold Coast Land Tenure and the Forest Bill* was published in London in 1913. Two years later his *The Truth About the West African Land Question* appeared. He continued to be at home in west Africa and Britain, working on legal matters and for nationalist causes until he died in 1930. His British-educated son Archie was a minister in the first independent Gold Coast government, in 1957.

Thomas Johnson's *Twenty-Eight Years a Slave* (1908), Salim Wilson's *The Ethiopia Valley* (c. 1906), Bandele Omoniyi's *A Defence of the Ethiopian Movement* of 1908, John Barbour-James's *The Agricultural Possibilities* (1911), Bishop Johnson's autobiography and doctors Bond, Strachan and Alcindor's medical research, which have been detailed earlier, should not be forgotten in this overview of Black Edwardian writers.

The actor-turned-journalist Duse Mohamed (later Duse Mohamed Ali), whose *In the Land of the Pharaohs* was a major book, contributed to various English magazines and, with the Sierra Leone businessman John Eldred Taylor, started the *African Times and Orient Review* in London in 1912. The original *African Times* had folded in 1902. The new enterprise attempted to survey the entire world of the 'darker races' which, Liberia and Ethiopia apart, were part of some White-run empire. The 158, Fleet Street, offices became a meeting place for Africans and people of African descent, as well as those from British India (India, Pakistan, Sri Lanka, Burma and Bangladesh) and Iran, Egypt, the Arab world and the Caribbean.

One of the regular contributors was James Carmichael Smith, who had retired from Sierra Leone to Jersey, later moving to London where his daughter was born.[74] He had published several leaflets and started a series of articles on financial and social theories in the first, July 1912, edition of Mohamed's magazine. That issue carried comments by some of those who had been approached by the editor. Meyer, the conqueror of Jack Johnson, suggested that an 'ordinary newspaper' would be the ideal place for publication of the views of African and Asian peoples.

The second issue dealt with the death of Coleridge-Taylor. It is clear that the two men were not close despite their common ancestry in Africa and domicile in greater London. The pages of the *African Times and Orient Review* reveal other Black people in Britain; for example, H. Hunt from British Guiana, first in Britain in 1900 when he was aged twenty-two, advertised for backing for his inventions. This was not a hopeless cause, for veterans recalled another Afro-Guyanese named Williams who had sold one invention for enough to settle near Marylebone High Street where he continued to tinker with mechanical matters into the 1930s.[75]

The *Review* reported the death, on 25 November 1912, of judge Francis 'Frans' Smith, the Sierra Leonean who had served the Queen and her son in the Gold Coast, before retiring to England where several of his sisters had homes. There were reports of successes, including Alain Locke who had returned to America from Germany, and was now teaching. That April 1913 issue also noted that Jamaican Benjamin de Cordova Reid was now an associate of the Victoria College of Music.

It published a photograph of Adeyemo and Olayimka Alakija, brothers from Nigeria, along with Debeshin Folarin, all having been called to the Bar, in April 1913 too. The month before it noted that Father Raphael, a Jamaican, had attended St Aiden's College in Birkenhead and King's College in London: currently he was based in Philadelphia.

The Middle East aspects of Mohamed's publication and his anti-imperial stance led to his Fleet Street offices being raided by the police in December 1914 when Britain was at war with Turkey (its Ottoman Empire included millions of people in the Middle East). In August 1914, as there began the war first known as the Great War and then the First World War, Mohamed wrote that the struggle would 'require years' for the combatants to recover. 'It may be that the non-European races will profit by the European disaster.'[76]

The first years of the *Review* involved Marcus Garvey, who founded and led the largest Black-led organisation in the world from 1920. Garvey wrote 'The British West Indies in the Mirror of Civilization – History Making by Colonial Negroes', duly published in the *African Times and Orient Review* in October 1913. Garvey stated that had the 1865 uprising, led by George Gordon and Paul Bogle, been successful, then Jamaica would be independent like Haiti. Under late Victorian rule, Jamaican Blacks won places in the local civil service. White Jamaicans pressed for such jobs to be filled by nomination 'and by this means kept out the black youth'. Garvey described the victors as 'an inferior class of sychophantic weaklings'. He suggested that West Indians 'will be the instruments of uniting a scattered race who, before the close of many centuries, will found an Empire on which the sun shall shine as ceaselessly as it shines on the Empire of the North today'.[77] Garvey visited his sister, the domestic servant in London, and eventually applied for assistance to return to Jamaica. First with the Anti-Slavery Society in July 1913, then in May 1914, reaching the Caribbean three weeks before the First World War began.[78]

After that war Mohamed worked in the United States for Garvey's Universal Negro Improvement Association, then moved to Nigeria in 1933. His autobiography appears in his *The Comet* of Lagos between June 1937 and March 1938. He lived until 1945, and most of what he claimed to have done has been found to be true.[79]

A younger man, who settled in New York from Jamaica and had a career in journalism, was Joel Rogers. He travelled around Europe in 1928 and found John Alcindor was recalled four years after the doctor's death; 'a Negro who was a physician for the Board of Health in one of the poorer districts'. Rogers observed:

> the British Negro, on the other hand, is usually ashamed of his color, and it is most amusing to meet in London coal-black Africans, Oxford accented and all, who pretend that they are Englishmen.[80]

An earlier visit had brought him into contact with Scholes who thought that 'England was a bad place for a Negro but when I told him of conditions in America he admitted that the former was nothing in comparison.' He also met Miss Aldridge.[81]

The reasons for Rogers's interest in British Blacks and the justification for the mimicry which he found odd were based in the financial and economic strengths of early twentieth-century Britain. They were colossal, and British institutions commanded enormous respect. Although the larger society's view of Africa and its inhabitants was based on ignorance and bigotry, the Africans observed by Rogers (and many described in these pages) were the elite. In behaving like an elite in Britain they were following a role. We are interested in *Ethiopia Unbound* because its author was an African, and we respect its author's achievements as a novelist and in law. We can relate to its scene when the nurse-maid walks out into the London fog as she felt she was unfit to be the partner of the highly-educated African professional man. Her partner had already asked himself 'And what would he do, if asked to Government house?'.[82]

This elite challenged the ways that Whites thought about their lands and their people. They challenged it by taking prizes at school, university and medical schools; in writing books and articles, by achieving within the rules that deliberately excluded most of the inhabitants of the British Isles. They also followed its rules: the new barristers posed for the camera in wig and gown, and councillors Williams and Nelson, doctors Easmon, Moody, Brown and Alcindor behaved as British professional standards dictated.

The Black writers whose novels, plays, histories, law books, economic studies, magazines, medical researches and humour were published in Edwardian times had respect. Class divisions in Britain in the 1900s and 1910s, which encouraged these activities, had made them something of an elite because of their education and through their writings. An outsider such as Rogers saw them as too English.

Many of these Black Edwardians had international connections. Indeed the reason some have been traced is because their names have survived in distant documentation.[83] Tracing these links and connections has relied on their published writings, and on a global focus. This is clearly seen from evidence around an imperial exhibition in London in the summer of 1914. Crossing class and geographical boundaries, making connections with others of similar appearance or race, we can see links between a man educated at the school for Africans in 1890s Colwyn Bay, a minister of the Baptist church, some musical entertainers, a slumland politician, the parents of a Black child living in Lancashire, and a writer who had been proud to have served the British monarch in Africa.

NOTES

1. Mathurin, *Williams*, pp. 107–8; Hooker, *Williams*, p. 56.
2. Mathurin, *Williams*, p. 108. Hooker, *Williams*, p. 129, n. 112 states that this was a 38 pp. book, reprinting two lectures.
3. C. Fyfe, 'Horton versus Blyden – An Educational Dilemma', *Sierra Leone Journal of Education*, 5, 1 (1970), pp. 30–33; see also H. Lynch, *Edward Wilmot Blyden, Pan-Negro Patriot 1832–1912* (London: Oxford University Press, 1967). My thanks to Fyfe for clarification on the complex Blyden.
4. E. Holden, *Blyden of Liberia* (New York: Vantage, 1966), p. 771.
5. Holden, *Blyden*, pp. 771, 809; H. Lynch (ed.), *Selected Letters of Edward Wilmot Blyden* (Millwood NY: KTO Press, 1978), p. 485 letter from 18 Greencroft Gardens, London, 24 September 1906; *Kelly's Directory for Sussex* 1905 and 1907 lists members of parliament T. McKinnon Wood and John William Benn, and the Anti-Slavery Society's Travers Buxton as other residents in the small Sussex health resort of Crowborough.
6. Lynch, *Blyden*, p. 245.
7. Harlan, *Washington: Black Leader*, p. 241.
8. Harlan, *Washington: the Wizard*, pp. 290–3.
9. Marriages registered Pancras January-March 1912 Ib 186; Deaths registered Islington January-March 1923 Ib 364; *Gold Coast Nation* 24 May 1919, pp. 2, 5, noted that Tandoh was now Chief Amoah III of Cape Coast; see also A. Locke, 'Nana Amoah: An African Statesman' *Survey Graphic* 8, 4 (January 1926), pp. 434–6; R. Wraith, *Guggisberg* (London: Oxford University Press, 1967), p. 282.
10. Harlan (ed.), *Booker T. Washington Papers*, Vol. 9 pp. 2–4, 500–1, 522.
11. Lewis, *Du Bois*, pp. 348, 414.
12. R. Jenkins, 'In Pursuit of the African Past: John Mensah Sarbah, Historian of Ghana' in Lotz and Pegg (eds), *Under the Imperial Carpet*, p. 122 using the *Gold Coast Leader* of 19 September 1903.
13. Ibid. pp. 109–29.
14. A. Merriman-Labor, *Britons Through Negro Spectacles* (London: Imperial & Foreign Co, 1909), pp. 72, 104. The publishers, of 65 Loughborough Road, Brixton, had already published his *My Earliest Miscellany* according to this book, which also

states there had also been *A Tour Through Negroland*. The copy of *Britons Through Negro Spectacles*, which I borrowed in 1983 from the Bodleian, had never been fully read as I had to cut the later pages.

15. Ibid. pp. 91, 134.
16. Ibid. p. 145.
17. H. Thomas, *The Story of a West Indian Policeman, or Forty-Seven Years in the Jamaican Constabulary* (Kingston: Gleaner, 1927), p. 368. Governor Sydney Olivier, in February 1907, said of Thomas that he had a 'permanent lack of balance and incapacity for right judgement' (CO 137/670).
18. *Medical Register, 1887*, p. 255.
19. Geiss, *Pan-African Movement*, p. 110.
20. Ibid. p. 111.
21. T. Scholes, *Glimpses of the Ages*, Vol. 1 (London: John Long, 1905), p. xvii.
22. Scholes, *Glimpses of the Ages*, Vol. 2 (London: John Long, 1908), p. ix.
23. Scholes, *Glimpses*, Vol. 1, p. 78.
24. Ibid.
25. Ibid. pp. 263–4.
26. Ibid. p. 257.
27. Ibid. p. 360.
28. Ibid. p. 371.
29. Scholes, *Glimpses of the Ages*, Vol. 2 p. 91.
30. Ibid. p. 167.
31. Ibid. p. 139.
32. Ibid. pp. 347–76.
33. Ibid. pp. 397–8.
34. Ibid. pp. 403–4.
35. Ibid. pp. 487–8.
36. Geiss, *Pan-African Movement*, p. 111.
37. *Crisis* (New York), 1 (November 1910), p. 5.
38. Lewis, *Du Bois*, pp. 439–40.
39. Ibid. p. 439.
40. Geiss, *Pan-African Movement*, p. 216. Lewis, *Du Bois*, has Gustav; Spiller's book is by 'G. Spiller'.
41. Lewis, *Du Bois*, p. 440.
42. *Crisis* 2, 5 (September 1911), p. 202.
43. Ibid. 2, 4 (August 1911), p. 159.
44. Ibid. 2, 6 (October 1911), p. 253.
45. Lewis, *Du Bois*, p. 452. MacDonald's letters and biographies show the House of Commons link.
46. Du Bois Papers.
47. Ibid.
48. Information from David Killingray; see Lobagola, *Story*, p. 337. One cannot imagine Du Bois reading the *Illustrated Police News*.
49. Reeve and Couzens, *Seme*, p. 22. See also L. Thompson, *The Unification of South Africa, 1902–1910* (Oxford: Clarendon Press, 1960), pp. 402–7.
50. E. Roux, *Time Longer Than Rope: A History of the Black Man's Struggle for Freedom in South Africa* (London: 1948; 2nd ed., Madison: University of Wisconsin Press, 1964), p. 72.
51. Ibid. pp. 73–4, 76–7.
52. Geiss, *Pan-African Movement*, p. 217.
53. D. Jabavu, *The Life of John Tengo Jabavu* (Fort Hare: Lovedale Institution Press, 1922). His daughter Noni Jabavu (Mrs Michael Crosfield) wrote *Drawn in Colour: African*

Contrasts (London: John Murray, 1960) in which she details the murder of her only brother, a medical student in Johannesburg. Her sister had married a Ugandan.

54. I am indebted to Ian Duffield for xerox copies of Mohamed's autobiographical journalism in the *Comet* of Lagos of 1936–7; see Geiss, *Pan-African Movement*, pp. 215–18, 221–8.
55. Lewis, *Du Bois*, p. 452.
56. Sayers, *Coleridge-Taylor*, p. 285.
57. Ibid.
58. Ibid. p. 286.
59. Geiss, *Pan-African Movement*, p. 218.
60. Willan, *Plaatje*, pp. 152–3 notes that Seme, back in South Africa, was speaking of African unity against oppression in August 1911, days after the Race Congress ended in distant London.
61. A. Cromwell Hill and M. Kilson, *Apropos of Africa: Sentiments of American Negro Leaders on Africa from the 1800s to the 1950s* (London: Cass, 1969), pp. 175–7.
62. Willan, *Plaatje*, p. 108.
63. Levy, *Johnson*, pp. 124–5.
64. Johnson, *Ex-Coloured Man*, p. 137.
65. *Crisis*, 5, 4 (February 1913), p. 168. His return was noted in *Crisis* 8, 1 (May 1914), p. 7.
66. P. Sherlock, *Norman Manley: A Biography* (London: Macmillan 1980), p. 61.
67. Du Bois papers; Lewis, *Du Bois*, does not mention Downing at all.
68. Discussion with Marjorie Evans, April 1987.
69. Published by Francis Griffiths in London in 1913, with copyright shared between Downing and Griffiths. It lists his *The Exiles, The Sinews of War, Human Nature, The Arabian Lovers, The Shuttlecock, Melic Ric* and *The Statue and the Wasp* and the husband-and-wife titles *Placing Paul's Play* and *Which Should She Have Saved*.
70. *West India Committee Circular* (London) 8 June 1922, p. 258.
71. Mathurin, *Williams*, pp. 134–5; Hooker, *Williams*, p. 96. Dr Garnett chaired Marcus Garvey's first London meeting in 1928. He and the League need investigation.
72. *Journal of the African Society* (London), 9, October 1903, p. 121.
73. A Liberian writer is now thought to have been the first African novelist.
74. Information from Donald Simpson, librarian of the Royal Commonwealth Society, London.
75. I am indebted to Leslie Brown who recalled, with enthusiasm, Williams's motorised horse.
76. I am indebted to Imanuel Geiss for bringing this to my attention.
77. J. Clarke, *Marcus Garvey and the Vision of Africa* (New York: Vantage Books, 1974), pp. 38–48, 77–82.
78. Ibid. pp. 47–8, using the CO Jamaica index of the Public Record Office.
79. Ian Duffield's research has yet to be published.
80. J. Rogers, 'The American Negro in Europe', *The American Mercury* 20, 77 (May 1930), pp. 3, 6.
81. 'England Offers Opportunity to Negroes of Wealth and Artists: No Place for Masses', *Norfolk Journal and Guide* (Norfolk, VA) 25 August 1925.
82. Casely Hayford, *Ethiopia Unbound* (London: 1911; repr. Cass, 1969), p. 13.
83. My research into Dr James Jackson Brown, Jamaica-born doctor of London, was stimulated by a London-printed leaflet found in the papers of Nigerian nationalist Herbert Macaulay by Brian Willan, the biographer of South African nationalist Sol Plaatje. In the Amanda Aldridge Papers (in Illinois) there is a letter from Roland Hayes, an American, introducing Macaulay's daughter to Miss Aldridge in the 1920s.

Connections at the empire's centre, 1914

CELEBRATING 'the centenary of peace and progress' of Britain and the United States of America, the organisers of London's Anglo-American Exposition contacted Daniel Jenkins of Charleston, South Carolina, in the spring of 1914. His orphanage in that Southern port city rescued Black waifs and strays from the streets and police courts, provided a formal education and trained the boys and girls in practical skills such as laundry, farming, shoe repairs, printing, and music making. Musical groups toured the nation, publicising the Jenkins Orphanage, gaining funds and friends, and exposing the youthful instrumentalists and singers to America. These children were both competent and a novelty, and theatrical impresarios Max and Jules Hurtig wanted them for the London exhibition.[1]

Aware of the demeaning role that exhibitions expected of Black entertainers, the Revd Jenkins insisted that 'the Band will be used only for Concert purposes for the Exposition patrons'.[2] Assured of that and promised one thousand dollars for ten weeks work, new uniforms, free accommodation and free passage, Jenkins gathered the musicians who left via New York on the *Campania* in May 1914.[3]

Twenty-plus musicians, Jenkins and his wife Eloise, and his assistant thirty-year-old Paul Daniels lived in London throughout the summer of 1914, for the band was so popular that the contract was extended until the autumn close-down.[4] Their work was no sinecure, for their schedule started before noon and ended at 11:30 with a maximum break of two hours.[5] A set of six postcards was issued. Copies of 'The Famous Piccanniny Band' reached South Africa, purchased at the exhibition by a proud African visitor named Solomon Plaatje.

Plaatje had travelled to Britain to protest to the imperial government and to explain to persons of influence that recent legislation in the Union of South Africa was destroying the stability of the Black people there. Funds for his trip came from the recently founded African National Congress (treasurer: Pixley Seme). There were five Africans in this group as we have already noted.

John L. Dube, the American-educated church minister from Natal,

Anglo-
American Exposition.   " Altogether."
    The Famous Piccaninny Band.

49. The band of the Jenkins Orphanage of Charleston, South Carolina, worked at the Anglo-American Exposition in London throughout the summer of 1914. These postcards were used by South African nationalist Sol Plaatje, who met the instrumentalists and their supervisors

was president of the group. Rubusana, veteran of visits in 1905 and 1911, was no longer a member of the South African parliament. Plaatje, who had been an interpreter during the legendary imperial adventure of the siege of Mafeking during the Anglo-Boer War, had spent months investigating the impact of the Native Land Act of 1913 which evicted Black farming families from nearly ninety per cent of the land of South Africa.[6] The others were Thomas Mapikela who had been to Britain in 1909, and Saul Msane who won the sweepstake on the voyage to England.[7]

They contacted the Anti-Slavery Society on arrival in Britain. Secretary John Harris, who had been a missionary in the Congo at the turn of the century, and was a friend of the Revd Frederick Meyer,[8] was expected to arrange a meeting with officials at the Colonial Office. Harris indicated that the delegation should make no contacts with the British press. Dube and Plaatje were newspapermen, and regarded this advice as very strange. Nevertheless they kept quiet until finally they had an audience with Colonial Secretary Lewis Harcourt at the end of June 1914.[9]

Plaatje noted that Harcourt made no notes and asked no questions. South Africa was a self-ruling (White) dominion and Harcourt and his advisers thought that the Africans should have made their case to Louis Botha in Pretoria. They were not allowed to be presented to King George the Fifth: he greeted traditional monarchs and kings, not journalists and members of the Black bourgeoisie who were complaining about the manner in which the imperial Union of South Africa was governed.

The five Africans turned to the British press. Plaatje wrote for the *Daily News* and was interviewed by the *Westminster Gazette*.[10] The nonconformist Brotherhood Movement welcomed them, as it had Edun some months before. They spoke at several Brotherhood meetings. Rubusana and Msane addressed hundreds of people, and were praised by Labour parliamentarian Will Crooks. Two Liberal members of parliament, primed by the Africans, asked questions in the House of Commons.[11]

Funds were getting short and Dube returned home. In August he cabled for the others to leave England. Harris was to pay their fares. Plaatje refused to accept his terms, for he was deeply suspicious of this professional pro-African spokesman. He decided to remain in Britain, explaining how the British empire's local rulers, as Scholes would have assumed, were failing to govern in the best traditions of Britain. Plaatje also decided to write a book on the African experience of White rule and the far from pro-British nature of many of South Africa's White leaders.

Plaatje knew Scholes, who in 1915 read the manuscript of his *Native*

Life in South Africa which was published in London in 1916.[12] In it he mentions lawyer Cambridge, who shared a platform with him in London in March 1915.[13] Other contacts included a Sierra Leonean lawyer named F. Fredericks, and Modiri Molema and James Moroka, medical students in Scotland.[14] He met Africans and people of African descent in London associated with Mohamed and the *Review*. And he went to the Anglo-American Exposition in late July, where he saw and admired the youthful musicians from South Carolina. He purchased postcards which he used for correspondence.[15]

At that time the Revd Jenkins was writing to governor Coleman Blease of South Carolina, advising that 'Nine of the Councilmen of London' had called on him on 22 July 1914 to congratulate him on his work.[16] One councillor may have been John Archer, the Black mayor of Battersea, who had written to John Bruce in New York that he intended to be involved with the exhibition.

Jenkins went to see his England-born daughter in Wigan, with her mother, now Mrs Jenkins. The band was managed by Daniels, whose name had appeared in a mid-1899 copy of the old *African Times* when it reported his departure from Colwyn Bay to South Carolina.

These connections, via Britain, linking the world of Africans and their descendants in Britain and the New World, continued. One of the two clarinettists in the orphanage band in 1914 London was Emerson Harper.[17] Overcoming race prejudice he became a professional musician in New York by the 1930s where he was a friend of author and poet Langston Hughes, whose *The Big Sea* autobiography of 1940 is dedicated to him and his wife.[18] Hughes travelled in Europe in the 1920s, spending months in Paris in 1924 where he had met Anne Marie Coussey, daughter of a West African lawyer with considerable links to Britain. Hughes, then a penniless sailor, was deemed to be unsuitable for the highly educated Miss Coussey, who had lived in London from the age of five.[19] Charles Coussey's friend John Alcindor went to Paris and escorted Miss Coussey back to London.[20]

Alcindor had been presiding over the African Progress Union of London, a role he had inherited from John Archer in 1921. His committee included Emma Smith and John Barbour-James (who had retired to London in 1917) and Edmund Jenkins, the son of the Revd Jenkins of South Carolina and Harper's fellow-clarinettist in the exhibition band. Edmund Jenkins spent seven years at the Royal Academy of Music in London, visited William Hughes in Colwyn Bay, got to know Du Bois and Coleridge-Taylor's widow, played at cosmopolitan gatherings where he met Plaatje, other Africans, Caribbeans, and Black Edwardians. He died in France in 1926, and Alain Locke attended his Paris funeral.[21]

By that time the world had changed irrevocably. The assassination

of an Austrian archduke in the Balkans led to the invasion of Belgium
by Germany, which led Britain to declare war in August 1914. The
Great War, later called the First World War, was hours old when, on
5 August 1914, Booker T. Washington wrote to Robert Park:

> The more I see of the actions of these white people of Europe, the
> more I am inclined to be proud of the Negro race. I do not know of a
> group of Negroes in this country or in any other country who would
> have acted in the silly manner that these highly civilized, and
> cultured people of your race have acted.[22]

In Liverpool, in Cardiff, in London, on Tyneside Black men volunteered for military service. The Manley brothers served in Belgium;
Canadian Blacks manned a battalion which served in France and
Belgium.[23] Africans fought in Cameroons and German East Africa, and
Caribbeans of the British West Indies Regiment served in France but
never in combat.[24] South Africans also served in France, and were
affected by their treatment by British and French Whites, which was so
different to that of their homeland.[25] Far away in British Guiana a
young man named Lionel Turpin fretted at the delays, and made his
own way to Britain where he enlisted and came close to death in
France. One of his England-born sons was to be a boxing champion in
the 1950s; another died in the summer of 1990.[26]

Amy Barbour-James, born in London in 1906, died in Harrow in
1988. Her father had known Blyden. Josephine Esther Bruce, born in
London in 1912, died in July 1994. She had known Marcus Garvey. In
early 1993 John Francis 'Frank' Alcindor died in southern England.
His father had witnessed celebrations of Victoria's jubilee in 1897 and
had qualified as a doctor in Scotland before the Anglo-Boer War
started in 1899. The last surviving veteran of that war died, in Canada,
in 1993. Was the Edwardian era really so long ago?

Has the Black presence in Britain at the beginning of the twentieth
century been forgotten? The vibrant memories of veterans who were
traced in the 1980s and 1990s exposed aspects of British social history
that had been overlooked but not 'forgotten'. Men and women who had
known Edward Nelson, John Alcindor, Margarita and Henry Downing,
the Aldridge sisters, the Grenfell sisters, Lou and Alfred Cambridge,
and Will Garland recalled them and their friends. It was possible to
meet people who had known Coleridge-Taylor, George Christian,
'Jags' Smith and ex-slave Thomas Johnson. Family photographs and
documents were retrieved, tales told, and fresh identifications were
made.

Many of these stories had not been written down before because
historians of British society had not considered that Black people had
made contributions to every aspect of life in Edwardian Britain. Those

who have investigated the Black presence in Britain have been faced with several difficulties. The ideas that had fooled Britons into thinking that they had a God-given right to rule a quarter of humankind remained powerful. Kenneth Little's pioneering *Negroes in Britain* appeared at the same time that the *Empire Windrush* brought Jamaican settlers to Britain in 1948. At that time, despite the recent independence of British India, there were many who welcomed plans to build a new colonial office in central London. In 1957 the Gold Coast became the independent Republic of Ghana; other colonies followed. The whole ramshackle empire of the British was dismantled within the lifetimes of multitudes who had celebrated Edward the Seventh's coronation.

British commentators on Black affairs had inherited many of the Victorian concepts of Africa and African peoples. They believed in an Africa that had been underdeveloped; people who had been enslaved; people who were pagans; people who had been held down, held back, restricted, limited to the production of foodstuffs and raw materials for Europeans. There was no concept of self-willed people who had settled in the British Isles over centuries.

There was a view, tinged with socialism, which saw Blacks as restricted by official and unofficial bigotry and thus prevented from reaching their full, human, potential. How could a people so widely despised make successful claims to nationhood? Historians examined the Black men and women who had led their people out from imperialism to independence. Studies placed leaders such as Kenyatta, Manley, Garvey, Nkrumah, Eric Williams, Banda and Nyerere as temporary visitors to 'the West' (meaning the world of Europeans in Europe and north America). It was and is comforting for the larger society to think of Black people as temporary residents: people with a home far away. Visible because of their colour, the migrants who settled in Britain from Africa and the Caribbean from the 1950s were not seen as participants in long-term global movements that had taken Scots to eastern Canada, Sikhs to Hong Kong, Irish to Chicago, Italians to the Argentine and Britain, English to Tennessee, Chinese to Trinidad, Malaysia, Australia, Cape Town and Calcutta, Gujeratis to Uganda, and as this study has revealed, Africans and Caribbeans to Britain.

It is a legend that schoolchildren in France and French colonial schools, stated 'Our ancestors, the Gauls': but that applied in the tropical empire of the British where clothing styles, names, games, social groups, religions, and language took on strong British elements by the 1900s. There were contradictions, seldom seen at the time: surely the most poignant being that Robert Baden-Powell, hero of Mafeking and founder of Scouting, was encouraging British urban youths to consider Zulu and Ndebele military behaviour at the very time when stiff-collared British teachers were training African and Asian youths to line up and behave as if they were members of British infantry regiments.

British concepts of Black studies are influenced by the imperial connections of Africa, the West Indies and Britain. This reinforces an underlying belief that people of African descent are 'from' somewhere and therefore will 'return' there. That Black people have lived in Britain longer than they have in the United States of America was a statement I made, with considerable impact, at an informal lecture I was permitted to give at Howard University in Washington, DC. That London-born Coleridge-Taylor had benefited from racial prejudice was a comment that also had an impact when stated at a conference in Edinburgh in 1994 – 'part of Mr. Coleridge-Taylor's enormous popularity is due to the African blood, although mingled with English, which so unmistakeably flows in his veins'.[27]

Over the years, and certainly when discussing matters with Peter Fryer whose *Staying Power: The History of Black People in Britain* (1984) begins 'There were Africans in Britain before the English came', I have concluded that there have been two reasons why the true history of Blacks in Britain has not been published in the post-colonial period. First, political and emotional enthusiasm for research has been restricted to those of the left who seek proletarian and anti-capitalist movements in history: and have found them. Secondly, that the ancient rules and precedents of universities failed to encourage original research in this field, leaving schools of Caribbean and African studies involved with Black people whose lives had temporary or no periods in Britain.

Blacks are known for success in sports and entertainment, and as victims in the horrors of civil war and famine. The heritage of Blacks in world history is not widely known. That there were men, women, and children of African birth or descent in Britain at the zenith of the empire, active in so many fields, strongly suggests that the modern world still fails to understand that Black people are merely members of the global human race.

That people at the beginning of the twentieth century believed that the British empire was a force for good could have no better comment than that of the African arch-nationalist Bandele Omoniyi whose *A Defence of the Ethiopian Movement* of 1908 was dedicated to British rule: 'the source and fountain of true liberty and politicial progress in the world'. The presence of Black people all over the British Isles, in all walks of life and of every class and style, must have made it possible for the end of that ridiculous empire to be so smooth and so swift.

Those inhabitants of Britain – Black, White, and indifferent – unable to get to grips with the social realities of the so-recent past will be guilty of failing to honour their history.

NOTES

1. J. Green, *Edmund Thornton Jenkins*, pp. 7–11, 37–9.
2. Ibid. p. 38.
3. H. Rye, 'The Jenkins' Orphanage Band In Britain', *Storyville* (Chigwell, Essex) 130 (June 1987), pp. 138–42.
4. Green, *Jenkins*, p. 39.
5. J. Green, 'An American Band in London, 1914', *Musical Traditions*, No 9 (Rochford, Essex) Autumn 1991, pp. 12–17.
6. Willan, *Plaatje*, reveals the tragedy and lost opportunities for Africans in southern Africa from 1890 to the 1930s.
7. Ibid. p. 175.
8. Information from his grandson, supported by letters.
9. Willan, *Plaatje*, p. 177.
10. Ibid. p. 179.
11. Ibid. pp. 179–80.
12. Ibid. pp. 188–9. Plaatje and Msane had visited Harry Johnston in Sussex in August 1914, but Plaatje rejected Johnston's introduction for his book.
13. S. Plaatje, *Native Life in South Africa* (London: 1916; repr. Johannesburg: Ravan Press, c 1982), p. 267.
14. Willan, *Plaatje*, p. 186.
15. Green 'American Band', p. 15.
16. Ibid.
17. Rye 'Orphanage Band', p. 138.
18. Langston Hughes, *The Big Sea* (New York: Knopf, 1940).
19. Arnold Rampersad, *The Life of Langston Hughes: Volume 1 – 1902–1941* (New York: Oxford University Press, 1986), pp. 86–7.
20. Ibid. pp. 89–90. Frank Alcindor recalled the Cousseys as friends of his father, when interviewed in 1981.
21. Green, *Jenkins*, pp. 42–82, 158–9.
22. Harlan, *Washington*, Vol. 2, p. 294.
23. C. Ruck, *The Black Battalion, 1916–1920* (Halifax NS: Nimbus, 1987).
24. D. Killingray 'All the King's Men?' in Lotz and Pegg (eds), *Under the Imperial Carpet*, pp. 173–5, 180–1.
25. S. Jingoes, *A Chief is a Chief by the People* (London: Oxford University Press, 1975), p. 92.
26. J. Birtley, *The Tragedy of Randolph Turpin* (London: New English Library, 1975).
27. *Gloucestershire Chronicle*, 17 September 1898. J. Green, 'Samuel Coleridge-Taylor (1875–1912): English Composer', unpublished paper, January 1994.

Selected bibliography

Echeruo, Michael J. C. *Victorian Lagos: Aspects of Nineteenth Century Lagos Life* (London: Macmillan, 1977).

Fryer, Peter. *Staying Power: The History of Black People in Britain* (London: Pluto Press, 1984).

Kennedy, Carol. *Mayfair: A Social History* (London: Hutchinson, 1966).

Longmate, Norman. *The Workhouse* (London: Temple Smith, 1974).

Mowat, Charles Loch. *The Charity Organisation Society 1869–1913* (London: Methuen, 1961).

Richardson, Ruth. *Death, Dissection and the Destitute* (London: Routledge and Kegan Paul, 1988).

Roberts, Robert. *The Classic Slum: Salford Life in the First Quarter of the Century* (Manchester: Manchester University Press, 1971).

Smith, Francis Barry. *The People's Health, 1830–1910* (London: Croom Helm, 1979).

Thompson, Paul. *The Edwardians: The Remaking of British Society* (London: Weidenfield and Nicholson, 1975).

Index

TITLES OF RELATED INTEREST

Reconstructing the Black Past
Blacks in Britain 1780–1830

Norma Myers, *Merchant Taylors' School*

> *'A valuable contribution to the understanding of the history of black people in Britain.'*
> **Race Relations**

This book examines the character and composition of the black population of Britain between 1780 and 1830, previous studies of which have been hampered by a lack of demographic evidence. Drawing heavily from data collected from parish registers, contemporary newspapers and journals, parliamentary papers and the records of merchants involved in the slave trade, the author ventures beyond existing research to examine the age structure and sex ratios of the black population; family marriage patterns; and the occupations of black men and women.

174 pages   1996   0 7146 4575 3 cloth   0 7146 4130 8 paper
Slave and Post-Slave Societies and Cultures Series No. 3

Africans in Britain
David Killingray, *Goldsmith's College, University of London (Ed)*

This collection of essays looks at the history of African people in Britain mainly over the past 200 years. Individual chapters focus on African writers in the eighteenth century, Afro-British men and women transported to Australia, the Kru community in Liverpool, African political activities particularly in the West African Students' Union, the part played by African students at Scottish and English universities, African service in the Royal Air Force during the Second World War, the formative post-war years spent by Kwame Nkrumah in London, and the impact of Tshekedi Khama's exile on British politics.

246 pages   1994   0 7146 4571 0 cloth   0 7146 4107 3 paper
A special issue of the journal Immigrants and Minorities

Imperialism, Academe and Nationalism

Britain and University Education for Africans

Apollos O Nwauwa, *Rhode Island College, USA*

> 'This book is compelling, brilliantly written and immensely scholarly, a remarkable account ...'
> **West Africa**

> '... a scholarly and welcome addition to the history of British colonial education.'
> **History of Education Review**

Of all the aspects of British 'cultural imperialism' the one which Africans found most seductive was formal western education. They were quick to realise that University education opened up prospects for economic advancement and would ultimately provide the keys to political power and self government. Using a wide range of papers from the British Colonial Office and colonial governments in Africa, the archives of several libraries and the writings of African nationalists, Dr Nwauwa examines the surprisingly long history of the demand for the establishment of universities in Colonial Africa, a demand to which the authorities finally agreed after the Second World War.

272 pages   1997   0 7146 4668 7 cloth

Ethnic Labour and British Imperial Trade

A History of Ethnic Seafarers in the UK

Diane Frost, *University of Liverpool and Merseyside Maritime Museum (Ed)*

> 'a significant contribution to our understanding of some of the non-Europeans who were increasingly significant in manning British ships from the mid-nineteenth century.'
> **International Journal of Maritime History**

This collection of essays identifies a neglected but significant component of Britain's maritime and labour history, that of ethnic labour drawn from Britain's colonies in West Africa, the Middle East and Asia. The interdisciplinary nature of the volume raises a number of important issues: race and ethnicity, colonialism and migration, social class and the complex nature of racial hostility meted out by organized white labour.

178 pages   1995   0 7146 4185 5 paper
A special issue of the journal Immigrants & Minorities

Arthur Wharton 1865–1930

The Forgotten History of the First Black Professional Footballer

Phil Vasili

With a Foreword by **Irvine Welsh** *and an Introduction by* **Tony Whelan,** *Manchester United FC*

Arthur Wharton was the world's first Black professional footballer and 100 yards world record holder, and was probably the first African to play professional cricket in the Yorkshire and Lancashire Leagues. His achievements were accomplished against the backdrop of Africa's colonization by European regimes. While Arthur was beating the best on the tracks and fields of Britain, the peoples of the continent of his birth were being recast as lesser human beings. His sporting career spans, almost exactly, those marker points of Britain's imperial conquest of Africa, the 1885 Treaty of Berlin and the ending of the Boer War in 1902.

The late-Victorian context of Wharton's career, in a Britain at the height of its economic and political power, shaped the way he was forgotten: it was simply not politically expedient to proclaim the glories of an African sportsman when the dominant ideas of the age labelled all Blacks as inferior. Arthur died penniless after working at Yorkshire Main Colliery. His absence from the histories of football, and to a lesser extent athletics, is now being revised. Yet this book shows that the deeds of many Black and working-class people suffered the same fate.

240 pages 25 photographs 1998 0 7146 4903 1 cloth   0 7146 4459 5 paper
Sport in the Global Society No. 11